THE BATTLE AT FORT ANCHOR

THE BATTLE AT FORT ANCHOR

PATRICK WHELAN

PW

First published by Patrick Whelan Publishing, 2022

Patrick Whelan Publishing
78 Pastures Hill,
Littleover,
Derby.
DE23 4BB

A CIP catalogue record is available for this book from the British Library.

ISBN 978 1 39843 233 8

Typesetting and origination by Patrick Whelan

Printed and bound in Great Britain by 4Edge, Essex

Contents

I dedicate this book to my lovely wife Shirley who provided the necessary encouragement and refreshments for me to get my book completed.

Also, to my grandchildren Bradley, Jayde and especially Lycia, for always being at hand to help me in navigating the intricacies of the computer.

About the author

Having had a good secondary education, Pat Whelan found employment in factories in Birmingham, becoming skilled in tool setting on capstan lathes. After marriage, he joined the GPO in exchange construction at Burton on Trent telephone exchange.

While there, he gained O level equivalents in BTEC as a fully qualified telephone systems installation engineer. He spent many years working in the fine breweries in and around the Burton area.

Influenced by his family's love for racing pigeons, he holds a real fondness for all types of birds. Pat, however, could always commiserate with anyone losing a 'good' racing pigeon to a killer hawk.

He enjoys cycling, walking his Samoyed dog and the compliments he receives from other dog walkers about his Nordic beauty. He also enjoys visiting Victorian forts, castles, and seeing historic armaments. His visit to Malta inspired him to write his fictional story about this giant cannon that others misguidedly derided as a seven day wonder.

Acknowledgements

I WOULD like to pay compliments to the wonderful Fondazzjoni Wirt Artna of the Malta Heritage Trust. It is a voluntary non-governmental organisation in heritage preservation that looks after many historic buildings on Malta.

Special thanks go to Mario Farrugia, the Curator of Malta's museums for safeguarding British heritage in Malta. Also special thanks go to the many part-timers for their really splendid re-enactment duties.

Fort Rinnela is highly recommended by me if you visit Malta any time. Do what I did and leave your inhibitions at home. I visited Fort Rinella and the saluting battery at Barrakka Gardens. I also wore the uniform, aimed and fired the Lee Enfield rifle and joined the volunteers in loading and firing the Howitzer in the adjacent field. All great fun to remember and treasure for life.

It's worth pointing out that if the booklet titled *Fort Rinella And Its Armstrong 100-Ton Gun* was purchased. At the rear of the booklet there is a drawing showing the layout of the fort and the reader can follow the Battle at Fort Anchor as it unfolds.

I would also like to thank Mike Darling of the Palmerston Fort Society for his help in giving me information along with phone numbers and email addresses. It was much appreciated.

Chapter 1

The vast Woolwich Barracks

ON A warm, cloudless day at one of the many parade grounds of the Woolwich Arsenal, rows of fresh recruits stood anxiously in anticipation of the next stage of instruction. Each of the men would soon be given a trained, sturdy war horse from the line of stallions tethered to the nearby hitching rails.

Standing in front of them on a raised platform was the stout, surly, whiskered figure of the drill sergeant, surveying his latest complement of cadets. Expertly, he barked out his instructions. He wanted to see which of the men gathered before him could listen to his commands and obey instructions. Having already put them through a series of orders, he had mentally noted any who were struggling to follow his commands. These he would weed out by the end of the day's exercises and have them usefully employed elsewhere. From his years of experience, he was aware that all recruits wanted to ride a 'War Horse' – it was only natural. He also knew that not all had the ability to stay up on the horse while galloping at speed, risking both life and limb of themselves and others.

"Draw sabres!" was his high-pitched, ear-piercing order.

A loud metallic scrape could be heard as the men in training drew the deadly, highly sharpened swords from their scabbards. The exposed blades glinted in the sunlight, reflecting flashes of light onto the shaded sides of the main building nearby.

"Present sabres!" His lingering cry hung in the air as the men saluted, the backs of the cold steel blades pressed firmly to their faces.

"Shoulder, sabres!" There was a rugged thud as the swords were sloped hard to their shoulders, the combined noise of the movement resonating beyond the confines of the square.

"Order, sabres!" The swords were instantly lowered to the ground.

"Return sabres!" was his final lingering command – half an octave higher and almost a full scream. There followed a similar metallic scraping sound as the swords were returned to their scabbards in one powerful movement. Seconds later, a slight murmur of profanities rippled through the cadets, spat out through the gritted teeth of those who had still not mastered the motions.

Blessed with sharp hearing and a keen eye, the instructor watched for any untoward 'after' movements that would betray the culprits who had failed him yet again.

A heavy silence fell across the parade ground as the disheartened men collectively realised they would have to repeat the exercise. Standing ramrod straight and hardly breathing, they waited for the drill sergeant to break the hush and vent his fury.

Exasperated and red in the face, he took an enormous breath before dementedly screaming at them, bending forward with a clenched fist to emphasise his point. "That's not good enough, is it?!" His voice carried across the parade ground, reverberating off the same building and wafting over each of the men's damp, sweating bodies in an audible, threatening wash. "That man there! It's not good enough, is it?" he demanded, pointing his swagger stick at the luckless figure who had somehow made another mess of it.

"No, it's not," was the man's feeble reply.

"No, it's not, what?"

"No, it's not, Sergeant," the man replied, straightening his back and shoulders in fear.

"You, man! It's not good enough, is it?" he repeated, asking another, who had also failed miserably.

"No, Sergeant!" he barked back.

"You two, see me later after we have finished here. As for the rest of you… if necessary, we will stay here day and night until we get you, fine gentlemen, into some sort of order that will pass muster on my parade ground. These sabres are awkward to use at first but are deadly in skilled hands – however, I should warn you now, they can also prove deadly in untrained hands.

"We had a sorry example of this when one ungrateful prick managed to spoil all my good work for a week – yes, a whole week! Yes, yes! It took me that long to get over it. He carelessly stabbed a colleague standing behind him. He is now working at the Arsenal factory, and he walks with a limp – his riding days over before they had even begun.

"Therefore, you will all be getting this right before you mount up. No one will be allowed to ride these chargers until they have mastered the basic sabre moves. I do not want these horses stabbed from the saddle, or parts of them missing, either! You will ensure they are not injured or put out of action, *or else*! Each of these chargers stands fourteen to fifteen hands high, is strongly built, and can move extremely fast, *and I want them to stay that way*. Horses are valuable and hard to replace, while you gentlemen are not! *Do I make myself clear?*"

"Yes, Sergeant," was their shouted response.

"Unlike the horses you trained on, these are war horses and taught to ride towards enemy fire. *Is that clear too?*" he bawled at them, still not satisfied. His eyes darted across their faces, looking for anyone failing to mouth a response.

"Yes, Sergeant," they repeated, though none dared to meet his threatening gaze.

"*I can't hear you!*" he yelled, his eyes alight with fierce passion.

Still not daring to look directly at him, they could only guess at the vengeance he could bestow on each of them in his present intense anger.

"*Yes, Sergeant!*" they shouted back, louder this time – no one wanting to be singled out and made the target of his wrath.

"Good!" His voice had now dropped to a calmer, more civilised tone. "I heard one or two 'sirs' in there somewhere. Do not call me sir; I am fully conditioned into working for a living."

And with that, he began his shouted orders again. "Draw sabres...!"

On another of the parade grounds, a single bugler was sounding the charge. Immediately, the drumming of hundreds of hooves could be heard as the cavalry intake accepted the challenge. This thunderous noise was accompanied by high-pitched shouting and screaming, designed to strike fear in the hearts of the enemy as they practised riding down imaginary foes at a gallop.

Being trainees under instruction, a few riders were soon unsaddled and lying in a dust heap on the ground – not having experienced the excitement of the charge before. While the main body of horsemen reassembled after reaching the end of the run, the unsaddled riders quickly remounted, chasing up their horses where necessary and rejoining their comrades, excitedly waiting for them to catch up.

Some of the gathering horses stomped the ground and whinnied in protest at their harsh treatment. In contrast, others expressed wide-eyed contempt and annoyance at their riders' incompetence by snorting loudly. These screaming, deafening cavalry charges always attracted crowds of men kicking their heels as they moved about in groups from one place to another in the Arsenal complex. It proved quite a spectacle for anyone fortunate enough to be passing at the time; it was compulsive viewing.

With his swagger stick tucked firmly under his arm, the drill sergeant stepped down from the rostrum and took to striding amongst the men, eyeballing those that had caught his eye. "Now listen, you men. When you return your sabre, you will grip the top of the scabbard with your other hand. You will then place your thumb and first two fingers just above the lip of the scabbard to guide the blade in. Do not lose any members, gentlemen, fingers or otherwise: that is an order! I do not want you to be picking up lopped-off body parts after your dismissal. You will need every one of your fingers later for holding the reins of your charger with and staying up in the saddle – otherwise, you will bloody fall off."

He heard chuckles coming from the lines of men standing behind him but none from those in front. He looked around at them with a thin, secret smile. Alternating between chiding them gently one minute and then screaming blue murder at them the next was his usual procedure. He used any delivery method at his disposal to get the best results, and the men usually obeyed him to the letter.

"Now practise returning the sabre to its scabbard a few more times while I get back to the platform. Continue, gentlemen."

The Woolwich Arsenal was also a venue for conferences and was known as 'The Warren' by military men. The nickname referred to the labyrinth of corridors in the Arsenal, the countless rooms and offices of different sizes, and its complex campus of buildings.

The whole site covered many acres and was fully equipped as a significant arms manufacturer, with tremendous industrial works situated on the site. Large steel and brass foundries, and the stress-testing laboratories for the finished articles, gave much-needed employment to many people. Swords and rifles were made there, as well as the more powerful muzzle-loading cannons.

The other large industrial factories in Birmingham and Newcastle helped increase the overall output of these armaments from the Woolwich Arsenal. However, the prevalent desire of the world's manufacturers to build ever-larger muzzleloaders continued; every day, new ways were being sought to deal with the expanding armour mounted on the latest warships and were thwarted only by the overall design frailties of their cannons.

At other times, the Arsenal was open to the public as a display area, and these visits provided splendid recruiting opportunities for the forces. The Royal Artillery – and other troops of the realm – put on great shows of discipline and artistry in marching, riding, and firing the guns. On these occasions, the soldiers wore their pristine dress uniforms, and the horses were beautifully turned out in polished brasses, fine saddlery, and leather harnesses. Field guns were highly buffed and shined, and the heady smell of leather hung heavily in the air.

Over time, such days would continually prove to be excellent opportunities for enlisting men into the forces of the expanding British Empire. Most days, the business of Empire and how to run it had to be addressed with raw recruits, although the parade ground could become an implement of torture for some of these fresh cadets, casting doubts on their reasons for enlisting.

Two men were gazing down at the drill instructor – both excellent, upstanding officers of the royal artillery, resplendent in their blue uniforms. Each had a blue cloth-covered, brass spiked helmet held safely and securely under one arm. They were chatting at the foot of one of the long windows in the large, empty meeting room, each one offering panoramic views of the parade grounds outside.

Captain Robert Townsend and Captain David Marsh, both previous officers in training, were taking a keen interest in the frustrated drill sergeant below. Townsend – at six feet two inches, with dark, chiselled features and brown eyes – used to be as carefree as his companion was apt to be. In the past he had gotten into various minor scrapes that had been the talk of his comrades, but since meeting and wooing the beautiful, gentle Victoria into becoming his wife, a deep maturity – and a desire to take care of her – had settled upon him. When confronted with a problem now, his approach was to solve it in a slower, more measured, and more thoughtful way.

Marsh, in comparison, was slightly shorter and unwed. At six feet tall, with blue eyes, unruly blond hair, and good looks, he had a boyish, carefree – and sometimes accident-prone – attitude to life. Annoyingly, he would brag to anyone who cared to listen about his ways with pretty women. Much of it, others claimed, was just boast and bluster. His sometimes reckless attitude towards matters concerning the fairer sex had frequently got him into trouble; therefore, his ability to make a swift exit was a bonus. In his defence, his family often stated that *David would settle down once he met the right woman. It was just finding her that was the problem.* The two men were sons of retired officers and had become firm friends during officer training – which, incidentally, had been given by the same drill instructor they were now watching outside.

"Remember when we were in training ourselves, David?" Townsend mused. "I still think the Army would do better if they stopped this emphasis on turning out 'refined gentlemen' and instead concentrated more on solid training and leadership. I feel so much talent is being lost."

But Marsh's mind had strayed from Townsend's philosophy as he recalled his first attempts at riding here. "Do you remember putting saddles on chargers for the first time, Robert?"

"Of course I do!" he chuckled. "You left the straps a little too loose and tried to mount the horse, only to end up on the ground with the saddle around the horse's belly. And you weren't the only one."

"That was good fun!" Marsh laughed before his happy mood darkened. Frowning, he added, "But it's the lower ranks I feel sorry for. You know, if we choose, we can have our uniform made to measure – unlike them. Lately, I've realised just how much the lower ranks are taken for granted. Although mostly illiterate, I might add, a large majority of recruits are considered incapable of learning anything, it seems, from those who lead us. Hence the constant drilling and shouting from the NCOs."

"Well, many had no future outside the Army, and discipline must be maintained," Townsend replied. "At least the men are clothed, fed, and have the opportunity for adventure." He paused for a moment, thinking. "But you make a valid point. I have seen how some new intakes swap and change their uniforms and shoes amongst themselves until a good fit is found. If you doubt me, let me tell you; I swear to have seen it," he added, emphasising the issue.

Then, as an afterthought – and bringing the loud tone of the discussion down – he added, "If we value our careers, it's best to keep our thoughts to ourselves."

At that moment, a polite cough interrupted their conversation.

Turning, the officers realised they were in the company of Colonel Downing, who had entered the room, unheard, behind them. Stepping away from the window, both immediately stood to attention, respectfully saluting their superior.

"Marsh and Townsend, is it? I see you two are watching the drill sergeant put our new intake under sabre instruction, eh?" he asked after glancing through the window behind them. "Have you noticed that little extra distance he's put between them since your day? An unfortunate incident happened recently, and he does not want a repeat of it. A recruit dropped his sabre and was regrettably stabbed by his colleague in front while bending down to pick it up. The silly arse missed his scabbard entirely, which saw the drill sergeant a man short. He was not happy about it. I can assure you. Why, do I hear you ask? Well, because it upset his marching and exercise routines for the whole week. Damned inconsiderate of the man, getting stabbed like that, he said. We never heard the last of it, gentlemen!"

Colonel Downing was a well-decorated man, known for his charm and wit. He could make lively conversations about most things. "As for your other remarks, I agree with everything I heard you two say. The Army is slowly changing, gentlemen, and for good – but the knack is not to rush the change too quickly and instead let it evolve naturally. Otherwise, we could lose that extra something special the British Army has over our enemies. But the point you raised about uniform fitting is a valid observation, and I have taken a mental note. I have heard others make similar remarks. Our men must be shown greater respect than that!"

Then, looking around the room, he added, "I see you two are the first here, good. It shows you are keen to find out what this is all about. Any sign of the others, Captain Townsend?"

He peered through the window. "Yes, sir, entering the building now."

From time to time, officers with impending service abroad came into the headquarters for consultations and planning. Today was one of those occasions, and soon the other officers began entering the room, beckoned in by the colonel.

"Do come in, gentlemen, and find yourselves a seat. Would someone shut that door while we study the Great Maps of Africa here on the table, which my aides have graciously got out for our use?"

Chapter 2

Urgent signal received. Centre of attention. Introduction to 'The Gun'

THE DUTY sergeant was sitting behind his information desk in the hall on the ground floor. His small team were there to meet and greet visitors to the premises, answer their questions, and direct them to whichever part of the vast complex they had their appointments. His speciality was the recruitment of men into the armed services, for which there were many applicants – especially after a successful public open day where the military displays, pageantry, and the romance of the uniform had caused the number of men enlisting to soar. The ever-expanding Empire meant that men were encouraged to join up and see the world.

Simpson was in the signals room, busy writing down another Morse code message from the War Office. During the translation – as he realised the importance of the message – his eyes widened, and his mouth dropped open. With a stern face, he dutifully wrote down the incoming message. On finishing his translated copy, he put his pencil to one side, took off his earphones, and gathered together the two important sheets of paper for the colonel's attention. He then hurriedly made off towards Colonel Downing's meeting room up on the first floor.

"*Stop there, that man!*" the duty sergeant called out, making the signals private instantly freeze near the foot of the stairs. "Where are you going to, running like that?"

During his unexpected quiet period, the duty sergeant had been concentrating on the mesmerising rhythm and rotation of a female cleaner's hips as she knelt down and took a scrubbing brush to a stubborn scuff mark on the highly polished floor. Now, he was upset at having his blatant attention to the undertaking of her task so rudely diverted, especially considering he had schemed to place the mark there in the first place.

The cleaner – just a few short weeks into her job – had noticed an increase in scuff marks near the recruiting desk, and was suspicious of the men there who often attempted to engage her in flirtatious conversation.

"Well? Answer the question!" the duty sergeant snapped, stamping grumpily over from his desk to confront the man.

"It's for the colonel, Sergeant," Simpson said in his defence.

"That's not unusual, is it?" came the low guttural tones of the sergeant, his face hovering mere inches from Simpson's.

Standing so close to the timid signaller, the sergeant's eyes seemed as wide as tin dinner plates. He loomed large above Simpson, a mountain of a man. Only the presence of the nearby woman forced him to suppress his urge to let loose and swear.

He circled the signaller until they were face to face again. "We get these things every day, Simpson, so why spoil my counting of the latest batch of recruits?"

"It's marked 'urgent' this time, Sergeant," Simpson explained. "I've just received it from the War Office."

"Urgent, you say? Well get a move on, then! But slowly, slowly, and don't scuff this lady's fine floor with those big boots of yours. I can see she's had enough of cleaning scuff marks for one day."

Behind Simpson, the cleaner looked up at the sergeant, impressed by his authority and his sensitivity towards her task. She smiled at him approvingly, her previous suspicions of him fading fast.

The duty sergeant noted her favourable reaction and felt the need to know her better – and to try to exploit the situation.

"Yes, Sergeant," Simpson replied, standing stiffly to attention with his chin tucked in and his eyes staring towards the blue skies through the nearby window. *Anywhere but here*, he thought as he promptly saluted.

Being keen to get away, he clumsily turned hard on his heels. It caused a high-pitched screech, and left another black scuff mark for the cleaner to remove. "Sorry, Sergeant! Sorry, Miss," he said, his persona and guise of a professional soldier beginning to slip as he hunched his shoulders in abject humility. He walked slowly up the stairs to the colonel's meeting room, knowing he was still under the sergeant's unfavourable gaze.

Arriving at the meeting room, he knocked sharply on the oak door and waited for a response. While waiting, he began eyeing his own tortured features reflecting back at him from the brass nameplate fixed to the door. He saw the rest of his body outlined in a distorted fashion across the contours of the panels of the highly polished door. Straightening himself up, he took out some of the creases from his reflection as he prepared to speak with the colonel.

After what seemed like an eternity – standing stock-still, with the duty sergeant's eyes still drilling into the back of his head – a voice called him in. *At last,* he thought as he opened the great door and entered, relieved to be out of the sergeant's sight. He saw the colonel and the other officers studying detailed maps of the African Continent, which were laid out on the large oak table in the centre of the room. Pushing back against the heavy oak door, it effortlessly and quietly shut behind him.

On seeing him approach, two officers released the corners of the map they held open, which immediately curled up on itself. All talk in the room had instantly stopped, and Simpson now found himself the focus of everyone's attention.

Feeling nervous and awkward under their combined gaze, he made for the colonel. Walking towards him, he became acutely aware of the loud squeak that had unexpectedly developed in one of his new boots, loudly marking his progress across the floor.

"What have you got for me now, Simpson? Can it not wait?"

Fully embarrassed, Simpson saluted. "Urgent message from the War Office requiring a reply, sir."

The colonel took the papers from him. "Wait there, Simpson," he ordered, irritated at the untimely interruption.

There followed a deep silence as he read the report. Occasionally, he would rub his chin or his earlobe as he perused and thoroughly digested the signal.

This meeting room was one of many in the main building, which faced the parade grounds outside. In the silence, the officers could hear the horse cavalry being drilled to perfection on one of the more distant grounds.

Colonel Downing finally looked up, thrust his shoulder gently back, and walked over to one of the large paned windows along the wall. Then, gazing into the distance towards the riders, he spoke. "Gentlemen, we have here what could be a potential crisis on our hands. We have been informed that Armstrong's of Newcastle have created another one of their splendid guns." Lifting his left shoulder up and then lowering it gently back again, he continued, "Nothing unusual about that, you may think, but this is special – and a monster. It is a cannon of huge proportions, with devastating power. They have designed and successfully built a gun that was deemed impossible by other manufacturers just a short while ago. Each is one hundred and two tons in weight, which – I'm sure you will agree – is enormous."

Upon hearing the size, they collectively gasped.

"That is... er... h-huge, sir," one managed to stutter.

"Yes, massive. It was first offered to the Admiralty but was turned down due to the cost. Then it was offered to the Italians, who accepted and bought the thing!"

"But why do they want it?" Townsend asked. "Several years ago, they were beaten by the Austrian navy at the Battle of Lissa, if my memory serves me correctly. Why re-arm so soon?"

"Correct, Mister Townsend, but I fear the incident you described hurt the political ego sufficiently that they decided to rebuild their navy – and they have gone for these guns. The order has gone in for eight one hundred tonners, as they are known. They are also building two super warships, each to hold four of them, which are far, far superior to any other gun that exists today. So, you see, they do not intend to be beaten by anyone's fleet in the future." The colonel sighed. "They never accepted that defeat gracefully. They have gone for fewer ships with larger guns; they want their ships armed with guns that could blast a navy of any size to bits without compromising their own safety. They appear to have set a precedent – this is how future warships will be designed and armed."

There was an uneasy shuffling of feet as his subordinates listened intently to what he had to say.

"There is no animosity between the two governments, so there is no reason why the sale could not go to the Italians, but now it seems the War Office are having second thoughts. They are worried that these guns could be potentially dangerous to the Crown, especially if the situation changes in the Mediterranean to our disadvantage. You see, they could position these ships off the coasts of Malta or Gibraltar. If they did that, they could use the guns to pummel our defences and knock the hell out of both with impunity. We would not be able to retaliate due to their greater firing distance."

"Stop the sale, then," one of the officers suggested.

"No. I have already said we cannot do that. Italy is not an enemy of the Crown," he stressed. "The War Office ordered the Inspector General of Fortifications to immediately review the readiness of the coastal defences of both Malta and Gibraltar. His report has been received and is in the throes of being acted on. In the meantime, the first of these guns to be manufactured by Armstrong will be loaded aboard an Italian naval vessel. It will sail to Tynemouth, then up the Tyne to Elswick and the Armstrong factory. Undoubtedly, the Italians will be the first country of many wanting to buy them.

"This gun has had our Intelligence people clambering all over it, so we know what they can do. But I want a couple of our men up there to see for themselves – and to show our faces," he said as he approached the corner of

21

his large oak sideboard that contained the drinks cabinet. Pushing a couple of decanters and whisky bottles to one side, he sat on its edge and continued, "They must then report back on this gun – now that it's completed – and get a feel for the finished article. It can be inspected and assessed in the Armstrong factory, where they built and tested their prototype before the sale."

"Any thoughts on breechloaders, Colonel?" asked another officer.

"What about them?"

"Well, I hear they're using more of them now, so...."

"Yes, Lieutenant, but they won't use them on the bigger guns. They are not popular with the gun crews. The gunners behind the firing breech were almost burnt by gases escaping from around the seals when they were tested. Escaping propellants also means less power from the guns, of course. Thorough tests are continually being carried out, but until the escaping propellants can be stopped, we'll stick to the more reliable muzzleloaders, which can shoot much further."

"I see, sir," said the officer, wisely backing down.

"The War Office is quite happy with the smaller breechloaders, but for the bigger guns, not yet! Also, there is something else we must get to grips with: namely, the modern warships the Italians are building. You see, from our Intelligence reports, we know that these ships are being constructed with hulls 20 inches thick, in wrought iron. These new guns can cope with that, whereas our existing smaller-bore cannons cannot – the shells would just bounce off! But not shells from these beasts." He shook his head knowingly.

"They are capable of sinking a ship of this type with one carefully placed shot. Therefore, we must be well prepared. The safe passage of British ships to the Suez Canal is of paramount importance and must not be compromised. We need the route to India to stay open for trading purposes, and for Gibraltar and Malta to continue as vital coaling stations for our merchant fleet." He paused thoughtfully, then continued, "Building massive cannons is expensive – too expensive by far – but the War Office is now prepared to go with these one hundred tonners because we can at least match anything an enemy could threaten us with."

"Does this mean we will eventually equip all of our Navy with these guns, sir?" asked Marsh, with boyish simplicity.

"No."

"I don't understand, sir."

"Well, Captain Marsh, the War Office has decided these guns are not for Admiralty use but for Royal Artillery use."

The seriousness of the situation curbed Marsh's natural tendency to joke with his peers; his attitude often lightened a conversation topic, but now he was listening more intently to what the colonel had to say.

Another marked silence pervaded the room as the men appreciated the enormity of the colonel's words. In the stillness, the faint sound of laughter could be heard coming from somewhere outside.

It transpired that a young novice cadet had been thrown from his horse and had ripped the gusset of his pants, exposing his 'blessings' in the process, much to the amusement of the others gathering there. He lay on the ground, winded, using both hands in an attempt to limit the exposure of his 'tackle' to his laughing, mocking colleagues.

Unaware of the incident outside, the colonel continued, "Because of the possible threat these guns would pose to our trading partners and to ourselves, the War Office has decided that in order to protect our interests in the Mediterranean and guarantee safe passage to and from India through the Suez Canal, we shall need five." His hand flicked at a perceived speck of dirt on his tunic sleeve. "With two on Gibraltar and three on Malta. It is what the Inspector General has requested in his final deliberations. As this was completely unexpected, we now have a lot to do, hence our visit to Newcastle. Is that clear, gentlemen?"

"Yes, sir," came the shared reply.

"Good. It will soon fall to us to put these plans into operation."

There was a short pause as the tasks facing them were absorbed by everyone in the room.

"We will shortly be obliged to look after these beasts – more so than the other cannons. These are the orders from the War Office, and we will execute those orders to the best of our ability. This is a great honour for the regiment, so we must guard them with our lives. I hope that is clear, too. Any questions?"

Townsend raised his chin. "There is something, Colonel. If the Admiralty are having none, and these guns are to be solely used by us, is there any perceived advantage to using the cannon over the other?"

"Continue, Captain."

"I can see a ship armed with these guns finding it awkward to aim and fire accurately over a great distance at sea," he explained. "The swell of the seas will lift and lower the ship in the water, making it almost impossible to pinpoint long-range targets, sir."

"Excellent, Captain, you are quite right – they will fire them. Of course they will, and with devastating effect, no doubt. But the secret here is not the amount of fire from a ship but the rate of fire our cannons can achieve – and with better accuracy. Nothing this size has ever been installed on a warship before, and to have four on one ship will mean the rate of fire from each will be slow and cumbersome. Our people reckon the firing rate will take about twenty minutes, from the time of firing to the time of reloading. This is because of the restricted space available to them aboard the ship – and bearing in mind the workforce involved to achieve it manually.

"Now, when it comes to loading and firing our guns, we have a clear advantage because ours will be housed in a unique fort. Three new forts are being constructed in Malta as we speak and will be converted to take these guns. Each will hold a solitary supergun and will become a single battery within its own garrison. The clear advantage we will have is being on firm ground to take aim and fire at will – without any of these distractions and problems – so the accuracy of our cannon fire will be far superior. Our people are working on a steam engine and what they call an accumulator to help fire our guns for us, but more on that another time. Now, are there any other questions? Time is growing short, gentlemen."

They shook their heads, satisfied.

"Very well, then. We had already decided that – when the time came – we would send Captain Marsh and Captain Townsend to Newcastle to look at this gun on our behalf and report back. Anything they can suggest will be much appreciated until we can get our hands on one. Now that we are involved, we must show a willingness on what we are about, bearing in mind that some of these superguns will have to be manhandled up hills without the benefit of roads, or big horses, to assist them. For convenience, the officers for the five garrisons will get chosen from those of you assembled here. Because of the accumulator and cannon size, the master gunner will be of captain rank and not NCO. However, before then, you will all get the opportunity to see the gun for yourselves, and full training will be given to successful candidates at Shoeburyness."

After politely coughing, Simpson – thinking he had been forgotten – asked, "Will there be a reply, sir?"

"Yes. Acknowledge that the message has been received and will be acted on at once."

"Very good, sir," said Simpson, saluting. He then did another of his unique about-turns –successfully, without losing coordination. The room fell silent again as he walked back towards the large oak door, his shoe continuing to squeak loudly with each alternate step.

Conscious of what had very nearly happened before – and that he was the centre of attention again – Simpson clumsily opened the heavy door and made his way back to the signals room. He passed the grumpy desk sergeant on the way, who heard him coming long before seeing him. He also noticed that the cleaner was kneeling, scrubbing away his newly created scuff mark – much to the sergeant's delight.

Once inside, Simpson quickly and efficiently returned the signal to the War Office. Away from the gaze of his superiors, he felt more at ease. Being a small cog in a vast war machine was how he preferred it – leaving it to others to make the decisions.

Cussing quietly under his breath, he rubbed dubbin into his new boot to soften the hard leather and to do away with the squeaking that had embarrassed him in front of the gathered officers upstairs. Then, sitting comfortably, he opened a book – *The Fundamental Theory of Telephony* – at his marker page and read on from where he had left off. It was all about the exciting invention of telephones – soon to be developed and rolled out as a matter of urgency to the forces.

***

"Right then," said the colonel, after erasing Simpson's attempted about-turn from his thoughts. "I will require both Marsh and Townsend to remain for further briefing. Everyone else will reflect on the talks we have had about the ongoing problems we are facing in Africa concerning Natal Province and the Zulu lands. Thank you, gentlemen. Dismissed."

The men filed past the abandoned jumble of maps spread out on the large oak table, the African Continent prominent.

Colonel Downing stood with his hands clasped tightly behind his back, again correcting his posture with an occasional backwards push of the shoulder after a soft sigh. He carried an old injury caused by his horse being shot from under him at full gallop in the Capture of Lucknow in 1858, from which he had never fully recovered. It was an all-too-common injury when on a real charge.

After the door closed on the last man, Townsend looked at the colonel in curiosity and asked, "Sir, do we believe the Eyeties could be a threat so soon after that mauling at Lissa?"

"Yes, we do," the colonel replied succinctly. "We would usually shrug something like this off, but it was what was said by Francesco Crispi, one of the Italian reunification programme architects, when he referred to Malta as 'ITALIA IRREDENTA' – which, when translated, means 'UNREDEEMED ITALY.' So, gentlemen, there is cause for alarm. Those two words have rightfully spread anxiety right down from Prime Minister Gladstone to the War Office, the Admiralty, and the Army here in Woolwich. We cannot leave it at that, so you two will be obliged to travel without delay to Newcastle. The *Landau* will lie rigged up and ready to sail at first light from London Docks. So, get yourselves on board for Newcastle. Is that clear to you both?" On their nods, he continued, "Just before you go, you will be pleased to know that Armstrong has laid on a little party, a celebration he has arranged for when the Italians receive their gun. He organised it to coincide with the opening of his new swing bridge across the River Tyne, which will replace the old, low-spanned fixed bridge they have up there. It will enable the Italian ship to dock right outside his works and will also allow larger vessels to get further along the Tyne to pick up cargo from other manufacturers. So, it is financially convenient for him to put on a show for international businesses, local businessmen, and his workforce's families.

"Enjoy it, gentlemen, while you are there, but remember to always stay focused and aware: this is a deadly and dangerous business, and a very grave matter. Some would kill for the gun's secret design," he continued, emphasising how important the matter was. "I have known about this for a while; I've just been waiting for the say-so, and that message from the War Department was our permission to proceed."

Marsh and Townsend both dutifully nodded.

"You will both report for further briefing and boarding passes," he added while pacing thoughtfully across the spacious room. "You see, gentlemen, we need to know how we should handle this gun from a practical point of view. I have not seen it myself yet, so we want you both to have a good look on our behalf. Please remember that we won't have the pleasure of roads or the big dray horses to help us out. They cannot be employed in Malta, where two of these superguns are going, which means they will have to be physically hauled into place – with all the back-breaking work that entails. But we will at least have the Royal Engineers' support, who will be working with us. Well, I should finish. Any questions, gentlemen?"

"No, sir," each replied.

"Good, go and prepare for your briefing. Dismissed."

He watched the two men file out. Now alone in the large opulent Victorian room, he poured himself a whisky, then reflected on the possible outcome of the orders he had received for the deployment of the gun – and if there would ever be good cause to fire it.

However, he was impressed with the way Townsend and Marsh complemented each other. No one need know it was his on-the-spot decision to send those two officers to Newcastle. They were well paired, he felt, for what he had in mind.

Outside, shouted instructions could be heard drifting over from the parade grounds beyond, along with the familiar metallic jingle and rattle that always accompanied armed riders on the move.

They were repeatedly practising the proven shock tactics of the charge just as the orders from the drill sergeant below boomed out again: "Attention! Draw sabres! Careful with those chargers you are sitting on, you men. Present sabres! Shoulder sabres! Order sabres! Return sabres! Careful, I say, *careful!* Come on, and bloody do it again!"

Chapter 3

Visit to Newcastle and the Blue Boar Tavern.
Birds of a feather

HAVING SPENT a leisurely two days aboard the *Landau* steamship, Townsend and Marsh soon arrived in Newcastle. The new, modern steamships made travelling around the treacherous British coastline much safer and far more enjoyable for the passengers. More direct and purposeful, these ships' risk of floundering in the dangerous coastal areas was significantly reduced and made for a more pleasant, relaxed way to travel. Indeed, the two had thus far had a reasonable time of it and had enjoyed the journey.

After collecting their baggage from the cabin, they sat on the open upper deck, enjoying the scenic sights of the coastal areas the vessel was passing. Eventually, the ship approached Tynemouth, and soon the Priory and the old, ruined castle could be seen off the ship's port side bow. After passing the familiar landmarks, the ship's speed slowed as it neared the River Tyne entrance – a signal of sorts for passengers on the upper deck to get themselves below and inside.

A mother, father, and son remained at the top level until, after sharp words between them, the father got up alone and descended the steps.

The mother let out a long, loud sigh. "Come on, Jimmy pet," she said, "let's get below, man. Yer da's gone off and left us again, as usual."

"Nah, I don't wanna. Yer canna meck me!" he said, stepping back a pace and defying her.

"If I go and get yer da back to meck yer, he will. Well, do I have to gerrim back here to yer? He will tan yer arse for yer again, just like before!" the woman said. Then, while the boy's guard was down, thinking of his previous punishment, she quickly reached out, grabbed him by the arm, and yanked him off towards the lower level.

Wrapped up in their conversation, Townsend and Marsh continued their discussion without noticing how the other passengers were gradually disappearing.

"Are you excited to see this wonder gun, Robert?" Marsh enquired. "From what we've been told, it must surely be an amazing sight."

"Of course I am, David! We should consider ourselves privileged to be the first of the regiment to see it and to discuss its merits with the famed Mr Armstrong. It should be interesting."

As he was being pulled past them, young Jimmy deliberately barged hard into Marsh, spilling some of the drink he was enjoying, which made him rise to his feet in anger. The sullen lad, looking back at him over his shoulder, was delighted with what he'd done; he smirked at him before being pulled below deck by his threatening mother, who was unaware of the incident.

"Little swine!" Marsh mouthed at him with a scowl before he disappeared – knowing full well it had been deliberate.

Minutes after Marsh had sat back down, the ship's speed dropped considerably as it prepared to turn across the sea current and into the River Tyne; the ship's engine's tone was reduced to a steady chugging as it turned to port to continue its journey.

The belching black smoke from the vessel's funnel caught up with the boat's slowing speed, covering the whole open upper deck with choking, acrid, soot-laden fumes. It instantly sent both men into fits of coughing and spluttering.

Abandoning the unfinished drinks, they smartly got themselves down to the covered lower deck, much to the amusement of the regular passengers – and especially little Jimmy. He pulled faces at both, highly pleased at their discomfort and embarrassment.

The *Landau* sailed into the port serving the garrison town of Newcastle without further incident. It was a bustling, thriving place where ships of various sizes were being loaded and off-loaded under a variety of heavy cranes. These stood like sentinels lining the quayside while other ships were preparing to set sail from this bustling, working port. Hundreds of people made a living amongst these vessels, and to ensure they kept their jobs, some took to sleeping there. Such was the widespread poverty in Newcastle, people were prepared to do anything to hold onto and protect any sort of paid work.

The longboat crews put their backs to the oars, rowing and steering the *Landau* to the outside of its regular berth. Then the shore crew took over, hauling out heavy lines from fixed capstans and securing them to the ship's side. Using the capstans, they then began to wind the lines in. This action pulled the *Landau* sideways on into its berth, where it could be securely tied up and made safe.

As they waited patiently on board – along with the other passengers – to disembark, the two men occasionally coughed up and spat out specks of blackened soot from their mouths.

"I hope you enjoyed the trip, gentlemen?" the captain asked, seeing their obvious distress.

"Why, yes, Captain. It was certainly an experience," answered Townsend diplomatically.

"Yes, we won't forget it in a hurry," said Marsh, annoyed, coughing another black speck into his neckerchief. "You gave no warning you were slowing down, sir. Only, this is our first visit to Newcastle, and we were not aware of being anywhere near it. A little more information about the journey would have been appreciated." He coughed again, this time noticing his spittle was beginning to clear.

"Well, you should have gone below sooner," said the captain, dismissing the barbed comment. "I said nothing, true, but there is a large sign on the door to the open deck. Educated gentlemen such as yourselves should have read it – or at least followed our regular travellers down!"

Their continued discomfort amused the captain of the vessel, which irritated both men further.

Having bid the man a cussed farewell, they stepped unsteadily down the gangplank while attempting to find their land legs. Once ashore, and having decided on the direction in which they would get off the dock, they set off with a firm stride to find their allocated tavern. They had been reliably informed earlier by a crew member that the Blue Boar would be somewhere nearby. It was a well-known watering hole with a good reputation, and it had been highly recommended by previous patrons from the military. Woolwich had considered it ideal, therefore, for two of their military officers.

The two men passed along the quay, where the young daughter of a local fisherman sat with a stick at the ready, squealing with a mixture of worry and delight whilst knocking back in any pitiable crab attempting to escape its basket prison. Likewise, her brother was employed brandishing a long stick at any gull that swooped in to steal a fish. Other fishing boats were tied up and heaving with their latest catch, while coaling ships were lined up nearby under huge coal hoppers, waiting their turn to be loaded. With the strong smell of fresh fish filling the air – and their lungs – they soon forgot about their uncomfortable bouts of coughing.

"I've never seen so many fish, David!" Townsend exclaimed.

He licked his lips before replying, "You're right. Just the smell has me feeling famished."

The two men had been spotted disembarking by several eagle-eyed ragamuffins, and they now found themselves being very quickly surrounded by these waifs – each begging for spare coppers while walking beside them along the quay.

"Hey, mister, let me carry yer rucksack for yer for a penny!" shouted one boy.

"No, don't. I'll carry it for a ha'penny, man!" called out the lass next to him.

"Aye, and I'll carry the small one for a farthing!" said her little sister, dressed in rags and reaching out to take one. She smiled sweetly, wiping away the snot from the end of her nose with the cuff of a sleeve.

Suddenly, arguments galore started amongst the children, with war threatening to break out as to who should carry the rucksacks. They followed the two luckless men out of the docks, harassing them and arguing amongst themselves, as they headed towards the streets.

On turning the corner in haste, Marsh's immediate reaction was to hold his nose. "God, it stinks here," he said. "It smells like an open sewer."

"Aye, it is that. Da said someone's had a huge turnout, like," the boy said with a snigger. "The sewer is blocked and cracked, like. That's why it's overflowing into the street, man. Look, are yer ganna let us carry yer rucksacks, then, mister, or what?" he asked, feeling mounting animosity towards Marsh, considering him to have dithered for far too long.

"Yes, alright, then," he finally agreed before being stopped by Townsend, who was worried the children might run off with the rucksacks and leave them stranded.

"I'll give you the pennies," he said, "but we will carry them ourselves. Are your parents aware you're out here, begging?"

"Oh, aye! There's me da, over there."

Opposite them was a man sitting on the cold stone floor, leaning his head on his raised knee. His arm was propped up across the other, and he was holding his hand out in the hopes something of worth would be dropped into it. He had fallen asleep in that position.

"Maybe yer da – I mean, your father – has got money?" asked Marsh.

"Nah! He ain't. He's got nothing on him."

"How do you know?" said Marsh. "Yer da – er, your dad – might have something in his pocket."

"Nah! He ain't. I've been through his pockets like me ma told us to," the child said wisely, wiping his wet runny nose on the back of his arm and then rubbing his arm down the side of his torn trousers, leaving a snail trail on the grubby garment.

31

Townsend could sense his friend getting sentimental and anxious at their plight. "Look, tell us where the Blue Boar is, and I'll give a threepenny piece to yer da – er, excuse me, your dad."

"You're not to give it to me da," the boy protested. "Ma won't see anything of it because he'll be down the pub to piss it up against the wall. I'll give it to me ma, though! She'll gerrus something to eat with it, aye!" He paused, pointing down the road. "That side is cut off with a great puddle of piddle halfway down the street, so don't go down on that side. You can cross over here and walk to the very end – staying close to the wall. Aye, then, turn right and keep going past the Clifford Fort. If you come back to the docks, take the next street along, which is clear right back into the quayside – then turn left, and it's halfway along there. Yer canna miss it, man, but I bet your mate would, easily." He ended his directions by pointing a grubby condemning finger towards Marsh.

Townsend flipped a threepenny piece towards their diminutive guide, who skilfully caught it. "Now, share that thruppence between you," he instructed before turning and saying, "Come on, David, let's get going."

They carefully crossed the street of small square cobblestones by stepping and balancing on top of any raised above the urine-contaminated mud.

"It's hard to see how some people live like that," Marsh commented sadly. "There's plenty of fish on the quay, yet some are starving! Given a hot summer, Robert, cholera could break out here again like before."

"You need money to buy food for the hungry; there's the problem," Robert answered scornfully.

Seasoned city travellers knew that the safest way to walk in a strange town was in the middle of the street, thus giving a nifty and well-heeled person a sporting chance to avoid anything unsavoury that might suddenly be flung from an open doorway or window.

It wasn't long before the men heard the fearful: "Gardyloo! Gardyloooo!" – the time-honoured warning cry for flying excrement and piss.

They both reacted instinctively by ducking down low and walking on quickly. Something unpleasant splashed in the gutter only seconds after passing one household, but they had no desire to find out what it was. The only way to safely navigate these streets of scruffy, thriving humanity was to be aware that everything and anything could suddenly appear at any given moment.

Then, only minutes later, they found themselves fending off shameless prostitutes and ignoring suggestions on what they could do to their bodies if they gave them money, all while keeping a wary lookout up and down the street for any sight or signs of constabulary approaching.

At last, they came across the Blue Boar.

Hurriedly, they pushed open the door so they could get inside and avoid being hassled by the beggars lingering outside the premises. As they stepped into the gas-lit room, the smoke from the drinkers' pipes hung in flat, undisturbed, layered wisps in the one unoccupied corner of the room. The building's frame was made of recovered oak beams set into thick walls that supported the bar's varying ceiling heights on the upper bedroom floors. The best timber, salvaged from long-forgotten sailing ships, had been put to good use. The room was full of merriment from happy customers: the complete opposite of the chaotic, impoverished scene they had witnessed outside.

Townsend and Marsh jostled and squeezed themselves between the crowd of drinkers to head towards the bar. On the way, Townsend showed a marked interest in the newly installed gaslights, which were spaced out where needed along both walls of the room. *Quite impressive*, he thought.

Marsh had noticed too. "Look, Robert, they have that new lighting in here. I've seen it occasionally when passing buildings, but I've never been inside one to experience its effect with a mantle fitted."

"Yes! I can see you quite clearly under it. It's much better than looking at faces and objects through flickering candles," Townsend replied. "It gives off a little heat, and it's better on the eyes… and safer. I should think most homes will have gas lighting soon. Welcome to the modern world, David – this is the future we see here!"

As they used their elbows and some belated apologies to get to the bar, they absorbed the conversation between the customers, confirming that big orders were coming in – with two shifts working extra time to fulfil them. To David and Robert, it seemed like the jobs market was beginning to thrive, with vacancies posted daily.

"Can I help you, sirs?" asked the ruddy-faced gaffer.

"Yes. We understand you have two rooms booked for us. We're both up from London," said Townsend, before giving him their names.

The gaffer went over to consult the ledger. "Ah, yes. Are you the two gentlemen from Woolwich?" he shouted back above the voices of his customers.

"Yes, we are!" replied Townsend, matching the shouted volume of the landlord.

"Good! Then, gents, if you would kindly pick up your belongings, I'll show you to your rooms. We have two at the back, so you won't be bothered too much by this jabbering prattle. Follow me, then." With that, he led them through the bar to the stairs in the corridor opposite the large kitchen.

Marsh, who hadn't spoken, brought up the rear as they climbed the creaking stairs. Passing the kitchen, he casually peered in through the steamed-up glass in the door and caught sight of a pretty lass working there. Indifferent to her surroundings and thinking she was alone; she was busily wiping away at a large spillage on her clothing. It had penetrated her dress at the top of her thigh, leaving her decidedly wet, itchy, and most uncomfortable.

He opened the door purposefully, considered her startled expression, and quickly said, "Oh, excuse me."

In that instant, she dropped the hem of her dress and blushed, but not before he had caught a glimpse of her shapely leg. She lowered her eyes, embarrassed as he smiled at her appreciatively. He lingered for a few seconds more, continuing to look, then bowed low at the waist with a sweep of his hand and quickly bounded up the stairs to catch up with the others. *She's pretty. Maybe Newcastle isn't as dour or grim a place as it first appears,* Marsh thought.

Sarah, the young woman in the kitchen, had tutted and glared at him, plainly thinking him rude, staring at her the way he did. While feeling angry with him, she had given herself a wry smile at being caught out so blatantly by his obviously planned intrusion. *Both bold and unmannerly,* she thought. She had never before been left so embarrassed, but she somehow enjoyed the confrontation.

***

"This is it, then, gents. You in here, and you in there," said the landlord, directing them to two good-sized single bedrooms. "After you settle in, come on downstairs and we'll get Sarah to cook you something. She's down in the kitchen now."

After the landlord had gone, leaving them alone in their respective rooms, Marsh grinned at himself in the tarnished mirror on the wall. *There's a good possibility down there of some fun, especially now I know her name,* he thought. *Hopefully, she has a sense of humour to sit alongside her beauty.*

Townsend had a strong physical presence, with his rugged good looks, but he also had a good strength of character. He was a man of complete sincerity, with a certain inner softness that women often found quite endearing and attractive. Lying down on the creaking bed, he placed both arms behind his head and then stretched out his tall frame, which filled its length. He felt tired from the journey and was about to slumber when his wife emerged foremost in his mind.

He dutifully thought of Victoria, alone in their bed, with her fiery auburn hair cascading down and caressing her shoulders. He was missing her already. They had got married only a short while ago and had been blissfully happy. He hadn't, however, seen her for some time, and her absence was beginning to tell on him. Married life in the military was cruel, always second to the regiment's incessant demands.

Restless, he sprung back to his feet and went in search of Marsh in the opposite bedroom, considering that he ought to keep his interest up if he wanted to avoid him getting into one of his frequent scrapes.

Agreeing that he was tired and hungry, Marsh traipsed downstairs after his friend, pausing for a quick peek while passing the partly open kitchen door – and confirming she was still in there.

Edging their way through to the bar, they gave out their drinks order: "Two tankards of your fine ale, please, landlord – and one of your cigars, if you will," added Marsh.

Once he had the cigar in his hand, he looked to light it from the tiny metal figure of a pixie sitting on the near side of the bar. It had a small flame of coal-gas flickering out from its mouth for smokers to use. He lit his cigar and inhaled contentedly.

A loud gathering of friends now sat in the once empty corner, and could be heard above the others in the room. They were noisy but well behaved, poking and prodding each other as the drink loosened their tongues. Their strange but heavy local accent had a jolly ring to it.

"Why aye, man. Yer was the spitting image of yer da when yer was a wee bairn. We put a pipe in yer gob ter meck sure, like."

They hung on to each other in fits of laughter, their slapping at one another disturbing and breaking up the layered wisps of smoke above their heads.

"Away, man. It was yer ma, mind, who said yer didna."

It was followed by more demented giggles and uncontrolled merriment while under the increasing influence of the strong ale.

"What do you think of this draft ale they have up here?" Marsh asked, watching Robert lift his tankard. "The drink is okay, isn't it? It tastes good and comes with a reputation," he said slowly, unsure of himself.

"Yes, it's tasty, all right. Good, in fact," Townsend replied, savouring the taste. "The trick is to check that no bits are floating around at the bottom, because it could be duff with the dregs of other, flat beers mixed in. It's become a habit now for me. You would soon know, of course, when you got the shits in the morning. But you're right – it's a nice, clear drink, with a good head on it, too. Back home in London, if you're not a local, they pass the dregs of the barrels onto you if they think they can get away with it – including the collected slops from used tankards if you're not careful.

But they wouldn't do it in a place like this," he said, with a nod towards the eavesdropping landlord. "Too swanky, with a reputation to keep."

Later, they gave their food order to the landlord and waited patiently, but he was being inundated with questions on racing pigeons from the various men he was serving at the bar. Feeling the first pangs of hunger, Marsh offered to take the orders to the kitchen for him, to which he agreed.

Pushing open the kitchen door, he saw Sarah with her back to him. "Ahem," he coughed.

She heard him but, at first, she only lifted her eyes to the window and carried on peeling the potatoes in the bucket. "Yes? What do you want?" she asked sharply, recognising the man's voice who had purposefully surprised her earlier.

"Erm, it's our paid order for two. The local bird fanciers are mobbing the landlord at the bar, so I volunteered to bring it instead, *Sarah*!"

Without looking, she gave herself an extra wry smile. *Another interested in me, it seems*, she thought. *One more randy bloke trying his luck, I expect. They can be such a bloody nuisance.* She turned and walked towards the figure in the doorway. "Thank you. I'll take that. It will just take a short while if you want to wait." Holding the order, she checked first for the landlord's mark to be sure. "This will be my last for tonight. Phew! I'm worn to a frazzle. Soon, someone else can take over from me."

"Oh good, I've made it, then?"

She looked into each of his blue eyes in turn, trying to determine if the remark meant anything else. "You haven't made anything yet," she retorted, knowing he was flirting. She liked what she saw, though. He was different from her usual suitors. "Are you passing through?"

"Yes, erm, that's right. My name's David. I'm here with my colleague, Robert. We're here on business."

"I would be foolish to believe that," she countered as she started plating the meals. "You being suited means nothing. You look too much like the military. It's the way you carry yourselves. Officer types, maybe?"

"You've seen through me, Sarah." He gave her what he always thought of as his winning smile. "It seems you're observant as well as beautiful."

"I have to be with the men that come and go here," she said, deliberately ignoring the compliment. "You need eyes up your...." Her voice fell away without finishing the sentence. She was too well brought up and mannered to say such a thing out loud to a stranger.

"Two slices, please," he said, interrupting her thoughts.

"Sorry, what did you say?"

"Two slices of bread. One each – and can I have the crust?"

"Oh, I see. Yes, of course. Well, here are your meals."

"I'll take them with me." Marsh leant across her for the bread, deliberately brushing her forearm with his hand.

She flinched and pulled it away before nervously patting down her hair for no real reason. After regaining her composure, she wiped her hands on the apron sitting comfortably around her waist, staying silent. Sarah knew what he was up to, and she felt that the 'deliberately accidental' touch had cleverly broken down the icy barrier between them.

He thought he'd unsettled her for a second time, so he changed his line of conversation accordingly. "Tell me, Sarah, is the landlord your father?"

"No," she replied, getting on with her work. "I stay here a few days, go home, and come back on the Sabbath. Father was injured in the mine when the tunnel collapsed. It's been left to my brother and me to keep a roof over our heads. I'd almost finished training for a professional career but I had to forsake it until Father got better. This job pays reasonably well, and I'm near home to help. Suffice to say, I have every intention of going back to my career when he recovers."

He heard the tone in her voice gradually soften. After a short pause, he asked, "Sarah, would you like to have a drink with me later? I'd very much appreciate your company – only, I don't know anyone else in Newcastle."

His charming while delving manner was beginning to affect Sarah, which irritated her. *You're a fast worker, aren't you?* she thought. "I don't know," she answered cautiously. He wasn't the first person to ask her out on these premises but being brought up well, and into a caring family, she was prone to decline such offers because of where it might lead. Her parents had made her aware of the many risks a young woman faces in the world today.

"Well, will you?"

Sarah considered his offer. She thought he was handsome – and different from those who lived around here. *I'm amazed he's had the cheek to ask me like this*, she thought. *But why not? I can't keep saying no to them all. Besides, we're not going anywhere. Surely, there can't be any harm in it.* "Mm. All right. I'm done here in a half-hour, so I'll see you on the hour after that?" She pushed the two plates of food toward him. "Now, be off with you before that food gets cold," she ordered.

She watched him go with a small shake of her head; she was beginning to feel friendlier towards him now, though his initial remarks had been far too forward for her liking.

Marsh carried the plates back to the bar with a little bounce in his stride.

"Where have you been? I nearly came looking for you," said Townsend, eyeing him with suspicion and mild concern.

"Nowhere," replied Marsh, thinking of Sarah and how he had successfully managed to manipulate their encounter.

"Must be a woman," said Townsend, with an impatient tut. "Here, give me my food. I'm starving."

***

Later that evening, Marsh waited for Sarah at the foot of the stairs. She wasn't in the kitchen, only another member of staff. He had left Townsend asleep on the bed in his room and had decided not to wake him. *The journey must be catching up with the old boy*, he thought, though there was barely two years difference in their ages.

Suddenly, Sarah appeared at the top of the stairs. Her hair was shiny and clean, and gone were the sticky curls she'd had from the heat and steam of the kitchen.

"Sarah, I didn't expect you to come that way!" he exclaimed. "What are you doing up there? Were you looking for me?"

"No. I've got a room in the attic," she said, pointing to the top of the stairs. "I sleep up there." She smiled shyly at him as he took her hand at the bottom of the stairway, gallantly steadying her down the last three steps. She lowered the front of her weighty cotton calico skirt – a well-mannered young woman's last line of defence against amorous suitors, meant to discourage any intended secret fumbling. A floral blouse completed the set, cut slightly low at the front; it fired Marsh's imagination about what the rest looked like beneath the dress.

Gazing down, he couldn't see her feet, but he knew they were in there somewhere. She had made every effort to look her best for this first meeting, and he fully appreciated the result.

In fact, he couldn't contain himself; he made a noise of approval before saying, "You look lovely, Sarah – quite stunning, to be truthful. If I get you a drink from the bar, will you sup it with me?"

She hesitated. Marsh guessed that she didn't ordinarily drink and would, therefore, not usually be found in the bar, socialising with the patrons. He was thinking about suggesting an alternative when she interrupted his thinking.

She nodded. "A light sherry, please, David."

"Do you mean a medium sherry?" he asked, suspecting that she didn't know what was on offer.

Sarah blushed. "Oh, yes, of course. I meant a medium-light sherry. Thank you."

He thought he would test her knowledge further. "Wet, dry, or sweet?"

"What?"

"Wet, dry, or sweet?"

"Wet and sweet, of course," she said, slightly swinging her hips at his silly question.

He left for the bar knowing full well she wasn't a drinker and was acting older than her years.

"Would you like to drink outside in the cool breeze?" he asked on returning. "It's still daylight, and it'll be much quieter away from all this noisy drunken chatter." At her nodded approval, he led her outside, carrying their drinks into the welcoming breeze. He gave her the sherry and then noticed the three wooden pigeon pens in the yard. "Sarah, who do they belong to?" he asked.

"They belong to Albert. He sometimes races them. You saw the pigeon owners in here already tonight," she explained.

Together, they went to peep through the wooden bars of the cages, which instigated the birds into cooing, dipping their heads, and bowing while walking in circles.

"They've eaten all the corn, so they probably think they're getting extra," said David. "You can see the different markings on the birds if you bend down beside me." He deftly slipped his hand to her waist and bent down to show her where to look. "Look at those tumblers in there, Sarah."

"Do they trip and fall?" she asked innocently, not knowing what he meant.

Marsh laughed. "No, just a different type of pigeon," he explained. "The name tumbler means they fly to about sixty feet up in the sky and then tumble backwards in mid-air. They put on quite a show for anyone watching. These in the next pen are skimmers. They fly in ever-wider circles, high above their pens, to between eighty and one hundred feet. Then they glide or skim over buildings and such back to their pens."

"Ooh, I'm impressed," said Sarah, dipping her chin and still not bothering to remove his arm from around her waist. "Where did you learn that? A book, I suppose?"

"No, my uncle keeps pigeons. He's a big pigeon fancier, and he encourages me to fly them whenever I stay at his house. Plenty of people keep pigeons and race them where I'm from, just like here. It's a sport. Sometimes they can be very keen and passionate with it, I assure you."

While his attention was elsewhere, Sarah took her first dainty little sip of the sherry, and her eyes lit up. She liked it. She had a larger sip, then another, soon finishing it off. Pleased with the taste, she drank it way too fast for a beginner. *Mm*, she thought, savouring it. *I didn't know it tasted like that – it's quite pleasant.* She decided to say nothing, however, about the effect it was having on her. "Very interesting, David," she fibbed. "Can I have another?"

Spurred on by her perceived interest, he continued, ignoring her question. "These, now, are what's known as tipplers. They fly so high you need a good eye to pick them out. They just appear as small dots in the sky. Eventually, they will all return to their lofts or pens, back to the hens in the nest. They're used in the military to carry messages. We always send two pigeons with the same message in case one is lost to a hawk or gets shot down. Also, they never mix the bird types in the same cage; it would ruin the different breeds."

"I see," said Sarah, not looking. Her thoughts were still on the drink. "David, can I have another sherry, please?" she asked again, appealing to his generous nature.

"What, so soon?! Of course, I'll get one each," he said, disappearing back inside the bar.

After he had gone, Sarah steadied herself by leaning against the side of the pigeon pen with one hand, the other at her waist. *Ooh, it does taste good*, she thought light-headedly, with one leg a little bent at the knee and the other straight. A slight curl of her pouting upper lip was all that betrayed her enjoyment. *Mm*, she thought, *I could bathe in that!*

When Marsh returned, he found Sarah steadying herself at the pigeon pen. Her speech was beginning to slur. It was becoming evident that she wasn't used to drinking, and he began feeling strangely protective of her.

"There's a lot of sherry in my glass, David," Sarah observed tipsily. "Why is my glass half-measure, the same as yours, when I'm not drinking beer? That's what I want to know. The standard measure is not a glass full, is it? Or is it me? They do seem to be getting bigger?" She pushed him playfully on the chest while snorting and giggling in his face.

"Honestly, they were short of smaller glasses, Sarah. These were all they had," Marsh explained. "Even the tankards are in full use, and besides, it saves me getting you another. There are quite a few in there tonight, even queuing to get to the bar. I think the landlord and his wife are just about coping." He realised she was getting drunk and unsteady, so he pulled her closer to him, so close that he was able to nuzzle his nose into her hair and could smell the essence of a beautiful, nubile lady emanating from each pore of skin around her neck: very fresh, and very desirable. He didn't want her to fall, so he held on more tightly, feeling even more protective towards her – for reasons he couldn't explain.

"And those three?" she asked, pointing between two birds.

He looked at her sideways, with raised eyebrows and a trace of a smile. She was becoming comical now, and he laughed both at her and her antics.

"Well, if you want to know, all three are called mixed-winged 'uns," he said, playing along. He slid his hand down from her waist, where it had been resting, onto her right hip. She didn't seem to notice or care. "The other one over there is called a blue-barred 'un."

"'Un, 'un, *un!*" She giggled while he drew her closer, kissing her neck – and still getting no rejection.

"Yes, and that one is called a 'good hen' and that one there is called a 'good cock'."

Overwhelmed by a sudden carnal passion stirring from deep inside, he drew her full on and kissed her – putting an instant stop to all such awkward, frivolous talk.

Tipsy, Sarah responded instantly, and with an enthusiasm that surprised her.

By the time they finished their drinks, they were still engrossed in each other's company, oblivious to everything else. Marsh was struck by her enticing, beguiling innocence, while Sarah appeared impressed by his knowledge.

Suddenly, she shuddered.

"It's getting cold, Sarah," said Marsh. "Shall we go in?"

"I want another," she said, slurring her words.

"You've had more than enough," he told her, holding her gently. "And, to be truthful, I feel pissed just trying to keep up with you! Tell me the truth now: does Albert or Rose know you're out here drinking with me?"

She dismissed his concern. "No, why should I have told them?"

"I see. Come on, let's go in where it's warmer."

They were walking towards the tavern, holding hands, when he asked, "Can someone wake me in the morning?"

He didn't receive an answer.

They got to the staircase and began climbing the steps, Sarah holding onto his arm to steady herself.

"Where's your room, Sarah?" he asked, and when she didn't respond, he nudged her and asked again, "Where's your room? Can I come in with you?"

"It'sh in the attic above the landlord's room, hish family room," she said in a giggling, drunken, whispering lisp. The sherry was beginning to take control of her senses.

"In the attic, did you say, Sarah? Above the landlord?"

"Yesh," she replied loudly, then hiccupped – no longer caring about decorum, convention, or conformity.

"Shit!" The word was silently forced from Marsh's mouth as he realised his plan to bed her was not to be. Then, he asked, "Sarah, will you give me an early morning call? I have to go to Elswick on important business."

"Yesh, yesh," she said, followed by another noisy hiccup.

"Good! Let me show you to my room. I'm in here, Sarah." They tottered in, and he lit the remains of a candle he had found on the small sideboard, dripping the hot candle wax onto its holder to safely set the candle in. "You will call me tomorrow, won't you? Promise me before you go back to your room."

She put her fingers to her lips and, after waiting for another hiccup to arrive, said, "You won't need me to call you, Davy. The cock'll be up cockering and crowing early in the morning, that's for sure." She giggled, holding a cupped hand to her nose.

Changing his mind, Marsh closed the door behind them. He then held Sarah by the shoulders, smothering her with more tender kisses before slowly tugging down on her blouse.

I'm about to find out about 'IT' for the first time, and I intend to enjoy 'IT' she thought happily, intoxicated. She remembered how her friend Bernice had once told her, on the quiet: *It's enjoyed better the first time if you're slightly inebriated, Sarah! He will also appreciate you holding it. You will find it fits well in your hand. Better still, both your hands will please him even more!* She took this as the obvious truth.

"Well, I've tried to get ininigburated," she said aloud, but Marsh wasn't listening; his mind was on other, more important things.

The blouse had suddenly halted. *Something's stopping it from coming down!* he thought. *Damn it! What the bloody hell is it?* He began to check his handiwork by the failing, flickering candlelight, which just about enabled him to peek into her blouse. He could see it was the fullness of her breasts that was causing the issue. One final tug and her breasts sprang back, allowing the material to drop silently to her waist.

He caressed one of her breasts, which felt firm under his touch, and then kissed her again passionately. As she responded, he drew her in closer, until the nipples of both breasts pressed firmly against his chest. He turned her slowly but deliberately, greedily desiring to feel the fullness of both in his hands. Cupping first one and then the other, he began to nibble slowly at the back of her ear, causing her to moan with pleasure. Delighted at her submission, he reached around to her front and undid the sizeable top button at her waistline, allowing the heavy calico skirt to drop to the floor – and taking her loose-fitting, stringed cotton drawers with it.

"Don't hurt me, please, David," she whispered. She was sobering up now and was well aware of what he was doing.

Before she had the chance to change her mind, Marsh quickly got out of his clothes and left them in a heap on the floor. Then, after wetting two of his fingers with spittle, he extinguished the candle's flame – burning a finger in the hot candle wax in the process.

Sarah heard him cuss in the dark, then felt him move towards her on the bed. Instinctively, she eased her legs apart; the same friend had also instructed her that entering was much more comfortable that way. *I can assure you that you will enjoy it if he's a considerate lover*, she'd told her.

As she felt his warm body eagerly pushing against hers, she let out a moan of unexpected delight.

***

"Cock-a-doodle-do!" crowed the rooster as it strutted about the courtyard below his room.

Townsend squinted through the window but couldn't see the animal. Using the back of his hand, he rubbed away at the build-up of condensation on the windowpane – but he still couldn't see it. *Why is it crowing? It's still bloody dark!* he grumbled to himself.

Although woken abruptly, he felt much refreshed – unlike yesterday when he'd been exhausted from travelling. He lay there for a while, thinking of the importance of their visit to Elswick later and the need to familiarise themselves with this ground breaking gun. The colonel had hinted – more than once – that both he and Marsh could go to either Malta or Gibraltar with one, which he felt would be an excellent career opportunity for himself.

Soon enough the dawn broke, and the bolshie cockerel finally stopped its incessant crowing. Hearing movement further down the corridor, Townsend splashed water onto his face from the water bowl and towelled it dry. Then, when he was suitably dressed, he opened the door to the first-floor corridor. Walking gingerly along the creaking floorboards – which sounded more like loudly snapping twigs in the early morning silence – he crossed the passage, pushed open his friend's door, and walked in.

"Bloody hell!" he gasped, upon seeing the bed's occupants. *There he is, lying naked with a woman! While I was asleep, he was having sex with someone. Probably drunk, to boot! Well, he's coming to Elswick with me today, whether he likes it or not! There will be no lie-in for him this morning.*

Picking up a metal plate and a wooden spoon off the small table, Townsend took a deep breath and bawled into his friend's ear, banging the spoon on the plate as he yelled, "This is your sergeant major speaking! Get up and stand to attention! Get up! Get up!"

43

Instantly, Marsh shot out of bed and stood rigidly to attention: naked, rock solid, and with his eyelids still welded together, but fully conditioned to early morning inspection.

Startled by the commotion, Sarah screamed as she grabbed the sheets to cover herself, now fully aware that a stranger had seen her naked. She felt ashamed and embarrassed at being found out.

Townsend, meanwhile, laughed devilishly at them both and quickly left the room.

Once he was gone, Sarah turned on Marsh angrily scolding him. "David, how could you do this to me? You had this planned, didn't you? You plied me with the drink and made out you were being friendly and chatty. And then you left me lying here so your friend could see my nakedness in the morning! I won't trust you again... never!

"Sarah, I'm sorry!" Marsh exclaimed, still bewildered by what had just happened. "I'm sorry! It wasn't like that at all. Yes, I did want to make love to you, but I thought that's what you wanted too?" he asked. "You completely bewitched me! But I won't take the blame for Robert walking in on us as he did. Honestly, I forgot about him – I only had thoughts and desires for you. Besides, he had no idea you were in here with me because he had fallen asleep in his room before I came down to meet you last night."

Sarah rolled herself into a ball, pulled the bedclothes over her head, and said nothing.

"I apologise for his behaviour, Sarah. I'll make it up to you... if you allow me," he continued. "Having said all that, he could have shown a little discretion and left the room, but he didn't. Instead, he thought it a good idea to bang a metal plate in my ear. It's still bloody ringing now!" he grumbled as he pulled on his trousers and boots. The more he thought of it, the angrier he was becoming.

After more futile attempts to convince Sarah of his true intentions, he grabbed a shirt to wear and then walked over to Townsend's room. When he found he wasn't there, he descended the stairs with clenched fists. Townsend's absence had taken some of the anger out of him, and he felt cheated; he had wanted a good argument, right there and then.

After ensuring he'd gone, Sarah swiftly dressed and then – realising that the bedsheet was marked – she gathered it up and took it to her room, hoping no one would see her on the way. She then stripped off her own clean bedsheet and took it down to Marsh's room to remake his bed with it. She had every intention of using carbolic soap and salted water on the marked sheet. Her embarrassment at their little escapade was now complete, and the future possible result of the dalliance deeply worried her.

***

Marsh strode purposefully into the bar to confront his friend. "Oh, there you are, Townsend, you twat face! I wondered where you'd got to, running out as you did." He walked over to where he was sitting at the empty bar. "I suppose you think that was funny," he said while rubbing his groin.

"Look, David," said Townsend, holding his hand out defensively, "we're off to Elswick today, or had you forgotten? While I was asleep, you were out romping for most of the night. I'll give you credit, though. She's pretty, all right: beautiful and a definite head-turner. Yes, I'll say that for you."

This comment broke the animosity between them, and – after a long stare out – they both smiled.

"Not bad, eh? That's what I thought too, Robert."

"I've spoken to the landlord," said Townsend, still smiling. "He's arranging for us to travel to Elswick by coach and horse. The other passengers are also going to the fair Armstrong has laid on for the locals. So, the Eyeties are collecting their first gun. The new iron bridge will be opened, and we get to see the gun being loaded aboard the *Europa*. Then we'll go back to the factory tomorrow to see it again for ourselves. The gaffer said it's only a short distance away, so I'll get Sarah to give us something to eat. Is she down in the kitchen?"

"She should be by now; I think she followed me down," said Marsh. "I'll order our breakfast, though, if you please. I want to see if she's calmed down any. I'll be back soon."

"You had better. There's no time for anything else," Townsend reminded him.

Marsh attempted to speak to Sarah in the kitchen, but she was having none of it, so he returned to the bar to wait. A short while later, Sarah brought their meals in but wouldn't look at either of them: her face was dark with anger as she placed the plates down hard on the uneven table. Marsh reached for her hand, but she snatched it out of his grasp before hurrying back to the kitchen.

Townsend watched her leave through the door. He was beginning to feel a tinge of guilt for embarrassing her as he did.

The breakfast was eaten in uncomfortable silence as Marsh thought about his predicament. Sarah had been very amusing last night, and he was beginning to feel a strong attraction toward her. Even after the third sherry, she'd been quite willing to hold the pigeon he took out of the pen. Sarah had clutched the bird in one hand, holding both wings just like she'd been shown: with its legs held comfortably between her first two fingers. Sarah was amazed that she had found the courage to handle it and, delighted at her achievement, she had happily stroked the pigeon as it cooed softly. It was only when the bird had touched her thumb with its beak that she gave out a scream and begged him to take it back and put safely away in its pen. Marsh admired her naivety and innocence, and found her charming – and extremely attractive. Which made her rejection of him even worse.

"I'll take the plates back to the kitchen, Robert."

"Leave them. Rose will clear them away soon enough."

"No. I want to see Sarah and make my peace with her before we leave."

Marsh got to the kitchen door and stood aside while another staff member came out and passed him by. Sarah was now left alone in the kitchen, and Marsh decided to take his chance. "Sarah, I've brought the plates back," he said cautiously, not knowing how she would react. "I thought I would save you a journey to the bar."

Without saying a word, she walked over to the door and snatched them out of his hands. After placing the used plates on top of the existing pile, she returned to the kitchen door, slamming it shut and locking it in his face.

Then, somewhat to his surprise, he said something completely out of character: "Sarah, do you believe in loving someone at first sight? I didn't until I met you, and then something happened to me last night to make me change my mind. Sarah! Sarah, I know you can hear me," he whispered through the door. "I hope you will forgive me, that's all. I must go, but I want to see you when I get back. Until later, then."

She ignored his pleading and waited for his footsteps to die away on the passage flagstones leading back to the bar. Once she knew he had gone, she unlocked the door and returned to her work of dealing with the used plates.

Chapter 4

Elswick Fair and the new bridge.
Loading the gun aboard the Europa

THE HORSE-DRAWN coach drove noisily over the cobblestones, through the high archway of the once-active coaching stage, and out into the disused stable yard behind the Inn, where it stopped to pick up the passengers. Inside sat two ladies dressed in their finery and two bad-mannered children.

"Good morning," said Marsh, opening the carriage door.

"Good morning, ladies," Townsend said courteously, ever the more refined of the two.

"Good morning," they both replied, impressed with their good manners.

"May we join you? We're going to the celebrations and the fair ourselves."

"Indeed, do," said the one, making room for them on the bench seat.

"And are you children excited to be going to the fair?" Marsh enquired of the two little ones.

They both shrank away from him. "I don't like you," retorted the little girl instantly.

"Mary, please mind your manners," insisted her mother, stunned. "I do apologise, gentlemen. She appears to be tired from the journey."

The boy just stared at him – unimpressed with his friendliness and clearly weighing him up.

During the short journey, Marsh occasionally shot a cursory glance at the boy, but little changed. The boy was still watching him. He began to feel decidedly uncomfortable under the child's gaze, which only ended when the coach drew to a halt at the Armstrong gates. The two men dismounted first and then helped the ladies and girl down. The boy was last; jumping from the top step of the coach, he landed between the two of them and said, completely out of the blue, "Well, I don't like either of you!"

Apologising for the outburst, his mum shook him and dragged him off by the arm, chastising both him and his sister for their bad behaviour as she went.

The finished gun trundling out from the Armstrong factory. Being pulled by a small steam engine on a narrow-gauge track. On its way to be loaded aboard the waiting SS Stanley.

I can see her having a difficult time with the two of them in the future, and she has my every sympathy, Townsend thought.

The celebrations were already in full swing. Following the sounds of a brass band playing nearby, they soon became immersed in a flow of bodies that swept them along in the excitement of the occasion. Many hundreds of people converged on the pathways and walked eagerly towards the river, keen to listen to Armstrong's inauguration speech.

When the crowded throng reached the banks of the Tyne, they came to a halt at the back of a much larger gathering. Armstrong was standing at a podium on a platform decked out in festival gaiety. He was expounding on the benefits of his bridge.

Along with the others, Townsend and Marsh listened with great interest to his intriguing but long-winded speech about his swing bridge's operation. As he spoke, the towering bridge behind him began to open as a demonstration for the gathering. It was surprisingly quiet and graceful, and both men – and the rest of the crowd – were very much taken with it. Armstrong had designed a most original hydraulic bridge, which swung fully open on its axis to allow the taller ships through.

The Italian ship the *Europa* gave several short blasts on its steam whistle before starting to move forward as arranged. When this first ship passed beyond the new bridge, several small cannons arrayed on the riverbank fired off a series of blanks in recognition of the occasion. The brass band struck up again – along with much whooping and clapping from the crowd – while the *Europa* passed safely through and along to its docking berth outside the Armstrong foundry.

This was the signal for the festivities to begin in earnest. Bunting danced in the breeze as if joining in with the merriment while children ran through the crowd, rolling hoops and laughing with one another. Some parents bought their children 'Whip the Top' spinning toys from the stalls, while others skipped or played hopscotch. Toffee apples were eaten with relish by many among the crowd.

Townsend watched as a woman chose the stick-pierced apple she wanted from the open boxes in front of the stall. Then, daintily – taking care not to dirty the lace-trimmed sleeve of her dress – she dipped the apple into the warm, mouth-watering liquid toffee and raised it to her lips. The man next to her was more impatient for his treat. Paying his penny, he snapped off his chosen cooled toffee apple – which had hardened on a chilled tray in cold water – and walked off with it.

Further on, there were yet more stalls, including coconut shies and penny pushing. Many were playing games using glass marbles. Every so

Watched by a large, cheering crowd. The loading crew are in the throes of welcoming the deadly cargo aboard.

often, a cry would go up when an opponent chipped their marble using steel bearings – a practice considered decidedly lousy form. By far the favourite attraction, however – especially for the little ones – was the hand-cranked carousel. The ride's length depended on the age and stamina of whoever was cranking the handle at the time. This task usually fell to fathers and elder sons, all of whom were eagerly encouraged by both the children and the owners of the ride, who were thankful for a rest from the demands of keeping the carousel turning.

"Come on, David," Townsend exclaimed, caught up in the excitement of the fair. "I'll treat you to a large toffee apple if you crank the carousel!"

"I'll do it for two," Marsh replied, taking up the challenge. "Excuse me, sir, can I give it a whirl for you?" he asked of the aged, overweight owner, who was most thankful for an opportunity to get his breath and strength back. He gave his permission willingly while dabbing a rag at his perspiring brow.

"Good," said Marsh, ushering him to one side and immediately blowing three loud, shrill whistles through his fingers to get the children's attention. "All aboard! All aboard for the fastest ride ever and ever, and never and never and never to be repeated after today!" he cried, getting rather carried away. With squeals and screams of delight, the children were soon clambering aboard, ready for the off. Then, Marsh shouted above the caterwauling, "Hold on for dear life, everyone! And so we begin!"

Townsend shook his head in amusement and watched as David's eyes narrowed. He followed his gaze to the swings opposite the carousel, where the two children who had disliked them in the coach that morning were sitting. At once, he guessed that Marsh intended to show them a thing or two, while slowly cranking up the speed of the carousel.

The impatient children on board were having none of it, however, and one disappointed youngster shouted at him as he passed, "Faster, mister, faster! Me ma can go faster than this, man!"

"Aye, she can that," shouted his chum the next time they passed.

Marsh looked immediately deflated, but he doubled his efforts.

Townsend just looked on, laughing. Marsh was indeed in his element. Though the two men were of similar age, he felt his friend had never grown up. Every so often – such as at this moment – Marsh would offer undeniable proof of this fact.

While watching the battle of wills play out between Marsh and the children, Townsend picked out a woman of wealthy means standing nearby the jostling crowd, facing away from the antics at the carousel. A filthy scruff of a man was standing a little too close to her. Townsend frowned.

Something about the situation seemed off, and a prickle of unease crawled across the back of his neck. With his suspicions aroused, he moved – slowly and subtly – closer to the unusual pair.

He knew that people were apt to become distracted by the numerous amusements on offer, making them easy prey for pickpockets and thieves. They made for particularly attractive targets since many people had saved up their meagre pay to have a good time on such occasions. No fair was immune to attracting the wrong sort of people, and now a small group of thieves were moving stealthily amongst the crowd, plying sleight-of-hand tricks, and cheating the gullible. More of their brethren were quietly robbing the fairgoers as and when the opportunity arose.

Leaving Marsh with his new-found friends, Townsend drew close to the woman and her harasser without the man realising. The ruffian was holding something in his left hand, hidden inside his pocket, and he unobtrusively used it to prod the woman while robbing her.

Having seen enough, Townsend quickly stepped forward, placing his right arm over the thug's left, and grabbing his wrist. He then brought his right elbow up into the face of the thief in time to prevent him from drawing a nasty-looking knife from his pocket. His arm connected with the man right on the nose, dropping him to the ground.

The villain released the woman, and she instantly began screaming with the shock of being threatened – and then the relief of being saved.

The man tried to clamber back up but, seeing his intention, Townsend instantly hit him flush on the jaw to deter him. After recovering his senses, the man's feet and hands scrabbled on the rough cobbles, trying to find a purchase to stand, but he only managed to fetch the skin from his fingertips. Blood dripped from his broken nose onto his shirt and sleeve, leaving them heavily stained.

"No! No more!" the thief pleaded, throwing up an outstretched arm in an attempt to fend him off.

Townsend ignored him. Turning to the victim, he asked, "Are you alright?"

The woman swayed a little, turning suddenly pale, and – fearing she would faint in shock –Townsend reached out to support her.

"Why, yes, sir," she replied thankfully, fanning her cheeks with her open hand, "I think I am, sir, but only just."

"Was anything taken? Before I deal with him?"

"Nothing, thanks to you, sir." She began to tremble with disbelief, outrage, and the embarrassment of being accosted.

"Good," he said as he turned on the spot, only to see the ruffian sloping away, aided by his partner.

The noise and scuffle had attracted a small group of onlookers, including Marsh, who had stepped away from the crank handle to assist him. But when Townsend looked for him, he found his friend sprawled on the floor.

"Well, where are the reinforcements when you need them?" he asked, looking down at him.

"Oh," Marsh moaned, clutching his skull. "I was coming over when I got a crack on the head. Their friend must have hit me," he insisted.

"Sure you were," Townsend replied, pretending to doubt him while scanning the heads of the crowd, looking for the fleeing robbers.

As he got to his feet, the two children from the coach skipped past, laughing their heads off.

"He's very funny," the girl said to her brother, who nodded while laughing at him uncontrollably.

Rubbing the back of his head, Marsh remarked, "A monster to a clown in two hours, eh!"

"Come on then, joker," said Townsend, aware of the larger crowd's late interest. He nodded to the woman he had rescued, whose companions were now looking after her. "Let's go find this Armstrong gun – or where the *Europa* is. It must be somewhere close to it."

The *Europa* was tied up immediately outside the factory, surrounded by even more spectators lining both banks of the River Tyne. Dotted about in the crowds were bare-knuckle fighting booths, trying to tempt cocky young men and drunks to try their luck with their very own 'champion.'

Over the racket, the caller's voice at the nearest booth rang out: "Come on, come on! Who wants to try their luck? Five pounds to anyone hard enough to last a single round with the Champion of Champions! What about you there, shrimp? Are you man enough?" He pointed directly at Marsh, singling him out, while the last man to try his luck was carried away in the background.

Already smarting from the knockdown he'd suffered near the carousel, the red mist descended over Marsh immediately. All he could think of was hitting the man for his blatant insults. "Hold my coat, will you?" He attempted to thrust his jacket into Townsend's hands, but Townsend refused, restraining him instead.

He gave Marsh a hard, cursory glance, followed by an angry question: "What do you think you're doing?"

"I'm going to tan his hide, good and proper. Unhand me, Robert!"

"No, you are not. It's not that big mouth you'll be fighting; you will find a man-mountain somewhere behind the curtain, just waiting to lay into you as soon as you enter. Maybe two." Townsend looked at Marsh with real concern. "Believe me – they're just waiting for the next drunken idiot to come swaggering past. Think about it... it's a trick. They won't allow anyone to walk off with five pounds, now, will they?"

"I suppose you're right, but I won't take any lip from that," he said, calming down, though the sincerity and concerns of Townsend's statement hadn't entirely convinced him to back down.

The fight promoter cussed under his breath. He had good reason to insult Marsh and relieve him of the easy money he'd planned to make. He watched, annoyed, as Marsh was ushered away from more of his well-rehearsed barbed insults, and then spat on the floor for allowing him to escape so easily.

***

The captain of the *Europa* was eager to get the cargo aboard as soon as possible; he wanted to get underway first thing in the morning as Armstrong knew the gun was due to be tested immediately on its return to Italy. Therefore, he was keen to assemble the crowds for the spectacle of seeing his special surprise. He was aware of how much power a double feature had to wow the crowd, and it would undoubtedly boost his sales when reported on by the local and national newspapers.

Somehow, the friends managed to fight their way to the bar and get drinks from the overcrowded beer stall, gladly following the rest of the crowd's example.

Edging closer to the foundry, they now found themselves in the shadow of the enormous crane towering high above the *Europa*. It was idling now, subdued streams of steam leaking from its hand-operated stop/start valves. It occasionally gave a loud hiss as the operator released the build-up of pressure in the boiler while waiting for the little steam engine with its precious cargo to appear.

With his feelings still bruised, Marsh took a pamphlet from one of the company clerks handing them out to the watching crowd. "According to this, that beast of a crane was also designed and built by Armstrong. It's described here as a hydraulic crane that could raise any load up to 160 tons. Yet another great feat of British inventiveness, of which we should be rightly proud! It also says that we ought to expect a big surprise in the vicinity of the *Europa*."

"That will be our gun, I'll wager," said Townsend.

Marsh grunted his agreement as newspaper reporters pushed wildly against each other to get a closer look at the soon-to-be-seen revelation.

Buoyed up by the atmosphere and the promise of a surprise, the crowd began chanting, "Where is it?" excitedly around the two officers, all giddy with anticipation of the surprise. No one but the two soldiers knew anything about what they were about to witness.

The crowd nearest the foundry gave a warm burst of oohs and ahhs as four men slowly slid the big doors back on their rollers. Then, a loud 'toot, toot!' from a steam whistle quietened the crowd down.

Those standing behind began craning their necks over each other's shoulders to get a better view. No one had, thus far, taken any notice of the small-gauge railway track running out from under the doors – that was, until the small steam engine emerged into the daylight, its drive wheels slipping before taking up full traction on the rails.

Out it came, pulling the supergun with it and spreading over two open-sided wagons for everyone to see. The gathered crowd gasped in disbelief as they took in its extraordinary size. They then cheered and applauded excitedly as the giant cannon rumbled forward into full view.

"I don't believe it!" exclaimed Townsend. "I don't bloody believe it," he repeated as he watched in awe. Marsh merely nodded, his mouth hanging open in shock.

Sitting across the two wagons in regal fashion – its nose in the air, with a half-ton collar attached – was the longest, largest muzzleloader Townsend had ever seen. The famous Armstrong Gun!

"I don't believe it either," said Marsh, echoing the words of his friend while staring at the massive, bottle-shaped weapon. "I'd like to get nearer, Robert." Marsh nudged him as he spoke, encouraging him to get a closer look. "I would unquestionably want to fire that big boy."

"Stay with me, David; leave it for the crowd to enjoy," Townsend advised, restraining him for a second time that day. "We'll see one just like it soon enough in Armstrong's factory. Remember, they've arranged a private viewing – for our satisfaction."

The little engine had built up a good head of steam and was now coping more easily with its load, trundling along the rail track until it reached the grabbing and lifting area for the steam crane. The crowd erupted with glee as several workmen attached large lifting chains to the gun's central and end positions. In contrast, others attached the chains to the large hook hanging from the crane's jib. When he was satisfied that everyone was clear, the crane driver started lifting it from its cradle.

The crowd fell silent again as the crane took up the slack in the chains and – under the guiding direction of the two men sitting along its muzzle – it slowly hoisted it up, accompanied by strained creaks from the chains and noisy clouds of steam escaping from the valves, rising high in the air over the historical scene.

Now the critical moment: will they be able to place it safely into the hold? thought Townsend.

The two workmen boldly sitting astride the gun barrel had no such fears. To the delight of everyone there, the crane easily lifted both the gun and the men high enough to clear the rail deck and gunwales of the *Europa* – still accompanied by the many gasps of the assembled crowd.

The crane swung it around on the jib's long arm, feeding the cannon towards the steamship. Once above the hold, it turned the gun again. Then, under the guidance of the two men sitting astride it, the heavy armament was lowered into the specially adapted hold. The empty cargo ship bobbed in the water before taking on the weight of the supergun. Once it was loaded, it settled down on an even keel.

Immediately, the crew in the hold began piling the ballast up and around the cannon for safety before daring to release the crane's holding hook and chains. The Europa's hold had been meticulously planned and prepared to take its only cargo, thus ensuring the massive gun couldn't roll about and sink the vessel.

The critical part of the loading was now done – to the obvious relief of the ship's Italian crew, who then began cheering along with the crowd. With much hissing and escaping of steam, the hook was lifted clear from the ship's hold by the crane driver, and, with that, the transfer was complete.

The successful inauguration of the first swing bridge demonstration had proved astonishing – especially when followed up with the world's most gigantic muzzle-loading cannon. It proved a real eye-opener when shown being loaded into the *Europa,* and the crowd loved it. As thousands of people found it a joyful relief from the grime and poverty that many knew they had to go back to, the merriment and drinking continued until late afternoon. Then, slowly, the crowds started to dwindle. It had been a fun-filled day, and a good time had been had by most, leaving the many visitors with pleasant, lingering memories.

Townsend and Marsh – who had only lunched on toffee apples and other festival fares – were beginning to feel hungry, and decided it was time to make their way back along the Tyne to the Blue Boar. The treats they'd gorged on earlier – along with the beer – were turning gaseous, giving them both bellyaches and flatulence, with Marsh occasionally rubbing at the gusset of his pants.

The trek back to the inn, therefore, was uncomfortable, but without mishap or incident. On the way, they noticed that the washing hanging out on the lines was visibly greyer than earlier.

Spying a woman in one of the gardens adorned with washing lines, Townsend called out to her in passing. "I should think it's hard work keeping clothes clean around here, madam?" he shouted cheerily over the low hedgerow separating her garden from the river's towpath.

She stopped collecting her pegs and washing before looking over at them. "Aye. It's much harder than that, man. Sometimes, it needs washing and scrubbing two or three times a week to keep the dirt down. The blessed wind always seems to blow it this way. The skin on me hands keeps cracking, so it does with all this washing. It seems, sometimes, they're forever in water. It can be painful with the natural oils washed out of them. But if you need anything washing, sirs, you know where I'm at," she added hopefully. "A little extra comes in handy – aye, it does that."

"Why, thank you kindly. We'll bear your offer in mind," said Marsh as they continued past the gardens and out of her view. "It's turning chilly," he said to Townsend. "I think she'll be huddled around the fire grate tonight with her little ones, like everyone else."

Townsend gave it some thought. "Well, with little ones or not, with all the coal burnt here, let's hope the wind takes it away. Otherwise, that smoke we can see billowing out of the chimney pots and smokestacks will turn to smog later; that will cause a few more coughs and wheezes, no doubt. I've seen people stay indoors all day in London to avoid going out in a real thick smog – unless they had to. I've had to feel my way along a street with both hands touching the walls a time or two. It wasn't pleasant at all."

"Why call it smog? I haven't heard that term used before, Robert."

"Some clever buggers were amusing themselves in a tavern I visited one foggy day. As it thickened outside with the smoke, they put the two words together and made smog. I thought it amusing and never forgot it."

"I see. Come on, let's get ourselves along to the Blue Boar. I want to have another crack at apologising to Sarah," said Marsh, unthinkingly rubbing his crotch again.

Quickening their pace, they arrived back at the inn in no time. The landlord noticed their return and was eager to learn how the day had gone.

"How was the bridge? And does it actually open?" he asked in jest. Albert had insisted on serving them personally because he wanted to know all the details.

They told him everything about how the day had gone, finding in him an interested and eager audience.

"The cannon was something else, though, and well worth seeing," remarked Townsend. "I hope you don't regret missing out, Albert?"

"I'll see the bridge as soon as I get a little time to myself away from here, but I'm not interested in the cannon," he told them. "Newcastle is a garrison town, with cannons and guns everywhere – so I should think I've seen them all."

As Townsend watched him walk off to give Sarah their orders, he shook his head. He decided that Albert simply could not comprehend or visualise the armament's size. After all, it was a rarity that defied description – one that had to be seen to be believed.

Following the landlord's departure, the two soldiers sat together to discuss their first glimpse of the gun and the sights they'd been privileged to see that day. Then, eager to complete their mission well, they began compiling a list of questions of a technical and mechanical nature they could ask during their visit to the foundry the next day.

They were swapping their thoughts when Sarah brought out their meals from the steamed-up kitchen.

Approaching the door into the bar, she spotted them through its small window. She wasn't looking forward to talking to either of them, but work was work. So, after hooking the door with her heel and tugging it open, she walked into the bar, startling them when she put both plates firmly down on the same uneven table.

"Oh, Sarah!" Marsh exclaimed, surprised at her sudden appearance.

She ignored him, still deeply angry with them both, her smouldering resentment not yet extinguished.

"Have you got the cutlery, Sarah?" he asked, clearly hoping to extend the conversation.

"It's over there. Get it yourself," was her terse reply. Then, with a swirl of the dress, she was gone, heading back to the kitchen.

"She's still upset," observed Townsend, with sympathy and another tinge of guilt.

"Shut up," said Marsh, realising there would be no truce between them. "Friendliness entirely out of the question, and all your doing," he accused. "Well, most of your doing."

Townsend shook his head without replying, and they ate their meal in silence until Townsend finally broke the stand-off. "I'm turning in," he announced. "Don't forget that we have our appointment at the foundry tomorrow, rather early. You don't want to inconvenience the colonel – and you don't need another night of carousing," he warned.

Marsh remained silent, ignoring him completely, so Townsend left him there and retreated to his room.

Left by himself, Marsh dallied a few minutes to finish his drink. Weariness was beginning to creep in, and he yawned uncontrollably. The festivities had taken their toll, along with a lack of sleep the night before. *It will be another walk again tomorrow, and I need the rest,* he reasoned.

Sullenly, he climbed the stairs, looking into the kitchen as he passed and hoping for a glimpse of Sarah – but he couldn't see her. Lying on his bed and fighting his tiredness, Marsh fell into a reflective mood. His mind turned over the many sights he'd seen that day, but he was restless and couldn't sleep. His mind was too active with muddled thoughts of Sarah.

After lying prone on the bed for a while, he heard the tell-tale creaking of someone on the stairs.

It could be anyone, he reasoned, but then he heard the unmistakable rustle and swish of the hem of a dress as it negotiated the tight bend in the stairs to the attic. He knew it was Sarah – there were no other women on this floor – and he was determined to speak with her.

Tiptoeing past Townsend's door to the end of the corridor without making any sound, he tentatively climbed the narrow staircase to the attic. Quietly treading on the edges of the risers, he was careful not to make any loud creaking sounds. Then, gently tapping on the single door he found there, he whispered, "Sarah! Sarah, can you hear me?"

There was no answer, only silence.

"Sarah, I'm sorry. Sarah, can you hear me?"

Marsh repeated his pleas several more times before she responded, "Go away."

"But, Sarah, I…" he tried again.

"Go away, David, or I'll scream! I mean it. I will – and I'll have Albert up here in a flash," she threatened.

Realising the landlord's family was immediately below, Marsh decided he couldn't risk it, so he returned to his room in despair. *After last night, I suppose I do need to sleep.*

He attempted to settle down and rest, but getting to sleep was another matter. He simply could not get the woman out of his mind, thinking of ways to regain her trust. As he racked his brain, he became aware of the occasional coughs and voices from a room further down the corridor, realising for the first time just how thin the bedroom walls were. In all likeliness, the entire floor had heard every moment of how he and Sarah had wrestled and cavorted together – although he hadn't heard any complaints.

He thought about their little caper a while longer, then shrugged the unwanted but pleasant thoughts out of his mind and fell into a much-needed deep sleep.

Chapter 5

Apology accepted.
Arrival at the Armstrong factory

THE EARLY morning crowing of the cock was followed soon after by the subdued noises of the household beginning to stir. In a well-ordered fashion, the family and their staff prepared to go about their early morning tasks and duties in the big house. Heavy bolts were eased then drawn across outside doors, and the occasional squeak of a dry door hinge requiring goose fat could also be heard. Whispered voices were talking downstairs, along with the scraping out of the burnt ashes from the fire grate.

With all the ashes cleaned out, a new coal fire was lit to take the chill from the large room. Rid of the ashes, the fire soon took hold. The wood crackled and spat sparks as the flames licked and danced merrily in the hearth, consuming the sticks and coal. It made a fine sight first thing on a chilly morning. Select windows were opened to let a clean draft of air through the house, refreshing the rooms from the stale overnight odours of flat beer, tobacco, and pipe smoke. Nearby, another helper was rinsing out the previous night's tankards and glasses in a water-filled bucket.

Albert started busying himself with the small tasks that needed attention before swapping the heavy beer barrels around in the cellar. The landlady, Rose, was a large, red-faced, jolly woman of ample proportions. She could heft a beer barrel around just as well as Albert, or so she claimed. She took on the task of wiping over the bar and tables to keep the persistent dust down from outside, and then went on to remove the sticky layers of spillage from the previous night. Before tackling the barrels, Albert (at Rose's insistence) began cleaning out several spittoons strategically placed on the floors of both bars – quite an unsavoury job, which always turned Rose's stomach – and replenishing any sawdust on the floor that had suffered from spillage or missed spittle shots.

At the same time, Sarah set about her tasks in the kitchen, reflecting on her reduced circumstances. As a colliery manager, her father and his family lived in a comfortable house supplied by the mine owners, asking only for a nominal rent in return. While enjoying her career in the newly formed Medical Nursing Auxiliary, Sarah had been upset at being given the news of her father's accident. So, she had hurried back from London, fraught with worry, to be with him and support her mother. A rethink of the family's financial circumstances became necessary, so Sarah and her brother decided to find temporary paid work. This enabled their mother to freely tend to their father's health, and his issues relating to his injury.

Her father had been injured while inspecting suspect props in the most awkward part of a tunnel in the deepest part of the mine. There had been a partial cave-in, trapping him there with several others, but the rescuers had dug them out. The company practitioner told him he would recover sufficiently to carry on with his job, but that he'd need time to recuperate first. The family, however, still needed to eat, so with very little savings and in desperation, the children were required to help. There was the nominal rent to pay for, as well as their food.

Albert Dobbins, a good friend of the family, had been able to give Sarah a job in his kitchen, where he intended to keep the young lady employed and away from his louder, rowdier clientele. Although safely ensconced in the kitchen, sometimes with only Rose or Albert for companionship, the presence of a young woman at the inn had not gone unnoticed. It had become a challenge among the younger men to woo her and become the first to seduce her.

Sarah thought back to her last suitor, the one before Marsh. He had been quite unashamedly forthright while turning on the charm.

"Will you walk out with me, Sarah?" Edward asked her. "Perhaps we could walk part of the Tyne together, eh lass? Get to know each other better, like."

"Go on, Sarah lass. He's got a job and everything, and he'll look after you if need be," his companion said, encouraging her to go.

She was always embarrassed at these offers and firmly turned them down; she was not the type to walk the Tyne or anywhere else with anyone, especially when her father lay injured in bed. She wasn't looking for boyfriends, only wanting to stay focused on her career. By the end of most days, she was too tired for such foolish pursuits.

Most of the time, her abject refusal was enough to put off all but the most persistent of suitors. When anyone refused to take the hint, the presence of Rose or Albert was usually enough for them to back off. Both Rose and Albert felt very protective of their young charge and always tried to look after her welfare.

Sarah went outside to hang out the washing – determined to take full advantage of the warm, refreshing breeze blowing in from the sea. She wiped away the settled grime from the line before pegging out her newly washed apron when she saw Marsh come downstairs, suitably washed and brushed, before taking himself off to the bar to await his colleague. To avoid a confrontation with him, she slipped back into the kitchen to busy herself with their morning breakfast.

Townsend came downstairs soon after and spied Sarah in the kitchen holding a knife. Her rear end shook provocatively as she sliced into the fresh, crusty farmhouse loaf.

"Sarah, can I come in?" he asked from the safety of the doorway. "I'm David's companion, Robert Townsend."

She scowled at him. "Yes, if you must, but you can't be here long. I'm too busy, and you're a distraction I don't need right now," she huffed.

"It's about the other morning," he said apologetically. "I thought David was alone. I had no idea you were also there, and I was horrified to see you! However, I admit that the devil got the better of me and I played the fool, and I am truly sorry if I've hurt your feelings and embarrassed you. Would you take this present from both of us? David told me about your family's bad luck, and we would both be delighted if you would accept it."

Sarah sensed the sincerity in his voice and, as she had never been the vindictive type, she took the handmade envelope from him. Opening it, she found five pounds inside. Her temper flared immediately. "Have it back, Robert. I'm not that sort of woman and I don't need payment!"

"No, no! It's not like that!" he retorted, his face flushing a deep red that suggested he was telling the truth. "I'm sorry. Can you forgive me?"

"Well…" She hesitated, still struck by his sincerity. Although it may wound her pride to accept the offer, she knew the money would be a godsend, given her family's predicament.

"Take it, Sarah," he urged again. "It's to help your family get back on their feet. That's all. We both feel deeply sorry."

"All right," she said, "I'll take it – against my better judgement. It's such a very kind gesture on your part, Robert." She put the money back into the envelope and carefully placed it into the large pocket at the front of her apron. Then, with a hand on each of Robert's broad shoulders, she lifted herself onto her toes and kissed his cheek. "Apology accepted." Her voice began to tremble; she was suddenly feeling incredibly emotional at this spell of good fortune. "Now get yourself in," she ordered, not wanting him to see her eyes welling up with tears. "Your breakfast will be along soon! And thank you so much. It means everything in the world to me."

"Just one thing before I go. Would you please smile at David?" he pleaded. "It would change his whole outlook on the day. He's normally a happy-go-lucky type, but right now, he's a pain in the backside... and I could slap him!"

"I'll think about it," she snuffled.

Townsend left her and walked into the bar to find his colleague seated at the window. They exchanged pleasantries, but he detected a less than enthusiastic response. *We'll soon change that*, he thought, hoping that Sarah would follow through and at least smile at him.

Minutes later, Sarah came through the door, making a show of happily humming a little ditty. As she gently placed down the two plates, he noticed they had an extra egg each, which he thought would go down nicely.

Marsh failed to look up, however, so – after a glance at Townsend – Sarah moved opposite, but still he refused to look at her. She smiled at him without a response. Then, partially bending at the knee and gritting her teeth, Sarah forced another. There was still no recognition from him, and she grew tired of repeating it.

"You're in a sulk, so I'll leave you to it," she said, with Townsend nodding in agreement. "Oh, and if you want that bread toasted, you can fork it yourself at that fire," she added, flouncing off.

"You idiot!" Townsend exclaimed. "Couldn't you see she was trying to talk to you?"

"No, she wasn't," Marsh grumbled.

"How do you know? You wouldn't even look!" Townsend told him, annoyed that his efforts had been in vain. "Get on with your breakfast, man. It will soon be time to go, and any chance you had of making up with Sarah has long gone. She came in here looking to speak to you, and what did you do, eh? You sulked! Sulking is what you're good at, it seems to me."

"Look, there are plenty more women out there; I don't need to be beholden to just one of them," he said churlishly. "I apologised to her more than once, and now I'm done with it!"

Townsend surmised from his friend's manner that his feelings ran somewhat deeper than he'd expected – and were far more profound than he liked to admit. He kept his opinions to himself, however. Today was the day they would see the gun for themselves, and that promised to be sufficient to lift David's ailing spirit!

After their filling breakfast they made for the door, encountering the landlord rolling along a beer barrel as they went.

"Are you both off, then?" he asked cheerfully.

"Yes, Albert. Hey, you could do with a little time off, so why not walk along the Tyne with us and see this new bridge for yourself?" Townsend suggested.

"No, not today. I've got trouble with the tavern's cesspit out in the far backyard. It's blocked and not soaking away. Some friends are coming by to help me fix it. It's a messy, stinking job, and I hate doing it, but thank God it's not often! That's all I can say."

"Well, we hope to return sometime after you're soaped up and washed down," Marsh quipped, raising a mocking brow. "Hopefully with a full pail of clean water and carbolic soap, just to be safe. No sense in you putting us all off our meals, now, is there? Cheerio, Albert," he added cheekily, before following Townsend to the door.

Even before reaching the end of the street, they encountered an overpowering reek of freshly deposited human excrement hanging in the air, the acidic strength of the stench suggesting its very close proximity. Bent-over figures hurried past them in the opposite direction, holding their noses and grimacing while clasping coats close to their chests to keep out the damp chill.

Turning the corner, the source of the gut-wrenching stench became apparent: fresh faeces, wet with piss, lay in the gutter, having been deposited by a chamber pot.

"Who knows which of these houses dumped it? Thank goodness most have cesspits. See, it's already attracting the flies," said Townsend as they hurried on their way.

Although less chancy than the night, daytime could still be dangerous to unwary strangers in the backstreets of Newcastle, so – on Albert's advice – they decided to walk alongside the busy Tyne again, which was now carrying all types of tall shipping vessels. They felt the air would be fresher there, given the stiff breeze from the sea, and so it proved to be true.

They passed comments on the various industries they could see as they walked on. They also saw many laundry lines strung between walls and posts, raised by various cut tree branches used as props. Some of the women they saw were skeletal, with dark rings under their eyes and small children hanging onto their dresses. It bore all the signs of a tough life, trying to keep a roof over their heads while earning enough to feed a family.

"You know, Robert, I had no idea what life was like for many of the people living here, and during our visit, I've realised it's as bad as London."

"It is bad, but better than some places," Townsend reflected. "The number of people that are getting attracted to cities like Newcastle is growing, with the local industry expanding so quickly. It's the same everywhere. As I see it, the problem is where to put the people once they're here. The answer to that is building many more hundreds of these back-to-back houses we can see here, but where are the services for them, David? I glanced at the local *Weekly Chronicle* in the Blue Boar, which said there were very few in the area. We saw near the docks; the sewers couldn't cope. People have left rural areas in droves, deserting the farms and villages to get here, and for what? Living in these hovels causes disruption and poor health on a grand scale. How can these people be fed if no one works the farms and grows the crops to feed them?"

"You're beginning to sound more like a politician than a member of the military," Marsh grumbled. "Don't bore me, Robert."

"I apologise, David, but that's how I feel."

"Hey, there's the constabulary over there," said Marsh, nudging him to look. They watched two Peelers chasing a man towards them, turning hand-held rattles that created a loud din to raise the alarm.

"Stop that man! Stop that man, there!" they shouted.

Doing their civic duty, Marsh and Townsend stood before the fleeing man, denying him his escape. On seeing his route blocked, the man sank to the ground in utter despair.

The two Peelers ran towards them, dressed in top hats and heavy blue tailcoats. "Well done, you men, and thank you for your assistance," said the first to arrive.

The second was larger and a much slower runner. When he finally arrived, coughing and gasping for air, his ample girth was threatening to pop the buttons on his waistcoat and trousers.

After arresting the man, they hauled him to his feet and escorted him back to their horse-drawn covered wagon and its existing occupants.

"That's another drunk they're hauling off the streets, then," Marsh commented.

It looked like an unsavoury task, as the fugitive was making a spirited attempt to wrestle and fight with them both. His futile efforts were wasted, however; they simply resulted in the policemen bolting shackles around both his ankles.

"These men are much needed to keep order in the streets," remarked Townsend. "I know they're a welcome sight in London; their no-nonsense approach to hardened criminals gives assurance to the public."

"Yes, what a state to get into, first thing in the morning," said Marsh loudly.

"Aye, you're right there," said the officer, "but they haven't drunk a drop yet, young sir. They're still pissed up from last night! These ones are suffering from too much mead mixed in with the ale – and anything else they can get their hands on. Some will drink all sorts of concoctions to escape the poverty of this place, I can tell yer. Aye, alcohol warms the spirit, all right, but the body gets cold at night without them being aware of it."

The jovial, ruddy-faced constable helped his colleague haul the urine-soaked man into the back of the wagon to join the others. It was plain that the officer was partial to a little tipple himself; he picked up the half-filled bottle of wine the fugitive had dropped.

"Oh, this goes up front with us," he declared. "Evidence if needed, see! If not wanted, it's just a perk of the job, as we like to call it, sirs," he said as he slammed the door shut on his prisoners.

"Ooh…" groaned someone inside as the officer took hold of the reins.

"Are they going to the cells smelling like that?" Marsh asked.

"No! Once we get them back to the station, they get washed down before being put in the cells."

"They should like that, with heated water?" he suggested.

"No, no. All these wretches will stand against the wall in the yard and have pails of the cold stuff thrown over them. We don't want them coming back too soon now, do we?" He shook his head. "We must discourage them somehow, sir! Well, we'll be away then. The sooner these men are introduced to the carbolic, the better. We bid you a good day, sirs, and thank you again for your brave response."

After a flick of the whip, the man clicked loudly from the corner of his mouth and shook the reins. The horse trotted on with the wagon and its groaning cargo.

The small children came out as soon as they'd gone, begging again; the little waifs stood there, hands out, pleading for spare coppers. Most had snotty noses, and some had no shoes. "Please, sir, spare a penny, sir, please, sir, please!" came the clamour of desperate begging.

Moved by the plight of these little children, they both willingly thrust their hands into their pockets for any spare change. It was part of the social malaise that better men had failed to tackle. Finally – pulling away from the pleading youngsters – they hurried on, having to run a little way to prevent the children from following them.

When they were finally in the clear and walking at a leisurely pace, Townsend asked, "Why did you not speak to Sarah this morning?"

Marsh cleared his throat, his demeanour darkening. "It was clear she only wanted to speak to you. She made it very clear she wanted nothing more to do with me."

"Yes, she did. She told me."

"Liar."

"She told me," he repeated.

"I don't believe you," challenged Marsh.

"Why not? Does she have to get her tits out to get your attention?"

"Are you telling me the truth?" Marsh demanded. "I'm warning you, Robert, it's not a laughing matter."

"How do you know? You wouldn't look at her," Townsend retorted. "You were the only man in the bar not looking at her. I'm sure they would all have gladly changed places with you." Then, picking his words carefully, he continued, "She's gorgeous. Or had you not noticed with all your scheming?"

They continued in silence for a while as Marsh mulled over the incident, then he remarked, "Thank you, Robert. I must admit, I've developed strong feeling towards her. I'm a little confused, that's all, but I'll apologise to her when we get back. You have my word on that."

With a new spring in his step, Marsh led the way to the metal security gates that marked the Armstrong foundry entrance.

Townsend detected a new sense of purpose in his friend, a lighter side to his manner. *It feels good to have the overhanging dark mood and tetchiness between us lifted*, he thought as he followed Marsh into the foundry.

They found the Armstrong factory's site at the Elswick Steelworks to be considerably different from the day before. Then, the area had been filled with laughing, jostling people in their thousands. Today, the crowds had all gone, and the site was under a complete security lockdown. Yesterday the factory itself had been silent, but now it was thundering with the noise of the great steam hammers forming white-hot steel into their intended shapes. The echoes reverberated across the courtyard and rumbled through the very ground they walked on as they approached the main gate.

The guards at the gate were alerted to the visit and, after identifying themselves, Marsh and Townsend were escorted to Armstrong's office.

"Good morning, gentlemen. Won't you come in?" said the tall, genial man, inviting them to take a seat with a sweep of his hand.

"Thank you, sir," said Marsh, with a frown, "but you're not Mister Armstrong who gave that robust inauguration speech at the swing bridge yesterday?"

"No, quite right. My name is Stepney, Charles Stepney. I'm afraid Mister Armstrong isn't here, but he's authorised me to meet you both. I am to tell you, with apologies, that he's gone to meet representatives from the War Office yet again. Things are very hush-hush right now. Therefore, your visit was cancelled until further notice by your commanding officer, whom I believe is a Colonel Downing?"

"Yes, sir, he's at Woolwich. It was a splendid show you put on yesterday," said Townsend. "It certainly put a smile on many faces, especially the children. Captain Marsh can vouch for that; he had a fantastic time." He nodded at his companion, knowing he would struggle to reply.

"Er, yes," Marsh agreed uncomfortably. "The trip was well worth it, if just for that, but I noticed when we arrived that the *Europa* had already gone from its moorings?"

"Yes, it has," Stepney replied. "They sailed at first light. With the niceties completed, the vessel's captain was keen to get going. They will be back for the other guns in due course." The two men nodded in response. "Now, the reason for your cancelled visit – and I don't see any harm in telling you this – is because we are developing a top-secret steam contraption to help you fire the gun on land. So, in your case, it may not require too much manual labour. We received the telegraph from Woolwich Barracks a few hours ago, but it was too late to cancel the visit. Your orders are to return tomorrow; you will board the same ship, the *Landau*, on its return voyage. Of course, it will sail first thing, so make sure you get yourselves on board."

"That is a disappointment. We were looking forward to seeing the gun and your factory," said Marsh.

"Well, I don't see why you can't, gentlemen," said Stepney. "You have both travelled a long way to get here; it would be very discourteous of me to deny you both the pleasure." He smiled. "And I have just the man to show you around! Jack Stamp is his name; Old Jack, we call him. Every factory and foundry should have a man like him, because he's worth his weight in gold. Stay seated, and I'll have him sent in. He's very experienced and knowledgeable – the best foreman we have here. So, good day to you both, and enjoy your factory tour!" he concluded, before leaving to summon Old Jack.

Chapter 6

Touring the factory before inspecting 'The Gun'

TOWNSEND CHUCKLED to himself, a chuckle that got louder and louder until he was forced to stifle the need for full-blown laughter.

Marsh also chuckled along, feeling it was becoming infectious. "Ha, what started you off? Ha, ha, what's so funny?"

"That man, Jack Stamp," Townsend said, between chuckles. "A name like 'Stamp' in a factory!" He dissolved into laughter once more, and Marsh joined him until they were interrupted by the sound of someone cursing in annoyance outside the door.

Realising their guide had likely heard every word, they tried to calm themselves down.

Jack Stamp gave them time to collect themselves before walking in. A wily old chap who had a roguish glint in his eyes, he was short in stature, with frayed sleeves rolled up to the elbows and grey sideburns. Wearing a skullcap on top of his head, he was bald as a badger beneath it. He was wrapped in a short brown factory gown and walked with both hands thrust into its pockets. From his appearance and walk, he seemed a Jack Russell Terrier type of a man – wiry and ready to snap.

"I'm Stamp," he said, sizing them up. His deep voice belied his height. "I have been told to show you around our factory. Dizzy you up a bit, I suppose. Blind yer with mechanics before kicking yer arses out the back gate. Well, I don't know any science, and I can't dance, but I do know a fair bloody bit about our factory. Are you ready?"

"Hello, Mr Stamp. I'm Robert Townsend, and this is David Marsh," Townsend introduced them, holding out his hand.

Stamp ignored it. "Let's cut through the chaff. I'm known here as Jack, and you can call me that. We will have to get you two kitted out with gowns. You can't go traipsing about here in those nice uniforms, getting them all dirty."

"What uniforms?" asked Marsh.

"We aren't wearing uniforms," said a confused Townsend.

"Yes, you are," countered Jack. "They are under those fine clothes you wear. I saw you both stiffen when I came into the room. I'm many things, but I'm not daft," he said sternly.

"Well, you are correct, Jack. We are both Royal Artillery."

Old Jack gave them a thin smile, eyeing them both up and down in a quizzical sort of way until the two men began to wither under his scrutiny. Marsh suspected he wanted to get his own back for their earlier snide laughter.

"Are they turning out better officer types nowadays, compared to the stuck-up arsewipes and gobshites they normally turn out?" the old man asked.

"Do you think our officers are like that, Jack?"

"Aye, and it's normally good men that get them out the shit," he said without hesitation. "It's always been the same. Anyway, get these on and we'll get going," he added, tossing a gown to each of them. "I ain't got all day to mess about."

Once they were ready, Jack led the way outside and across the yard to one of the many buildings that made up the vast industrial complex.

"I'll take you in here first," he said as he slid open the heavy metal door.

The noise from the substantial steam hammers was tremendous, forcing the red hot metal into workable shapes while sending dangerous sparks flying high and wide. Townsend and Marsh instinctively covered their ears with their hands and watched, amazed. Neither had seen anything like it before.

Further along in the workshop, men were operating vast furnaces. They wore heavy protective clothing with gauntlets on their hands, and rags and cloth wrapped around their faces and heads – protecting themselves from the intense heat. Even standing at the door, Marsh and Townsend began to wither from it. A high crane spanning the workshop's width was being used to lift large metal loads of different shapes and sizes from place to place on the workshop floor.

Finding space while keeping the production line moving proved difficult but manageable for the crew. Loads of varying tonnage of castings had heavy chains wrapped around them, ready for lifting – all to be hooked up in turn to the crane, which was rolling steadily and effortlessly along on its well-greased wheel tracks, up and down the factory floor.

Leaning towards the men, Stamp had to shout to make himself heard. "I can't take you closer than here because they're about to pour molten metal from the rotating furnaces into the formers and castings. Look down there – you can see the hot steel on the rollers being cut and fed into them hammers there." He directed their gaze to another part of the factory floor. "A man had his eye out the other day from a spark. Yer needs to be careful. Those men don't want us down there when they're doing that. They have enough to be worrying over. Come on!" he bawled, leading them outside into the fresh, body-cooling air.

"Bloody hell! It was hot in there, Jack," said Marsh, busily wafting his open gown to draw in the cooler air. "I could never do that job. Could you, Robert?"

There was no answer.

"Could you, Robert?" he repeated.

"What?" Townsend said, rubbing his ears. "Oh, no. I'm glad to get out. My ears are ringing like ruddy church bells. How do you put up with it?" he asked Stamp.

"Oh, you get used to it, boys. You have to." Jack shrugged. "Stay here a day or two longer, and the wax will build up in yer ears. It helps a lot working here, that does – although you're always shouting, even at home: habit, see. My wife Hilda keeps thinking I'm having a go at her, she does. It leads to unnecessary arguments... and doesn't help my love life either."

He took them to another workshop. "In here we have the results of all that forming and casting," he explained, taking them up on a platform for a better view. "Like the first one, it's got a moving crane running the length of the workshop. Look below it on the floor in the middle, and you'll see the small-gauge rail track used to move the work into the other sheds. There are castings of different shapes and sizes stacked up on either side of the line, waiting for attention. Those men there are working with the castings on the floor." He pointed them out to Townsend and Marsh. "After the castings have cooled enough to work on, which takes a few hours, they bring them in here on that little steam engine you saw yesterday. They break out the work from the moulds, and then it's off to be finished to the shapes and sizes required."

The two officers looked on as the skilled work progressed.

Marsh gave a low whistle. "I've never seen anything like it, even in the military. So, what will happen to the castings, Jack?"

"That's called felling," he explained. "The cast's shape is left when broken out of the sand formers, but it's very rough, see? They have all sorts of lumps and sharp edges and corners on them, and they must come off. Too dangerous to work with, like that!" Jack cackled. "They're broken off with small hammers and chisels. Aye, it's a bloody hard job, I can tell you. A lad lost his long middle finger in here a few weeks ago; his lass wasn't best pleased about it. He's doing light duties now, he is. They will never put him back on that job, though. Good company, they are – look after you here, they do."

"Could we see your cannon?" Townsend asked, having noticed that Marsh was looking a little queasy. "We want to see the big bugger, Jack. The sooner, the better."

"I know, have patience. I'm giving you a little background on the processes involved to give you a feel of the place. Next, I'll take you to the lathe shop; we are heading that way."

"It's a dangerous place to work, isn't it?" Marsh enquired, in awe at the foundry's vast size.

"Well," replied Jack, "if you lark about, you'll have an accident sooner or later, that's for sure, but these men are well-trained." He said this with a touch of professional pride. "Having said that, accidents still happen. Of course they do."

As they crossed the second yard at the back of the building, Jack stopped them in full stride by placing his hand on Townsend's arm. "Was it you that thumped the scoundrel at the fair?"

"That was Robert, alright," piped up Marsh. "I heard the crack of his knuckles in the cad's face," he added, exaggerating.

"Was he trying to rob the woman?"

"Yes. How did you know?"

"I was there too and saw it, and I have to say it was a fine fist you put on his chin," he declared approvingly. "When he ran off with his friend, he was lucky I wasn't closer, or he would have got a kick up the arse to help him on his way!"

Marsh nodded, then grinned. "He's always quick to help out the ladies, Jack!"

His friend's face flushed in embarrassment, as a result of both Jack's praise and Marsh's double meaning. "I was there and saw it, so I stopped him in his tracks, that's all," he said modestly.

"Good lad," said Jack as he rolled open the door into another of the many lathe shops on site.

Again, as they stepped inside their ears were assailed by the tremendous increase in noise, and they felt the soles of their shoes sticking to the tacky floor as they walked along. Small metal off-cuts – that had been trodden into the dirty, oil-soaked work area over the years – cut at the leather soles of their boots.

"This shop turns out the bits and pieces that go along with the armaments," Jack told them, his manner much friendlier than before.

"Triggers, rifle barrels, nuts and bolts – that sort of thing. All the small stuff that's needed. The forty-odd lathes here are all belt driven, powered using spindles turned by a single steam engine up yonder. Watch that chap there, making those rifle barrels. They feed out a length of tubing to the stop on the lathe and then close the rotating chuck off, which grips it tightly. As it spins, if it's not turning true, he'll tap it with the short solid bar he keeps on the lathe, see? A sharp tap with that bar, and it will spin true so he can cut it."

"What's the white stuff, Jack?" Townsend asked. "It looks like milk spurting from the pipe."

Jack barked a laugh. "You can't be drinking that, old son. They call it suds. It's a mixture of water and engineering cutting oil. Stops the cutters burning out it does, aye."

"And what are the squiggly bits coming from the tube?" queried Marsh, pointing.

Jack sneered at his ignorance. "I can see you've never been in a factory before. No, that's called swarf. Its metal cut off the tube as it rotates. It'll be collected at the end of the day and sent back to the furnaces for reprocessing. Nothing gets wasted, I can tell you. Now, if you're happy, then we'll go back out. I want to show you some smaller cannons we make. It will put the big bugger into proper perspective, I can tell yer."

"Just before we go, how dangerous is it working on these lathes, Jack?" Marsh asked, thinking of the severed finger.

"Well, a few months past, a young man working on a similar lathe dropped his measuring gauge into the suds bowl," Jack told him as they descended the gantry. "He hadn't switched his bloody machine off, and as he bent down to recover his gauge from the suds, his long hair got caught by the wet metal turning, and it ripped his hair right off! From forehead to crown, all in one go, just like that," he said, snapping his fingers to emphasise the point.

It made Marsh step back, horrified at the thought of it.

"It lay wrapped around the pipe like a new bloody wig, it was! It damn near scalped him. He was off for weeks with a terrible headache before coming back, and the hair on his head never grew back properly. Ripped out at the roots, it was! He's here somewhere. He's only twenty-five or so. He wears a cap now, but yer can never get him to take the damn thing off for a good look at the mess it made of his scalp!"

"Bloody hell, Jack, you've got us both cringing now!" said Townsend as he hurried out after Marsh, who'd beaten him to it.

Jack chuckled to himself while following behind, looking amused with them both. He slid the heavy door shut on the workshop and then ushered them to another building nearby. "Here you are then, what you're both interested in." He pointed to the large sign pinned to the front, which read: 'BIG GUN LATHE SHOP.'

Putting his shoulder against the sliding door (after seeing how Stamp had done it before), Marsh quickly opened it. Upon entering, they could see many cannons of different sizes currently in production.

"This is where we turn the cannon muzzles and cut out the bore size," said Jack, gesturing towards different factory floor areas. "If you thought the other lathes were big, how about these beauties? They're our pride and joy. This is where we lathe turn our 50-inch guns. When these operators have finished with that lump of metal over there, it will be more recognisable as a cannon."

"It's turning now," said Townsend. "How do you stop it?"

"By pulling that cord hanging there. It will disengage the belt drive from the pulley on the spindle. With the large-gauge callipers, he can then measure what has been cut after it stops turning, of course. Not like the other silly bugger. He can then–"

"But where's the big 'un, Jack?" asked Marsh, interrupting him eagerly. "You know, like the *Europa* took with it this morning?"

"–check his work," Jack continued after a pause, ignoring the question. "Three men work on this lathe as it cuts and turns. It's a very skilled job, and the men working on it can earn themselves a few pennies more for their skills. Armstrong is always on the lookout for skilled men, but we won't go in any further. A man had his foot crushed in there last year, so we'll stay well clear. The state of the floor is too dangerous – with all the splashed oil – for those with no experience."

"I can see now why they're always looking for skilled men, Jack. They get through quite a few of them here, don't they?" Marsh said jokingly.

"Oh, aye, they do. Are you interested after you finish your service?" the man quipped.

"No way! It's too bloody dangerous working here! I'll stick with the Artillery and risk being shot at instead, if you don't mind. It's probably safer."

Townsend nodded in agreement before saying, "Tell me, what is that rather large, unusual building I can see over yonder, Jack? Are you taking us in there?"

"Not today, lads. We have the 'Great Crane' working in there on one of the hundred-ton guns you are interested in. Visitors aren't allowed. We're in here next," he said, guiding them through a connecting door into another large area, leaving the noisy lathes behind them.

They now found themselves in front of up to fifty cannons, each sitting on pairs of sturdy trestles, standing side by side along the floor.

"This, gentlemen, is one of our inspection areas," Jack told them. "The guns come in here after they've been finished and polished. The ones in here now, as you know, are the six-inch-calibre type. They shine a light down the barrel, and the chap you can see standing at the other end looks through it. They have well-trained eyes and know what they are looking to find. If it's a smooth bore, there will be no protrusions. If there are protrusions, it goes back to the finishing shop to have it polished out. If we want a rifled bore, they will ensure the rifling goes all along the bore. Again, anything untoward will get sent back and fixed. Everything has to pass inspection here before it gets shipped out." The older man paused, expecting another of Marsh's questions.

"Any accidents here?" Marsh asked, leaning against the nearest gun.

"Not yet. Only yours if you keep loafing on that gun like you are. If you're not careful, the trestles and gun will topple over, and you could lose a leg! It will be the first time in here if you do."

Not wanting to become another statistic, Marsh apologised sheepishly before moving away.

"Though it's tempting to leave bits of Marsh here with you, I am impatient to see the big gun," said Townsend, beginning to sound a little testy. "Is it nearby?" he asked.

"It's out the back, here at the end of the sidings," Jack replied. They followed him out and across another much longer yard, where he stopped them for a moment, allowing another little steam engine to trundle past. "We're coming to the special testing area along here, which is behind this high wall, so you must follow me past it – but stay close to me and the wall. We can give what's behind it a wide berth if you two don't mind. It's best to show it respect."

"Why?" Marsh asked, eyeing the wall in alarm.

"We have a man here by the name of Noble," Jack explained. "He comes and goes, and he's working on some new type of explosive with Armstrong. There's a race on with other factories to perfect it. It's called cordite. Well, he's blown a few things up in a fashion, and it is powerful when it works: otherwise, not so good. But it's where the bloody bits come down, that's the trouble. That's when you need to be on your toes and get dancing. Someday it will replace gunpowder entirely, but what do I know? I'm just the foreman here. Anyway, we seem to be in luck – I've heard no explosions today, so they're not testing. We had better get a move on, though, just in case, so keep up!"

He led them across the small-gauge track at the end of the long protective wall, and past the greasing station to an offshoot track that wandered off behind the sidings. They followed it around a corner and there, in its magnificence, stood the gun they had come to Newcastle to see. The hundred-ton cannon had been parked on its two wagons in the sidings away from the other well-used tracks and amongst worn-out rail stock, well hidden from prying eyes.

Struck dumb, they could only stand and stare up at it. It dwarfed all the vehicles around, standing nearly twice the height of either man: the most massive muzzle-loading gun in the world. Both felt very privileged to be standing beside it, though it stood unpolished and slightly rusted along with heavy black gunpowder burn marks around its snout. Even unfinished and open to the elements, it presented itself in a very threatening way, leaving them both feeling rather inadequate in comparison.

Awed into silence, the two officers clambered up onto the wagons, each lost in thought. They took turns to stare down at the rifling inside the muzzle, only to pull back sharply from the thick, burnt gunpowder fumes of its last firing. They began checking where the huge charge went and figuring out how the expansion joints would react and cope with the stresses of firing a one-ton missile. They saw how it could be shot by either a lanyard with a drawn friction tube or a LeBlanc battery with an electric priming tube.

While checking the gun thoroughly, Townsend couldn't help but notice Marsh's grimace as he rubbed his manhood again.

Finally, Townsend found his voice. "I could see it was big, Jack, when they loaded the other onto the *Europa*. But to get the feeling of its true size, you must stand next to it. It's truly gigantic. What will happen with this one? Will it be sold? Is it damaged in any way?"

"This one is our prototype," their guide explained. "It's been tested to death so it won't be going anywhere soon. It's thirty-four and a half feet long. It pierced a solid mass of wrought iron thirty inches thick at a thousand yards. It can sink a ship with a single shell, going right through it, and is deadly up to eight miles. The calibre is 17.72 inches wide and constructed with twenty-eight different sized tubes inside it, hence the bottle shape. That's why, gents, you won't hear of an Armstrong cannon of any size misfiring or blowing up. Not if it's used correctly, at any rate. It's unheard of for our guns to either malfunction or for the barrel to split," he bragged. "All of us here are enormously proud of our reputation. I know Mister Armstrong is hopeful more orders will follow for the gun because it's far superior to anything else out there. So, this cannon will have its bore relined: a job only we can do. They are talking of having it shipped to Shoeburyness for you boys to practise with. If you get the same gun, look for my initials. I'll scratch them on here," he said, pointing out the exact spot.

"Having seen action with the Royal Artillery, we appreciate what this can do to our enemies," said Townsend, as Marsh continued to peer at the cannon. "I should think this cannon of yours will guarantee safe passage for us in the Mediterranean for years to come – or I hope so, anyway. Will the Eyeties buy more?"

"Oh, yes, the cannon they took is their first," said Jack. "They've paid for seven more. We have already started work on the rest of the order. More orders will follow when they see what it can do, you can be sure of it."

"Well, we have to go," said Townsend, pulling his friend away from the extraordinary armament. "We appreciate your time and expertise in showing us around the factory, Jack."

"Yes," Marsh agreed, "we've learned plenty about your gun today. You know, it is most likely that where these guns end up, there won't be any convenient railway to help us move them or set them up."

Jack immediately looked interested, and Marsh cursed his overeager tongue.

"So, the British Army will be ordering some?" the foreman asked.

"Yes, they will, but keep it to yourself, will you?" said Marsh.

Jack nodded, looking pleased. "I had guessed as much. This visit seemed too covert and secret to be anything but a reconnaissance trip."

Marsh nodded back. Then he thought of all the horrible injuries Jack had revealed to them. "I wouldn't be able to work here, though," he said aloud.

Scratching the crown of his head, his cap in hand, Jack replied, "No, probably not. Two fine gentlemen like yourselves have got your futures already drawn up, I'll warrant. Here, give me back them cow gowns and be off with yer. I have better things to do than pettifogging with you two."

After a little more good-hearted banter, they shook hands with Jack and took their leave through the security gate.

Jack had been impressed with the two men. After they left, he turned to the guard on the gate. "These new officer types are better than the arsewipes I've encountered, that's for sure," he remarked, before spitting on the ground. "The Army should be much better for it – that's a fact."

Leaving the large foundry behind, Townsend and Marsh made their way back towards the Blue Boar Inn; the only subject on their minds being the supergun.

Being inside the foundry and seeing the gun up close had made a significant impression on them both. It was, naturally, the main topic of conversation between them walking back, and they spoke – in hushed tones

– of little else. Talking to old Jack Stamp, they had discovered tips on its manoeuvrability and how to fire it, no doubt much to the delight of Colonel Downing.

"Just think of all the stories we can tell our fellow officers when we get back, Robert!" Marsh said as they carried on along the pathway. "There should be a few free drinks in it for us. It's just a case of spinning our story out for as long as possible," he figured.

"Don't forget it's all hush-hush," Townsend advised.

"I did say our fellow officers, Robert," Marsh said, correcting him.

They walked on further before suddenly halting, immediately stopping their discussion of the armament. Four men were barring their way to the small footbridge running across a river tributary flowing away from the Tyne. They just stood there, slapping cudgels in their hands menacingly.

"Hello, soldier boys! We saw you enter the factory, and have been waiting here for you," said the smaller man standing in front of three much larger thugs, one of which was the caller at the fighting booth who had cussed Marsh for his cowardice. "You stuck your noses into something that didn't concern you," he said, pointing his club at Townsend. "Aye. You broke my brother's nose, and now yer gonna pay for it!"

Marsh glanced at his friend, realising that he meant the robber at the fair.

"You have the wrong men," Townsend replied, attempting to bluff his way out of a confrontation.

"No, you're the men, alright," he spat. Then, pointing at Marsh, he asked, "Do you still have that lump on your head I gave you, fella?"

"So that was you, you little bastard!" exclaimed Marsh angrily.

"You'll have bumps all over by the time we're done with yer!" the man threatened.

"We've got nothing to defend ourselves with, Robert!" Marsh cried, searching for a way out of their predicament. "I'll tell you what – you keep them here while I go and fetch help!"

"No, you won't! Remember your training – anything is permissible. I'll take these two on while you tackle the other two," Townsend calmly informed him.

They didn't have time to argue since, at that moment, the four ruffians took the opportunity to attack.

The smaller one stepped aside to enable the fight promoter to wildly swing a club at Marsh, who managed to avoid it. However, his sidestep carried him into the other man's path, who grabbed Marsh by the throat, pushing his head into the overgrown hedge and holding him there – giving his little mate a chance to severely damage his legs. The leader raised his club and took a wild swing at Marsh's knee – aiming to dislocate the kneecap – but in kicking out his leg and attempting to fight back, the blow caught his upper thigh instead, causing him to howl out in pain.

Townsend, meanwhile, hadn't stood on ceremony. The first thug received a well-aimed kick to his testicles; the man doubled up, dropping his club as he fell to the ground, clutching his groin. Townsend immediately seized it to even up the fight.

Still with his head wedged in the hedge, Marsh kicked out blindly at his tormentors, catching the smaller man sharp in the ribcage. He staggered back, surprised; he hadn't expected to get hurt himself.

With his new-found weapon, Townsend brought the club down hard between the shoulder blades of the man holding Marsh by the throat.

"Aargh!" he shouted, straightening up, both his arms and shoulders being forced back. Finding it difficult to breathe, he let go of Marsh instantly.

Marsh was immediately on him with flailing fists, continuing until the man slumped to the ground, unconscious. He then turned to see Townsend grimace at a blow to his upper arm from the other attacker's club.

Before Marsh could act, Townsend quickly turned, bringing his club down onto the man's hand, breaking fingers as he connected with it. The ruffian cried out in pain, dropped his club, and ran off, clutching his bloodied hand close to his chest.

Having dealt with the three taller fighters, Marsh and Townsend turned to face the smaller thug, who suddenly became meek and scared.

"I swear we didn't want to harm yer – it was supposed to just be a warning. I'm sorry!" he cried, cringing and cowering like the lickspittle he was.

Marsh – who was having none of the little man's incessant wailings – hit him square on the nose, which broke with a sickening crunch on impact, knocking him out.

"They won't forget us in a hurry," he said, rubbing his knuckles. "Since when should a coward and thug like him be listened to and shown mercy, Robert? Now he and his brother should remember us both long after we have gone from this place."

Dirtied and ruffled from the ambush, the two men dusted themselves down and continued across the bridge. The blow to Marsh's thigh was tender, and he limped for most of the journey, but by the time they approached the Blue Boar it had straightened out – though his skinned knuckles were sore and bloodied.

Inside the inn, they decided to put it behind them and mention nothing of the attack to anyone, including Sarah.

So, they both relaxed, enjoying a refreshing beer near the warmth of the open fire. It crackled in the hearth, casting out mesmerising sparks dancing amongst the flames. One missed the fireguard and landed on the wooden floor beyond the fireplace, at which point Townsend immediately stamped the life out of it.

Tired from his exertions but not displeased about how things had turned out, Marsh decided to have one of his occasional cigars. Unwilling to walk to the bar, he knelt in front of the fire with the cigar and placed the poker tip deep into the flames. Then he waited a few seconds until he saw its tip glow red with the heat. Withdrawing the poker, he held it up to his cigar, dragging on it until it lit. Finally, he sat down, satisfied, puffing out fat little smoke rings towards a window, where they dispersed into the colder air. He found the fire itself mesmerising; he watched as a burnt log collapsed, the subsequent large profusion of sparks being sucked up the chimney.

As both reflected on their eventful day, their thoughts turned back to Sarah, who was nowhere in sight. Even after moving to a table with an open view, they still couldn't see her. Marsh was ever anxious to talk with her and apologise for his previous bad behaviour. Therefore, when Rose came over to collect their empty glasses, he decided to enquire as to her whereabouts.

"Can I get you something to eat?" Rose asked. "We've got a sweet stew on the go tonight – a rabbit stew. I know you'll both like it."

"No thanks, Rose. Where's Sarah? We haven't seen her since we returned."

"Oh, she's gone home, Mr Marsh. I'll be cooking for you tonight. Is there anything else you may want? We have a tasty pheasant laid out on the platter, ready for cutting."

"Damn it," he spluttered, the words escaping from his lips in a hiss.

She stood back in alarm. "Pardon me, sir? There's nothing wrong with the pheasant. Bought legally as well, it was. This very day too," she said defensively.

"My apologies, Rose," he said, placating her. "I was hoping to see Sarah before we return in the morning; our stay in Newcastle has been cancelled, and we have been ordered back to London."

Rose narrowed her eyes a little; from Marsh's marked tone of voice, she suspected a romantic attachment. She was still protective of her young charge and was annoyed he'd flirted with Sarah without her knowing. "Yes, and she will be back long after you have taken your leave," she admonished. "Would you like me to give her a message? I can get my daughter to write it down for me."

"Not now, Rose."

"No, sir? Maybe later then," she said, showing a slight sensitivity towards him, before moving to another occupied table, where an abandoned empty bottle had caught her eye.

"Who's a clever lad, then?" quipped Townsend, mocking his friend. "I gave her five pounds from both of us. She only wanted to thank you personally for the gift this morning, that was all."

"You're lying to me," Marsh growled, savagely flicking ash from his cigar.

"It was to help Sarah's family get back on their feet. She just wanted to thank you for it, but you had to go and sulk! I could see she had feelings for you because you were her first, you know. She certainly wasn't any sort of loose woman."

Marsh sighed. He realised he had been a fool, and he was belatedly understanding that not all of Sarah's groans were down to his skill at lovemaking. "Are you sure?"

"I saw the evidence for myself when I walked in on you. I thought you must know, did you?"

"No," he stammered. "I was just too headstrong after the ale. It wasn't intentional, despite what you think. I should have taken greater care. Sarah said something, but I ignored her and just got on with it."

"You idiot! She wasn't a knock-up, you know," Townsend admonished. He was angry now. "And why do you keep rubbing your groin? Have you got the clap or something?"

"No. I checked my member that same morning and found I had ripped the foreskin around the helmet," he explained. "It was bloody sore, I can tell you. I only managed it once," he added flippantly.

"A prick unable to use his prick. Now I find that justifiably amusing," said Townsend. "Will you leave her a message about where she can contact you?"

"No, I don't think so." Marsh frowned at first, then carried on. "It's too late now. I'll look at it as an experience. I can't believe I've been such a fool, though, and I hope Sarah forgives me."

"Oh, snap out of it now!" said Townsend, tired of his excuses. "Let's get our food ordered with Rose, have a jar or two of the fine ale they serve here, and get to bed. We had better climb aboard the *Landau* first thing in the morning – if we can remember where she berthed. Otherwise, we could suffer for it back at Woolwich."

***

Waking up to the noisy crowing of the cockerel, Townsend peered out of his window into the grey morning light. He caught a glimpse of the bird strutting about the courtyard through a small gap in the smog. It lay like a thick blanket across the gardens and buildings. Most of the smoke from the many chimneys would normally lift by morning – being gone during the night – but it had stuck fast that morning. The coastal winds that usually blow it away had virtually dropped overnight, leaving the now common sight of smog hanging in the air, suffocating and deadening any sound.

Is it my imagination? he pondered. *Even the pesky cockerel sounds hoarse from the effect!*

Soon afterwards – washed, dressed, and with their baggage packed – the two companions ate a hearty breakfast to sustain them and then made their farewells to the landlord and his wife. After that, they ventured forth into the smog, searching for the *Landau*, pressing the damp cloths Rose had given them to their mouths to protect their lungs from the unpleasant burning miasma.

Taking the children's advice, they fumbled and felt their way along the walls of the next street and onto the quayside. After going this way and that, unsure in the smog, they were relieved to find the ship still tied up at its landing berth – though it had seemed an age to them before they found the vessel, rocking gently against the side of the dock where thick ropes still held it fast.

As they drew nearer, the vessel's rigging loomed eerily in front of them from out of the grey mist at the water's edge. The dull creaking of its timbers and the high-pitched, intermittent squeaking from the ropes made it a haunting sight. Another most challenging view to the men there was how to separate the smog encroaching on the Tyne from the town, from the mist rolling in off the Tyne; it all added to a claustrophobic sense of density surrounding the harbour. Meanwhile, the crew's usually sharp, clear sounds – making ready to sail – were muffled in the enveloping smog.

They boarded the *Landau* as it rolled gently from side to side, with the swell and flow of the water slapping continuously along its length. Sometime after, a more urgent movement was detected among the crew; the ship was visibly lifting in the water on the incoming rushing tide. They knew it would soon be time to leave. A crew member checked the water depth table on the side of the dock wall to confirm it.

Excitement stirred both the experienced crew and anxious passengers alike as the movement told them they would soon be gone. It always affected seafarers the same way.

The *Landau* was a three-mast hybrid steamship that carried an auxiliary sail and travelled by steam. It had proved profitable and economical for the shipping company, with regular sailing between Newcastle and London. As was the custom, a sounding bell – muffled by the smog – was rung as loud as possible by a crew member to announce the ship's pending departure. It was the signal the crew had been waiting on.

So, the team pulled up the gangway under the bosun's dull-sounding whistle and let the slimy, seaweed-covered mooring ropes drop with a muffled splash into the water at the ship's sides before clambering aboard themselves. The vessel drifted slowly away from its berth as the mooring ropes were hauled aboard and, very soon, it was underway.

The steam engine turned the screw and pushed it forward slowly and gently. Simultaneously, the harbour pilot's boat – adorned with lanterns and a ringing bell or two – guided them beyond the clinging smog towards the open sea and complete visibility. Only when the ship was in deeper waters did the harbour pilot signal the all-clear.

Upon seeing it, the captain gave the orders to unfurl the sails and turn off the steam drive to the engine. Once the sails dropped, they billowed out into their fullest shape, with the ship's helmsman pointing its prow south towards London.

***

The following day, Sarah arrived back at the Blue Boar in a good mood. All was well – the extra money Townsend had given her was a godsend. It had helped the family enormously with their outstanding bills, and her father's health was finally improving.

Looking about for the two officers, she asked Rose, "So, where have the two soldiers gone?"

"Gone back to Woolwich," said Rose. "They left here yesterday morning to sail back on the *Landau*." She caught her young charge's downhearted expression. "I'm so sorry, Sarah."

"Did David leave a note or anything?" she asked, trying not to look as hurt as she felt.

"No, nothing at all," Rose replied. Then, after a very awkward silence, she asked, "Did he deceive you, child? Did he play with your heart?"

Sarah struggled momentarily for a suitable answer. "Yes, Rose. He told me about racing pigeons. I know all about mixed winged 'uns, blue barred 'uns, tumblers, skimmers, and tipplers. I know what a good hen is and a good cock. I know they were used for carrying messages to the military and why a cock bird always flies back to its hen in the pigeon pen. I know so much about pigeons; I could write a book."

She paused, shaking her head.

"Oh, Rose, I've been such a fool! I had deep feelings for him," she admitted as tears formed in her eyes. "I had hoped he felt the same way.

I spent the time away thinking of him constantly because he said he was falling in love with me. Well, I fell in love with him that night! I was saving myself for the right man, and I thought it was him, but it all happened so fast. Now I can see it was just some sort of game. He soon cleared off," she finished, the bitterness evident in her voice.

Rose put her arms around the young woman and held her close. "I didn't know, dear. Matters of the heart can be so cruel. As I see it, the trick in life is to learn from your mistakes," she said softly, stroking Sarah's hair and attempting to console the younger woman. "Aye, learn from your mistakes, and you will have a good life, girl. And if there is ever a time you want to talk about pigeons, you come and speak to Rosie. I know all about them too; I'm married to a bloody pigeon fancier! I can tell you they are all bloody boring. I swear to it, child, you have missed out on nothing there, so forget him. Let him be gone – and good riddance!"

Rose's words forced a hint of a smile to grace Sarah's face. *Typical of Rose to help lift my gloom*, she thought. Her short-lived passion for David had turned rapidly into love for the man. She had missed him while away with her parents and had been eager to see him again and renew their friendship on returning – only to find him gone.

Now she was feeling the hurt and hopelessness of it all, and she hated him for leaving her the way he had.

Maybe Rose was right; maybe she was better off without him.

Chapter 7

Officer selection and deployment

A SMALL, select band of officers had learned to cope with the new one-hundred-ton gun at the School of Gunnery in Shoeburyness. They were taught to load, fire, and maintain the cannon efficiently, and were now ready to serve in the Mediterranean coastal forts in Malta and Gibraltar.

The excitement was high, but the work was hard, especially as none of them had ever had to deal with a weapon of this size before. Each of the men fired it against the latest thickness in modern ship's armour, assisted by its dedicated steam engine. The steam engines used hand-cranking valves that regulated and controlled the steam-driven hydraulic power flow, thereby controlling the gun's movement. It was explained to the men that these steam pressure storage devices were called accumulators.

With a small company of men acting as their gun team, the individual officers were assessed and put through their paces on how the gun was to be loaded using this new concept of steam power. Range-finding and its translation into firing trajectories were also repeatedly drilled into them; the training was intensive.

It was repeatedly stressed to the men that getting their readings right the first time would give them the edge over the enemy in combat, and they experienced all aspects of loading the cannon mechanically with the steam engine's aid. This included how to fire it, and – most importantly – how to physically load and fire it if, by some mishap, the steam hydraulics failed.

"Did you recognise the gun, David?" Townsend asked on their final day at Shoeburyness.

"Yes, the type we'll be using."

"No. Did you recognise *it?*"

David shook his head, confused. "No, Robert, afraid not. Should I have?"

"Have you forgotten so soon? It's the same one old Jack Stamp showed us at Elswick," Townsend told him with enthusiasm. "Remember when he said he'd scratch his initials in it for us to find? I checked today, and there they were: J.S. He knew it was for training purposes, but the old devil chose to keep us guessing! I would put my life on it. It's the same one!"

"But the one we've been using was painted up in grey," Marsh argued. "Not like the rusting specimen we came across at the Armstrong factory."

"True. The Armstrong engineers must have replaced the old inner lining and rifling on the prototype with new ones. Stamp told us it was a specialist job only they could do, which increases the gun's working life in service. I found a slight indentation under the paint, so I scratched it off to reveal his initials."

They were still discussing Jack Stamp's mischief when a training officer pinned a list of successful names up on the notice board. On reading it, both Townsend and Marsh were delighted to see their names among the ten selected officers, confirming that their postings would be to the Mediterranean. For some it meant a promotion; for others it would be, at the very least, a great adventure abroad.

Their training at Shoeburyness had now ended, and the named few were expected to attend a meeting at the Warren regarding their Mediterranean placements the next day.

That morning, the officers found their way into the colonel's meeting room at the Warren – under the guidance of the grumpy duty sergeant. They were all busily engaged in an enthusiastic discussion of which fort and island they could be going to in the Mediterranean. There was a pleasant stir around the room as they wondered what adventures the mission might have in store for them.

Standing apart from the others, Townsend felt a sharp slap on his shoulder. Assuming it was Marsh messing about, he turned sharply to confront him. It wasn't Marsh, however, but the guffawing, pompous Cuthbertson.

Marsh and Townsend – along with others whose families had a history of serving as officers for many years – possessed trained, curious minds and therefore did not sit well with the likes of Cuthbertson in the ranks. He had obtained his commission through entitlement; his father had made his money as a successful merchant and had taken full advantage of the new-found social mobility his money had given him, buying his son a commission. After meeting the man, many privately agreed it was probably to get the inadequate out from under his feet and thus protect his company.

"I say, Townie, old boy, I wonder where our postings will be, eh?" Cuthbertson guffawed. "We may even be posted to the same battery, with a bit of luck, what!"

"One never knows, Captain Cuthbertson," replied a voice behind him. Marsh had finally turned up, saving Townsend from being alone with the man.

Cuthbertson, however, was not dismayed at all. "Why, the three of us could even end up on the same island – if chosen. Spiffing if that happens, what? We will soon find out, too! What fun!" He then moved away to take a seat, much to Townsend's relief.

It took a concerted effort for them both to suppress their sniggers. "Who would think either of us would want to be on an island with him for any period, eh, Robert?" said Marsh, in an undertone.

"True. Although Cuthbertson does show a degree of idiocy, he is a forthright and demanding character," Townsend remarked thoughtfully. "I hope he has earned his place at this meeting, for all our sakes. Otherwise, him being in charge of one of these guns doesn't bear thinking about."

At eleven o'clock sharp the door abruptly swung open, curtailing all conversation.

"Attention!" an aide barked, and – directly from muscle memory – every man in the room snapped into the straight-backed salute.

"Alright, alright," said Colonel Downing, entering the room along with his aides. "Be seated, gentlemen." He took a position at the head of the table as they settled down expectantly. "I hope you all enjoyed your little foray to Shoeburyness; your few days there appear to have been highly informative, judging by the discussions I heard when I entered. Now, I had you convene today to discuss this artillery piece and the provision of ammunition for them – and, of course, your postings. After seeing and experiencing for yourselves the action of this new gun and firing system, it is hoped you will be able to at least aim and fire the bloody thing without making a mess of it… or one another." He paused to allow them to chuckle amongst themselves.

"As you should all be aware by now, this firing system should allow us to maintain a steady rate of fire. It will allow the Royal Artillery to load and fire these guns in double-quick time, to the great disadvantage of anyone out there who might want to take us on. The forts in Malta and Gibraltar that have these guns will be defensive, and those of you now selected will be a very privileged band of men indeed. The Royal Artillery, gentlemen, will again make history – aided and abetted by the Royal Engineers, you can be sure." He paused again to let his words sink in. "Right! I know you gentlemen have plenty of questions to ask, so let's get on with it." With that, the colonel motioned towards Marsh, who had his hand in the air almost before he'd finished speaking.

"What advantage will the steam engine and accumulator give us over an enemy ship armed with a similar gun?"

"Ah, Captain Marsh, is it? The report you and Captain Townsend filed on your return from Newcastle helped in no small part with this," the colonel said, making a steeple shape with his fingers. "Although cut short, the visit was invaluable. Therefore, with great pride, I can tell you that the steam engine and accumulator will give our gunners a considerable advantage over anything on the high seas. Their firing rate is one shell every six minutes. Thanks to this system, we can defend our interests in the Mediterranean around Malta and Gibraltar.

"Compared to ours, the guns aboard a ship will have a rate of fire of one every twenty minutes due to the time it takes to reload the gun manually in a restricted space. They will also be disadvantaged by the rise and fall of the seas, complicating accurate aim. In contrast, our guns will be on solid ground, with no such distractions. This means, gentlemen, that our guns will be deadly, devastating, and final. This enormous armament will be entirely independent of human error in working and loading. But, if for any reason these mechanisms failed, the gun could still be armed and fired conventionally, using a contingency of forty men. So, everything has been carefully thought through to ensure we have the appropriate resources to hand."

Feeling he should support his friend, Captain Townsend asked, "How many will be needed on the islands, and where will they be stationed, sir?"

"A good question, Captain," the colonel replied, congratulating him. "You have a sense of practicality. There will be five of these superguns, which we think will be enough to protect our interests in the Mediterranean. Two will be in Gibraltar. The first will be the Victoria Battery, sited at Grand Parade. The second will be the Napier of Magdala, situated on the cliff above Rosia Bay. The firing positions for these guns are already in place, so only the front part of these batteries will be built.

"In Malta, because of the geographical constraints, the requirements for the batteries are entirely different," he explained. "Three forts – each with the intention of housing one supergun – are being built from scratch and are currently in various stages of construction. The first fort is at Sliema and will be called Fort Cambridge; the second is at Kalkara and will be named Fort Rinella. These two guns will be able to traverse the whole of the bay and, if needed, both will be able to bear down on the same enemy ship. It would provide formidable protection against any warship trying to gain access to Grand Harbour. Finally, the third fort will be positioned at Anchor Bay and be known as Fort Anchor. This last fort will be able to cover any possibility of incursion onto the smaller beaches and islands. Anywhere in between, the defence can be provided by conventional means. Each gun will have a dedicated fort large enough to house these beasts and all the paraphernalia that goes with them – as well as the men required to load and operate them, should their automated mechanisms start failing."

Another officer – who Townsend knew to be a sensible fellow – asked, "What size and shape will the new forts take on, and how will they differ from the existing forts, sir?"

"Excellent question, Major Phillips. Given the new armaments' size and shape, the forts cannot be the so-called 'traditional' shape and build. These new forts will be wholly symmetrical polygons, identical in layout. Access to these forts will be through a bent entry to protect the single gate from long-range artillery fire. The fortified gate will also have a Guthrie bridge – which, as you know, can be immediately withdrawn in times of danger – spanning a ditch running around the whole perimeter of the fort."

"If the Italians are all we are worried about, with those newly equipped battleships of theirs, why go to such lengths to house these guns, sir?" Major Phillips asked.

"The short answer to that, Major, is that they are not the only threat," said the colonel darkly. "We have intelligence that the German Krupp factory is, at present, in talks with the Turks – amongst others – to manufacture and provide them with similar large guns. Remember, gentlemen, the renewal of the Napoleonic threat is not long behind us. Germany and now Italy are in the act of combining their states into nationhood. So, I'm sure you are aware we have a duty to the realm to protect the Empire in the Mediterranean with these fortresses – and the sooner the better, lest we regret it!"

The questions were coming in thick and fast now as another officer asked, "How tall will the finished forts stand, sir?"

"With new mechanical techniques, we must explore a new approach to fort construction," said the colonel. "It's not how high it will be, but how deep they get excavated."

The men looked at one another, puzzled.

Seeing their blank looks, he elaborated: "Each fort under construction will eventually have a full garrison of about forty men. These men will be in barracks in shell-proof accommodation below ground level. These lower-level rooms will have loopholes, so as well as barrack rooms, they will also serve as a musketry gallery, allowing our forces to suppress infantry invasion via the perimeter ditch and beyond."

"A glacis, sir," Marsh interrupted in his eagerness.

"Yes, Captain, a killing field," confirmed the colonel. "If necessary, these individual forts can withstand a large army. Food, water, armaments, and the latrines will all be within the confines of the fort – basically, everything that is required to ensure the continual firing of the gun. Or, at the very least, to keep things going until assistance arrives."

"Presuming we are being fired upon, in return, by an enemy with an equally devastating armament, I assume the wall of the fort will be extremely thick – to withstand incoming fire, sir?"

"No, Mr Cuthbertson. The cannon will be almost invisible from the sea, so the fire is unlikely to be concentrated upon the fort walls," the colonel explained. "This single artillery piece will be the battery. Its firing position will be sunk into the ground to afford maximum protection from any incoming shot, negating the need for thick walls. Each will also have a reinforced roof. There will be two magazines below the gun to store the various ordnance, one for different-sized shells and one for the various charges."

"Earlier, you spoke of our ability to fire the gun every six minutes, but it took longer in training. How would we achieve this, sir?" asked Townsend, who had been trying to work it out ever since the exercise had ended.

"The gun you gentlemen have been playing with had one loading turret, but the guns in these forts will have two loading turrets, each with two sixty-foot hydraulic rammers. The rammer will shove both the charge and shell down the gun's barrel first before it's fired. Then it will be swung mechanically to the other turret, where another charge and shell will be waiting, and rammed into it. After each firing, the inside of the muzzle is to be washed with running water – to douse any glowing embers – and then emptied. Alternating the two turrets will achieve the six-minute turnaround and maintain an effective firing rate. At the close of this meeting, each fort commander will be given a series of drawings offering greater details of the forts' layouts and the required resources. I must stress that these are for information purposes only. More detailed plans will be awaiting you on arrival at your assigned fort, including how to deal with any gun malfunction or mechanical failure. That should satisfy you all for now, I think."

"When will we know our postings, sir?" Major Phillips enquired. "And how long will they last? Also, what provisions are there for men with families?"

Townsend was pleased this question had been asked because it had been nagging away at him. His family members were important to him, and too long of an assignment could become a problem.

"Single men need female company too, sir," said Marsh. "What provision will be made for us – um, I mean, *them*, sir?"

The comment broke the tension in the room; the pressure they felt under – coupled with the weight of waiting – was slowly beginning to lift from the men.

Colonel Downing had been standing with one hand in the crook of his back when the barrage of questions hit him. He took half a step backwards, fully recognising the group of officers' nervous excitement before him, having seen it many times before. He lowered his hands slowly, in a calming fashion.

"When I leave here shortly, you will be at liberty to find your postings and how long they are likely to be, which my aides have posted on the board at the back of the room. You may apply for your wives to join you personally, and I will consider each case individually. Only wives with no children will be considered. The wives' temporary accommodation will not be within the fort itself; alternative arrangements will be made. After all, these forts are not suitable for wives. They are, first and foremost, fighting units explicitly built to service and fire the single gun battery. We cannot have our men worrying unduly about the safety of their kinsfolk while under fire. Anyone wishing to discuss this further may come and see me."

His voice trailed off as he paused for breath, slowly rocking back and forth on his heels.

"As for the second question," he said, looking directly at Marsh, "officers and their men will find the ladies of Gibraltar and Malta beautiful and fun-loving, from what I recall, though they also possess solid family ethics. Saying that, our men are expected to conduct themselves with dignity befitting soldiers of the Crown. If for some reason they cannot, then I hope God shows mercy on them if they get caught by the locals. Suppose, by chance and good fortune, they do escape the locals. In that case, I will personally deposit their testicles somewhere south of Sicily using this fine gun of ours."

The colonel smiled coldly at Marsh, who was squirming at the thought of his careless womanising being curtailed. The other officers openly grinned and laughed at him. "If they are stationed in Gibraltar, the said extremities will probably end up somewhere between 'The Rock' and Morocco. Either way, they won't be found easily. Do I make myself clear, Captain Marsh?"

"Yes, sir. Of course, sir," he gulped, shuffling uncomfortably in his seat. His barely audible answer became almost lost in the belly laughs of his fellow officers.

"You should also note," continued the colonel, "there will be no smoking permitted anywhere near the fort, and most definitely *not* inside it. As you might imagine, the results would be catastrophic. Smoking will be completely out of the question. You do not smoke, do you, Captain Marsh?"

"Oh, no, sir. Not anymore."

"And when did you stop, Captain?"

"Just now, sir!"

"Good! Because if there was an explosion in a fort of this nature and the munitions were to go up, your balls would be on the surface of the moon. Do you all take my meaning? Especially you, Captain Marsh?"

"Certainly, sir. Most eloquently and persuasively put, if I may say so." Hysterical laughter ensued amongst the men yet again as they noted his further squirming embarrassment.

After a loud double cough from the colonel, the meeting came to order. "Excellent. You will find that two among you have earned a promotion to battery commanders – both were thoroughly examined by the Promotions Panel of the Royal Artillery and have excellent character references. Congratulations to those men. Each battery commander will have under their command a master gunner, with nine gunners to assist him. Twelve men will deal with ammunition provision. Three men will act as the position finders, while four will act as rangefinders. There will also be a trumpeter, a storeman, a cook, and a lamp man, with a telephonist-cum-signaller maintaining contact with all the other fortifications. In Malta, these will be the three new forts and St. Elmo.

"Besides the new telephone, signals backup will be provided by semaphore and signal mirror. Fort Cambridge, Fort Rinella, and Fort Anchor will each have a well within the fort to provide fresh water for drinking and the latrines.

"It's with immense pride that we hope – no, not hope, but expect – that with repeated drills, the rate of fire will be increased to once every four minutes. As your placements are imminent, you must take your home leave immediately, so you can come back here suitably refreshed for the tasks and rigours ahead. Tie up any loose ends you have and get everything in order."

"What happens when the guns get to Malta and Gibraltar?" Townsend asked. "Will the Royal Artillery move them using traditional means, such as shire horses and platforms? Also, sir, if I may be so bold, the gun is no lightweight, and if we were to use sheer muscle power, we would need somewhere between eighty to ninety men to move it. Of course, that would be with horses and such."

"Thank you, Captain Townsend. You have raised several relevant points, which will be answered more thoroughly in due course. For today, I just want to deal with the basics. As far as Gibraltar is concerned, the hauling up of the gun will be straightforward, as you surmised. The road infrastructure is in place, so it would be correct to assume muscle power aligned with shire horses will get them to their garrison. At the New Mole docking area, the guns will be lifted off the cargo ship – the *SS Stanley* – with one of the heavy shears they have there, and then onto a carriage, to be delivered with the aid of the shire horses.

"Malta will be a completely different proposition. Two of these guns will be required to protect the Valletta Harbour approach from the sea; the garrisons will sit on either side in the hills above Valletta Harbour. The Cambridge garrison will have an easier approach because there are roads in various states between the harbour and the fort. Forts Rinella and Anchor, on the other hand, have no road structure whatsoever. These guns will get to their garrisons by manpower and capstan alone. There will only be horsepower at Fort Anchor once it has reached the top of the hill, and then only for a short distance. In the Anchor Battery case, they have thoughtfully considered constructing a landing stage by deepening the water in the bay using underwater explosives. The gun will get transferred from the *SS Stanley* to a barge, which will bring it to the new landing stage. The Royal Engineers will have their gantry erected, ready to raise the gun. It will lift the gun clear of the barge and deliver it to ourselves on shore at Anchor Bay."

"How will the guns be delivered into the forts, sir?" Marsh asked, overcoming his embarrassment.

"The Royal Engineers are building the forts," he replied. "An opening will be left in the defensive wall to allow for the entrance of the gun, and will be sealed up once it's in place. Another group of Royal Engineers will construct a temporary gantry, which will lift the gun into place between the two loading ports. Many men were required to build these new forts, so the Royal Engineers employed local labour where necessary. Because of the difficult terrain, each gun will have a contingency of about one hundred men to deliver them. It's hoped, Mr Marsh, that your efforts will leave you far too tired to be thinking about women if you are selected. You should be thinking, instead, of getting some much-needed rest after the day's exertions."

Feeling awkward under the colonel's gaze, Marsh wisely kept quiet.

"Well, gentlemen, I believe I have covered everything," said the colonel, clapping his hands together and twisting both palms. "As I say, all the information is on the board for you to digest at your leisure. Applications for wives are to be put on my desk after the meeting for due consideration. However, I will give the answers now if any of you want me to. Just come to the office next door, and we will get it sorted before I depart for the War Office in an hour. Then I must advise you to take any leave you may have coming to you, so you can come back fresh and alert for the tasks ahead. You will certainly need it! Good day, gentlemen." With that, the old warhorse left the room with his entourage of aides jostling behind him.

As soon as the door closed, the men gathered at the noticeboard, all keen to discover who had gained promotion and which of the forts they had been assigned.

The first to the list took it upon himself to read the promotions aloud: "Captain Peters, you have been promoted to commander along with Captain Townsend."

The congratulations started immediately, and both had to fend off good-humoured banter while wilting from slaps to the back.

Marsh finally rescued Townsend by shaking his hand firmly and dragging him out from the melee by the elbow. "Congratulations," he said as he saluted, "Commander Townsend of Anchor Battery."

"Is it Anchor Battery, David? I failed to get close enough to read it."

"It is, Robert – with me as your master gunner!" he exclaimed.

Elated, Townsend made an enormous effort to appear unhappy. "Not so good."

"Why, Robert?"

Townsend stared at him, waiting to provoke a reaction.

Realising he was teasing, Marsh gave a broad smile, and they shook hands vigorously, congratulating each other on their success. "Oh, and if you never heard it, Captain Cuthbertson is being sent to Gibraltar with Major Phillips, so that's one less worry for us."

Feeling relieved, Townsend began thinking of Victoria, and he left Marsh to seek permission to take her with him.

***

After leaving the Warren, the two friends visited a convenient hostelry where they planned to celebrate their good fortune, now that they were officially on leave.

"I bet Victoria will be pleased with your promotion and deployment, Robert," said Marsh, swishing around the remains of his ale in his tankard.

"I certainly hope so," Townsend remarked. "Now is the time to do these things before any children come along. I do worry that she may not want to go with me, though, and if that's the case, I will be away too long and she won't like it." He blew out his cheeks, concerned, as he leaned his elbow on the upturned empty beer barrel being used as a table. Meanwhile, the bar was filling up fast with customers and others who made their living locally.

"Can I get you boys anything?" Belle, the barmaid, asked, standing and looking down at the two men, her hands on her hips. The snug corset and low-necked chemise she was wearing left little to the imagination as she leaned forward. Belle was the star attraction at the pub, keeping the men drinking in there entertained – earning thruppence a night extra for herself on top of her wage and anything else she could get.

"That's a very kind offer, although I don't know you personally. I'll have a pint of ale, please, and the same for Robert."

Townsend spluttered at his cheek, losing a mouthful of beer in the process.

"You know what I mean, soldier," Belle purred.

"Oh?" Marsh asked innocently.

"You've got a cute face," she said, running her finger down his nose. "When I say anything, I mean *anything*." She made a conscious effort to lean forward even more, pushing her breasts almost into his face.

"Landlord, can we each have a handful of your fine pork scratchings over here?" Marsh called, wearing a wicked grin. "Belle said she would pay!"

"Smart arse!" she retorted.

"Alas, I can't stay, but I'll dream of you tonight, Belle," Marsh promised.

"I don't mind, soldier, but there will be a charge for that service too," Belle said seductively. She was always very forward where money was concerned.

"So, what do we get for our dreams, Belle?" asked an eavesdropper.

"A smack in the face if you keep it up," she threatened.

At least it took her attention away from Marsh, leaving the two men to enjoy the rest of their drink together. They watched as Belle sashayed away to the far side of the room, over to another group of men that hadn't been involved in the bawdy incident. She circled the group, joining in with their chatter while thrusting her ample bosom close to their faces, fishing for another client.

"I can't figure out what manner of charm you possess, David, that attracts the women. But looking at her, I don't want to. You can keep it to yourself." Townsend clapped him on the shoulder. "Look, I must go soon, but I don't want to leave you in her clutches. Therefore, let me pay for one more drink, and then we both must be off. I can't wait to tell Victoria the news. The same again, David?" he asked as he wiped the beer froth from his lips with the back of his hand.

"Yes, Robert, of course."

Casually striding over to the bar, Townsend called, "Two more beers, please, barman," before adding, "tell me – does Belle abide here?"

The barman gave him a castellated, toothy grin. "Our Belle's got a room out the back. The lass has been there a year or two now, aye. She works the tables for the gaffer because she gets them to drink more!"

Townsend pulled back at the smell on his breath. "Not exactly pretty, is she?" he asked, rather rudely, though he felt he was stating the obvious.

"The day's young yet, man," the barman laughed. "Ask me again after a few drinks; the men here reckon Belle gets prettier by the tankard – especially after dark, when the candles are lit!" His grin broadened, showing a complete set of rotted teeth.

Joining in with the laughter, Townsend brought the generously overfilled tankards back to Marsh, dripping two beer trails across the sawdust-covered floor and up onto the barrel top.

"Where will you go from here, David?" Townsend asked, concerned he might end up in Belle's clutches.

"I'm not sure. I'll think of something."

"Well, as long as it's not with Belle. I do not want to join my command at Fort Anchor with a good friend and master gunner short."

"Ha! No fear of that happening with her, Robert. I'll be coming with you, that's for sure."

An hour later Townsend was eager to be away and, after wishing each other well, they went their separate ways. Marsh had embraced secret thoughts of seeing Sarah and strode off to make the booking. Similarly, the newly appointed major was ever keen to share his good news with Victoria and tell her she would be travelling with him. He selfishly needed her feminine presence alongside him for the duration of his time in Malta – however long it may be.

Taking advantage of his leave, Townsend felt a little shopping was required, so he headed off to Powis Street in Woolwich. Victoria wouldn't forgive him for coming home empty-handed – and she would be sure to let him know it.

When he was finished, he slung the heavy rucksack containing the gifts – and other things necessary for the family – over his shoulder and went looking for convenient transport.

Chapter 8

Woodside Cottage. A welcome few days leave with unexpected news

THE NEWLY promoted Townsend hired a horse and cab to take him home and, a while later, it halted at the top of a narrow lane just four miles outside the Woolwich village. Although it bore no name, the road was known locally as 'Bluebell Lane' after the flowers' profusion in the woods on either side of it that came out each spring. He fondly recalled seeing the blue carpets of flowers many times.

He paid the driver the fare and then slung the heavy rucksack containing candles, friction matches, and presents for the family over his shoulder as the driver began to turn the horse.

"Are you sure you want me to drop you off here, sir? I could get you down that lane," he offered.

"No, leave me here, driver. I want my homecoming to be a bit of a surprise, and I wouldn't want you getting stuck down there; it's quite narrow in places. Besides, I need to break in these new army boots and stretch out the leather. They feel a little tight, just now."

"Very good, sir, and thank you for your custom," he said, turning the horse's head with the reins. After giving them a firm shake and letting out a whistle, he was off – back to the Woolwich Arsenal, his usual pick-up spot.

Townsend watched the horse flicking its tail as it disappeared over the brow of the hill with the carriage in tow. For a brief moment he stood at the top of the lane, savouring the complete silence after the clamour of the day. It was for the silence and beauty of the place that he and Victoria had moved here in the first place – being lucky to buy a cheap ramshackle farm. Other parts of London had a smutty look to them as local industries sprang up, requiring more and more people, and with the extra people came more crime. But this little part of heaven had seen none of that.

Before long, the birds started up one at a time as the perceived danger – in the form of the horse-drawn carriage – passed. A curious robin discovered Townsend first and chirruped at him while a thrush hurriedly crossed his path, searching for its mate. Within a few more steps he'd disturbed a blackbird – which had been turning over fallen leaves, looking for a tasty morsel – which then flew off, alarmed, clicking a loud warning call as it went.

Townsend smiled, thinking of the day he and Victoria had decided to move away from the noise and clamour of Woolwich. They had had the option to stay in married quarters but had instead elected to find a place where he could relax when on leave, away from the barracks' regimented protocol. After Townsend had completed his army service many years into the future, the dream was to retire there. Although his captain's pay was better than most, it was still meagre compared to some professions, so it excited him to tell Victoria of his promotion.

The welcoming rain had stopped moments before he stepped down from the carriage, leaving a lingering sweet freshness in the air that assailed his senses as he walked towards the narrow, smog-free lane without a soul in sight. He descended into the shaded upper part of the lane, appreciating the place's solitude and noting how 'loud' total silence can really be. It was a marked difference from the ever-clamorous presence of the Army.

The line of trees on either side of the lane had spread into a canopy aloft, entangling leaves in each other's branches and creating a shaded tunnel below – almost a hollow way. In the early afternoon, the scent of numerous wildflowers hung in the air. The colder nights and bright days had kissed the trees' upper canopies, which had begun shedding a few leaves, fluttering silently down to the floor. Shafts of sunlight broke through these gaps, giving a magical feel to the place.

Soon it will be winter, but Victoria and I will not need to face the cold again this year. He felt happy at the thought.

Carefully, he walked on the higher-ridged middle of the track to keep his new boots dry. Over the years, water seepage from the woods and the passage of carts had slowly washed away the ground on each side of the lane, leaving the partial roots of some trees exposed. Following the recent downpour, water was leaking out of the higher banks into these tracks, where it trickled down on either side, flowing and combining towards the water splash crossing the lane further down.

It was his second spell of home leave since the trip to Newcastle and, during his last visit, he had installed a new cesspit from a construction guide. It delighted him to see that the controlled outflow into the ground was working a treat. With a plentiful supply of wood at hand, a natural well to draw fresh water from, a carefully stocked larder with wild game in the woods, and a good number of candles to hand, they had everything they needed, and life was good.

He stopped abruptly when a prowling fox crossed the path below him. It started towards him for a few brief seconds before scurrying off into the undergrowth; now hidden, the fox watched him from a safe distance as he passed it by. On rounding the bend at the bottom of the lane, the ford came into sight.

Good, he thought, pleased. *It hasn't flooded yet.*

Also during his last home leave he had placed large stepping stones across the shallow stream, then hung a sturdy rope between two stout trees to steady travellers when crossing over. He knew it could be dangerous after heavy rainfall, so he congratulated himself on his forethought as he confidently stepped over and across the slowly rising stream to the other side.

What will the cottage look like now, with the new roof? he wondered.

The old roof had needed attention from the local thatcher, having seen far better days. They were due to start the day after he returned, and now he was eager to see the result.

When it came into view, it looked visibly attractive, and – for a moment – he simply stood there and gazed at the house that was his and Victoria's home. Smoke was rising lazily from the chimney, its whitewashed walls gleaming in the aftermath of the rain, making it stand out from the muted green tones of the woods behind. It was beautiful.

He was pleased to see that Steven – Victoria's brother – had cut plenty of wood for the fire and piled it up undercover near the side of the cottage. The overall effect was stunning and picturesque. *I will paint it on canvas one day – after I retire,* he promised himself before starting down the slope.

While descending the incline, he caught sight of Victoria in the distance, coming out of the cottage. Even at a few hundred yards, her auburn hair was quite distinctive.

She was hanging out the washing with a spare peg in her mouth when he first called her, but she hadn't heard him. He could see her pushing back the wisp of hair that had dropped across her face, knowing how much it annoyed her.

He whistled next, and this time the ears of their dog, Cassie – a spirited mongrel terrier – stood up. She immediately started barking, recognising both the whistle and her master.

Then Victoria did look up, scanning the landscape with her hand shielding her eyes from the sun, looking around for any signs of anyone. Gazing up the hill, she squinted at first, and then the realisation dawned as she picked him out, waving at her in the distance.

"It's Robert, Mum, Robert!" she squealed delightedly. "Mum, where are you?" she squealed again, dropping the empty wicker washing basket. Suddenly, her appearance was of the utmost importance; she tucked the wisp of hair firmly into place, unable to contain her excitement as she brushed away dust and specks of dirt from her dress.

Then, what had started as a timid walk towards him, quickly developed into a run.

"Mother! Mother! It's Robert! He's home! Where are you?" she shouted. Pulling open the gate, she lifted the front of her long dress and ran up the hill, squealing with glee at the unexpected sight of him approaching.

The dog quickly outstripped her and reached him first, yapping with great excitement at his feet, desperately wanting a fuss as she lashed his legs with her tail.

When Victoria finally got to him, he swept her up in his capable arms, cradling her head in his hand and kissing her lovingly. Eventually, he put her down, telling her how much he had missed her.

"I have missed you too," she said as she gave him another kiss on the cheek.

"I bet I've missed you more than you missed me," he said with a grin.

"Don't start that again, Robert, you fool!" she said as they laughed together. "Oh, I do love you, Robert. You make me laugh at all the silly things you say!"

"I bet I love you more than you love me."

"Stop it," she said as she slapped him gently. "We have all missed you *so* much," she told him again as she held him by the arm and led him down to Woodside Cottage.

As they neared the door, he stopped her. "Where's your mother and young Steven? I heard you calling them, even from way up the hill."

"They must be down at the hollow," Victoria told him. "Only this morning, Steven thought that one or two of the cows might have wandered off. They must have gone to look for them, which is all very well, as I've got something important to tell you."

She paused, and he gazed at her blankly. "Robert, darling, I have the most wonderful, wonderful news." She placed her hands on both his shoulders, raising herself on her toes. "Robert, I'm pregnant," she whispered in his ear.

Townsend stepped back a pace, trying to read her expression. "You're fooling with me, aren't you?" He couldn't believe what he was hearing, and his face creased in a confused frown. "What did you say?"

"I'm pregnant," she said again, bursting with delight. "I saw the physician the other day because I wasn't feeling well, and he confirmed what my mother and I both thought! It must have happened during your last home leave."

"Hurray!" he cried. "At last! Not that it wasn't a pleasure trying to achieve it, you must understand," he added quickly, success written across his features. "I thought I was about to surprise *you* with good news, but you've bettered it!" Then, suddenly, his whole attitude changed. "You shouldn't lift anything heavy. I cringe now at you running up the hill towards me. What if you had fallen?"

Victoria rolled her eyes prettily. "I'm pregnant, Robert, not an invalid. Besides, it wouldn't have mattered yet – it's far too early, silly. What were you about to tell me?"

"I've earned my promotion to major at last! With the title of Commander of the Garrison."

Smiling coquettishly, Victoria placed a finger to his lips to quieten any further concern. Speaking softly, she said, "Robert, I want you, and I want you right now. I swear if you say no, I will rip your uniform off, so I will. Right here and now – to celebrate our good fortune and your promotion!"

"But what about Tilly and your brother? They could walk in on us!" he cautioned, though he felt the same way.

"No, Major. You won't get out of it that easily," Victoria told him in a voice that brooked no argument. "If they are where I think they are, they won't be back soon. Besides, this is your wife speaking, and I'm not taking no for an answer. Give me a few minutes to titivate myself, and then come in. That's an order, Major!"

She disappeared inside the cottage, leaving Townsend with the dog, who was pleased to nuzzle into him and lick at his face.

"Good girl. Good girl, Cassie," he said, standing there now with her in his arms.

After Townsend had married Victoria, the dog had become the first addition to the family. He had found her one evening alone, lost, and hungry, just a bag of bones. Her sad eyes had bored into his conscience, and he just had to take her home, where he gave her food, water, and a sense of belonging. Since then, the dog had repaid him with slavish devotion toward the whole family.

Conscious that Victoria was waiting for him, he placed the dog gently down and strolled towards the house. Lifting the latch, he walked in, firmly closing the door behind him; he wanted her to hear him enter and get nearer.

My, he noticed, *what a difference a new thatch roof has made! Before, the heat escaped up and out of the roof, which leaked in places. Now it feels so much warmer, comfortable, and inviting.*

He followed her scent towards the bedroom, thinking that, in her excitement, she had been a little heavy-handed with it. Honestly, he thought, she hadn't needed it at all. She was already a very feminine woman – *his* woman – and he wanted her just as badly as she wanted him.

He found her lying in their bed with a cotton bedsheet drawn up over her nose, her gorgeous auburn hair splayed across the pillow. At the same time, her eyes peered up at him with a sexy, enticing look, the few freckles on her face only adding to her beauty.

She moved the bedsheet down a little and pouted her lips suggestively, delighted to see that her feminine charm was having the desired effect on him. She meant it; she wanted him. She was already moaning and moving her hips suggestively beneath the sheet.

Townsend sat on the stool awkwardly; he wanted her too, but he was struggling a little. "I can't get these blasted new boots off," he muttered as he tried again and again. "My bloody feet have swollen from all my walking, Vicky. Damn it! I knew they felt a little too tight."

"Oh, let me help," said Victoria. "I can't wait all day." She bounced off the horsehair mattress, completely naked, and then – straddling his legs – grabbed for a boot. With his help, she yanked it off his foot and then grabbed at the other one, but it wouldn't budge. Putting his foot on her bare bottom, he pushed her with it, and eventually they got the blessed thing off. She quickly rushed back into bed, but he had seen her in all her glory, and his penis immediately stiffened and throbbed with the view.

"I have no idea how long I will last for, Vicky," he said huskily, "but I can always make it up to you later tonight, darling." With that, he dove under the covers alongside her.

***

Victoria's brother, Steven, and their mother, Tilly Smith, had managed to drive the two escaped cows back into the field, where Steven made busy repairing the hole in the hedge to stop any further attempts to get out. After her father's death, they had moved in with Victoria – and Robert – and had both been very happy in their new surroundings.

Steven stopped and listened. "Did you hear Cassie barking a while ago, Mum?"

"Yes, I wonder who it could be?" she pondered aloud. "Let's go and see," she added, tying the gate behind them.

"Come on, then," said the young man, pulling her hand.

Then, linking arms, they made their way back to the cottage – along the path Steven and Robert had shored up with stone in the spring. Both were delighted to find Robert framed in the cottage doorway talking to Victoria, his braces dangling in loops from his waist.

"Where have you two been? I've been back half a day now," he teased, putting a companionable arm around Steven's shoulder.

"Oh, you are a liar," Tilly rebuked him as they embraced. "We've only been gone for a short while, so you haven't."

"What's the problem?" he asked.

"Those cows got out again – that's the second time this week!" she complained.

He listened as he slipped his hanging braces back up over his shoulders. "Don't worry, Tilly. If they are safe for today, I'll get down there tomorrow and sort it out."

"We've fixed the hole for now," said Steven.

"Good, well done. Now come inside and see what I've got you both," he declared. "I've bought you that new fox stole you've always wanted for the church, Tilly – and for you, Steven, a wooden model of a British Man O' War."

"Wow!" exclaimed Steven excitedly as he hurried inside to find it.

"I've also got a mixture of news to tell you both," he said, ushering Tilly inside, along with Victoria. Opening the rucksack, he took out the candles and friction matches first before giving out the gifts.

He was delighted to hear how much they were appreciated. He had secretly bought a sexy undergarment for Victoria too, but he chose not to mention it to her until later, when they'd be away from prying eyes.

When the excitement had died down, Victoria urged him, with subtle gestures, to tell them the news of his promotion.

Clearing his throat, he began, "You both know how we have struggled at times to make ends meet, and you know we've had to get essentials – such as roof repairs and animal fodder – and how hard it's been, at times, to find the money." He took a deep breath, treasuring the moment. "Well, I'm delighted to say that should be a thing of the past... because I have finally got the extra money we need – along with a promotion to major."

"Well done! Oh, well done, Robert!" Tilly cried as Steven whooped with excitement. "We knew you could do it! But what's the bad news?"

"Well," he said, with a sigh, "my official title will be the Commander of the Battery, but with that comes a posting abroad to Malta. My home leave here will be for two weeks. Sometime after that, I will get shipped to Malta. I could be gone for three years or more... I'm afraid it's impossible to say. Now, because of the uncertainty, I want to hire someone from the village – preferably someone with muscle – for when any hard manual work is required here."

"I can help there," said Steven, once he had recovered from the shock. "I know someone in the village that could do with a job. More importantly, he'll be able to get here daily."

"Good! At least that's one worry less," Townsend replied, followed by a sharp exhalation of air. "I would like him to start before I'm back at the barracks, just to get to know him and fill him in on one or two things – and to organise payment and such."

Tilly asked, "How will Victoria cope now she's pregnant?"

"Well, now I know she's pregnant, it's put a rather different colour on things," said Townsend. "I have special dispensation to take her with me, but now that she's expecting our baby, it's changed everything. I couldn't possibly expect her to go."

"Hush, Robert," Victoria ordered, while blowing that wisp of hair from her face again. "Typical man. One minute, they roll about, wrestling with you: the next minute, they imprison you in overbearing protection. We have two weeks to decide, and the matter is by no means settled," she added, tossing her head and turning before her husband could even start to argue. "Meanwhile, Robert has plenty of work to do here at the cottage before then."

***

During his time at home, all the jobs that required attention were made right. Anything he could do, he did. Fencing got nailed, and the recent storm-damaged barn roof was repaired. To Tilly's delight, he also cleared out the rubble that had fallen from the walls inside the well, blocking the water pail from fully submerging into the clean drinking water flowing below.

Victoria and Robert also found time to ride their horses together, pointing them across the ford to ride in the lanes and dirt tracks, as they had done many times before. They were, as ever, incredibly thrilled and in love. He wanted her to ride side-saddle because of the baby, but she would have none of it. She had already cultivated the habit of deflecting his charming concern with the promise that she would stop riding horses altogether the day he returned to the barracks.

As the days passed, Victoria also had time to work on his stubborn refusal to take her with him – she insisted that she wanted to go, no matter what.

Finally, on the last day of his leave, she lost patience with him. "Look, Robert," she said, when they were all sitting in the kitchen, "I'll take any ship that's going to Malta. I'll pay my passage on one, and you won't know about it until I come knocking on your drawbridge. You won't keep me away. Not for three years, you won't!"

Her determination drew fond laughter from him. "You sweet thing, but it's not a drawbridge – castles have those – mine is a fort with a gate."

She rolled her eyes at his pedantry.

"Well, I can't wait here for the next two or three years, hoping someday you may turn up," she suggested. "It would kill me. Don't you understand? In any case, if I'm going to travel, now is the best time. My bump doesn't show, and you have admitted that officers' wives can go with their husbands. All I want is to go, too. I want to be with you, for heaven's sake!"

"All right," he said in defeat, then stayed her excitement with a hand upon her arm, "but I never said you were pregnant, so we ought to keep it quiet until after we get there. There's no way I would allow you to travel independently, either. I love you too much for that.

"For serving soldiers, the usual method used is a game of chance in the lower ranks. If your names are picked, you can take your wife along on your posting, or she may qualify as a camp follower. Only one married man in ten or twelve is permitted to take their wives abroad. The women need to earn their keep, though. They are expected to wash and launder, not only for their menfolk but also for the other soldiers. They will have to sew and darn clothes for them too. The women receive half-rations for these services, and they are only allowed private space in the billets with their man if screened off by a curtain! There are various roles for women in the Army: cooks, nurses, midwives, launderers, sutlers, and seamstresses.

"As my wife," he continued, "I need you to understand what life is like for the ordinary soldier and his family. Also, you will be expected to earn *your* keep by supervising these ladies and holding them to account for any misdemeanours, such as fights, theft, and the like."

"I never realised how complicated it was," she said, raising an eyebrow, "but I shall manage. I run our small farm when you are away, so you will not dissuade me, Robert."

"Victoria, as the commander's wife – if I take you – you will travel on a troopship with me, where we will have the courtesy of a cabin for ourselves."

"And when she arrives at Malta, Robert? Where will my daughter live?" asked Tilly, showing concern.

Townsend smiled. "As I understand it, there will be temporary accommodation at hand for us, but I have no further information yet. It's a chance we will have to take on where, but it will be somewhere close to the fort – just not within it." He scratched his nose. "Since your position would make you responsible for the general well-being of the women, you will likely be billeted with them. Do you think you could cope?"

"I'm willing to do anything required, Robert, as long as you are beside me on our adventure."

"I know you are, Victoria, but I need you to be aware of the hardships involved."

"Hardships?" She laughed, a sound to gladden his heart. "I know all about hardships. My mother, Steven, and I know all about the hardships we've had to endure while you were gone," she replied cynically.

He loved it when she threw her head back in defiance. He couldn't resist – and she knew it.

"Right, you have managed somehow to persuade me," he said, holding his hands up in abject surrender. "When I get back to the Warren tomorrow, I'll ask for a right of wives' passage ticket. As I understand it, we'll be setting sail for Malta one or two weeks after that. I will send a hansom cab for you, and then you will stay with me in married quarters until we set sail. I'm sure that your mum and brother will be fine with the help at hand until we get back. Will you, Tilly?" he asked Victoria's mother, who was sitting across from them.

"Yes, of course we will," she replied robustly. "We don't want you both worrying about us while you're over there, now, do we? If you must go because of your promotion, then you must go. We will be here when you return. Our only concern is for Victoria. You will take care of her, Robert, my son, won't you?"

"You know I will. I'll guard *both* with my life," he added, with a smile and a wink at his wife. "Oh, come here, Tilly. Cuddle me and blow your nose, or else you will start us all off."

Later, as he and Victoria walked the dog together, he tossed a stone into the distance for the dog to chase. She tore away after it, and as the two of them watched Cassie run at full pelt, Victoria glanced up at him with a knowing smirk on her face.

"Oh, Robert, I'm so glad you finally came around to my way of thinking," she mischievously declared. "As you have hardly got off me these last few nights, it would have been quite cruel of me to deny you tonight. But I would have, you know."

He shot her a cursory glance. Her green eyes flashed back at him in a way that told him she knew she would get her way, yet again.

"Why, you little bitch," he snarled, not remotely serious.

Victoria laughed and ran ahead of the dog.

"Why, you! Come here!" He laughed, too, as he ran after her, the dog yapping at their heels along the way.

***

The morning of Townsend's return to Woolwich soon came, beginning with a concerted effort on his part to get out of bed and untangle himself from his wife's splayed legs. Following a wash and shave, he shared a light morning meal with the family before venturing inside the barn to groom and feed the two horses – all between giving Cassie some extra heavy petting.

Sometime after, Victoria followed her husband out and found him saddling up both horses.

"Victoria, darling. Will you ride with me to Barney's farm over yonder and bring back my horse as before? I've arranged a lift into Woolwich on his horse and cart."

She nodded her agreement, disheartened that they would be separated again so soon.

Later, after his goodbyes to Steven and a tearful Tilly, Townsend set off with Victoria to meet Barney at his farm gate, as arranged. They rode away from the cottage, only stopping occasionally to allow their horses to graze on the rich, abundant pasture. Talk between them was infrequent and strained until he finally caught her downturned eyes. She gazed back at him, knowing he would ask her to stay yet again.

"Are you beginning to worry that the time to leave is getting nearer?" he asked her gently.

"A little. I know I haven't travelled anywhere as you have – certainly, not out of the country. And, yes, it's difficult for me to be leaving both my mother and brother. But you said so yourself – your commission could be anything up to a few years, and I am not prepared to waste that much of our lives apart. It will be difficult, I know, but I will take the opportunity and go with you."

Tenderly, he took her hand. "Look, Victoria, you don't have to, you know. If you are unhappy about leaving your mother and brother."

"No, Robert," she replied defiantly before continuing in a louder voice, "That's not right, because my place is with you. We married to make a life together, and if that means going halfway around the world, I will. If only your dear parents had been alive to see you take up your post; they would have been really and truly proud of you, I'm sure."

A lump came to his throat as he recalled the sadness of his parents dying in a most unfortunate bizarre accident. His father had driven their carriage too close to the edge of a crumbling roadway, and the wheels had slipped off the verge, plunging them down a steep hill. They were both tipped out of the carriage and struck by the overturned vehicle that had followed them down. The news of their deaths had hit him hard; he'd been inconsolable for days.

"I won't wait years and years for you to turn up again," said Victoria. "I'm a young woman, and there are certain things a lady wants – and I swear to you, I would go off with a one-eyed, one-legged pig farmer to get it if you were gone for years, so there!" She spat the words out at him in no uncertain terms, her unusual declaration breaking the nervous anxiety between them.

"Hah!" he barked a laugh. "I'm beginning to think you would too. The world must be full of one-eyed, one-legged pig farmers, so there's no way I'm leaving you behind now. Oh, Victoria," he sighed, "you know I couldn't go off and leave you, even if I wanted to. Come and hug me, and then I'll help you back on your horse. We must be off to meet up with our neighbour if I want that lift to Woolwich. I couldn't possibly walk it in these boots." He smiled, attempting to lift the gloom. It nearly worked, but she still kept a straight face.

A long, sad silence descended again after the easy chatter, something that continued until they reached the farmer's gate. Victoria had become tearful and was trying to hide it, but Townsend saw the raw effect their parting was having.

As soon as they dismounted, he turned her to him, wiping away the tear from her cheek with a light brush of his thumb while she clung to him, wanting him to stay longer but knowing better than to ask.

"I've got to go," he whispered before kissing her again and tasting her slightly salty response on his lips. He took a few seconds longer to run his hands over her delightful curves before adding, "I will get word to you as soon as I know, and we will meet as planned. Now, please go before you upset me too. Tilly nearly started me off blarting earlier!"

Victoria nodded, tears still in her eyes, but she was smiling a little now too.

Townsend helped her back into the saddle and then handed her the reins of both horses. She turned them about and looked at him one more time, drinking his features in while she still had the chance.

After taking a moment to look up at her, Townsend gave both horses a helpful slap on their flanks, sending them back home at a gallop.

Chapter 9

Setting sail for Malta on 'The Esmie'

THE OFFICERS' married quarters stood well back from the parade grounds and barracks to protect the wives' ears from the often unsavoury cacophony of soldiers under instruction. It also discouraged any familiarity between the officers' wives and the troops, which could have disastrous consequences. Of course it still happened – though rarely – and if improper fraternisation was proven, it carried severe repercussions for those involved.

Seeing the carriage arrive, Townsend descended the married quarters' steps and held out his hand to help steady Victoria with as she stepped down. He glanced briefly at the small amount of baggage secured to the rear of the carriage. Then, holding her at arm's length, he said, "Hello, darling. You're looking lovely as usual. Is this everything you want to take?"

"Oh," she said, glancing around. "This is all I need for now. I've arranged for the rest to be delivered to the London Docks in five days, ready for us to sail. We won't be living in style out there, anyway."

"Excellent, darling," he said, pleased. "I'll pay the driver, then show you where our quarters are. It should be suitable for a few nights, and I hope you find it comfortable."

At once, Victoria became suspicious. *That's twice Robert has called me darling in a few seconds*, she thought. When she narrowed her eyes at him, he realised he had perhaps overdone it with the endearments.

"I'm surprised you were able to meet me, Robert," she said, with an air of nonchalance he did not believe. "Should you not be involved with the other officers and men? Like doing shooting or fencing or something of that nature?"

"How simplistic, uncluttered, and non-military your thinking is!" he declared, causing her frown to deepen. "Is it any wonder I love you?"

He showed her inside, his eyes quickly taking in the shapely feminine charms he so adored and had missed as she surveyed their married quarters. "Come here," he ordered.

With a mock salute, she replied, "Yes, sir."

His hands quickly stretched out and pulled her in close. "I have my final orders," he told her softly, enjoying having her in his arms again. "The cannons are to be shipped out when the forts are near completion. Fort Anchor will be the first operational fortress to be up and running, and I feel honoured to be its commander. Our fort will be followed by Cambridge and then Rinella, in that order. So, for now at least, I've been stood down from duties to concentrate on family problems and welfare." He kissed her lightly on the lips. "You are my family problems and welfare," he added, kissing her again.

"But I'm not a problem, am I?" she asked, crestfallen.

He cut her off with a firmer, more eager kiss.

"But Robert..."

He kissed her again, gently stifling her protests.

Sensing he was becoming too passionate to argue with, she pulled out her hatpin and dropped it and her hat, blindly, onto the table beside her, just as he deepened his kisses.

Recognising that she was giving ground spurred him on. "How's my baby doing?" he enquired, helping her off with her dress.

"It's fine, Robert. It's doing fine and still not showing," she gasped, drawing fresh breath between his kisses, "but shouldn't you abstain? It's only been days, you know. You have waited longer."

"No, I shouldn't. No," he replied quickly, peppering his answer with passionate kisses.

Exasperated, she gave up the argument and succumbed to his lovemaking. She knew what pleased him best at amorous times like this – her total submission – and she didn't mind.

***

Days later, they were travelling the narrow lanes along the London Docks, looking for the *Esmeralda*. The troopship they had passage aboard was due to stop at Malta before sailing on to the Suez Canal and Egypt.

"Are you sure the *Esmeralda* is in this part of the docks, sir?" the driver asked, his voice betraying his concern. "I can't see it anywhere."

"It's here somewhere, driver; just keep looking," Townsend instructed confidently.

"Indeed, sir. Then it must be further over there," he added, pointing a finger.

The docks were vast, with many ships berthed there. Various flags were flying, flapping noisily in the brisk wind, their worn corners frayed from the continual slap. Beyond the docks, a large backdrop of chimneys belched out the familiar choking black smoke.

The horse and carriage continued slowly along the narrow lanes that connected each section of the docks, searching for the *Esmeralda*. Animal hides, destined for tanning, festooned the many small shops and stalls in the lanes. Around these premises, the stinking smell of the urine used in the process hung heavily in the air. It fused readily with the stench emanating from the soap factories, which were boiling down animal bones – sourced from abattoirs local and further afield. Nothing was left unused. Other shops had the latest maritime gear for the ship and sailor, such as sextants and compasses, oilskins, and even weapons. There were also grocery stores dotted amongst the higgledy-piggledy storefronts, displaying leaded, tinned cases of meat and biscuits. 'Guaranteed to keep in any climate' proclaimed the posters on the walls. The premises they traded from took on weird shapes, each haphazardly built without any planning or foundations – often encroaching over the lane and looking to be in various states of duress and disrepair. Such were the London Docks.

Both the driver and his passengers were unaware that disaffected dock workers had chosen that day as a day of protest for the widespread use of cheap casual labour. They wanted everyone working there to take the 'Dockers' Tanner' to make sure the dockers could feed their families. Tensions were already high, and, on their approach, several large, threatening-looking men blocked the road, stopping all movement. Immediately, they began to intimidate the cab driver, threatening violence if he attempted to travel any further.

"Get ye back, I say, before I maim thy horse!" one rough fellow cried. "Wait until we say thou can go if we say thou can go!" He raised his cudgel threateningly, just inches from the horse's head.

A few seconds later missiles were hurled from the crowd of protesters, some hitting the carriage and frightening the horse, causing it to rear up and neigh wildly. The loud thuds resounding inside the carriage made Victoria shriek with fear – worried at what the mob would do next.

Townsend instinctively put a protective arm around her while reaching for a pair of loaded pistols he had in a carrying case. Picking both the wieldy guns up, he displayed them openly to those that would do them harm. They were all made aware he intended to shoot the first miscreant that opened the carriage door or harmed the horse.

Despite the chaos caused by the demonstrators all around them, working cranes creaked loudly as the men refusing to strike worked on, cranking cargo ashore regardless of the gathered protesters.

The unruly mob succeeded in delaying the cab significantly until, finally, the constabulary regained control and made room for them to drive through. The driver expertly guided his horse around the obstacles the dock workers had deliberately thrown down to stop free passage – including lumps of wood with protruding nails designed to maim the horses of anyone getting past the pickets.

Ignoring the threats and roars of the men on either side, the driver chivvied his horse up with an encouraging whistle and a slap on its flanks.

Each ship they passed had different odours wreathed around it, assaulting their senses. The stench of freshly scraped animal hides assailed the nostrils from one, where a broken crate with several cattle horns protruding from it had been carelessly dropped from a crane and left scattered across the ground. At another, the air became fragrant with the smell of coffee and spices, only for it to turn sharp and acidic with the reek of tobacco leaf at the next. Heady vapours from the many hundreds of rum barrels laid out beside another ship thickly permeated the air as they passed by.

"Why, there's the *Esmeralda*, sir!" the driver shouted down, gesturing towards lines of troops on the quay.

The *Esmeralda* lay at berth at the very heart of the docks. Townsend was later told she had been captured by the Royal Navy and then pressed into service. She was then bought privately and leased back to the navy whenever they needed more troops abroad, as they did now in Suez.

Finally, the cabbie brought his horse to a halt alongside the ship.

"Well done, driver, well done!" cried Townsend as he jumped down. "There's an extra tip for you for getting us through that mob back there."

In response, the cabbie tipped his hat at Townsend.

"Phew! I thought we would never find it, Robert," exclaimed a very shaken but relieved Victoria, stepping down from out of the cab.

"Where's the rest of the baggage?" Townsend asked her, looking around.

"It's over there, on that other horse and cab. Look, the driver is waving at us." Victoria pointed to a carriage a few yards away.

Before they could meet with him, they were interrupted by the call: "All aboard that's getting aboard!" They looked around to see the time caller ringing a loud bell. "Three hours to the *Esmeralda* sailing!"

The soldiers about to board stood idly talking, patiently waiting their turn. Finally, when they were ordered to, they clambered aboard using both the forward and aft gangways.

Townsend began unloading the baggage along with the other cab driver. It was starting to make a pile on the dockside when a voice of authority shouted down to them from the ship's bridge, "Ahoy there! Who are you, and where are you going with that?"

"I'm Major Townsend, and this is my wife. Boarding for Malta," he replied.

"Not with that lot, you're not. Who told you to bring the entire contents of your home?"

Taking umbrage at the harsh tone, Townsend looked at his wife and then back at the figure. "Well, I did. I'm Major Townsend of the Royal Artillery. Commander of Fort Anchor Battery in Malta. And who are you, may I ask?"

"Yes, you may well ask. I'm the captain of this vessel, Captain Faversham, and I'm ordering you to quickly sort out from that lot what you're taking and what you are not. Good god, man! There are troops on board – there's hardly room as it is. Sort out what's necessary, like clothes and such, and I'll get some men down there to get you and your luggage aboard. We sail in two and a half hours, sir, so get on, do it!"

He saluted. "Yes, very well, Captain," he replied, giving way to his higher authority.

"Robert, I didn't mean to get you into trouble," groaned Victoria. "It's all my fault. Can you forgive me?"

"Yes, of course! The man has his job to do, that's all. He is responsible for the ship and his passengers' safety. We do have too much, though, looking at it. Let's sort out what we need, and I'll pay the driver to take what's left back to your mother. I'm sure we can get those things in Malta. Although we have plenty of time to board with our baggage, I'm feeling uneasy knowing the ship will be leaving, and we are still not on it. So, as far as I'm concerned, the sooner we get on board the better."

After they'd finished arranging the baggage to be sent back, four of the ship's crew members came down and escorted them aboard, each carrying a trunk as if it were lightweight. The muscle-bound sailors then showed them to their cabin – their home for the next few days.

"Is this it?" Victoria asked disappointedly as she looked over the cabin. "Not much room is there?" she added dismissively.

"Aye, this is it alright," one sailor told them. "It's a lot bigger than most aboard the Esmie, for sure. The cap'n has sent his compliments and said to tell you not to empty all the cases. Only take out what you wear. That way, there'll be more legroom," he said, lashing down the cases Victoria indicated as being unimportant. "So that you know when we hit the open sea, there's bad weather due. Even more so when we pass close to the Bay of Biscay, ma'am."

"Why is it called the *Esmeralda*?" Victoria asked. "It's an odd name for a British ship."

"The Esmie is a Windjammer with three masts for sail and steam. It's iron-hulled with timbered structures inside throughout its length," another sailor replied proudly, apparently fond of his ship. "She was converted for carrying passengers and sold on after our navy captured her without hardly firing a shot – the captain being a bloody coward, with all cannons trained on it – and they simply kept her name. It suited the old girl. Oh, I nearly forgot... to make the journey more comfortable, the cap'n said to tell yer there's a balcony behind them curtains for you landlubbers to enjoy the view. Well, cheers for now."

Townsend and Victoria could hear the sailors' laughter as they made their way back into the ship's depths.

Once they were out of earshot, one of the crew, Jake, turned to the others and asked, "Did you see that woman he's got in there with him? I know what I could do with a wench like that! I could churn out a whole ship's crew for free. The problem would be how to afford to buy the bloody ship to crew it!"

"Aye," came the reply from his sniggering companion. "He'd kill ye if ye did, mind. You can be sure she's prized, that one."

After ringing the bell, the call went out: "All aboard that's getting aboard. Two hours to the *Esmeralda* sailing!"

Victoria turned to her husband and declared happily, "Robert, we have a balcony!"

"I think he is having fun at our expense; let me look." With a purposeful stride over, Townsend lifted the stained, oilcloth curtain that separated the small amount of standing room from two plank-built bunk beds and a porthole. "I thought so. Faversham was upset at me for challenging his authority and had the crew pass the information on. Come and see for yourself. There might not be much room, but we can open the porthole and let fresh air in – it sits well above the waterline. I pity how some of the other poor wretches are having to travel. It would be most uncomfortable for them, as we have seen."

"Yes," agreed Victoria, disappointed, realising now how space on the ship was precious.

"I'll have the top bunk then," he said, secretly hoping she would agree so she would feel the full benefit of the porthole. She nodded, and he smiled, relieved. "Look, Victoria, I need to leave you for a while. I'm going to walk the ship. I haven't seen Captain Marsh yet; I hope he's aboard somewhere. There should be others from my regiment, but I haven't seen anyone. I'm getting worried, and I'll be back to you soon. When I find them, there should be a small group of officers' wives for you to meet up with during the voyage, so at least you'll have some female company and won't be alone."

Victoria smiled back in response to his thoughtfulness.

***

Having made a brief, cramped tour of the ship, Townsend found himself on deck when he heard the one-hour call to sailing. He leaned on the rail, a deep frown on his face. Marsh was nowhere to be seen. *Where is he?* he wondered, annoyed. *It's just like him to be bloody late.*

He made his way below again, squeezing past soldiers as they settled down below deck, milling around among the hammocks and tables set up for everyone's use. He ducked down frequently to avoid hitting his head on the iron beams forming the vessel's skeleton – or on the lanterns and other gear hanging from them. Then, finally, he saw David a little further along, swaying from side to side.

Why is he walking like that? We're still at anchor!

He soon realised that David had been supping ale again.

"Captain Marsh! Attention!" he snapped, and the many months of training kicked in. Marsh stood immediately to attention, though he was slightly tipping forward.

"Ah, it's you, Rob, ish it?" he slurred, recognising Townsend. "Where the hell have you been? I got here early and spent the best part of the morning with other buggers, singing shea shanties with Shandy at the bloody Shore Inn. Are we off, Robbie?" he asked, making a valiant attempt to focus his eyes on him.

"No, not yet," he replied, a little curtly.

"Well, why the bloody hell is the boat moving? I can't shwim, you know."

"Where's your cabin?" Townsend asked, despairing of his friend.

"I'm in with the whiff-whaff," he replied with disdain, unable to pronounce the words.

"Show me, Captain," Townsend ordered, now aware that Marsh feared both the sea and the sailing upon it.

"Shertainly. I'm in bloody there, Robbie," he moaned.

"Well, it's the same size as our cabin," Townsend observed, glancing inside.

"Yesh, but you have a woman in yours," he slurred. "There are five bloody hairy men in there with me."

Suppressing his urge to laugh aloud, Townsend helped Marsh into the lowest bunk, where he fell asleep almost at once.

Crikey, he thought. *I have never seen him in such a state. He's drunk more than he's letting on, I know. I pity anyone sharing the cabin with him tonight, though. However, his head should be clear by morning,* he reasoned. So, he stepped out into the corridor, leaving him to sleep off his stupor.

Suddenly, he felt the ship lurch, and he grabbed out at something – anything – he could hold onto. *I must get back to Victoria and calm her. We are about to set sail.*

"The final and last call!" came the now urgent cry, with much bell ringing. "All aboard that's getting aboard. The Esmeralda is sailing!" After waiting patiently for a few more minutes, the man then shouted, "Pull the gangways back, men. We leave!"

This task was performed with much noise and clatter. The high tide made its presence known, visibly lifting the ship – and other vessels – in the calm harbour as the sea waters violently rushed throughout the docking area. Feeling the ship give another lurch, Townsend grabbed at a rope embedded into the nearest wall to steady himself.

"Heave, lads!" came the command after the ship up-anchored and slipped its moorings. With tug ropes attached both fore and aft, the longboat crews carefully pulled the ship out of its berth under the naval pilot's expert guidance, from where he was standing on the bridge. He, and his crews in the boats, safely manoeuvred the vessel away from the dangerous sandbanks before taking the deeper centre channel, winding its way out towards the open sea.

"More to port side, helmsman!" was his final order as they straightened the ship up in the deeper waters mid-stream. "You are all clear to go, Captain. Just give me the time and grace to get into my boat first," said the naval pilot.

The captain responded to the shouted order on the ship's bridge by hollering back, "Thank you for your assistance, officer. I will indeed." He waited while the pilot scrambled down the grab nets and into his longboat with a cat-like surety – having done it many times before – then his crew rowed themselves safely clear of the much larger vessel.

Under Faversham's orders, the steam-driven propeller began to turn, churning up the dirty, muddied waters at the stern and slowly pushing the ship forward. Fingers of water appeared to form at its bow, attempting – magically, it must have seemed, to anyone watching – to hold it and shove it back.

The ship's captain returned the salute of the naval pilot now standing in the longboat's bow, and his crew behind him upended their oars in salute as the much larger ship passed them by.

"Slow ahead!" he ordered the coxswain.

"Slow ahead it is, sir," came the helmsman's calm, forthright reply.

Returning to Victoria, Townsend shoved and squeezed his way through the men crowding along the corridors. At their twin berth cabin, he found her standing bent at the porthole, watching the land they loved slip away. He joined her for the last look, the both of them bidding farewell to England.

"It doesn't feel too bad, Robert. I thought it would be so much worse," she remarked boldly.

"Well, at least we have a cabin, unlike others on board," he said resignedly, "but when the ship hits the open seas, there will be more movement than this, and it will be much rougher." He brightened then, thinking of where they were going. "Sailing abroad to Malta is the start of a new life together. Does it scare you?"

"No, darling. Not while you're with me," was her brave reply as she pecked him on the cheek to reassure him.

They busied themselves in the cabin, sorting out the baggage they had access to while, all around them, the ship's timbered skeleton creaked and groaned in a ghostly manner as it lifted and fell away with the waves. They soon felt the surge of the steam engine turning the ship's bow, forcibly powering its way forward through the choppy seas – and leaving behind the customary smoke trail so often seen from the shore.

Frequent checks at the porthole saw the land swiftly disappearing behind them. The different figures and buildings on the shoreline were now long gone, having been replaced by green-brown terrain as the solitary ship sailed on grey seas that merged into greyer skies around them.

All passengers settled down to wait out the journey while soothing each other's fears regarding the ship's safe passage to the Mediterranean. They were now totally dependent on Captain Faversham, the ship's crew, and the Good Lord to deliver them safely to Malta.

***

The following morning, Townsend met with the other artillery officers. It was evident none of them were happy with the threatening weather conditions. "How are you coping with this sailing? Do you think you could do it yourselves?" he asked while attempting to act brave himself.

"No!" Captain Roach answered instantly. "I would rather do hand-to-hand combat than this constant dipping between the waves," he moaned, increasing his grip on some conveniently raised woodwork. "Although I have experienced worse, gentlemen. Why, I was once aboard a ship that leaked through cracks in the joints, drenching all those huddled on the floor – along with their belongings."

"Aye," Major Stevens agreed, equally affected. "Dropping into chasms between the waves before lurching back up again is unnerving, until you come out the other side on top. You think this is it – the end. Well, I do, and I'll be most grateful to get off. My wife and I prayed last night, like we'd never prayed before, for Him up there above to keep us safe."

After more similar chatter, Townsend noticed someone was missing. "Has anyone seen Captain Marsh?"

"Aye, he's over there, Major," replied one of the men, pointing him out. He was currently being sick overboard.

Townsend hobbled, penguin-fashion, across the heaving deck towards Marsh before stopping at a safe distance and watching as he retched over the side. "How are you feeling, David?" he asked, having to shout his words above the noise of the wind whistling every which way through the rigging. "It was foolish having all that drink yesterday, you know."

Marsh had just about heard him and was now straightening himself up with difficulty, clearly in a poor way, with an ashen face utterly devoid of colour. "Not now, Robert. I can't stay up here any longer. I'm off to my bunk." Holding a flat hand across his mouth, he disappeared below deck.

The enormous rolling waves they found themselves amongst threatened to immerse the ship and sink it until, somehow, it miraculously rode out on top of the swell. The sea's immense and ancient power now held the ship forcefully in its grip, seemingly playing with it.

***

For the rest of the voyage, they kept themselves well out of the way of the crew as they carried out their duties with calm professionalism – gaining new-found respect from all the watching passengers.

The days passed slowly with the monotony of being unable to do anything but wait. The passengers' only relief from this tedium was when it was their turn to walk the decks twice a day – or thrice if they were lucky and the weather held. Then they would be ordered below and once again entombed in their billeted berths, under threat, if necessary (though it seldom was), by the naval marines attached to the ship. There was a strict rotation of walking the upper decks and taking their ablutions. To spare any embarrassment, it was always the women first, later followed by male civilians. Finally, the soldiers had their turn. Then the whole process would start again. Discipline on the ship was maintained under the ultimate threat of a flogging ordered by the captain.

Unable to wash, the men and women without cabins lived below deck with limited privacy. Sweat and a heavy stench hovered in the air above the open hatches, despite the strong winds blowing fiercely across them. The latrines were communal buckets lashed to the sides of the ship. Once used, all contents were emptied over the side before lowering the bucket to be washed clean by the sea. They were then hauled back up to await the next customer. Every so often, a man would piss on the ship's gunwales – unable or unwilling to wait to use the buckets – only for the stiff, swirling winds to blow it back in on him.

When the wind dropped and sailing slowed, Captain Faversham had the lifeless mainsails gathered in under the supervision of the master rigger. He then had the steam power take over to keep the ship from straying off course. The passengers and soldiers alike always marvelled at the gutsy performance of the crew while going about their duties performing tasks. They watched them working and merrily singing sea shanties alongside the bosun's shrill whistle – seemingly without a care in the world.

Townsend tactfully left their cabin each time Victoria required privacy for her ablutions. Although awkward and sometimes embarrassing, they managed the situation between them. Fortunately, their porthole was large enough to pass through their private pail for night soil.

Victoria often sought out the other officers' wives' company to gossip about shipboard life, the journey, their husbands and families, and what they might expect to find in Malta. Those amongst them that were new to sailing quickly learned the sea was never to be taken for granted. One minute the ship could be in ideal sailing conditions; the next saw a heavy squall developing above and around them, threatening its very existence.

Days into the voyage, when Townsend and his wife were lying below, talking about the life they had left behind, a confrontation broke out above. Heavy footsteps running across the open deck interrupted their conversation, and raised voices rang out, shouting and cussing as men pushed and chastised each other. Buckets of human slop spilt over as they collided with the other passengers performing ablutions.

"Why, you bastard!" they heard one complain, presumably standing there with wet feet.

Suddenly, the running stopped.

"Get back, you dogs! Otherwise, the first man to put another step forward will get his brains blown out. I mean it! Come on, if you fancy your chances. I'll fucking show you!"

"Steady, Sam, me old matey. Don't be doing anything rash now!" someone else shouted. "Put the gun down before you do anything you might regret. Now, what's going on? What are you accusing him of?"

Townsend and his wife exchanged glances as they listened to the commotion.

119

"My woman said he interfered with her while we were sleeping," said another voice. "We were lying down with her here, turned into my back. We lay like that for a while, and then she here screamed. She sat upright, kicking out at all and everyone around her. Didn't you, Mary?"

"Aye, I did that, Will!" a woman agreed, sounding angry and upset. "I thought it was a bloody rat or something. Goodness knows I've seen a few of them while aboard this ship, I can tell yer."

"Is that all that happened then, Mary?" the calming influence asked.

"No, it wasn't," she replied. "We settled down again, and I had just got to sleep when I was disturbed once more – finding Sam here too close for comfort – and then I felt a hand under my dress, right on the top of my thigh. I know it belonged to him there because Will was on the other side of me – lying on his side, see."

"Oh, Sam, it's not looking too good for you, is it, matey?" the calming influence asked. "They could have you flogged for something like that. Everyone was warned."

"Do you think so, eh?"

Before he could answer, more footsteps stamped over. Townsend whispered, "Those sound like military boots."

"Marines, perhaps?" Victoria suggested softly, whispering as they strained to listen.

"What's going on here?" someone barked, sounding none too pleased to be on deck with more heavy weather on the way. No one replied. "I said, what's going on here? What's all the fucking arguing about?" the man in charge demanded to know.

"Definitely marines," said Townsend, agreeing with her.

"Oh, it's nothing," said Sam, who had concealed his gun. "I had a grope of her tits with his blessing, but now he's asking too much money!"

"You wench. Is that right?"

"Aye, that's right. But the dirty bastard put a hand up under my dress," said Mary, who – it seemed to the eavesdroppers – sounded like she was doing some quick thinking.

"Aye, that's extra, and he ain't paid up!" said the husband, Will. "He still owes me a full penny for the grope of the wife!"

"Pay up, or I will throw you in the brig," demanded the marine.

"Here you go, Will," said Sam, and Townsend imagined him ferreting around for a grimy penny.

"Right! Now behave yourselves for the remainder of the journey. You're lucky the cap'n is not aware of this," said the marine. "I warn you; he would have the skin stripped from all your backs. Keep a tight rein on that woman, you! With all these men about, she could start big trouble. I don't think they should allow them aboard –too much distraction for the men, showing their bits and pieces. Full of temptation, I say! Now get back in the hold where you belong."

"What about the shit they spilt from the buckets?" asked the man with the wet feet.

"Aw, leave it. This storm's building up to be another big 'un. It'll wash the decks for yer." The heavy footsteps receded as the three naval soldiers went below deck, back to their card game.

"Thanks for that, Mary. I'll have my penny back now!" said a relieved Sam.

"Oh no, you won't," said Will. "We've just saved you a flogging, and I think it was worth a good penny to get you off the whip. The cap'n would have flailed his name across your back, man, if he'd been made aware of what you were doing! Look, I know what you were after with your hand up my Mary's dress, and I'll have none of it."

"It was the smell of a woman and her closeness that drew me to her, Will. Honest, it was!"

"You are a liar!" Will cried indignantly. "You knew she had our money under there, in a body purse, and you were after it. Well, tonight, she'll be on the other side of me, Sam, and if your hand wanders again, I'll pin it to the floor with my dagger. You see if I don't!" he yelled, before repeating, "You just see if I don't, Sam, you bloody scoundrel!"

"Well," Townsend remarked when all was quiet again, "I feel sorry for Mary, stuck between those two."

"I don't know," said Victoria. "She got her hard-won penny. Though I would have told the marines what that blackguard was at if he took the opportunity to revenge himself upon you as we slept!"

"Heaven forfend!" sighed Townsend heavily, and the pair chuckled together in their bunk beds at the thought.

***

Days later, the crew passed a message by word of mouth to all onboard: "Due to making good progress with strong winds behind us, the cap'n reckons we will be entering Grand Harbour sometime tomorrow morning."

The cheers and gasps of relief travelled along the length of the ship as the good news spread. Outside, the *Esmeralda* was ploughing on while black, threatening clouds collided and mixed high above them.

With all the open hatches safely battened down, the ship headed towards her destination – and into another rain-lashing storm.

Chapter 10

Relief on arriving at Grand Harbour. Meeting the Governor of Malta

THE *ESMERALDA* had made reasonable time, despite the poor, inclement weather; Malta was now visible to the lookout in the crow's nest in the high upper rigging of the ship as a strip of bright rock they were approaching on the horizon. The master rigger informed the captain standing on the bridge that Malta had been sighted in the distance. On seeing it himself, Faversham, in turn, ordered him to have his crew close the rigging down to part sail. This order was soon followed by a marked slowing down in the ship's speed.

Clippers and other small, faster vessels were seemingly skimming across the heaving seas. Other ships were also involved in moving troops, passengers, and cargo in and out of the busy harbour, done under the careful watch of two ships of the line – both bristling with guns, and guarding the seas around Malta.

With the outbreak of the Russian-Turkish War two years earlier, the British were taking no chances on and around this small, strategic island. Minor skirmishes often took place on the beaches of Malta's many natural harbours as criminals continually attempted to secretly come ashore. Smuggling and piracy had gone on for hundreds of years in the Mediterranean. When it was discovered in Malta, it was dealt with efficiently by the ever-watchful Maltese authorities, aided by the British.

The grey, rocky island stood proudly above the sea, with its several forts high up in the cliffs. It greeted visitors with an open embrace of cold granite, enticing the weary mariner into the calmer waters of Grand Harbour.

With word spreading below deck regarding their arrival, a shout went up: "Three hurrahs for the captain!"

The reply was bellowed from every quarter, resounding throughout the ship with enthusiasm and relief: "Hurrah! Hurrah! Hurrah!"

As the *Esmeralda* sailed past, some of those onboard waved to the crew of a three-masted sailing ship in the middle of dropping anchor. The crew members had climbed into position on both sides of the masthead, waiting to gather in the sails, and they warm-heartedly waved back. The crewmen below them on the deck were busily untying all the ropes holding the sails in place, allowing the captive air its freedom. After the release, riggers gathered up the heavy sails and safely tied them off, all under the expert direction of the watching master rigger's whistle.

The *Esmeralda* finally stopped and downed anchor herself at the harbour's mouth. When it dropped, the anchor caused a large splashback of water to the ship's bow as it noisily dragged its chains down to the bottom of the ocean floor.

On spying the White Ensign fluttering aboard the ship, a naval pilot from the HM Dockyard was sent out to bring the ship into its docking buoy. They rowed out to the ship, but a fleet of smaller craft – aptly named bumboats – had arrived before them and were busily selling their wares to those on the ship, despite the lively sea. It was a bustling trading opportunity to sell to passengers for some much-needed money before they disembarked.

Once the vessel was permitted to berth, they knew many others would be waiting to sell to them, and their potential earnings would be lost. Therefore, it was essential to get to any newly arrived ship first. Most of the new arrivals who had been at sea for many long days or weeks were thankful for the offerings and would be happy to pay or barter the asking price. Some of the small craft also carried prostitutes, who brazenly called out to the crew, telling them what they could expect to get for sharing their rations with them.

From the porthole, Victoria watched the shenanigans and sheer audacity of these vulgar, bad-mannered women. "What's happening, Robert? What rations are they talking about?"

"It's the crew's beer rations they want," he replied. "Each of these sailors gets rationed a gallon a day – or the equivalent in wine or spirits. That's what they're after, plus any money for favours, of course. I hear they save most of it for the end of each voyage when they can cavort with these lovelies."

In their enthusiasm to trade, the sellers began to scale the ship's sides – a common problem at the harbour approach when a ship was lying at anchor, waiting for its clearance to berth.

"Keep away and off this ship!" shouted Captain Faversham, before being forced to repeat his words. When that failed, he had the marines summoned; they appeared around the vessel's decks with their rifles at the ready, waiting for his next command. "These passengers are aboard Her Majesty's ship, and I am ordering you to keep off and let the naval pilot climb aboard!" he yelled.

The marines raised their weapons, threatening the sellers and keeping them in check. In response to the threat, the sellers took to haggling the prices for their wares from the bumboats; they threw up their goods in exchange for the agreed money, which was dropped down to them in the attached pouches.

"Ahoy there! Do I have permission to come aboard your ship, Captain?" the naval pilot called up while standing, braced, in the bow of the bobbing longboat. His front crew members were busily attempting to seize the rope ladders with their boat hooks to draw the longboat closer. Members of the ship's crew – the side boys – were at the ready, on the bottom steps, to catch the thrown lines from the oarsmen when the boat hooks failed. They caught them with difficulty before fending off the bow of the longboat, thus preventing it from colliding hard with the side of the ship.

"Yes, please do, sir!" the captain yelled down. "I've passengers aboard keen to land."

After several seconds, the naval pilot hauled himself up the ropes. He almost fell headlong through the open entry gate at the top, but Faversham steadied him with a firm hand.

"No passengers, crew, or troops will be allowed off until I have confirmed by inspection the general well-being of everyone aboard this ship, Captain. Those are my orders for all new arrivals."

"Aye, then you must do it, sir," replied the captain, shaking the British naval pilot's hand as he steadied himself.

After a detailed examination of the passengers and crew throughout the vessel, he returned and confirmed they carried no illness and that none of the civilians were wanted criminals – as far as they could ascertain.

Then, taking over the navigation, the naval pilot expertly steered the *Esmeralda* into the harbour and on towards its allocated holding buoy in the Naval Dockyard. The helmsman at the wheel had to instantly react to each of his shouted orders. His crewmen in their longboats safely guided the ship along, aided by the ship's subdued steam engine and the experienced naval pilot's knowledge. Slowly and carefully, they coaxed it expertly across the harbour, where many of the smaller sailing craft gave way to its passing.

They passed one unfortunate ship held in quarantine; it had reported the carrying of an unknown sickness on board. The sad and anxious faces of the ship's crew and passengers watched as they tacked the ship past, cursing at being denied the clearance to land. They were anchored there, waiting for a government physician to identify any suspicious sickness before they would be allowed entry. Meanwhile, the *Esmeralda* soon became one of many ships laid up in the beautiful setting of Malta's Grand Harbour.

True to the rumours they had heard, Valletta bristled with fortifications, all quite capable of confronting an enemy. A cacophony of lively sounds reverberated in the Maltese air. Men, women with children, and marines and sailors alike went about their various duties, all of which made up the typical hustle and bustle of this busy and vibrant dockside. It belied that the island was recovering from a severe cholera outbreak that had ravaged the colony for many years, causing countless deaths and poverty in its passing. It was the reason for the strict conditions of entry set by the authorities.

Below the loud, piercing squawks of the circling and swooping seagulls, more traders were lining up to hassle the new arrivals into buying their wares from the moment they disembarked. The passengers moved eagerly among them, looking for fresh fruit and trinkets. Ne'er-do-wells were also there, loafing about on the steps, ever watchful of the baggage the passengers carried as the pickpockets melted into the arriving crowd.

The civilians disembarked first, followed by the military, who leered lustfully at the line of wenches they passed, waiting patiently for the ship's crew. They were keen to get to them first and share in the money and drink rations they all knew they had.

"You there, sailor! Where's that lying, thieving mate of yours?" demanded one such woman, raising her voice above the clamour of the crew members making sure the *Esmeralda* was firm and fast at its allocated buoy.

"He'll be down to you soon enough after we finish here. Why, he's been missing yer, Maggie Maguire, and could hardly wait to get back – just show a little calmness."

"Well, he can stay that way until he pays up what he owes me!" she shouted. "The rat ran out on me, so he had better have a good excuse. A girl has to live, too," she said, patting down her large bust with indignation.

With all the strangers milling about, Townsend was wary of taking his eyes off their baggage as he waited for Victoria, who – desperate to taste the fresh fruit she'd so been longing for – had gone off to buy oranges for them both. He felt a sense of relief when Marsh finally joined him. He had introduced him to his wife during the voyage, and it had become a jest between them that Marsh would whisper, "You lucky bastard," whenever he felt so inclined.

"Excuse me, sirs, are you Major Townsend and Captain Marsh, by any chance?"

Surprised, Townsend raised his eyebrows and turned to find a neatly dressed civilian standing behind him. "Why, yes. And you?"

"Why, I'm Minton, sir. I've been sent from Governor Johnson's office to meet up with you and your wife."

Victoria re-joined them as the young man introduced himself, listening quietly as she enjoyed a large, juicy orange.

"If you would follow me to your quarters, you will be able to refresh yourselves after your tiring journey."

"What about the others?" Townsend asked as he took hold of Victoria's arm.

"Don't concern yourself, Major," Minton assured him. "You are all in temporary quarters. There is little space here – as you will soon no doubt appreciate – but you will all meet up again later this evening, I can assure you. Governor Johnson wants you to dine with him and Mrs Johnson tonight, where he will pass on your regiment's orders and details."

"The baggage?"

"These men here with me will see to it. Don't worry; they are in safe hands."

Minton was without uniform, so it appeared to Townsend that he was likely a civilian clerk, a not unusual placement in the modern governor's office. The chap was visibly wilting in the Maltese sun even as they spoke.

Longing for his shaded office, no doubt! presumed Townsend.

"So, if you will follow me," continued Minton, "I can get you out of this chaos and over to your quarters; it's only a short walk from here and just off the harbour." He led them away, fending off the beggars and peddlers in the process as they escaped the rousing clamour of the harbour.

"Where is the governor's residence?" enquired Marsh as they walked.

"Oh, it isn't here, sir," Minton replied. "The governor's official residence is at the San Anton Palace over at Attard. Because your presence here is of great importance to Her Majesty's Government and the realm, the governor did not wish to waste time expecting his guests to travel there. Your mission is of the utmost secrecy, so he felt it prudent to meet you here in Valletta at his secondary residence to convey your orders and his expectations. The cooks there will be preparing your meals for tonight. Of course, rooms here have been made ready for everyone, appropriate to rank and status," Minton added, with a gracious smile at Victoria, who dimpled back prettily.

All three were taken to stay at the officers' quarters near 'City Gate'. It was a welcome relief for Captain Marsh, who – on being shown his room – flopped onto the bed, ever thankful to be off the cussed ship with its creaking timbers and people farting.

Major Townsend and his wife, however, were taken to more substantial rooms befitting his new rank and marital status.

While inspecting their rooms, Victoria suddenly felt weak. "Aah! Robert," she gasped, grabbing at him for assistance.

His hands reached out quickly to support her, concern etched in his voice as he cried, "Victoria! What's wrong? Victoria?"

"Oh, I'm sorry, Robert – I suddenly swayed as if I was still on the ship. The room felt as if it was moving!"

"Here, let me help you lie down on the bed, darling. It will take a few days to put the rigours of the journey behind us both and get our sense of balance back," he said, reassuring her.

***

That evening, they met the governor and his wife for dinner, and, after the meal, the women turned the conversation to more feminine, delicate subjects – such as where high-quality material could be bought for things like dresses, curtains and the like, and which were the best seamstresses to do it. For practical matters such as these, the governor's wife, Agnes, was an excellent source of information. She told them to be wary as she explained some traders' underhand tricks to get customers to purchase their wares, as well as where to buy the most beautiful lace. Then, becoming sensitive to her husband's need to talk privately – and wholly aware of how vital his talks were – she ushered the ladies into a separate room to continue their lively conversation.

After they left, the governor took out some cigars and offered one to each of his guests – all of whom declined, remembering the wise words of Colonel Downing. "I am also to inform you that, after recovering sufficiently from your journey, you will report to your regiment in Valletta. After all, I am sure it was an arduous, uncomfortable sea crossing," he added, lighting his cigar. "Officers there will confirm what we will discuss tonight, but in greater military detail than I can do. I know they are eager to meet with you too. Now, I want to know more about this cannon you have."

The men were standing in a group, enjoying the governor's hospitality, with each of the six officers holding a drink of their choice. They explained the new gun's workings, its colossal size, and how it would be brought ashore at Anchor Bay. Throughout the evening, Marsh kept an eye on his favourite tipple and topped his glass up whenever the opportunity arose.

Finally, when the governor's curiosity was satisfied, the topic of conversation moved on to the Italians.

"How are they coping with these guns in their navy, sir? We were told they were having two ships fitted out with four on each, or so we believe."

"Well, rumour has it they had a hard time firing the guns at the ship's sea trials," Governor Johnson told them cheerfully. "In fact, firing off a full broadside with these monster cannons catapulted one spotter from the crow's nest into the briny! However, the ship vigorously righted itself, despite the combined recoil of the guns," he explained. "A section of the ship's crew not involved in the firing had permission to stand in two lines along the deck on the starboard side to watch. Some were standing at the back, while others leaned against the safety grab chains running along the sides. These, it turned out, were the lucky ones, who managed to brace themselves on the chains against the ship's violent bucking after firing the full volley. The poor devils standing behind were less fortunate; they were thrown like limp rag dolls over the top and into the sea, swiftly followed by anything lying loose or not fixed to the decks, such as mops, pails, and other paraphernalia. They had to stop the ship to perform a rescue – something not normally done by a fighting ship at sea! That was the rumour but, you do understand, I have nothing official to go on."

His eyes twinkled with mischief as they all laughed together – very much aware that the governor had his own private means of gathering information on potential enemies.

"As I was saying," he continued when the mirth had lowered to a level over which he could talk again, "the ship righted itself while pandemonium broke out inside the ship's bridge."

More laughter.

"The ship was superbly built and is regarded as the best in the world – and they're lucky it is," he declared, "as it withstood the full recoil force of the guns. We can consider ourselves lucky, I think. In other circumstances, it could have happened to our navy. Back to today, though…"

Mindful of the secrecy of their mission, the governor lowered his voice; two of the servants were newly appointed and unknown to him, so he wanted to avoid any security lapse. Many other countries had informants in the area, and he knew they could be anywhere. He had to be very careful, especially considering how the Mediterranean situation was threatening to change to a war footing almost on a daily basis.

But this caution came too late; the man serving at the governor's table left the room with the remnants of the meals, well pleased with his evening's work. He walked down the servants' stairs and into the kitchen, whistling to himself. He was eager to return and hear more.

"So, there you have it, gentlemen," the governor concluded. "You will find everything in the order papers I've given you from your regiment, but don't hesitate to ask if you have other questions. Your forts are in various stages of completion and will soon be homes for these guns. I should mention that Fort Anchor is further along the road to being finished than the other two because its construction is close to a quarry, so Major Townsend will be in the thick of it as soon as he gets there." He clapped Townsend on the back. "You must get on with it because Anchor will be used to smooth out any little snags encountered along the way. It will help no end with the two remaining forts that are nearly twelve months behind in their development. So," he added, smiling, "you other gentlemen can rest easy for the time being. The pressure is off you for now."

He levelled a much less chirpy look at Marsh and Townsend. "You fellows will have the additional problem of insurgency raising its head in the area around Fort Anchor, including mutineers against the Crown – protesters of this and that, rioters who have no respect for the law or anything else. Rebels who rebel against everything and anything and insurgents who want the British out of these islands.

"As you know, the forts will not have married quarters. Those of you with spouses will have temporary quarters in the form of a cabin, set up in the confines of the camp," he told them. "The gun will always be your number one priority, though. After the forts' completion, and before being commissioned, officers' wives will be moved here, to Valletta, for their safety. My wife Aggie will be most happy to greet them and oversee their stay.

"Forts Rinella and Cambridge will both have adequate backing by our troops around the harbour area," he continued, after taking a sip of brandy, "whereas the fort at Anchor Bay will be in a very remote part of the island, so reinforcements will take longer to get there. On that note, it seems banditry has become more common in the area. In the past, these people have been staked out on Comino Island, causing all manner of disruption by waylaying travellers between the islands of Gozo and Malta. The Maltese authorities have kept it in check in the past with an occasional, systematic sweep of Comino Island, but it seems the matter is getting out of hand again. It's hoped the very presence of this fort there will bring back a vestige of law and order to the region and, above all, a sense of stability and confidence back to the local population."

"Why are they doing it?" asked Marsh. "Surely, it's foolhardy?"

"It's because these islands have seen conflict for hundreds of years, Captain," the governor explained. "As well as the Italians, both Tunisia and Libya – and one or two other countries – regularly remind the Maltese authorities of their claims to them, so we need a presence in the area and to be on our guard. Over the years, local people have been attacked and murdered, women raped, and children carried off, undermining the local authority and putting the fear of God into the locals. It appears to be starting up again and it must stop, gentlemen. There may be a ship involved in landing these cut-throats. If so, they can only be brought ashore on the island's Tunisian side at night; anywhere else would prove too reckless.

"This is where Fort Anchor will be invaluable," he went on, gesturing towards Townsend and Marsh with his glass of brandy. "The fort will virtually guarantee the local people's safety, and force them to think again about further incursions. Major Townsend will take full responsibility for achieving this. This area is Malta's weak spot, and it's why a third fort and gun were requested for Malta, instead of the two originally planned."

"With an urgent need for military patrols, sir?" asked Townsend.

"Yes, of course. The patrols began as soon as they started on the fort," stated the governor.

"How often do they go out? Is it two or three times a day?"

"No, Major. They go out early in the morning, and we find that adequate. Our presence there constructing the fort has quietened things down, but it still exists."

"What about the other two islands, sir? I think they are Gozo and Comino? Are they patrolled regularly?"

"Not as we speak, Captain Marsh. But it is hoped that once Fort Anchor gets established, patrols to both islands will get underway more frequently from the fort. That should be enough to bring stability to the far side of these beautiful islands. Then the occasional sweep with our troops will no longer be necessary. We hope that should help satisfy the Maltese authorities."

"Have we been able to capture any insurgents, sir?" enquired an officer while admiring an oil painting hanging on the wall.

"Not up to now, Major Simms. If only we could!" the governor exclaimed. "These men have a different mindset than any others we have encountered over the years. They are true fanatics and, as such, are unafraid to die to further their cause – thus, avoiding capture."

"If we can capture any, what are we to do with them, sir?" Townsend asked.

"Have them brought back here to Valletta straight away and let our people deal with them," he replied grimly. "They will get them singing out loud; you can be certain of it."

"Why wasn't the fort built on Gozo or Comino?" Captain James asked.

"Simply because, if reinforcements were ever needed, it would take another twenty-four hours to get them there," Governor Johnson explained. "We could be too late to help in an emergency. The other reason, of course, is if Valletta were to face attack, Fort Anchor's gun could be trained at near maximum rotation to back up the two forts of Rinella and Cambridge."

Townsend looked down and thoughtfully swirled the rest of the whisky in his glass before speaking: "It seems Fort Anchor will be up and running quite a while before either of the other two. Therefore, I'm eager to get out there and make a start."

The governor nodded. "When the gun gets commissioned, it will require firing practice to iron out any faults. Therefore, we have arranged target practice for you on an old ironclad that's no longer seaworthy; it will be towed out beyond Anchor Bay for your gunners to have a few shots at. It's to help you get your bearings and experience for yourself how the gun handles under firing conditions in this wonderful climate. It will be quite a spectacle, no doubt. A few invited dignitaries and I will be aboard a frigate to assess your competency and expertise. I'm sure that will be no problem?" He smiled and opened his hands expansively. "We live in both exciting and dangerous times, gentlemen, and I have no idea how long you will serve here. Please take that up with your regiment. Why, you could all be returning to England at the same time – even on the same ship!"

The drinks were beginning to have a happy effect on Marsh. "Or even on the same ship at the same time," he repeated cheerfully.

"Not used to the quality stuff, eh?" the governor chided lightly at his demeanour, unaware he had helped himself. "Now, gentlemen, I'm rather eager to hear more stories of what's been happening back home. Five years is much too long to be away."

The evening slipped swiftly by as they spoke of England. The governor had been in Malta for too long; both he and his wife were becoming homesick and missing their beloved opera.

"You are all welcome to spend a day or two here with us in Valletta to get your personal supplies and such and recover from your voyage," he told them. "Then you will be judged ready for your trip to each of your batteries. Major Townsend and Captain Marsh, your journey will be long, difficult, and laborious, I'm afraid. There is no road, just a track of sorts, and it will require an early start. The others will wait a little longer to depart – and traverse much easier terrain, you will be glad to hear!"

He gazed thoughtfully at Townsend and Marsh for a moment. "It cannot be stressed enough, the enormity of the task waiting for you two gentlemen. These forts need to be completed as soon as possible, with their guns fully operational – just in case the present situation in the Mediterranean turns ugly. We must be ready to protect the interests of the Crown and Malta in this area. But, until then, my wife and I would like you to enjoy the many attractions to be found here in Valletta – and believe me, gentlemen, there are lots for you to explore. If any of you are particularly religious, you will find plenty of religious history and artefacts here too."

The governor then launched into a fascinating history of the island region, which went on late into the evening.

After spending an enjoyable and friendly evening with Agnes, Victoria and the other ladies rejoined their menfolk, tired and wanting to be escorted to their quarters.

Before taking his own leave, Marsh remarked, "I enjoyed the evening, Robert. Especially finding out what happened aboard the Italian ship. It was quite a comical anecdote! Goodnight to you both."

"Yes, it was amusing listening to him, but I think he exaggerated it a bit to liven things up," replied Townsend, grinning. "The governor deals in rumour at times, whereas our military act on fact. The put-down is typical when two countries compare armed forces. Goodnight to you too, David."

Outside, the spy who had served at the governor's table that evening handed a small bundle of hastily scribbled notes to an accomplice lingering in the darkened shadows of the outbuildings.

"Take these back to our leaders, immediately," said the renegade server.

The shadowy figure nodded, without saying a word, and then departed. The informer watched him go before heading back inside, delighted that they hadn't been discovered.

Chapter 11

An incident on the trek to Fort Anchor

AFTER SEVERAL days spent recuperating from the sea crossing, the party prepared to split up. Townsend had agreed with Victoria that he and Marsh would travel on to Fort Anchor and prepare to command the garrison there. Then, after purchasing the things they would need during their time at camp, Victoria would follow on later – as advised by her new-found friend Aggie Johnson. What she was required to bring depended on the information in the message her husband promised to send her as soon as he had inspected their living accommodation at the fort.

On the morning they were making ready to leave for Anchor Bay, there was a loud knock on the door of the officers' quarters.

"Corporal Collins, reporting to the captain, sir!" The man saluted. "The Royal Artillery supplies detachment has orders to escort Captain Marsh and Commander Townsend to Fort Anchor." Collins was a career soldier who had enlisted after attending a public open day at the Arsenal. While imagining riding a charger in uniform, having adventures, and seeing the world, he'd quickly made his mark and joined up, later to achieve the rank of corporal. His many friends claimed he was as dependable as a British Martini-Henry rifle.

"At ease, Corporal. I'm Captain Marsh, and the commander will be out shortly. I understand you are here in Valletta collecting the provisions for the fort?"

"Yes, sir. We arrived last night, to make a start this morning with the supplies."

"Thank you, Corporal. We apologise for the delay. How long will it take to get to Anchor?"

"Best part of the day," he replied, "but we should reach there before nightfall. It's a difficult trek to get there with the wagon, and near impossible in the dark, sir."

As they were speaking, Commander Townsend stepped out through the doorway.

"Attention! Detail awaiting your orders, sir," said Marsh.

"Very well, Captain," he replied, confidently and assertively. "Corporal, see to it that the baggage gets put in the wagon; we can then depart. Where are our horses?"

With a wave of his arm, Collins signalled to have the two horses brought up. "Here they are, sir. I personally selected them for you," he said, wanting to make a good first impression.

Outside in the courtyard, the sun's strength was already visibly increasing, burning off the early morning haze; behind Marsh, a tiny Maltese wall lizard gulped down a roaming spider that was stuck to its tongue and then scampered away into a crack in the wall to escape its growing fiery gaze.

"I have a gentleman here to meet you, sir," Collins reported. "His name is Edoardo Galea, and he's the contractor for Fort Anchor. He's the gangmaster for the hired labourers assisting our men in constructing the fort."

"Welcome, Major Townsend, to our islands," Galea said, shaking his hand. He was a man of dark, swarthy features, brown eyes, and part Sicilian extraction. His pencil-thin moustache and slicked down black hair – combined with his expensive clothes – gave him the air of a man born to delegate rather than a man who dirtied his hands.

"Thank you, Mr Galea. I understand we will be working closely together in the coming months to finish the fort for our new gun?"

"Yes, Major. When and as required."

"But should you not be at Fort Anchor with your men? We would have met later."

"Of course, Major, but I had important business to attend to, so I thought I would travel back with you and your soldiers and introduce myself to you," Galea replied.

Somehow, Townsend suspected he was not what Galea had been expecting. "It's hard to think what could be more important than Fort Anchor, Mr Galea," he remarked. "Will these trips of yours be a regular occurrence, sir?"

Galea inclined his head. "I can assure the major they will be a rarity until after the fort's completion."

"Very well, Mr Galea, I'm sure they will be. Right, Captain, if all is ready, I'm keen to get going and see Fort Anchor."

"Yes, sir. Mount up your men, Corporal," Marsh commanded, signalling to Collins.

"Mount up, men!" The corporal relayed the command to the others as he climbed aboard and sat next to the driver. Once they were all mounted, the small detail of men was led out of the entrance gate by two troopers, followed by the two officers, Galea, the supplies wagon, and two more mounted troopers at the rear.

Eventually, they passed the last of the foot patrols on the outskirts of Valletta. Townsend and Marsh had noticed how the area surrounding Valletta was in a perpetual state of military readiness in case the island was threatened at any time.

"There's plenty of Russian and Turkish sabre-rattling activity going on between those two countries in the Mediterranean, so a high alert level has to be maintained here," Townsend commented. "I should think the Maltese themselves are well used to it by now and therefore get on with daily life as normally as possible. I would assume it must be second nature for them."

"Yes," said Marsh. "I think you could be right, Major. They must be ever watchful and organised due to the many enemies they have in the region."

Before long, the carefully constructed road gave way to a dirt track. It was a typically hot day, and lively dust clouds were kicked up by the horses' hooves as they trudged on through the swelter. The wagon wheels jarred on protruding rocks and stones littering the track, making more speed impossible.

The heat was causing the soldiers to sweat freely, making their buttoned-up uniforms increasingly uncomfortable. Slowly, they began loosening their tunic collars to let fresh air circulate on their lower necks and to allow more body heat to escape.

The first eager gallop out of Valletta had long since dropped to a steady pace.

"Where are we, Corporal?" Marsh called back. "We will soon be needing water for the horses. Are we close to a stream to give them – and my backside – a rest?"

"We will be nearing a stream soon, sir," Collins assured him. "There are very few of them on the island, but we are fortunate to be crossing one. We are just outside Mosta, on the way towards Mġarr. We stay out on the trails instead of riding through small villages to avoid local... sensitivities."

"Sensitivities, Corporal? What sensitivities?" Townsend asked.

"Well, er," he stuttered, looking decidedly uncomfortable, "the ladies of Malta are beautiful, sir. They are renowned for it, as you may have noticed?"

"I have, sir. It's true enough," advised Marsh.

"Well, the men are a long way from home, sir. It's not unknown for some to try out their animal attraction on the local women." He scratched his head and continued," I think that's what they call it, and the women are just as quick to try out their wiles on them. You know how the ladies always like a chap in uniform. Well, these little… affairs, shall we call them?... sometimes don't go to plan, shall we say. They can play havoc with the family, sir. If the men in question are recognised when they ride through a village, all sorts of unsavoury rotting vegetables are thrown at them. It's not good to see, sir. One family I know has two gorgeous daughters, and they have huge stockpiles ready to let loose, sir, all stacked up outside the front door – er, so they tell me!"

Glancing at a grinning Marsh, who knew exactly what Collins was referring to, had reminded Townsend of his sad courting attempts with Victoria. He nodded towards the man and said, "I think it best to carry on with tradition then and stay well clear, Corporal."

"Oh, good! I mean, yes, sir," said the corporal, much relieved.

Reaching the gently trickling stream, they dismounted and allowed the horses free rein to drink their fill. The horses had notably quickened their pace as they drew nearer, having become accustomed to this regular stop on the journey to and from Valletta. One horse lay down in the cooling waters, wetting its leathers and flanks as it wallowed before shaking its head and mane free of water and snorting.

Nearby, men supped at the water with cupped hands, scooping it eagerly into their mouths. They then sat back on the ground, refreshed and invigorated after drinking their fill from this godsend of a stream.

Although Anchor Bay was no great distance for riders, it took a day for them to get there from Valletta with the cumbersome wagon in tow. The rough, hilly terrain was certainly challenging for the first-time traveller. Therefore, it was imperative to avoid dehydration, so the men replenished any water left in their canteens while at the stream.

Mindful of being vulnerable to any attack, the major was impressed to see how Collins organised a guard to overlook the men's safety at the stream at all times. "Corporal Collins, will you see to it that the guard up there is relieved of his post? I'm sure he would like a drink too!"

"Straight away, Major."

"Just a minute, Corporal. What's the man's name?"

"Ned Savage. He's hot-tempered at times – got the Irish in him, he has. He once told me his parents were from Tipperary, and his father made a living as a bare-knuckle fighter."

"I don't recall giving him permission to take his tunic off!" added Townsend as he gazed up at Savage's silhouette.

"No, sir, you didn't," said Collins. "Savage is an excellent soldier, but he has a problem with the drink. He's been a sergeant at least twice, but he always goes and ruins his standing with the officers with his drinking and gets demoted for stepping out of line. His evident leadership qualities always win them back, though. He looks parched with the heat, but I'm sure he would prefer the stream to trickle with the hard stuff."

"I see," said Townsend, as Marsh considered this dubious character reference. "Go and order Savage to put his tunic back on and get down here and take a drink. Then put another in his place. We will be leaving in about fifteen minutes."

"Yes, sir."

Townsend and Marsh watched Savage as he slithered down the rock face from his vantage point and walked over to the stream. Kneeling at the water's edge, he filled his helmet and let its contents spill down the back of his neck – but he didn't drink any. As he did so again, he sensed a shadow fall across his body, directly blocking out the sunlight.

"You haven't drunk yet, soldier," Marsh pointed out.

"I don't drink this stuff, sir. I only swim in it."

Resisting the urge to let his mouth twist in amusement, Marsh remained resolute. "Drink, man, I say. You may not know it, but your damn body's drying out. You need water, not the bloody stuff you've got in it now. So, drink it! That's an order, and I mean it."

"Do I have to, sir?" he said as he stood up: a big man in every sense of the word.

"Yes," Marsh confirmed. "We are not leaving until you do. Alcohol is no good for you in this heat."

Eventually, Savage did as he was ordered – pulling a distorted face as he tentatively sipped from a cupped hand. "Urgh, horrible stuff," he moaned as spilt droplets clung to his chin, finally merging before dropping back off into the stream.

He looks like I'm torturing him, thought Marsh, standing at his side. He made sure Savage took a few more mouthfuls before finally turning away, satisfied.

All suitably refreshed, they mounted their horses and continued the trek, but it wasn't long before trouble found them; presently they came across a small group of people with several children, hurrying towards them while cautiously looking back over their shoulders.

"Halt!" Townsend ordered, stopping the riders in their tracks.

"Thank God! He's answered our prayers," said the bearded leader of the group, stepping to the side of Townsend's horse. "We were shot at and had to turn back – we have no idea how many there are! We didn't stop to find out, and we demand you do something to protect us, Major."

"Corporal Collins, you and the driver stay here with these people, and Mr Galea, we will travel on ahead and see if we can find these men and flush them out."

"Yes, sir."

"Forward, men!" Townsend commanded, indicating the order with his arm.

Ready for anything, the six men moved off on their horses at full gallop, intent on finding these miscreants before they got away. Riding hard, they soon disappeared from the view of the wagon before unexpectedly being forced to rein firmly back on their horses. A dust cloud enveloped the riders as the horses dug in their haunches on command.

Spread out for a few yards in front of them lay an exceptionally harsh, unyielding rocky terrain, making riding at speed nigh impossible. Fearing for their mounts' safety, Townsend cautiously ordered his men to walk the horses through this short part of the trail. Now with the awkward stretch negotiated, the trail flattened out again ahead of them.

"Right men, on the gallop again. Forward!" he ordered, leading the riders on once more.

Minutes later, a shot rang out; the rider behind the two officers was hit and fell from his horse.

More bullets hit the ground around them as they jumped from their mounts to seek shelter. Being the nearest, Ned Savage grabbed his injured colleague by the back of his collar and then unceremoniously dragged him under the cover of the nearest shrub. The salt tree was an excellent shrub that offered plenty of space to hide in, but it afforded little protection from searching penetrating bullets.

"How are you, Jim? Where did they hit you?" Ned whispered.

"He's taken a small lump out of my arm, Ned. Apart from that, I'm okay."

"Good," said Ned, lying down flat next to him. "Did anyone see anything?"

"No, but there are two of them, Ned. The shots came from two different directions."

"That's what I thought," confirmed Marsh while hugging the ground beside them. He wiped away the excessive sweating – brought about by the encounter – from his brow with the back of his hand. Then, justifying their suspicions, four more separate shots were fired into the undergrowth around them – searching them out.

"There are two, all right. That confirms it. Fired from just two positions."

Townsend was noticeably quiet as his eyes scanned the trees in front of them. A small, speckled gecko-type creature alarmed him when breaking cover and scurried away to safety from beside his knee. Then, easing himself gently along the ground on his stomach, he caught a glimpse of sunlight reflecting off something in the tree in front of them.

A rifle barrel, perhaps, he thought. "Who's the best marksman here?" he whispered hurriedly.

"Ned is as good as any and better than most, sir," said a trooper.

"Let's put him to the test," Townsend whispered back. "Right, Savage, I want you to aim for that tree there. About 250 yards away. Can you see it?"

After making sure there was a bullet in the chamber, Ned carefully lined up his rifle barrel. "Is it the mature laurel tree, sir?"

"Yes, and about three-quarters of the way up, to the right."

"Got it, sir," Savage answered before bracing himself and his rifle hard against the granite rock beside him. "I'm ready, sir," he said, looking through the sights of his Martini-Henry rifle he had pointed towards the laurel tree.

"Good. First, we need a decoy or some sort of distraction to get him to show himself."

"I'll do it, Major," said Marsh.

Tutting at the sometimes-foolish bravery of his friend, Townsend hissed at him, "How do you propose to do it, Captain?"

"Considering we are hidden from the one man. We only need to worry about the man in front. So, if I step out like *this*," he said, raising his voice and briefly leaving cover.

At that instant, the gunman exposed enough of himself for Savage to let off a shot. The bullet found its mark, hitting the gunman in the chest and throwing him backwards off the tree's bough. His rifle dropped through the foliage to the ground, whereas his body slipped and slid in the branches before falling and hitting the ground with a dull thud. It was immediately followed by muted cheering from the men in the bushes who saw him fall.

"Good shot, soldier. You got him," Townsend congratulated Savage quietly as he rolled over and patted him on the shoulder.

"Thank you, sir," said Savage, proudly looking around at the others before adding excitedly, "Well, it was, wasn't it, lads?" Pleased with himself, he caressed his trusty rifle.

"Has anyone seen the other?" Townsend asked, anxiously looking around him.

"Sir, I've just spotted him. He's down out of the trees and making off yonder," a soldier said, pointing off into the distance.

"Let me hunt him down before he gets away and we lose him, sir!" pleaded Marsh.

"Yes, Captain – but be careful," Townsend agreed.

At once, Marsh was on his feet. "Yes, sir. Come on then, soldier. Let's find him. On your horse and show me!"

Remounting, they rode in search of the fleeing man, only to realise he had vanished.

"He must be near, sir. I thought we were after him quite quickly," said Watson, frowning.

"That means he's hiding somewhere in these thick shrubs," Marsh guessed. "There's plenty of it around here. We'll spend a few minutes looking for him, and then we must get back to our men."

The two soldiers poked and prodded at the thick shrubs from their saddles, one with his sword, the other with his rifle and bayonet. They were still methodically searching for him when a fully defined click was heard from behind.

They turned in alarm to see the man frantically attempting to reload his rifle; in his desperation to get away, he had forgotten to refill the rifle chamber.

After giving away his advantage, he cursed as Watson quickly aimed his rifle at the potential killer and coldly waited for him to make another aggressive move. Slinging down his rifle in despair, the man drew his sword. He brandished it at the two men, threatening them as he slowly backed away, his eyes continually searching for an escape route.

Both soldiers followed him on their horses as he continued to back away – one on either side, with a short single salt tree shrub separating each of them. The man kept muttering something under his breath that neither soldier could understand. *A prayer, perhaps*, thought Marsh. Knowing he was trapped, the killer slashed at them wildly with his sword, threatening them each time they rode too close while desperately looking to flee.

This cat-and-mouse game continued in complete deathly silence, save for the falling of the horses' clopping hooves on the stony ground and their quarry's gasps due to the effort of lashing out.

Wild-eyed, and with the tension rising unbearably, the man suddenly broke out into a run. As soon as he showed his back, they were after him. He had managed just a few yards weaving in and out of the shrubs when Marsh caught him with a deep slashing cut across the back with his sabre, bringing him down. The trooper was fast out of his saddle and bayonetted the man where he fell.

They felt the killer had shown no mercy and therefore he received none in return.

"Well done, soldier," said Marsh. "He will cause no more harm to the people around here. Bring his rifle back with you to show the major."

"Yes, sir! Thank you, sir," Watson replied. He picked up the rifle and tied it to his saddle before riding back to the others behind his captain.

Townsend had recovered the first killer's rifle near the body at the foot of the tree. He spent a little time inspecting it before sliding it down into the empty rifle holster on his horse, just moments before the two arrived back. "Business finished, Captain?" Townsend asked.

"Everything sorted, sir," was Marsh's swift, satisfying response. After months of training and a week or so on that dratted boat, he was delighted to have been involved and seen action.

Townsend marshalled his small group together. He paused awhile to allow the man's injury to be bound, then he rode the party back to the rest of their troop, Galea, and the worried family.

***

Edoardo Galea was in a philosophical mood as he awaited the return of the small party of men. It was a hot day, and he found the inconvenience of making small talk with the distraught family a little irritating. However, it was a worthy sacrifice for something much more significant that he'd planned to happen, so Galea put up with it. Soon, the tell-tale dust cloud of the returning troopers was sighted, and he watched, worried at the professional way they had performed.

Arriving back, Townsend confidently assured the civilians they could resume their journey without fear.

The relief the group showed on hearing the good news was understandable, and they made ready to go.

"Did you get them all, Major?" one of them asked.

"Yes – there were only two, and they won't trouble you anymore."

Galea joined in with his congratulations. "Well done, Captain! Well done! It seems the rule of law has expressed itself admirably." His eyes flickered as he spoke, and his smile dropped to a scowl as soon as their attention was elsewhere, taking great care not to let his chagrin show. Like others in the Mediterranean region, he held no love for the British uniform, and these two officers were no exception.

The gunmen were part of an envious group of cut-throats who still believed Malta would be a prized possession. These were the descendants of the Barbary corsairs, a dangerous group of people whose ships had once reigned supreme in the Mediterranean. These privateers were allies of the Ottomans and brought terror and fear of death to the area, where ships got robbed for their valuables and passengers and crew were hived off into slavery. Any older men who were caught were shown no mercy and put to the sword, while the women were savagely raped. At times, whole villages became involved in this lucrative business, as privateers placed no importance on anyone's religion; it was of no concern to them. Godless atheists and Muslims intermarried, creating new alliances to wreak havoc in the Mediterranean. Soon after the Great Siege of Malta's failure against the British, the disintegration of the Ottoman Empire and their allies began.

Over the next three centuries, the Ottoman Empire got driven back to the very shores of Turkey itself. These people became stateless, existing in scattered villages along the coasts of Algeria, Tunisia, Libya, and Sicily, in the very places they had once reigned supreme and moored their ships safely without fearing attack. They would receive due retribution for the cruelty they had bestowed on others.

Over time their villages, in turn, were looted and plundered by gangs of marauders. Long gone were the ships and power they had once enjoyed. So, they began to nurture a dream of uniting their like-minded peoples by occupying Malta and calling it their spiritual home. To achieve this aim, the prominent families of the tribes gathered to hatch a daring plan.

It had begun with gathering information and putting people in key positions. Loose talk by the Italians – describing the superguns they were having manufactured – filtered out and was picked up by well-placed spies. These spies soon gleaned information about the British installing them in Malta. When this news reached the leading families, they concocted a strategy to turn the guns against the British. As the men entrusted with bringing these plans to fruition would become very wealthy if they were successful, local merchants were only too willing to back the venture and pay for a veritable army, ready to strike at a given signal. They had unanimously agreed that this signal would be the firing of the Anchor gun towards the forts at Valletta.

As they schemed and plotted, Galea had quickly emerged as the favourite to lead them. Born into a wealthy family, he had been fed on a steady diet of anti-British rhetoric since his infant days and had grown determined to end the corsairs' suffering. Now an adult, he was intelligent and quick-witted, with a deep-seated grudge against the British for the Ottoman Empire's final defeat and, alongside it, the glory of the Barbary.

He was elected to take charge of taking over Malta and getting rid of the British but, for the plot to work, he needed others to assist him. Most of these recruits were mixed nationals with little education from various villages around the Mediterranean. Others were cut-throats and robbers who would do anything for anyone who paid them. It was a ragtag army of dispensable, dangerous men – though they were well organised and vicious, nonetheless.

Most of the men Galea employed at the fort to assist the sappers in the handling and moving of the granite boulders from the quarry, plus any labouring in general, were locals. Others were employed to hack out more of the rugged granite around the fort, making way for the dry ditch that would replace it. These labourers were innocent of Galea's real motives – and that was exactly how he wanted it. Fewer people in the know meant fewer mouths that could talk when plied with money or drink.

Galea's initial impression of Townsend was not favourable, however. The intelligence supplied to him by the informant at Governor Johnson's dinner described him as lax and careless, with the friendly nature of a fool who enjoys his whisky – an entirely different animal to the man standing in front of him, barking out his orders and marshalling his men for the rest of the trek to Anchor Bay.

Galea had taken over the position as head of the construction gang – after having the original owners murdered – so he could be at the very heart of their precious new fort. From there, he could work with his contacts across the island – some of whom were financing the initiative – to undermine the British involvement in Malta. He would stop at nothing in his endeavours to wrest control of Malta from them.

After years of indoctrination by his elders, he could not see it as a betrayal to seek to claim a land that he thought should belong to him and his allies. These once mighty descendants of the murderous Barbary pirates had plundered riches galore when they were aligned with the Ottoman Empire. Now, however, the majority were desperately poor and looked towards Malta for their salvation. Many among their number felt that the shame they'd suffered had stemmed from their defeat at the Great Siege of Malta at the hands of the British, and their hatred for them overruled all other considerations. To take Malta would mean that their scattered tribes would have somewhere to congregate and live – it would also mean they could be dominant and feared in the region once again.

It was a good thing Galea had purposely schemed to be there in Valletta solely to travel back to the fort with these two officers; it had allowed him to get the measure of the new commander and his ability to lead, as well as offering his friendship. The result from their first meeting, however, wasn't to his liking. Unfortunately, his attempt at comradeship and civility was rejected out of hand, but he did not intend to give up. He now knew the man was no fool; the utmost care and due respect must be shown to him if their grand plan was to succeed.

So far, the major's minor skirmish with the bandits had barely tested his capability. Both Major Townsend and his captain had responded with courage and intelligence. It was hard to see any weaknesses thus far that could be exploited, but Galea knew they would have them. Everyone had them.

***

Thanking the soldiers profusely, the family gathered their belongings and walked on. The small military contingent moved off with the injured soldier propped up in the back of the supplies wagon, taking some friendly teasing from the others.

"I would wager you being up for a medal for volunteering to stop that bullet for us," one man quipped.

"Argh, stop making me laugh. It bloody hurts!" the injured soldier complained, trying to entice some sympathy – to no avail.

Riding along together at the head of the party, and enjoying a slower gait, Townsend turned in the saddle towards Marsh and asked, "Why did you make yourself a target for that gunman back there? Why were you so cocksure you wouldn't get shot?"

"Hearing the guns go off, I guessed they were typical Arabic guns and not particularly accurate," he explained, shrugging his shoulders. "I've seen plenty of them and thought if they missed us both upfront and at that range, the risk couldn't be so great… so I stepped out."

Townsend withdrew the rifle from the saddle holster that he'd taken from the gunman's body and threw it across into Marsh's hand.

"Well, they happened to be the latest Russian rifles, and very accurate," Townsend informed him through gritted teeth. "You bloody failed to check them out."

Marsh stared at him, wide-eyed, then gulped hard.

Townsend watched the colour drain from his face. "The gunmen missed us because we were low in the saddle," he said. "That's why the man behind was hit. The bullet went between us. I sensed the bloody thing pass me. It wasn't the quality of the gun that was lacking, but the quality of the gunman."

Marsh listened open-mouthed.

"You're a *bloody idiot*!" Townsend hissed. "If you do anything like that again, I'll have you on a charge. Do I make myself clear, Captain?"

"Yes, sir," he replied, straightening his back in the saddle. "Sorry, sir!"

They reached Fort Anchor late that evening, dust-covered and saddle sore but otherwise in good health.

"Halt! Who goes there?" rang out the challenge from Adams, the sentry, who knew it was Collins. He thought he would have fun with him, having no idea he would be returning with the commander of the garrison.

"Corporal Collins and party are returning with the supplies from Valletta."

"Step forward and be identified, Collins. That's a false accent if ever I heard one."

Visibly irritated and knowing the sentry was about to be shocked, Collins stepped forward from the shadows, followed by both officers a few paces behind. As soon as the sentry recognised them as officers, he froze to attention.

"At ease, sentry," was Townsend's command, wanting to start on the right foot and encourage the men. "Good to see you so alert, by the way."

"Thank you, sir," said Adams, looking relieved at not being scolded for so obviously playing the fool.

Townsend and Marsh walked into Fort Anchor over the temporary bridge. The duty officer then stepped forward as they were, dusting down their clothes. Saluting his new commanding officer, he said, "Welcome, sir. I hope you had a good journey?"

"Thank you, Lieutenant. You are?"

"Lieutenant Berry. Royal Engineers, sir. Duty officer for the evening for Fort Anchor." He stood there, fresh-faced in his pristine uniform, eager to make a good impression. "We were only made aware you would be arriving – by semaphore signal – about two hours ago, sir. Your permanent quarters at the cabin are in the process of being made ready, but bell tents are available for you both tonight."

"Good. I'll have a wash and brush up to rid me of this dust," Townsend decided. "If you made sure two brandies were available for Captain Marsh and me, it would be appreciated. After which, I will be turning in for the night. Going by how Captain Marsh is rubbing his backside as we speak, I'd say his brains have been taxed to their uppermost limit during the journey here today."

"Of course, sir," said Berry, amused. "Would you like anything to eat? Cook would be only too pleased to get you something."

"No, Lieutenant," Townsend replied. "I've eaten my fill of trail dust already and haven't the appetite. Tell me, Lieutenant," he added, taking the man aside as the supplies troop made their weary way inside the camp, "what do you know about any insurgency activity around here?"

"There have been a few instances just lately," Berry reported, "but it's difficult to put it down to being organised, or anything other than occasional banditry, sir."

"I see, Lieutenant." Townsend gazed around at his new station, impressed. "So, this is Fort Anchor, eh?"

For a few minutes, Townsend just stood there amidst the towering grey walls of the fort and looked about him in the faltering evening light, with Marsh and Berry waiting patiently at his side. He saw that the main camp lay adjacent, with campfires and oil lanterns lighting up the gloom of the evening.

"I look forward to seeing more tomorrow," he said at last. "Now, if you can show me my tent, I think I'll get some sleep. After the brandy, of course – oh, might as well make it a small bottle. We must get rid of this blasted dust somehow!"

"Certainly, sir. Follow me – I'll show you both to your quarters and have that bottle of brandy and two glasses sent over to you."

A few minutes later, the two officers poured their brandies and sat outside the tent, surveying the peaceful military scene around them and watching the horses they had ridden being led away to the stables.

After a strained silence, Townsend blurted out, "Our first signs of action out here in Malta, and you nearly get yourself killed! What were you thinking of?" he asked angrily.

Marsh gulped at the question; he knew it was coming. "Too eager to help the family," he said quietly, on reflection. "But what did you think of the gangmaster?" he asked, not wanting to dwell on his unexplained irrational decision.

"I've no opinion of him yet. That will come in time, no doubt. Still, I do know that, as the gangmaster, he should be here with his men, supervising them, and not be gone for two days at a time on a jaunt into Valletta," Townsend replied a little testily. "Now, excuse me – I'm off to sleep," he said abruptly, still angry with him.

"Goodnight, Robert," Marsh replied sheepishly, and left. It was pointless attempting to defend the inexcusable, and he walked to his tent just as the bugler began playing 'Lights Out'.

Pausing at the open flap, he watched over the scene outside, lingering for a few more minutes – as the oil lamps were dimmed and extinguished – before lying down on his bunk.

Extinguishing his lantern, Marsh lay in the dark and thought about the earlier incident. To begin with, sleep wouldn't come; his mind was far too active for sleeping, thinking about what his recklessness might have brought him. *I could have ended up in a burial casket, in permanent residence on these islands,* he reflected in horror.

He shuddered at the thought, his body breaking out into an uncomfortable cold sweat that abated only slowly before he finally escaped his anxious thoughts of stupidity and fell asleep.

***

On his return, Galea hurriedly convened a meeting with his foreman and two of his trusted men in a tent belonging to the civilian workforce on the edge of the camp.

Wearily, he said, "At least my journey to Valletta wasn't entirely wasted, Khalif. I found out the fort commander is far from the careless oaf our man described. It seems the fool was describing someone else, certainly not the commander. He was quite strict in his dealings with me, and he was also brave when leading his soldiers into action after being ambushed by our men. Those two fools were the instigators of both their deaths, Khalif, by ignoring our wishes. None of our people should mourn for them." He ran a hand through the dust that had accumulated in his slicked hair, thinking over the day's events.

Khalif listened closely. He was a bearded, muscular man of few words. He was there to do Galea's bidding along with his two companions, one being Asif, his cousin. "Try not to worry about the commander, Edoardo. We have many days of quarrying stone ahead before the gun is even close to being fired."

But Galea, who had become fixated with the major, continued, "The commander deployed his men like an expert. He is no fool, and we need to carefully observe him, which I fully intend to do in the coming weeks. After that, I will know what his weaknesses are and will be able to exploit them. In the meantime, we help the British build their incredible fort and wait until this supergun has been delivered and is in full working order. Their practising will be, no doubt, heard across all these islands. It will be the signal to secretly land all our forces in readiness for the attack on Valletta. Go then, my friends – but first, have Fatima prepare herself well. Then have her sent in here to me. I am in much need of her companionship throughout the night. Now go."

"Yes, Edoardo," Khalif replied.

All three bowed before leaving him alone with his thoughts, still fixated on the major. The fort's commander increasingly worried him, with his proven ability to function and fight under the most unexpected circumstances.

His obsessive thoughts of the major only ceased when Fatima made her appearance, at which point his thoughts turned immediately to the more urgent desires of the flesh as he beckoned her towards him.

Chapter 12

Taking command in Camp City.
Discharging one's duty with the Sutler

'BELL TENT City', as the soldiers called it, lay outside the fort's walls. Over the months, it had slowly grown as more men with specialised skills and knowledge arrived to build up the fort's robust defences. Around the edge of the camp, guards were posted day and night to protect all those working on the fort.

At the break of dawn, the bugler on the musketry parapet worked spittle and suppleness into his lips to help seal the mouthpiece. Filling his lungs with air, he raised the instrument and sounded out the morning reveille, the bugle forcefully encouraging the men to wake and rise with its ability to penetrate the minds of even the deepest sleepers.

"Charley, Charley, get out of bed. Oh! Charley, Charley, get out of bed!" rang loud across the camp. The different bugle calls were a second language of orders to military men, each with a distinctive melody and urgency.

With the sounds of the bugle in their ears, the camp began to stir and then spring into life. Some soldiers playfully pushed and scrambled with each other to get over to use the communal latrines before the usual morning rush; no one wanted to linger there due to the build-up of gut-wrenching fumes in the unforgiving heat of the morning. 'In and out fast, not last,' was often chanted by the comedians in the camp, with the others fully understanding the reasons. The mantra was also scrawled in paint on the flimsy screen guarding the entry point. Some men, mainly the new arrivals, were not as eager or speedy – and they suffered for it.

Having washed and completed their morning ablutions, the men made their bunks and cleared their tents of clutter before getting outside and standing in line, followed soon after by the NCOs, for their daily inspection. If he thought even they were too slow, the sergeant major would also make an early appearance for a personal round of inspection; that morning, he came in early to the surprise of the NCOs, who knew they were not late in rousing the men.

"Come on, get a move on. Get outside and stand to attention. Move it! Move it!" he shouted as he roamed from tent to tent, looking for possible victims for latrine duty – a necessity due to never having the volunteers. He was followed by the NCOs, trying to keep pace with him.

"Outside, you men! Get a move on! I said outside!" he repeated. "On the double, get out!"

Striding into the next tent, he suddenly stopped at a bunk bed, the occupant of which showed few signs of movement. Bending down, he gently lifted the corner of the army issue blanket, exposing the soldier's face. His own began to distort in the evilest of looks as he screamed into the ears of the horrified man.

"Prosser, you bloody tosser, I should have known it was you! Leave your old man alone! Get the fuck out of bed now and get your arse outside this tent and stand to attention this second!"

"But I wasn't doing anything! I had a cramp and…"

"Out this fucking second, I said!" he roared, snapping down at the man. "Corporal, has this man had that new bromide stuff in his tea as I ordered?"

"Yes, Sergeant Major."

"Well, give him a double dose then. It's not bloody working!"

"Very well, Sergeant Major."

He strode out and continued the same pantomime in each tent until all the men were lined up outside, many of them feeling particularly surly at the methods he was using.

After his cramp eased, Prosser caught up with the rest of the men in triple-quick time and, after stumbling, managed to get himself onto the end of a row.

When the sergeant major emerged from the tents, the NCO shouted, "*Attention!*" The assembled men then heeled for the morning roll call.

Standing in front of them, finally satisfied that no one was missing, the sergeant major exclaimed, "Good! Well done, men! That even goes for you, Prosser." Then his face twisted. "It must have been a challenge to drag your huge manhood onto the parade. Well, I'll tell you this, Prosser: if it happens again, I'll be using your dick for bloody bayonet practice, and then, later, I'll have it sliced and fed to the dogs in the camp, like an Italian sausage! Do you get my drift?"

"Yes, Sergeant Major," Prosser said, his face ashen at the very thought of where his body parts could end up.

"Yes, *sir*! Prosser. The officer on parade." He had quickly calmed down after his sudden, demented tirade.

"Yes, sir," said Prosser.

"So long as we understand each other, Prosser," he said, before turning to face Captain Hill and saluting. "All men present and correct, sir."

"Thank you, Sergeant Major – sterling work by the way," said Hill before addressing the troops. He was an officious character with many years of service. His use of the men was solely to achieve an objective and give himself a less stressful time. "Last night, we were pleased to welcome the commanding officer of Fort Anchor, Major Townsend, and Captain Marsh, both Royal Artillery. These officers will be here at Fort Anchor long after the Royal Engineers have packed up and gone. Make every effort to fully answer any questions, if asked, from these officers."

As you all know, work on the lifting gantry at the bay must be completed in time for the arrival of their gun. It will be needed to take this exceptional ordnance off the barge when it arrives. We can start and finish the other gantry at the fort in good time, well before it gets there. This artillery piece will arrive sometime in the next week at Valletta Docks. Therefore, I propose concentrating on finishing all work on the lifting gantry at the bay first. Since it will take many days to get the cannon up to the fort itself, we will have more than enough time to finish the roadway and gantry at the fort to accommodate it. Right, then. Apart from anyone on latrine or guard duty, the rest of you will make your way to the cookhouse in good order. Thank you, Sergeant Major. Dismiss the men."

"Thank you, sir. *Dismissed*!"

The bugler took up another refrain, one that beckoned the men: "Come to the cookhouse door, boys! Come to the cookhouse door!"

The men formed orderly queues into the cookhouse tent, which was the largest in the camp. Here, some of the soldiers' wives worked, earning their keep, assisting the cooks or serving the men. The men always appreciated the females because they kept everything in perspective – and they were also good to have fun and banter with, brightening up the dull camp days.

"Here, Sally!" shouted one. "When are you going to leave that old man of yours? I get more money than him because of my stripe. You won't regret it, Sally darling. Come to me tonight."

"Keep your thoughts to yourself, Bill," Sally responded, without it getting heated; she knew he was teasing her. "He'll be along in a minute. You know he doesn't like you turning my head. I see he gets that bit extra because he excites me more than you. Get off with you now, you randy old bugger."

Raucous laughter followed, as Bill was ushered out of the tent.

***

That evening, Marsh and Townsend were invited to eat with Major Carter in his bell tent along with Captain Hill. While doing so, they were to discuss the fort's progress.

Before the commander arrived, Hill had been the highest-ranked officer at the camp, and he would often use his standing to influence anything that would afford him status and comfort. Seated in the tent, they were to be served by two stunningly beautiful women.

Carter introduced them. "This is Daisy," he said, running his hand over her hip and thigh, "and this is Molly, who takes good care of Captain Hill. These girls are our personal sutlers. Anything we need, these girls will get it for us." He looked up at Daisy in a lustful way. "Even wash and darn our clothes if required," he smirked.

While he spoke, Daisy placed plates of broth, potatoes, and bread down on the table for

Carter and Hill to start. Marsh and Townsend sat on much lower seats with a table between them.

"And here's yours," said Molly, the other beauty. Showing her suppleness, she bent low at the waist to place the plates on the table. In doing so, the front of her blouse ballooned forward, exposing her full, ample breasts. She put the plates down with the bread and stood upright again, obscuring the tantalising view. Townsend took the sight in his stride, but Marsh felt his groin stirring – reminding him he needed a woman.

God, he thought, *it's been a long time since I got my hands on a pair of tits like that.*

"So, if there's anything you need washed or repaired, the girls will do it, gentlemen. But that's *all* – if you understand my meaning."

"Thank you, Major Carter," said Townsend, asserting his authority. "My sentiments entirely, and as Mrs Townsend is due to join me soon, perhaps you may have thoughts as to suitable quarters for her stay?"

This question refocused his mindset. "Why, of course, I do apologise. I had forgotten your, er, wife," stuttered Carter, taking his hand from Daisy. "I will have someone show you the cabin being made ready for you both."

Once they had finished their meals, Carter offered them a tour of the fort and the land surrounding Anchor Bay. Then, after being shown over the fort, they mounted their horses and rode out to the granite ridge on which the fort was built.

Sitting astride their animals, they took in the beauty of the place. The west's view was an endless sea, which stretched as far as Tunisia's golden beaches. To the east was the curvature of Mellieha Bay. Beyond the small island of Comino, to the north-west, was the larger island of Gozo, easily seen in the distance and surrounded by a beautifully clear azure blue sea.

"I cannot understand why the fort has to be built here and not on Gozo. There are easier and more open positions of choice over there that would still cover the whole of this area," Carter remarked.

"I can remember that point being raised with Colonel Downing at Woolwich," Townsend replied. "He, and Governor Johnson, made it clear that if the fort came under attack, it would be easier to get reinforcements to assist the battery here than to get them to Gozo, where they may arrive too late to help. We would most probably lose any battle in that scenario."

"Yes, I see it now – and entirely agree," said Carter. "If you follow me down to Anchor Bay, I will show you where the gantry is being built to get your gun ashore. Also, you can see that the construction of the roadway to your fort is on our left and is well underway, so be careful; it's quite steep in places."

Allowing the horses to make their sure-footed strides, he led them down the hillside, up which the gun would torturously climb.

On reaching the bottom, Marsh looked back up the incline and frowned. "Excuse me, Major Carter, but how will you get our cannon up there? It's many times larger than any ordinary cannon. You have yet to see one, sir?"

"Well, the answer to your first question, Captain, is by the men's raw strength and cussed willpower, aided and abetted by the sturdy capstans we will have positioned on the roadway. As to your second question, I've not seen it, but I know its overall weight is 102 imperial tons, which is huge, I grant you. That is all there is to know to get it up this hill," Carter said, confidently thumbing behind him, "and into your fort. I do share your concern, however, Captain, and both Captain Hill and I feel the roadway should have an extra level added to take out more of the steepness of the hill as a wise precaution. The bay itself has been sufficiently deepened with explosives to allow the barge carrying it, in. The gantry base has been reinforced with metal piles and is sturdy enough to lift the gun's weight. When your cannon arrives at Valletta Harbour – on the *Stanley* – it will be offloaded and left temporarily at the docks under a twenty-four-hour armed guard. It will stay there overnight before being loaded onto a barge and brought here."

He ended by gesturing along the track towards the new landing stage. "Well, that's about it, gentlemen. I can see my men are on the way down here to get started. They must have all eaten by now, so we will get out of their way. Both Captain Hill and I will be back here later, for the rest of the day, if you should want us. There are still a few problems to sort out."

Passing the sappers, the three officers returned their salutes, and Carter urged them to ride on with him and see other parts of the roadway under construction.

They came across a detail of men under Lieutenant Berry's supervision, who had restarted work on the roadway on which they were to haul up the precious cannon. Their combined efforts began releasing a dust cloud, which hung in the air over where they toiled.

***

Captain Hill rounded up the extra men needed for the afternoon's exertions and led them down to Major Carter at the bay. Townsend and Marsh, with detailed plans of the fort, took themselves off to inspect the various areas. Of special interest to them was where the steam engine, accumulator, and boiler were to be located. Everything was looking good as they made their inspections together.

They were looking out from the musket counterscarp into the ditch below when Marsh turned and said, "Did you see the tits on Molly, Robert? God, I could have stared at them all day. What I'd give to stand behind her with those in my hands!"

"Although it's extremely pleasurable, I think you have a thing about that particular position," Townsend remarked knowingly. "I saw the effect they had on you and how you were captivated by her beauty."

"It seems such a long time ago now since I last had that pleasure with Sarah. I wanted to tell you about it during the voyage here, but I didn't get the chance to finish with Victoria about. Well, I fell for her. I fell in love with Sarah, all right."

"You fool. Why didn't you speak up and say how you felt? It's far too late now; she's long forgotten you. No doubt someone else will be appreciating her more than you were inclined to."

"Because I didn't realise it until after we'd left," Marsh explained. "You remember the home leave we had before coming here?"

"I do, and I made the most of it, I must say."

"Well, I went back to Newcastle, looking for her. I stayed at the Blue Boar Inn and spoke to Rose and Jack Dobbins again. They told me her father had made a complete recovery and was working again at the mine. Sarah, though, was so hacked off with how I left that she took herself off somewhere – back to some profession or other she had before her father's accident."

153

"How do you know that?"

"Rose and Jack told me," he replied. "Though they wouldn't say what or where. Rose gave me the sharp edge of her tongue, I can tell you, especially when I told her about my feelings for Sarah. She was angry and accused me of taking advantage of her behind their backs."

"Good! You deserved it. Well, you will have to forget her now because it's finished. But look, you're feeling frustrated, as any man sensitive to your particular situation can tell. Come back to my tent in about, say, twenty or thirty minutes after I have spoken with Molly about your... er... predicament."

Marsh thought about it. "But Hill and Carter are about," he stammered, knowing exactly what he had in mind.

"No. Both officers are down at the bay all afternoon. You know all about supervising and what that entails. The hill is too steep and requires that extra level put into the roadway somewhere to take it out. That is what they are looking at – making four in total."

"Would you do that for me, Robert?"

"Yes. I'm a bloody idiot too, aren't I?" Townsend gazed down at his pocket watch to check the time. "Twenty or so minutes should be long enough for me to at least ask her. What do you say?"

Eventually, Marsh nodded, smiling.

***

Townsend had one of the wives find Molly under the pretext that he wanted her to get some things for him, what with her being the officers' sutler. Not long after, she was asking permission to enter his tent, so he called her in.

"Ah, Molly. I need to ask a favour, and I'm prepared to pay well for it."

"What's that then, sir?" she asked in puzzlement.

"Captain Marsh, who you served with me this morning, caught an eyeful of your elegant and ample feminine charms. He's spoken of nothing else to me since. I want you to help him discharge his frustrations... if you follow my meaning."

Molly immediately realised what he was asking. "But I don't know if I should, sir. What if Captain Hill found out? Have you asked Daisy?"

"No, it has to be you, Molly," he insisted, fully aware of Marsh's obsessive infatuation with her. "Look," he added, holding her reassuringly by the elbow, "I'm the commander of Fort Anchor, and I promise you nothing will come of it. You have my word."

"Would it be regular, sir, or a one-off?"

"Oh, you can be sure it would be a one-off, Molly. I need him to think clearly, and this seems the only way to achieve it. I'll give you a full pound if you will?"

"That's very generous of you, sir. It will be our little secret, then?"

"Yes, Molly. I promise."

She came and stood in front of him, stroking the underside of her chin for him to see the natural attractive allure of her neck. "And yourself, sir. Can I help you in any way?" she asked, looking at him provocatively – testing his resistance.

"No! No, Molly. I am well serviced in that respect," he replied, starting to blush. "My wife is in Valletta and will be joining me soon, I hope."

"Oh, goodness me. What was I thinking of?" She quickly smoothed down her loose hair, embarrassed now at her foolish questions.

"That's all right, Molly, forget it. Captain Marsh will be along in a few minutes. Thanks again. I knew I could rely on you."

He left her there in the tent, only to see Marsh walking towards him.

The things I do for him, thought Townsend. *If this gets out, we could both be in serious trouble.*

"Sir," he said as he crisply saluted his commanding officer. "Is everything ready, sir?"

"Yes, it is," replied Townsend as he returned the salute. "You are cleared to discharge your... er... duties, Captain."

"Thank you, sir," was Marsh's delighted response. Entering the tent, he could see Molly sitting there, fully clothed, waiting for him. Not wanting to be disturbed, his fumbling fingers doubly secured the tent flap from the inside.

"Thanks, Molly," he whispered to her in the shaded gloom of the tent.

"Do you want me now?" she asked, her voice purring sexily.

"Yes, Molly. But first, I want you to bend down to me as you did this morning. I want to look down at that same blouse you have on now, then turn around and leave the rest to me!"

"That's awful," she giggled, "but if that's what you want." She bent herself forward at the waist with the same feminine suppleness she had shown earlier. It exposed her breasts again, and then she shook them a few times to tease him. "Is this what you want? Is this what you saw? Does it please you, Captain Marsh? You can hold them now if you want."

He moved behind her and, without answering, delved into her blouse. He cupped her breasts softly in the palms of his hands before exploring their fullness and shape, closing his eyes as he did so. Disregarding his fumbling, she began to gather the back of her dress up to accommodate him.

155

"No, Molly, not like that. Get it off! I want you properly! For God's sake, Molly! I will turn you in good time, I swear to it."

A long hour later, Molly began to ease herself from his embrace.

"Don't go, Molly. I think I can go again!" Marsh grabbed at her to bring her back, but she swivelled out of his clutches.

"I've got to go, David. Major Townsend gave me a full pound to do this, but I reckon you've had a good two pounds' worth," she said, smiling down at him while she dressed. "Well, in excess, if you ask me, but I did enjoy it," she added, nodding her head.

"Oh, Molly, I'll pay for it. Just come back."

"How much have you got?"

"Mm, I'm not sure," he said in a tired, relaxed drawl, with a hint of a smile in his eyes.

"Captain Marsh, I would have to be a complete fool to believe you. You just want more – you're a greedy bugger, you are. Have you not had enough? Have you not been satisfied?"

"Come on, Molly, I implore you. God gave men these urges to do it and get it done. It's not all my doing."

"Don't bring Him into it. No. You've been inside me too long as it is. I'm off for a wash before I live to regret ever doing it. Another time, if you want to, but not now. Why – you can hardly keep your eyes open as it is."

Smoothing down her dress and tying back her hair, Molly took the pound and a few coppers offered by Marsh. She looked down at him on their makeshift bed and asked, "Is that better?"

"Yes, Molly. Thank you so much."

She bent down low and kissed him warmly, full on the lips, allowing her blouse to balloon open again, teasingly reminding him of what he had just enjoyed. Untying the tent flap, she looked back at him; he was yawning and beginning to settle down and doze.

Nature's way, I suppose. Ha! I've done well though, being paid twice, she thought.

She placed the coins he'd given her into the same pocket that contained the commander's pound and stepped outside into the harsh, bright sunshine. Molly let the entrance flap drop behind her and then she headed towards the ladies' separate washing facilities.

From his vantage point, Townsend watched her depart. *I will give him two hours to get over his strenuous activities,* he thought. *Then he had better be ready for some hard soldiering – or else.*

156

Chapter 13

Attack on the Signals working party.
The jailed gang leader

AS THE days passed, Townsend made himself familiar with the complexities of a fort of this type. He wanted his fortress ready in good time to receive the ordnance it would eventually hold.

The doctor in camp saw the occasional injury from careless accidents, but he knew the situation would change once the gun arrived. Occasionally, there was a casualty caused by criminal activity, but this was becoming a rarity of late due to establishing law and order in the area. Criminals who chose to steal or rob were quickly arrested by the military and sent to Valletta to stand trial – after Townsend had signed the transit papers. Banditry was becoming less frequent but when, on occasion, it did happen, it was dealt with forcibly to discourage illegal activity. The Maltese had always known that other countries in the Mediterranean claimed these islands for themselves and felt open hostility towards those causing the problems they faced. Apart from some minor setbacks, the fort continued on towards its completion.

Suddenly, a shout went up from the parapet: "Rider approaching fast! Alert the commander!"

The man rode hard to the command post before pulling his horse up sharp in front of Townsend, who was waiting to meet him. The horse was panting and sweating heavily with its rider's effort to reach the fort, its lathered sweaty smears sticking to its neck and flanks.

"Sir!" he gasped. "Sir, the working party of Royal Signals are under attack! At a guess from about twenty-five, I'd say."

"Where?"

"About two miles back, sir," he said, with a heaving chest.

"Captain Marsh, give this man a drink and find him another horse. I want you to follow him back and teach the murderous swine a lesson."

"At once, sir!" Marsh answered before selecting from gathering volunteers, all keen to leave the camp drudgery and go with him.

Leaning over the water tub, the soldier eagerly gulped down his first fill of water, then dunked the cup again and drank it dry before leaving it swinging free – clanking on the chain attached to the tub.

"How much ammunition have they got? Can they hold out until we get there?"

"They have some, but not much," he replied, wiping his mouth with the back of his hand. "We were mostly kitted out to bring the new telephone cable to Fort Anchor. We should get back in time if we go now, sir."

"Are you able to show my men exactly where the working party is?"

"Of course, sir," he said, now refreshed. "I said I would get back with help."

One of the soldiers rode up with a replacement horse, allowing him to take the reins and mount up.

Taking charge, Marsh ordered: "Detail at the double. *Forward!*"

He led his men from the fort at full gallop. The displaced dust kicked up by the horses' hooves in the dry atmosphere rose, swirling into the air before settling down onto the roof of the command tent.

Riding hard, they came within earshot of the gunfire, at which point Marsh brought his men to a halt. "Where's the enemy position, soldier?"

"Our men are on the trail further over there, and the enemy ambushed us from the west, sir."

"Right! They have no idea we're here, but when they find out, they'll try to escape by going back the way they came. We can get the better of them by setting up a prepared ambush. Bugler!" he called.

"Here, sir."

"Get climbing up on that high rock where I can see you. We'll get in hiding behind them, over there," he said, pointing out the area. "When we are in position, I will wave my helmet at you. When you see my signal, blow the charge as loud as you can. They will take off back the same way, where we will be lying in wait. Get up there now and keep watch on where we are."

"Yes, sir. I'll be watching for your signal."

"Very good. Follow me, men – and keep the noise down."

They rode a little further before dismounting and tethering the horses. Clasping their swords and rifles tightly, so as not to make a noise that might warn the enemy, they outflanked them and began to set the ambush.

Marsh got his men into the favoured positions with frantic last-minute hand signals while the firing continued up ahead. Once he was completely satisfied with his men's positioning, Marsh waved his helmet towards the bugler on the higher ground. He waited a few seconds but nothing happened, so he signalled again, shaking it forcefully from side to side.

"Is the man blind?" he muttered before waving his helmet again in frustration, but this time the bugler spotted it.

Responding to the captain's signal, the call to 'charge' rang out clearly above the sounds of gunfire. On hearing the bugle, the shooting stopped as suddenly as it had begun. The bandits' only thought was to make their escape as swiftly as possible before the soldiers got there.

Rushing back to get away, they ran into a hail of gunfire directed at them on Marsh's orders.

"Keep firing, men, and take them out!" he shouted.

The killers were trapped by soldiers to the front and rear, completely taken by surprise and having no idea of the number of troops ranged against them. They fled every which way in a blind panic, intent on getting away.

Marsh let off a shot that felled one man as the killers closed in on his hidden position, but another was on him before he could bring his pistol to bear again.

The man lunged, bowling him over into the ground. Marsh attempted to rise, but it was too late; the man was quickly on his back. The brute had him in a chokehold, with his hand scrabbling for the knife in his belt to finish him off.

Instinctively, Marsh reached back over his shoulders and grabbed the man's head with both hands. Using sheer strength, he lifted him by the head and threw him with all the power he had over his shoulder. The man landed on a part-buried granite stone protruding from the ground, and an audible crack was heard. Marsh very quickly picked up his pistol and, as the man struggled to rise, shot him twice, instantly ceasing his attempts to stand.

The enemy fought like demons to escape the trap, but there was only going to be one result; now they were out in the open. Some were cut down with sabres, while others were shot or run through and finished with rifles and bayonets.

The rescue party had gotten off lightly, having only two men wounded with cuts. All the insurgents were killed except for one man, who, on seeing the soldiers, had thrown his hands up immediately in the act of hasty surrender.

"Good lord, we have a prisoner," said Marsh in disbelief. "We've got ourselves a bloody prisoner!" he repeated, looking around and doing a quick visual tally. The scene was one of a massacre, with the body count reaching twenty. None had wanted to surrender and so had paid the ultimate price, except for this one apparent coward. The Signals' working party suddenly came running up to Marsh and his men, panting, and with much relief, heartily shook hands with their rescuers.

"Well done, boys. What a welcome sight! We thought you'd never get here," said the lance corporal. "I just had six bullets left, you little devils."

"What kept yer? I had less than that!" demanded another engineer, grinning with relief.

"Make your report, Sergeant," ordered Marsh loudly above all the thankful small talk.

"Well, we had just erected a pole, sir, and Lance Corporal Durham had climbed up it on a rickety pair of rotten ladders he'd been using. He should have had them changed long ago, sir. That was when we came under fire, and they killed two of the men. Good men, they were too! Durham was making a connection to the cable when the gunfire startled him. That was when the rotted rungs of the ladder gave way, and he dropped like a stone to the ground."

"Nothing like a small stone, with his weight," some joker said, butting in.

"No, more like a bloody heavy boulder," said the sergeant, nervously shrugging off the incident while attempting to add humour. "But it saved your life, didn't it?"

"Too bloody right it did," said Durham with enthusiasm. "At least two bullets hit the pole exactly where I'd been working!"

"We then returned fire and kept our heads down, and sent a man to the fort to raise the alarm," concluded the sergeant.

"Thank you, Sergeant. Where are you from back home, Durham? I don't recognise your accent."

"I'm from Burton-on-Trent, sir. It's where the best beer comes from, the finest of breweries, and I'm proud of the place. The water there is the best for brewing in the whole country. I've worked in the big breweries, and it's what we mostly get rationed with over here."

"Mm, good stuff," said Marsh. "I'm partial to it myself. Tell me, Durham. You weren't intoxicated while up that pole, were you? Tipsy, maybe? You know it's a serious offence, drinking on duty. Only I caught a strong whiff of the stuff on you," he said, secretly winking to the others.

Coming stiffly to attention and then saluting, Durham whined, "No, just spilt early rations, it was. I've got witnesses, sir."

With his friendly jibe lost on Durham, Marsh assured him he was speaking in jest, then barked the order, *"Attention!"*

Immediately, the anxious banter between them ceased. "Bring the prisoner to me, Lance Corporal. Maybe we can get some vital information from him."

Durham got hold of the man and yanked him over before pushing him down at the officer's feet. He cowered there under the hostile gaze of the captain and his men, still refusing to answer any questions Marsh put to him, so Marsh decided to ask him again at the fort.

He ordered the two dead soldiers to be taken back to the fort for identification purposes. "Everyone else is to return to their respective units, unless injured. I will arrange for a burial party to come back here and bury the dead."

The journey back was at a more sedate pace – their physical exertions in the heat had taken a heavy toll, and all were exceedingly thirsty. Wearily, they approached the fort and heard the guard shout their presence.

On arrival, the horses were led off to the stables for feeding and watering, and any wounded men were taken to Doctor Charlton of the Army Medical Corps for treatment. The two dead soldiers were placed in a temporary mortuary the doctor had set up himself, with the intention of seeing them afterwards. At last the tired men could safely relax, and sit and enjoy their refreshments together, as the insurgent they brought back was taken off to the small guardroom, lying empty of the usual miscreants.

Marsh blew the dust from his helmet before attempting to brush it off his tunic. Once he was satisfied, he entered the command tent to file his incident report.

Listening intently, Townsend asked, "Were all the others killed, Captain?"

"Yes, sir. We took them completely by surprise. They were focused on the Signals' party, and therefore unaware we were behind them. It was all over in minutes. I need to get a large burial squad out there to bury the bodies – there's twenty of them – so I'll see to that now. I'll get Savage over there with a few others to get it done."

"Good! You can write your report up while I get over to the guardhouse to see what this man has to say for himself."

***

Saluting the major as he arrived, the guard unlocked the door and showed his commanding officer inside. The prisoner was seated at the open barred window with his hands tied firmly behind his back and his inquisitors standing beside him.

"Has he said anything?" asked Townsend.

"No, sir. He refuses to talk. We think he's Arabic. That's about all we know of him.

He's unduly stubborn, sir, and won't answer any questions our translator has asked him."

Townsend stood up close and looked into his eyes. He saw anxiety in them but also abject defiance. They were indeed the eyes of a killer.

161

What is it about these men who think nothing of death? he pondered. *Except for this one, who was very quick to surrender, for some unknown reason. But a coward? It's hard to believe.*

He turned to the translator and asked him to relate his questions to the prisoner. "Why the sudden rise in crime in this area? How many of these men are out there?"

The man remained unshakeably dour and silent, and Townsend realised it could be a long afternoon trying to loosen his tongue.

As he continued his questioning, news of the captive spread throughout the camp. It soon came to the notice of Galea, who walked briskly over to the guardroom to see if he could recognise the man they were holding. He stopped outside the open window, amongst the others jostling to get a peek at him, and momentarily caught the prisoner's eye. He then quickly walked on. It was Hassan, and they had recognised each other.

Although Townsend had his back to the window, he saw the man suddenly flinch and sit slightly higher, holding his head up as if he'd seen someone he knew. He looked out of the window but saw no one suspicious. "Guard! Who's just walked past this window?" he asked.

"A few to glimpse the prisoner, sir. No one suspicious."

"Thank you, soldier." Turning towards the prisoner, he asked again, "Why the sudden rise in criminal activities?"

But there was still no answer after translation.

"I see. Tell our guest he can have the night to think about the questions I put to him. If there's still no answer by morning, tell him I'll get the truth out of him another way!"

"Yes sir," he answered as Townsend left them and stepped outside the guardroom.

"Ah, Major. Just the man I'm looking for."

Turning to face the voice, Townsend saw the gangmaster. "Hello, Mister Galea. What can I do for you?"

"We need your final inspection of the barrack rooms and kitchen, Major," he replied, "but it can wait if you have other things to do. The word around the camp is we have a prisoner in there. Tell me, have you managed to get anything out of him?"

"No, not yet. But by this time tomorrow, our friend should be talking. You have my word on it. Why do you ask, are you concerned for his welfare?"

"I don't agree with any form of torture, Major," Galea stated. "It's barbaric."

"Well, I may have to use it," Townsend replied, glancing back at the guardroom. "If it pleases you any, I don't think he will take much persuading."

The simple statement shocked Galea into pondering what information they may get out of Hassan when he began to talk, but he kept his composure. "I'll meet up with you sometime later for the inspections, Major," he added, before walking away.

***

The day passed without further incident; the final inspections were undertaken by Townsend and Galea, along with the architect.

Towards the early evening, after all the men had visited the cookhouse, most were enjoying their ration of beer or wine – and, for some, the company of their wives. Privacy for them inside the tents was non-existent, apart from attaining a sweaty encounter with a blanket fixed up to contrive their own space.

The conversation throughout the camp had been subdued out of respect for the men of the Signals that had died that day. As the men relaxed after another arduous day building the road, some started joking to lift the cloak of gloom that had descended over the camp.

They told stories of the places they had seen and the things they had done, their beer rations loosening tongues and lifting hearts. The officers thought it healthy for the men to relax in this way – as long as discipline and decorum were maintained. As far as Townsend was concerned, he positively encouraged it.

Sitting outside their tents, Marsh and Townsend took in the late scene. Small groups of men broke out in song – like night warblers – usually with some good voices and some not so good. Occasionally, a fine tenor or bass singer was heard. Either way, it would all end in laughter when rude lyrics were added.

"You know, David, I had a feeling the prisoner recognised someone walking past the guardroom window when I spoke to him today. I wish I could be sure, though," Townsend remarked. Then, in a more reflective, lighter mood, he added, "I spoke to Molly a little while after your frantic get-together. She said you were greedy. Four times was well over the top. Was she right, I wonder?"

Marsh grinned. "She's got a lovely body, Robert. The first time, I just needed release. You must know what it's like. The second time... well, I thought the first time was just too bloody quick. The third time, I began to feel Molly was enjoying it as well by how she was responding to me!" he chuckled, "Then the fourth time... because I *was* bloody greedy! There, I've admitted it!"

163

Shaking his head at the detail given, Townsend threw his gauntlet hard at Marsh in a playful manner, in an attempt to rid himself of all thoughts of them cavorting together. It only served to remind him, however, that Victoria was yet to arrive from Valletta.

***

Late that evening, the camp's shadows darkened considerably while the moon and stars lay hidden behind a mask of black cloud. The bugle call for 'Lights Out' was sounded across the campsite, and unnecessary oil lamps and candles were extinguished, one by one. The NCOs had barked out their last orders of the day and, aside from the snoring, silence began to settle over the many tents that made up 'Bell Tent City'. The lone campfire left burning for the guards' benefit flickered in the night air, highlighting the fort's darkened silhouette in the background. The guards on night duty were placed in strategic positions in the camp and changed throughout the night.

After midnight, a figure emerged from the darkness, moving silently through the shadows towards the guardroom that housed the prisoner, hiding behind anything that afforded him concealment as he neared the guardhouse window. He waited and watched for the single guard to walk by on his round. After he passed, the figure counted in a slow, measured way, timing the seconds before the guard reappeared: two hundred and two counts later. That would allow him enough time to get to the barred window and speak with the prisoner.

He allowed the guard to make another pass to confirm the timing and then took the opportunity to quickly stride up to the window and whisper through the bars: "Hassan! Hassan! Can you hear me? Hassan!"

The prisoner got to his feet and made towards the open window; his hands were still tied behind him. When he recognised the speaker, his whole body began to shudder.

"Hassan, have the British any idea of our plans? Have you said anything to them?"

"No! They know nothing," he said at once. "I have told them nothing."

The shadowy figure's whole demeanour changed. "But why did you disobey your orders, Hassan? You were all told to stay in hiding. Our hard work to capture Malta could have been put at risk and destroyed. We would have lost everything to the British, along with the sorely needed twenty men today! Tell me, why have you let them capture you alive?"

"I was frightened. I did not want to die!" he admitted. "I have a young family, and I wasn't ready. My time has not come, but I have said nothing. Nothing, you hear me. Please believe me!"

The dark figure placed both hands between the bars and embraced the luckless Hassan. Stroking the back of his head, he whispered slowly into his ear, "Do not worry, Hassan. I have come to get you out of here and set you and your spirit free."

He heard the man whimpering softly and could feel his body shaking with fear as he attempted to find the words to thank him. He calmly stroked his head again, then, after a few seconds, spun the hapless man around, pinning him against the bars of the window. While holding the crook of his arm over Hassan's mouth to stifle his cries, he quickly reached for the knife in his belt. He slipped it through the bars and, with a sharp upward thrust, sank it into the man's stomach and forcefully levered it inside him.

The surprise on Hassan's doomed face soon gave way to a glazed look as his life quickly expired.

The dark-clothed figure wiped the blade of his knife clean on Hassan's clothes and then let his body slide gently to the floor. His exertions resulted in him having to stifle his heavy panting as he listened to find out if anyone had overheard them, feeling confident that no one had. He was still counting in his head as he slipped back into the enveloping darkness and waited. On the two hundred and first beat, the guard reappeared and carried on past, totally unaware of what had just taken place.

"Now you won't be able to say anything, Hassan, my friend," muttered the figure in black before stealthily making his way back the way he came. Cleverly and silently, he flitted between each of the dark black shadows – avoiding the guards as he went – safe and confident in the knowledge that the British would now learn nothing from their captive.

Chapter 14

The arrival of 'The Gun' at Grand Harbour.
A coincidence or what?

THE MORNING bugle disturbed two mongrel dogs as they roamed around the camp. Throwing their heads up, they howled back in mournful protest at the sounds, further disturbing the stillness and silence of the encampment. The bugle's musical pitch was painfully assailing their ears, or so it seemed. But, unknown to most, a small group of soldiers had purposefully made pets of these scavengers and had secretly encouraged them into howling for leftovers – often to the buglers' dismay, but to the wicked delight of the culprits. Each morning after the bugle call, they fed them food scraps as a reward before quickly waving the animals away.

Townsend had dressed, apart from his shirt, needing to wash and shave. The braces attached to his trousers hung in single loops on either side of his waist as he lathered up. Then, while humming, he began shaving away the soap and bristles from his face with the straight razor he held. He stopped for a moment to sharpen the cut-throat and to take out the burr developing on the blade's sharp edge; he took it off by running the blade up and down the leather strop he had hanging inside his tent. Satisfied with its cut, he finished off by splashing water onto his face to rinse away the lingering soap.

He was just putting away the small mirror he had – usually used for mirror flash signalling – when he heard a commotion in the distance. At first, he put it down to some luckless soldier getting bawled out by an overeager NCO, but it grew louder and louder until it stopped outside his tent.

"Major Townsend! I need to speak to the commanding officer now!" The voice was insistent, repeatedly saying it to others as they arrived and congregated outside his tent.

Townsend towelled his face quickly and pulled up his braces. Then, donning his shirt, he left the tent, still doing up his buttons. "Yes! What's wrong?"

"It's the prisoner, sir; he's dead. Someone killed him during the night."

"What?" he exclaimed, astonished. "Show me."

He followed the man back to the guardroom. Once inside, the crime was there for all to see: the victim still had that surprised look on his face as he lay there, his life's blood having drained away into a congealed pool on the floor next to his body. Townsend saw that someone had stabbed him – and used brutal force to do it! "Was nothing heard? Was the guard asleep or something?"

"No, sir," replied the corporal briskly. "The guard was changed twice in the night. Neither of them heard a thing. It could have happened at any time."

"Get this place cleaned up and have the body taken out and buried as soon as possible," Townsend instructed. "And someone tell Captain Marsh I would like to see him in my tent at once."

"Yes, sir."

A few minutes later, Marsh entered the tent. Townsend was seated, spinning the handle of his dagger on his desk, deep in thought.

"You wanted to see me, Robert?"

"Ah, David, come in. Have you heard what happened last night?"

"Yes, I went to see him: he's not a pretty sight."

"It means we have a killer in the camp. Someone did not want him to talk."

Marsh gaped at him. "Surely not any of our men, Robert? It can only be one of the labourers working for Galea, although we have no evidence..."

"My thinking exactly," Townsend agreed. "It would not be any of the ladies, either! It took brute strength to do that to a man, so we must keep our wits about us and keep watch until Galea, and his men, have gone from here."

"His workforce consists of some friendly locals, although there are a few dubious and unsavoury characters too, Robert."

"I agree. What has happened here is a grave matter, and we must always be wary." Townsend sighed. "I'm about to write up a report on the incident now. I will also have to speak to Galea about it and see if he has any thoughts on who could be responsible for the deed. Right," he said, clapping both hands together, "back to other business, David. Victoria arrives today – this afternoon, to be precise. You're not the only man in need of female company, you know!"

"I'm glad to hear it, Robert. I was beginning to worry about you, I admit. Is she travelling back with the supplies wagon? I saw the extra men with it when it pulled out yesterday. Now I know the reason."

167

Townsend nodded. "I want my wife to arrive here safely, David. I've given specific orders to ride back carefully and carry plenty of water. Also, to allow comfort stops for stretching her legs, because she won't be used to the hard wooden bench seat in the wagon – and, besides, she's pregnant. She is in no way a hardy woman in the military sense, though I'm sure she will prove me wrong; she usually does. I suppose I'm beginning to sound like an old woman myself now. She's told me I do at times."

"Well, you have a right to worry for her safety," Marsh told him. "Has the cabin been made ready? She will want to see it for herself when she gets here."

"Yes, it has," Townsend replied. "One of the ladies here will undoubtedly help with the finishing touches and the sensitive feminine things she will need. Also, I need someone to show her the running of the camp – Sally, the head cook, would be ideal. After all, she is taking over her role of ordering fresh stock and replenishing other used stores."

They then heard the guard outside shout: "Rider approaching, inform the major!"

Dismounting, and with his helmet held under his arm, the dispatch rider handed over his message. "Orders for Major Townsend from Brigadier Parker. Urgent dispatches. I am to return with your reply after deliberations, sir."

"At ease, soldier. Whatever it is, it must be too important to send by semaphore." Townsend cast his eyes over the soldiers milling around them. "Will someone see that this man is suitably refreshed with any food and drink he needs? And then have a fresh horse at his disposal." He turned back to face the rider. "I'll give you my answer shortly."

"Yes, sir." The dispatch rider was then led away to the cookhouse.

Returning to the tent, Townsend opened the heavily sealed envelope and read the contents. "Crikey!" he exclaimed. "It's here, Captain Marsh. It's here in the harbour. At last!"

"When did it arrive?"

"It's been under heavy guard at the docks for the last two days and will arrive here in another two – after a barge is made, ready to bring it." Parting the tent flap, Townsend ordered: "Soldier! Find Major Carter and Captain Hill. Tell them to stop what they're doing. I wish to see them here now."

"Yes, sir. Right away."

The meeting was convened and went on for over an hour, with strict instructions not to be disturbed. Now that the gun had arrived, they needed to urgently re-prioritise everything to accommodate it.

When the meeting finally ended, Townsend had the dispatch rider summoned and gave him his written reply to Brigadier Parker's message. Also, he gave him another short note to take with him. "You are to give this note to Mrs Townsend. You'll encounter her on the way back – she'll be with the supplies wagon. Do not get them mixed up, soldier. I do not know the brigadier on a personal level and do not wish to," he said jokingly.

"I'll try not to, sir," the dispatch rider said, chuckling at the ridiculous assumption – knowing full well the meaning of his words.

"Then you are free to go when ready."

He saluted the commander before mounting his fresh horse and galloping out of the camp, mentally pacing himself for the journey back. Within an hour's ride, he came across the covered supply wagon bumping along the rough track with its mounted guard.

"Whoa, there!" shouted the driver, pulling on the reins and bringing the horses to a halt beside the courier.

"Is Major Townsend's wife inside the wagon, Corporal?"

Before he could answer, a voice inside replied, "Yes, here I am." It was Victoria, seated behind Collins, in the wagon's shade and out of the glare of the full sun.

"A letter from the major," he said, handing it over. He then saluted and rode on.

Opening the letter, she found it contained just the three words: 'I love you.' "Oh, how sweet and typical of Robert!" she exclaimed.

Her travelling companion moved to her side. The two women were engaged in well-mannered gossip when the rider stopped them. Her companion frowned, leaving Victoria perplexed.

"Victoria, did he say your name is Townsend? Mrs Robert Townsend?" she asked.

"Yes, why?"

"Is he with a certain David Marsh?"

"Yes, he is. Why do you ask, Sarah?"

Her companion's face fell. "Oh, Victoria, I find this hard to tell you. It's embarrassing, really, and I'm beginning to wish I had never volunteered to come out here!"

"Well, you must, Sarah, and I insist you tell me. It's not about Robert, is it?"

As Victoria finished the sentence, a wheel jolted against a jutting rock in the ground. It shook the wagon hard, causing Sarah to cling to the inside while Victoria grabbed for the rear of the bench seat to steady herself.

The driver called out to them, "Are you two all right back there? I couldn't avoid that one, ladies."

"Yes, yes, driver, but please have care, will you?"

They settled back down again as the wagon and horses tackled the rock-strewn track.

"Carry on, Sarah – you were beginning to say something," said Victoria, smoothing down her layered dress.

"Well, I met both Robert and David in Newcastle. David flirted with me, and we had that extra bit of fun together, if you understand my meaning?" She began to blush.

Victoria offered her an understanding smile. "I do – and having met Captain Marsh, I'm not overly surprised. He has such a charming manner, and my husband trusts him completely."

"I was told they were both recalled to Woolwich, and I didn't believe it. David had broken my heart, and as soon as my father recovered from his injury, I went back to finish my last year of student nursing at the Florence Nightingale Training School for Nurses in London." She smiled unexpectedly. "The course was wonderful. I learned all sorts of things – bandaging, conventional medical instruments, and a good grounding in anatomy, medicine, and surgery. My tutors also encouraged gentleness, respectability, responsibility, and – of course –cleanliness."

"But why nursing?" Victoria asked, intrigued. "It's a noble profession, but one of my friends told me it can be very disorganised at times."

"That's all changing, Victoria," Sarah assured her with enthusiasm. "Have you heard of the Lady with the Lamp?"

"Florence Nightingale?"

"Yes!" Sarah exclaimed. Her facial features became animated with the passion of her chosen calling. "I've so admired Florence Nightingale for the care and compassion she brought to nursing. I feel the same as her and want to help anyone unfortunate enough to fall ill or injured. I have even bought two of the books she wrote along with me: *Notes on Nursing* and *Notes on Hospitals*, and I've read them through and through! Her influence means that a defined structure for nursing is emerging. It's setting new standards for cleanliness and reducing infections in areas such as orthopaedics, neonatal, and psychiatric nursing. Oh, I'm sorry," she added with a laugh. "I do rattle on when I get started on the subject, I'm afraid. At any rate, after qualifying, I volunteered as a military nurse here in Malta. A whole group of us came out here together."

"Not at all. One should be enthusiastic about one's passions!" Victoria was curious about this bright and ardent young woman so close to her age. "So, why Malta?"

"They said nurses were desperately needed because this is where many of our injured soldiers from the African war campaigns are brought to recuperate from their injuries and to restore their shattered minds before going home. You may have seen them yourself, convalescing in Valletta," she suggested. On seeing her new colleague's nod of agreement, she continued, "So, I thought: why not?"

"Have you just arrived here yourself, then, in Malta?"

"No, I came over by ship weeks ago – long before you and your husband – and I've been working at Valletta Military Hospital ever since," she told her. "A few days past, there was a request for a nurse to assist Doctor Charlton at Anchor Bay, and-" She shrugged, blushing. "I suppose I've made a name for myself, so the matron recommended me rather highly. I'm not sure if she thought I could handle the job or if she was just keen to see the back of me!"

Both women laughed at the thought.

"Either way, there's a real shortage of nurses, I can tell you. Fort Anchor sounded such a romantic name; I just couldn't resist it." Her face fell a little. "So, here I am, but I'm not sure what David will say. I can't believe this has happened, Victoria, I really can't! If I could return to Valletta right now, I would. I feel so embarrassed."

"Don't let it worry you, Sarah," Victoria assured her. "Just face him out if he asks. I'll back you up if need be. We women must stick together," she said confidently.

"Thank you," replied Sarah, looking much relieved. "Oh, I'm so glad to have met you!"

"As am I – ooh!" cried Victoria as the wheels glanced off another rock, jolting and jarring them yet again.

Aware of their discomfort, Collins stopped the horses. Then, pulling open the canvas curtain that separated them, he said, "We are stopping here at the stream for a break and to give the horses and yourselves a much-needed rest, ladies. Give me your hands when I come to the back, and I'll help you both down."

During the remainder of the journey, Sarah explained the rest of the saga, amusing Victoria with her new-found and extensive knowledge of pigeons. While they talked, she helped keep her cool with a cold-water flannel to her brow, for which Victoria was grateful. Victoria had dressed cleverly to look suitable for her husband, only for the garments to become uncomfortably hot in the baking heat of the day. She had a mild suspicion that Sarah, as a nurse, had guessed at her condition, but she elected not to mention it to her for a few moments until she'd thought more of her predicament.

Eventually, the small party arrived at the fort, confirmed by the Corporal's shout of greeting and the guard's subsequent reply: "Provision detail approaching. Inform the major!" It was late afternoon as the wagon trundled into the camp, with the armed guard heading off to take care of the horses.

Victoria couldn't stop smiling when she caught sight of her husband, waiting to greet her at the command post.

Corporal Collins saluted and declared, "Mrs Townsend safely delivered, sir."

"Thank you, Collins," said Townsend as he took her by the hand and helped her down from the back of the wagon.

Victoria looked beautiful in her pale mint green outfit, and she could tell he was eager to say so, but not here: he had to maintain his professionalism in front of his men. However, he kept hold of her hand, and she forbore from flinging her arms around his neck.

"Hello, Robert. It's good to see you at last," she said knowingly as she forcefully pulled her hand away from his.

Standing with his back to the wagon, he whispered, "My, you're as pretty as ever, darling."

"Thank you, Robert," she replied, slightly embarrassed but aware that the wink meant he was secretly up to something. "You're not so bad yourself, although it's only been just over a week and a half since we last saw each other!" she added, her tone of voice warning him off.

"May I also present Miss Cummings," said Collins. "She's come from Valletta to–"

"Who did you say, Corporal?" Townsend interrupted, surprised.

A voice behind him spoke. "Hello, Robert."

Victoria watched as her husband spun around and stared at Sarah in shock. "Sarah!" he spluttered. "I can't believe it. What are you doing here?"

"I've come to assist Doctor Charlton as his nurse," said Sarah, unflustered. "Unless you want me to go back to Valletta. If so, I will return as soon as possible."

And if you do, I'll have a thing or two to say to you, thought Victoria.

But Robert quickly recovered. "No! No, of course not. Welcome – welcome to you both."

Taking a lady on each arm – and rewarded by a broad smile from both – he escorted them into the tent and out of the overbearing sun.

"Mrs Townsend tells me you're the commander here," said Sarah once they were inside. "You were just a captain the last time we met, and look at you now. A major, no less. Congratulations, Robert."

"Thank you," said Townsend politely.

He looks uncomfortable, Victoria thought, *and no wonder, given Sarah's story of what happened in Newcastle. But he is hiding it well.*

"Where's David?" Sarah asked simply.

"He's in the fort somewhere," Robert told her, flashing her a sardonic smile. "No doubt getting in everyone's way as usual."

"No doubt," said Sarah, responding to the thought with a broad smile.

With all the awkwardness between them forgotten after Robert's amusing remark, the three began talking like old friends. Once they were suitably relaxed, Victoria turned the conversation to more practical matters.

"Right, then, Robert, will you show me where we'll be living?" she asked. "Sarah is to come with us too."

Robert looked perplexed. "I don't understand!"

"Well, you told me we had a spare room in the cabin, so I've asked Sarah to stay with us, if that's agreeable with you?"

Townsend kept quiet, and Victoria tutted. "Oh, don't be silly, Robert. I'm pregnant, thanks to your efforts, and because she's a nurse, it makes sense to have Sarah at hand in case of any little emergencies. She has kindly offered to assist me when required. Do you agree, Robert?" She asked this question with a knuckled hand on her hip, daring him to disagree.

Wisely, he decided discretion was required. "Looking at it like that, I suppose it does make sense, and we do have a spare room – although much smaller than ours. But my men must have the first call on her services, as with the doctor," he blustered, caught unawares.

"Of course, darling," agreed Victoria, placating him. "That's as it should be. You are the commander here, after all. Now, let's see where we will be living."

Robert took them to the cabin and showed them inside, pointing out the small wood-burning stove, handy for colder nights.

Victoria looked around her, inspecting it, and eventually nodded, satisfied. "It's sparse but comfortable and clean enough," she declared. "I've brought the curtains with me, Robert. I'll have them up tomorrow, and it should make a big difference. More homely, I should say." Then, pulling a face and frowning, she loudly exclaimed, "But Robert, where is the kitchen? How am I to cook? They have forgotten the kitchen!" she cried in anguish, both hands pressed to her cheeks as she looked forlornly around her.

Her husband chuckled. "Why do you need a kitchen? There's a whole cookhouse nearby. What more could you want? You won't be cooking while you are out here."

"Oh! Oh, of course!" She laughed, along with Sarah, at the absurdity of her thinking. "I'm sorry, it must have been the journey – all those jolts in the wagon have temporarily addled my brain!"

"I know the remedy for that," Sarah declared. "A good cup of tea!"

"The wonders of nursing school!" Robert teased, but there was no malice in it. "Look, Sarah – you and Victoria unpack. I will have your baggage brought in by the men. I want to tell Doctor Charlton you're here. I'll also have a word with Cook and ask her to send something over for us to eat tonight."

"What about David?" asked Sarah quickly, not wanting him forgotten.

"I'll ask him over to dine, too, but I won't say anything about you," he assured her. "Gosh, what will he say and do when you appear?! He went back to Newcastle looking for you, you know."

Sarah gasped. "No, I didn't know," she insisted. "I thought it done with and forgotten about."

Robert was about to reassure her further, but Victoria laid a gentle hand on his arm and shook her head to deter him. Wisely, he left them to their unpacking and each other's counsel.

***

Marsh duly arrived outside the cabin at the appointed time, smartly returning the salute of the sentry positioned nearby before rapping on the cabin door. He had made a genuine attempt to look smart for Victoria, with his hair slicked down and his tunic buttons cleaned and polished. He had initially thought his friend a fool for marrying but, having met the lady, he had formed a favourable impression of her – and, after Newcastle, he fancied he could almost see the attraction of settling down. An evening with a pretty lady, a drink, a meal – and all in good company – was as good as it got. Therefore, his mood was high as Townsend opened the door and ushered him in.

"You made an effort, I see," he remarked, looking him over. "We are in here, so come on through."

"Hello, David. It's good to see you again," Victoria began, rising from her seat as soon as she saw him.

He placed both hands on her shoulders and kissed her once on each cheek. "Hello, Victoria. You found us at long last. My, it's good to have more gentle, feminine company amongst us. Both Robert and myself would like to know how you two have been getting on," he said, pointing to her abdomen.

"Er, I told him about the baby," Robert replied in response to her dark look.

Victoria smiled. "I'll tell you over dinner. Now, you are to sit here next to me; Robert is to sit on my other side. Cook will bring our meals in now that you're here. I'm so hungry, aren't you?"

"Yes," he agreed. Looking at the table, he was puzzled by the extra place setting. "But who are you expecting? The table has been set for four."

Was it his imagination, or were Robert and his wife exchanging mischievous looks?

"Oh, er, Cook's coming now, David," said Townsend, nodding to the doorway behind him.

A familiar perfume filled his nostrils when 'Cook', standing behind him, leant across with his meal. He looked at Robert and then up into the face of the cook.

"Hello, David."

His jaw dropped as he gasped, feeling all the heat leave his body in shock. "Is that you, Sarah? I don't... er, I don't... b-believe it," he stammered.

"Yes, it's me," she said, noting the jolt it gave him.

"But – how?" With real effort, he managed to close his mouth. It had been quite some time since words had so utterly failed him.

"I'll explain over dinner," she promised. "It's an amazing string of coincidences. You won't believe it – I hardly do, myself."

Marsh listened, still shocked, until Sarah finished her story and then expertly steered the conversation away from herself and over towards Victoria. Marsh let them talk, still digesting the sudden reappearance of the woman who had haunted his thoughts since leaving Newcastle. He could tell Townsend was keeping a close eye on him, so he gave him a weak smile, letting him know he was all right with this sudden shift in circumstances.

"So, how long will it be before Fort Anchor is operational, Robert?" Sarah asked.

"Oh, not for many weeks yet," he replied. "Not until the gun is sitting on its firing platform and fully commissioned to our satisfaction. Then the camp goes, leaving a selected crew to man the garrison's battery. Everyone else will have to leave, including the cook. Victoria, you will return to Valletta to have our baby, along with Doctor Charlton and Sarah. Unfortunately, there will be no protection for anyone outside Fort Anchor. The governor's wife assures me that she will help take good care of Victoria's needs when the time comes."

"But Robert, the gun won't be here for a long time yet, will it?" Victoria asked, concerned.

Placing his hand over hers on the tabletop, he looked at her and said, "Darling, it's already here, carried into Valletta Harbour on the good ship

Stanley, where it's been under heavy guard. I'm afraid it will be brought here by barge the day after tomorrow. Major Carter estimates it will be another seventy days or so to get it up here. So, I'm afraid your stay will be rather limited – although there will be enough time for everyone to appreciate your efforts, no doubt."

Sarah seemed to sense Victoria's disappointment. "They told me I'd be here temporarily, too," she put in. "That's one of the reasons I volunteered to come out here in the first place, knowing it wasn't permanent. From what you told me, Victoria, you'll be seven months into your pregnancy by then, so you should be able to travel back to Valletta in comfort when it's time to go. And Valletta's a lot closer than England."

"At a push," said Marsh, eliciting giggles from the ladies. When the amusement subsided, a little sadness crept into his voice. "Well, I think it's time to get going. I must do the rounds tonight, as our glorious leader is temporarily indisposed. Thank you for inviting me, Victoria. I did enjoy the meal, and it's been a pleasure seeing you again."

Sarah rose from the table after David. "I'll, er, walk you to the door, David. I ought to apologise for shocking you the way I have."

They stood outside the doorway, staring up at the clear night sky. Sarah leant back against the cabin wall with both hands clasped together behind her back.

He couldn't help but gaze at her. "You look more beautiful than ever, Sarah."

Sarah held her tongue, perhaps remembering how he'd left her.

"Tell me the truth," he said at last. "Did you purposely come out here looking for me?"

Sarah's face clouded as she scoffed. "Ha! Don't flatter yourself, David. I left England to forget you, not to bloody find you! If someone had told me you were here, I would never have come, I swear," she informed him with bitterness in her voice.

David hung his head, knowing now how deeply hurt she was. She had been little more than a conquest when they first met, but how quickly his feelings had changed after being forced into leaving her!

"Look, I am sorry for everything," he said quietly. "I was an utter cad."

Sarah tutted at the suggestion but didn't reply.

He glanced at her stern face and, wanting to see her smile again, he cheekily asked, "You can walk me to my cold, sparse tent if you want? Then I can walk *you* back to make sure you arrive safely."

"Huh, safe with you?" she huffed, not seeing his intended sense of fun.

There was just something about the set of her mouth that gave him hope. She still held feelings for him, somewhere deep inside her, and now he knew it.

Sarah looked him straight in the face, trying to gauge his true feelings, but unfortunately, he was wearing a cheeky grin, which gave her the wrong impression. She folded both her arms together, putting up an invisible shield against his advances.

"Oh no you don't, David. I'm not falling for that again. If that was some sort of joke, I'm not laughing."

With that Sarah stepped inside, firmly closing the door on him. Then, standing indoors with her back pressed against the door, she wistfully reflected on his clumsy attempt to charm her again – which had nearly worked, to her mild annoyance. A secretive smile formed on her face, acknowledging that at least his brazenness made his advances easier to recognise and guard against. Not that she entirely wanted to.

He did look good in that uniform, she thought. Shaking her head at herself for her mixed thoughts, Sarah went back to the others, only to find that Robert had left the room.

"Oh, Sarah, while you meet the good doctor tomorrow, Robert has arranged for someone to take me around the camp. He thinks I should introduce myself as soon as possible to the ladies here and establish my authority. It's exciting, don't you think?"

"Of course!" Sarah replied. "They are your responsibility now. Are you to do any cooking or repairing clothes yourself?"

"Oh, no, I won't be doing any of that, although I'm well capable," Victoria assured her. "No, my role is in a supervisory capacity, managing the ladies and suchlike. Robert suspects one or two of them are providing the men with things they shouldn't, and he wants me to find out." She and Sarah shared a look of amusement. "That would most likely make an interesting story for a good gossip afterwards," she continued. "One of my main jobs is to order the supplies and provisions for the cook. Robert tells me it's becoming too difficult for her due to the rapid comings and goings of the soldiers at the camp; she needs to focus solely on running the cookhouse."

"I suppose I must call you madam now, then?" Sarah said playfully.

"Don't be silly!" Victoria laughed. "Gosh, it makes me sound quite ancient. Just bend at the knee; I'm sure that will suffice."

The women giggled loudly, already fast friends.

***

Marsh took a slow walk around the camp, offering a salute back to any guard he passed. He still couldn't believe Sarah had been leaning over him, serving his meal. *Had she deliberately set out to find me? Was it really just a coincidence, her turning up here of all places? She said she hadn't sought me out, but ought I believe her?*

His head was swimming with doubts and unanswered questions by the time he came across Molly, sitting between two oil lamps and using a needle and thread on a damaged shirt sleeve. "Hello, Molly. Keeping busy, I see."

"Hello, Captain Marsh," she replied, then narrowed her eyes suspiciously. "What are you doing wandering over here at this late hour?"

"No reason," he said – for once, quite honestly. "The camp is so peaceful I thought I would take a stroll. Besides, Molly, we've not spoken since–" He paused and smiled. "Are you and Captain Hill still together?"

"Yes, we are, although he can be rough with me at times."

"I wasn't, I suppose?"

"You were different," she replied. "With you, I felt a sense of duty to help after the sad story the commander told me. He nearly had me in tears and I pitied you. Although you were a little rough with me at first, I enjoyed it because I knew there was desperation involved. You were much more considerate after that first time. You told me you felt all your birthdays had come at once."

"Did I say that, Molly?" he asked, laughing.

"See, you can't remember that, even!" She shook her head, amused. "I knew it had befuddled your mind. I said it was plain greed – and I was right," she added knowingly.

"Be quiet, Molly!" he hissed. "Otherwise, the whole camp will hear."

Molly – wearing her signature loose, excellently flattering blouse beneath her dress –made a great play of leaning forward to put the needle and thread down, giving him a lingering look at her breasts. She deliberately held her stance, ensuring he had seen them, before lowering her voice to a silky whisper. "Are these what you want? If so, you can have them. Are they what you want, David? I said you can if you want to. Front and back, as you desire, with no charge. It would be my pleasure," she added, teasing him without a second thought.

Damn! What should I do? he pondered. *I'd like to put her over my shoulder now and carry her off to my tent. Her tits are gorgeous. Aargh! What am I to do? No. Captain Hill is nearby. I can't! He outranks me, and that would make things most awkward between us.* Then his thoughts turned to Sarah, and his love for her came rushing back. "You know, I want to, Molly, but not tonight," he told her. "Remember what you said to me about being greedy and the rest of it?"

"Yes, you were," she said, still purring. "Not that I'm complaining now, David."

"Well, I think you were right," he admitted. "I'm beginning to see it now, so I'd like to do something to show you my appreciation for coming to me in my desperation. You had a lot to put up with, after all."

"I handled it alright, I thought," she said, a little confused as to what direction the conversation was going.

"You certainly did, Molly, and I would like to give you this extra pound to show my complete satisfaction."

Molly frowned, perplexed. "Thank you," she said, taking the money off him. "You don't want anything more of me tonight, then? Are you sure? I found you such good fun too. I can be persuaded if you try, Captain."

"You are very desirable, but not tonight, Molly," he said with a hurt smile. "I'm tired, so I've decided to be a good little soldier and turn in. No naughty thoughts, nothing."

"Oh, very well, then. Goodnight," she said, bewildered.

"Goodnight, Molly." He walked off, wondering if he was doing the right thing. *Would I regret not taking advantage after she so graciously offered it?* he thought as he made his way back.

But, of course, there was Sarah to think of.

***

Townsend walked back into the main room of the cabin, where the ladies were amusing each other with anecdotes. Looking up, Sarah mused upon the difference in him, dressed in his splendid commander's uniform and the authority he wielded wearing it. He was seemingly more focused and more mature now than the man she'd met in the Blue Boar. To his credit, although the responsibility of his command was ever-present, he'd shown none of his new-found power or authority while talking to his wife and friends.

Pomposity is undoubtedly not one of his vices, she reasoned.

"I have been in the bedroom, Sarah, to check the bed was correct," he told her. "Taking care of minor details does not come naturally to my men, I'm afraid."

She chuckled. "Thank you, Robert, you are so kind."

Victoria stood up and stretched. "Come, Sarah, we'll sort out the blankets for the beds, and give them a good shake."

Entering the bedroom, Sarah remarked on how handsome Robert was in his uniform.

"Why thank you," said Victoria, with a pretty smile. "I think so too. He carries his responsibilities very well, and I'm so proud of him." Then she put her head to one side, fixing Sarah with a piercing stare. "Captain Marsh cuts a dashing figure too, don't you think?"

Sarah thought long and hard about the question before the slightly tense silence was broken. "It remains to be seen, Victoria. I would rather not say what I think of him right now. I was younger and naïve when I fell in love with him that first night, but I don't feel it's in a man to change his ways as much as I'd hoped David might."

Realising David had hurt her most deeply somehow or other, Victoria made a mental note to ask Robert about it. Perhaps he could explain the story's finer details to her.

Chapter 15

Sergeant major Horrocks taking drill and bayonet practise

THE BUGLER sounded his regular wake-up call, comically followed by the howling of the dogs. Then the order to the cookhouse was made – but today, it was to be different. Everyone in camp was made aware that the gun was at Grand Harbour and would arrive the following day. Real excitement ran throughout the campsite, even affecting the overwrought bugler, who had blown the call with zest, ignoring his canine hecklers. At last, after many months of demanding work and sweat spent, they were eager to see what it had all been for.

The surgeon, Doctor Charlton, visited the cabin to meet Mrs Townsend and his long-awaited nurse. A thoughtful, military man nearing middle age, he presented himself politely to the camp's newest inhabitants.

After a brief interview, he declared himself delighted to find Sarah qualified for all the tasks required of her. Her maternity expertise from her time spent in the new Military Nursing Service was a bonus, considering how many women worked in the camp.

He and Sarah escorted Victoria over to the cookhouse to make the head cook Sally's acquaintance. Leaving her there, they carried on to the surgery, where they would be working together.

"Well, here we are, Sarah," he said, showing her around. "What do you think of it? You'll find that most of our patients over the coming days will have aches, sprains, and bruises from getting the gun up here – as well as bruises to their egos, I'll wager! It's where a nurse such as yourself can play a big part. Treating their injuries is half the battle, but showing concern and expressing sympathy from a lady can do wonders in getting them back out where they're most needed: on that gun. Occasionally, though, we may have to deal with crushed limbs and such. Still, we should manage between us, and any we can't deal with will be sent to Valletta for treatment as soon as possible. We shouldn't see battle wounds, with any luck, but one must always be prepared for it in the military. Can our small team cope, Sarah? What do you say?"

"Of course, Doctor," she replied at once. "I find it so exciting being here, knowing what's about to happen at the fort. I deem it an honour to play a small part in it with you, sir."

"That's just the response I was expecting," he replied, delighted. "Well said! I feel, working together, we should make an effective team. Do you agree?"

Sarah smiled, and nodded back. She was ready to get to work as soon as she was needed.

***

On the perimeter of the camp, Sergeant Major Horrocks was taking drill with the men of the Royal Engineers. His booming voice could be heard clearly by everyone assembled – and several further afield! 'Horrible Horrocks' was the nickname given to him by the men, though never used to his face. But he knew, of course, and took the moniker as a point of honour. In his opinion, if the troops liked him, something was very wrong. He was a burly, broad-shouldered man who had seen plenty of action in Africa and was not to be messed with.

He scrutinised the faces of all the men standing in front of him. "Right, men. Your marching over here wasn't pleasant to watch," he informed them, seeing several of their faces fall. "Shabby and undisciplined, if you ask me. But it must do for now, 'til I can get you all square-bashing again. We will get it right! Yes, you lot heard me: we will! I will not have slovenly, sloppy marching in any man I command." He paused, letting the statement sink in. "Now, as our little hands are heavily calloused and sore from building this fort, I have decided to find out if you lot have forgotten how to fight as much as you've forgotten how to march. So, in my wisdom – which I have in abundance – I have set up a little bayonet practice for you here in these most beautiful surroundings.

"Now, as you run around at a leisurely pace, you will be able to appreciate the lovely islands of Comino and Gozo in the distance," he continued, gesturing expansively across the azure sea. "I want you all to feel blessed at how lucky we are to be here. Right then! After I split you lot into groups, I shall stand over here, away from everyone, because I don't want to get hurt, intentionally or otherwise. Your section NCOs will be coaxing you – verbally, at all times – to put on a little show just for me!"

He then quickly split the men into four groups of fifteen, one group for each hanging straw sack, and each with a non-commissioned officer to shout encouragement of sorts to any strugglers. Stepping well back, out of the way, he politely said, "Carry on, gentlemen."

"Attention!"

Loud stamping of feet greeted the order.

"Shoulder, arms!" bawled the section NCOs. "Present arms and fix bayonets! On order, charge, and stick enemy! On order: *Charge!*"

The first four men ran over and put their bayonets clean through the sacks of straw, shouting and screaming as they did so. Then, twisting them to enable withdrawal, they ran back to their position in the group. The second four men then ran over and did the same, repeating it down the line, until the last four had completed the exercise.

Upon finishing, the men were ordered to attention once more. The Sergeant Major then strode purposefully in front of them. "Well, how am I to describe that?" he barked. "Some of you were truly frightening, and I'm truly blessed to be on the same side as you. Some were bloody scary, and there's no doubt about that – they bloody scared me, all right. I shall be looking under my bed tonight! Some, however, were more interested in the lovely scenery they have here, and some looked as if they were out catching fucking butterflies!"

Laughter rippled through the gathered ranks.

"Shut up, you lot," came his direct order, with real menace behind it. "There's always one, isn't there? There's always one that takes the queen's shilling under false pretences. But in this case, there's half a bloody dozen. Prosser, we know about your impediment, don't we? It's not your dick you're holding and thrusting with both hands – it's a fucking rifle and bayonet, with a pointy bit at the end! Bailey, you're no fucking better! I want more shouting and screaming from you. Don't worry about waking the neighbours; we have none! We need to confuse the enemy with our strength and bad temper – not ourselves. You there, Hart! I don't like that bit of skipping you do before slapping the sack. You will stop that, Hart?"

"Yes, Sergeant Major."

"You can see those actions anytime down the bloody Edgeware Road. I will not stand for it while you are under my command! Do I make myself clear, Hart?"

"Yes, Sergeant Major," the man answered, more timidly this time.

"Corporal, you will dismiss the men – apart from these three," he ordered. "They will be made to practise and practise until *you* are blue in the face. I want them screaming and shouting. I want them lunging and plunging. I want them to stick and twist. But primarily, I want real hate shown towards the enemy: those sacks over there! I do not want airy-fairy

Nancy-boys in my army. Then, when you think you have somehow got them up to scratch, I want you to tell me so I can see for myself."

"Yes, Sergeant Major, they will be."

"Good! You know where to find me. Carry on."

There followed a half-hour session of intensive training. Most of those watching swore the NCOs conducted it with hate in their hearts, encouraging the men into screaming profanities, sticking, running, and sticking more. By the end of it, two of the three men had worked themselves up into such a frenzied state they screamed out loud, running back and away from the straw sacks until they had to be calmed down.

Finally thinking he could do no more with them, the corporal summoned the sergeant major, who returned from his harassment of other hapless troops.

"So, they are ready, are they? They are ready to show me what real soldiers are capable of doing?" He walked behind them, looking over each of their shoulders as he passed by. "Are you ready, Prosser?"

"Yes, Sergeant Major."

"Are you ready, Bailey?"

"Yes, Sergeant Major."

"Are you ready, Hart?" He waited. "Hart! I said, are you ready?"

"Yes, Sergeant Major," Hart growled back, his upper lip curled and determined.

"Right! Starting with Prosser, then Bailey, then finally Hart. Start them off, Corporal."

"Attention!"

The men stood stiff and upright.

"Shoulder arms! Present arms! Fix bayonets! On my order, charge, and stick enemy. On order: Charge!"

Prosser ran up, feeling thigh sore from the continual slap of his impediment. Sounding like something demented, he stuck the targeted sack of straw and then twisted the bayonet before withdrawing it smoothly. Bailey followed next with a similar demonstration. Hart then ran forward, screaming like a banshee, and stuck the battered sack of straw. He pushed the bayonet in once, then in further, toppling the hessian sacking from its frame and spilling the straw contents onto the floor. Holding his stance and growling for longer than was necessarily healthy, he twisted the bayonet and withdrew it while continuing to shout and whoop unconvincingly back to the others.

"Attention!" shouted the NCO. The order stopped the sniggering and brought them upright.

The sergeant major complimented them, saying, "Excellent, I'm impressed. You must now keep up that level of aggression." Feeling slightly uneasy with Hart and his performance – though it was much improved – the sergeant major sniffed then asked, "Tell me, Hart, when you stuck that thing, and you killed it, why did you push even more until you destroyed it? It's of no bloody use now! You've ruined it!"

"I hated him after he said you were ugly and horrible, sir."

The sergeant major looked at his NCOs, then back at Hart, then back to his smirking NCOs. He looked at Hart once more and then shouted, "Get this man to the washroom for a cool washdown. He's got bloody sunstroke. Get him away now!"

"Yes, Sergeant Major. It will be a pleasure."

The NCOs marched Hart off to the men's washroom, where they ordered him to strip. But instead of the cooling waters he was expecting, they threw buckets of chilled water over him for their depraved amusement. It was payback for the rollicking they kept receiving because of him.

***

Extra men were brought into the camp throughout the next few days, ready to assist the Royal Engineers once the cannon was ashore. It quickly turned into a logistical nightmare for Victoria and the cooks but somehow they coped, planning extra trips to Valletta for more supplies. It was something of a confusing initiation for the commander's wife.

First-class reports were beginning to filter back to Townsend concerning big Ned Savage, who was moderating his drinking somewhat. Clearly, Ned was also good at man management; therefore, Townsend had no qualms calling the man in to see him and giving him back his stripes. The ratio of men to NCOs showed he was a sergeant down. As Ned was now beginning to control his drinking – repaying the faith Captain Marsh had shown in him – and because Townsend was impressed with his improved attitude, he invited him to be a permanent member of his garrison.

He felt men such as Savage would be sorely needed over the coming weeks to get the gun up where it was needed – inside the fort. He required men of determination and leadership, ready to drive the gang forward, exercise sheer brute force, and overcome any obstacles they encountered. Savage had all the necessary requirements.

Meanwhile, all talk around the camp concentrated on just one topic: the gun.

***

When the time finally came, the steam-driven barge announced its presence in the bay below, with shrill blasts on the steam whistle that everyone in the camp above clearly heard. The vessel's skipper played on the steam whistle again, switching it on and off several more times to ensure everyone knew they were there.

Many non-military personnel were thrilled; they took themselves off to the cliffs with drinks and sustenance to sit and watch the unloading. The news of the gun arriving also attracted small fishing boats and their crews across to the bay, and they too settled in for the spectacle.

Soon, it was time for the Royal Engineers to take centre stage as they busied themselves with the complexities of safely offloading the precious cargo. In a short while, the whole camp lined the brow of the hill above the bay, all eager to see how they would cope with moving the massive gun.

The skipper and crew expertly manoeuvred the vessel into the landing bay, where they moored it securely. The lifting gantry, with its large chains dangling from the hook, was then lowered into position above the barge, ready to start the lift when required. The tension began to rise amongst the onlookers above as they discussed how the engineers would make the lift and transfer the gun safely ashore.

Colonel Havers had travelled over with the gun from Valletta, bringing Mr Copperfield with him. On his previous visit, Copperfield had left specific instructions on the erection of the massive wooden beamed gantry and how to complete it. He was, therefore, pleased to find they had followed his guidance precisely, and he expected a clean lift.

Finally, the call went out: "In position and ready to lift, sir!"

"Thank you, Captain Hill. Get more men on board and help uncover the tarpaulin," ordered Major Carter. "I speak for everyone when I say we are all intrigued to see the thing."

"You won't be disappointed, Major. Neither will the onlookers," Havers promised.

The men pulled back the hefty tarpaulin sheet to expose the enormous cannon, and the whole crowd of onlookers gave out a collective gasp as they saw it. They had all heard the rumours about the weapon, but that was plain tittle-tattle compared to seeing it for real. Everyone agreed that they had never seen such an enormous armament before.

It was, indeed, a monster.

The engineers began to shackle it with heavy chains and guide ropes to lift and swing the gun as necessary. The trunnions – the gun's point of balance – had the heavy chains fitted over them and into the lifting gantry hooks. The half-ton balancing collar – only used for lifting –

stayed bolted onto the muzzle end to maintain an even balance at the trunnions.

Only when he was entirely satisfied did Mr Copperfield allow Major Carter to take over from him.

"Thank you, sir," said the major. "Captain Hill, get your men clear and start the lift."

"But take it slowly to begin with, if you will," insisted Mr Copperfield, concerned that they should test the gantry first.

"Yes, sir," replied Hill as he ordered his men to start the hoisting.

Given the weight of its extraordinary burden, the gantry frame's oak beams creaked alarmingly with the compression of the wood as the gun began to rise slowly from its cradle in the barge. As it did, the barge also began to rise, as if still attached.

Then, when the gun was fully liberated and raised clear, it left the barge riding freely on the undulating swell of the sea. Now the men on the guide ropes worked hard to hold it steady and stop it from swinging in the wind. All the men involved were fully aware that a load of such weight and proportion could easily damage the hoist's wooden structure if allowed to swing about uncontrolled.

The skipper, however, showed great concern for his barge floating free underneath it, knowing that if anything failed now, the gun would drop and smash its way right through his barge, sinking it. Worried it might do, he quickly steered it clear from below the enormous weight.

To keep time, a sailor sang the lyrics to a shanty work song while the rest of the crew sang the chorus, getting into a rhythm while lifting the load. The sailors encouraged the soldiers to join in as their muscles strained with the lift. Shirts, soon wet with sweat, clung to their backs while bent to the bars of the capstan.

With each chorus sung, the men put on a fresh push to raise the gun higher. Slowly, the gun's incredible body was lifted clear and swung over to the landing bay. The tendency for it to swing in the wind and spin was again held in check by the men on the guide ropes.

Then, much to the men's relief, it was safely lowered onto a sturdy sleigh – purpose-built and sitting on metal rollers – before being unshackled from the chains that bound it.

With all military discipline forgotten, the crowd watched the arrival of this colossus; carried away with the day's excitement, they broke into a cheer as the chains came off.

Finally, after being loaded onto the sleigh, the half-ton collar was taken off, accompanied by yet more cheering. It spontaneously swept through the throng, as a large group of soldiers waved their helmets and hugged each other after safely getting it ashore.

The cannon was the reason for all the weeks of working in the scorching sun with blistered hands, but everyone felt it had been well worth it. They were tremendously proud of their country's achievements in manufacturing the gun – and of the small part they played themselves.

"Wow! It's like a giant bottle of beer," someone observed.

"If only it were," responded another, licking his lips at the ridiculous thought.

Townsend and Marsh, also standing on the cliffs, joined in with the general merriment as the spectacle unfolded below them. Having seen the gun several times, they felt no urgency to get themselves down there and so enjoyed the spectacle with the rest.

"It's here at last," said Marsh with a sigh. "Once we have it up here in the fort, I feel its presence should deter all but the foolhardy."

"Yes," Townsend agreed. "And it will soon be handed to us to begin ascending this little hill here. Then the real hard work begins, David."

Further up the hill, standing amongst the cookhouse staff, Victoria cast her eyes down to look at it herself. Initially, she had been curious to see why her husband and the other officers spoke so highly of the gun, but now – as she gasped with the rest at her first sight of it – she understood why.

Her casual gaze below then wandered over the heads of the crowd, gauging their reactions to the thrill of seeing it for the first time. She eventually settled on the sight of a swarthy gentleman standing apart from the rest, busily writing notes while watching both her husband and the scene taking place below him. Shielding her eyes from the incessant sun, Victoria recognised him as Galea, the man in charge of the work gangs, whom Sally had pointed out to her earlier. Something about him made her thumbs prick. *It is undoubtedly strange for him to be taking notes and not to seem as excited as the rest of them,* she thought.

Curious, she casually made her way over to him without him being aware of her standing there. "You take great interest in my husband, Mister Galea," she remarked.

"Huh, Madam Townsend!" he exclaimed, startled. He quickly pocketed his notes and took her hand. He kissed it gently and, looking directly into her eyes, replied, "Only to fathom out how he attracted such a beautiful woman as yourself. What is his allure? I ask myself."

He's obviously flirting with me, attempting to turn my head, and I want none of it. "You disrespect my husband, sir. Please, let my hand go," she said, pulling it away. "My husband has a quality you will never know and can only guess at." As she flounced away to continue with her duties, she was glad to be rid of his company, instantly disliking him and his silky chatter.

He, however, had enjoyed the encounter. His lustful eyes settled on Victoria's body until she'd passed out of sight. *You will change your attitude and disdain towards me once I have defeated your military – starting with your husband's command here in this very fort.*

At this thought, his lips curled in a cruel grimace of wry amusement.

***

Many of the onlookers descended the hill to the bay, following an irresistible urge to get down there for a closer look, touch the gun, and compare it in size to the cannons with which they were all familiar with.

Standing close, the sheer scale of it was even more astounding. The men stood around gaping as it towered above them while others just stared, transfixed in wonderment.

"They won't dare attack Malta now," said one, with deep satisfaction.

"Who won't?" asked a second.

"Any bugger, that's who!" cried the first man in delight.

"Why, it's even bigger than Prosser's weapon!" shouted a joker, causing much laughter and backslapping.

"That will stop him bragging, then, won't it?" said another, as they held on to their aching sides.

"Aye. There won't be any more bets to make easy money off the young ones. There'll be no more comparisons with weapons, not while this is here."

Major Carter and Captain Hill approached Townsend and Colonel Havers. "Major Townsend, I have the pleasure of handing over this powerful gun to you for safekeeping," Carter said with an air of joyous formality. "I'm not sorry to see it go, but I feel sure you will find an appropriate use for it," he grinned. "As for myself and Captain Hill, our task is nearly done. We will be leaving camp after this gantry is down and loaded back onto the barge. The smaller gantry will be enough for future deliveries here. The sergeant major will take over the task of getting it up to the fort for you. You will find his powers of persuasion most useful, no doubt, in these circumstances."

"Thank you, Major," said Townsend, shaking the man's hand. "All the shells, gunpowder, and the rest of the armoury – plus most of the provisions – can now be transported aboard the barge. There will be far less cause to use the wagon. I'm sure Collins will be pleased."

"Yes, everything will come here by barge, saving the arduous journey by wagon," confirmed Colonel Havers. "When the gun gets to the fort, a small detail of engineers will mount the gun on the traversing platform with you. The gantry will then get dismantled to join Mr Copperfield and me at the next fort."

"Thank you, Colonel. Sergeant, arrange for ten armed men to guard the cannon, with changeovers every four hours. This cannon is to be under constant, twenty-four-hour protection until we can safely get it into the fort. That will be all, sergeant."

Savage left them and walked away to enlist the ten guards he needed from the men watching the spectacle, all of whom were absorbed in the scene below. "You, men! Yes, you four, you four, and you two. I need all of you for guard duty throughout the night, down there at the gun. You are to be excused from all other duties. Get your rifles, men, and follow me down there."

They passed the smithy, Tom, at his forge. "Come and see the gun, Tommy lad! It's here!"

"I know, I can hear them," he retorted. "I had a look, but I can't go down now; I'm too busy. I'll see it soon enough! Right now, it's more important to finish this repair."

Tom was a large, muscled, salt-of-the-earth type who liked a gamble and, because of the forge's heat, was allowed extra rations of beer, for which he was most grateful. Working at his furnace, it soon got sweated out of him. The camp's blacksmith had seen his workload increase significantly in the run-up to the arrival of the big gun down below.

His orders were to check on suitable capstans and the array of various jacks to be used to move it up the hill; any broken or damaged would need repairing. He knew that any failure with his repairs could result in men losing their lives, so he didn't mess around. It was a critical job that had to be done as soon as possible, especially now that the gun was here. He knew, very soon, his handiwork would get thoroughly tested.

While he focused on the jacks and capstans, the jobs of fitting horseshoes and repairing wagon wheels – often damaged from the rough terrain – had fallen to his younger assistant, Arthur. Regular wheel inspection was essential, and Arthur had risen to the challenge. Often, a small crowd of idle soldiers would gather and watch him in amazement as he put his learned skills to the task of fitting new wheel bands alongside his mentor, Tom.

Tom saw no need to waste his wage on extra beer; instead, he would engineer a friendly argument over anything trivial and talk the man into challenging him after drinking a beer or two. If the man thought he was right, he should lift the anvil. If wrong, he would forfeit the beer after Tom raised it. The ploy worked well in Tom's favour with the continual changing of the men in camp. He often shared these extras with Arthur, whose part in the grand plan was to urge the soldiers to take Tom on.

Finally, the last of the soldiers began returning to camp. Nightfall had rapidly approached as the burnt orange sunset sank swiftly into the waters on the horizon.

The glow of the campfires in the night sky beyond the brow of the hill, and the rhythmic banging of Tom's hammer, was all they had to guide them back to camp. Reaching the top of the darkened hill, they could see Tom at his forge. He was hammering away with showers of sparks flying around him – the flashes lighting up the camp and throwing shadows onto the grey fort walls. Occasionally he stopped and doused the repair in water tubs he kept at hand, at which point the water bubbled under clouds of steam, sizzling and spitting.

"Are you not done yet, Tom?" one man called out as they passed by.

"Aye, I am now, lads," he replied, tired, while ineffectually wiping his sweating, soot-stained hands down his leather apron. "The gun won't be going anywhere; these jacks and capstans will see to it. I'd stake my life on it, lads."

Then he grinned and asked, "Any bets on it?"

Chapter 16

Ascending the hill to Fort Anchor.
The gun's first movements

TWO DAYS later – after sorting out some minor technical details – the four officers, along with Mr Copperfield and Colonel Havers, walked down the length of the unfinished roadway. To allay any possible fears, Major Carter pointed out what his engineers had done to help facilitate the raising of the gun.

"As you can see, gentlemen, we will have two capstans in use on each level. Hydraulic jacks are positioned and fitted top and bottom, on each level of the road, under the instruction of myself and Captain Hill.

"The capstans are to be used to move the gun upwards, while men on the heavy hydraulic jacks will force turn the gun on each corner and onto the next level. The ground has been cut back on each corner and flattened to allow the gun's muzzle to turn with it," he explained.

"I can see why we can't use our big boys; it's too steep!" exclaimed Marsh to everyone.

Resigned to the daunting task that lay ahead, Townsend agreed. "Our heavy horses are out of the question, Captain. I don't believe, even with those powerful beasts in tandem, it would be enough. Besides, I feel that forcing the horses to strain throughout each day would be cruel; therefore, we won't use them. So, it's down to raw muscle and mechanics to get the job done."

Major Carter nodded in agreement and continued, "The roadway consists of four continuous gradients, each made of a flat, solid road surface, skilfully prepared by my engineers under Lieutenant Berry's guidance. They have spent many hours getting the surface hard and flat to support the gun's weight. This will enable the rollers, positioned under the sleigh, to roll and function properly. We ensured each corner would have a thick metal plate sunk and set into the ground to brace the turning jacks. The capstans and jacks will not be enough to move the gun, so they will be used in conjunction with our men using crowbars and pull ropes." He nodded. "That's about it,

The 100-ton Armstrong gun with its half ton balancing collar, being unloaded at Malta Docks with the lifting derrick using hydraulic power.

The hundred-ton gun in transit.

gentlemen. We are now ready and eager to begin the move. The sergeant major has already informed his NCOs and the men on how we plan to do it."

"Splendid, Major. Let's get on with it then," urged Colonel Havers.

The gun sat on its sleigh at the base of the hill way below the fort, with heavy duty chains leading from it to the first capstan. Also attached to it were four thick, stout ropes. Each rope had a contingent of twenty men assigned to it – under the separate supervision of an NCO – ready to pull and guide the gun up each part of the hill with the aid of the capstan, which, on stopping, was to be locked off. Wedges would then be placed behind the rear rollers for safety, preventing the sleigh from slipping back. It was to be a significant operation.

Great excitement and expectation filled the air as the moment the supergun would start its epic climb neared. Some local Maltese stood about with other soldiers to witness the spectacle, swapping tobacco and comical quips.

"You've got no chance getting that up there!" one shouted.

"No, I haven't, but with these other lads pulling alongside me, it'll be in the fort by nightfall!" a soldier replied cheerfully, encouraging a throw of hands back towards him.

Others in the expectant crowd shouted encouragement to the teams of men as the time edged nearer.

Concluding his conversation with Copperfield and checking his pocket watch, Colonel Havers turned to face the commander, proclaiming: "Because the gun is in the care of the Royal Artillery, Major Townsend, you may have the honour of officially starting the move, sir. Then the capable Sergeant Major Horrocks will take over."

A hush fell across the scene as all eyes settled on the commander of Fort Anchor.

"Thank you, Colonel," he said as they saluted one another. Then, turning to look at the teams, he shouted, "Let's get this gun moving then, Sergeant Major. *Capstan ready?*"

"*Capstan ready, sir!*" he shouted back.

Looking over at the four sergeants in charge of the teams, Townsend bellowed, "*Sergeants ready?*"

"*Sergeants and teams ready, sir!*"

"On my orders, then. Altogether. *Heave!*"

The sleigh visibly moved but then stopped after two turns of the metal rollers.

"*Heave!*" ordered the NCOs as they took over. The sleigh moved again, then stopped. "*Heave!*" they ordered, and it shifted a little

195

further, only to halt yet again. *"Heave!"* came the order once more, but it wouldn't budge.

"Lock-off capstan and make safe," ordered Horrocks.

"Capstan locked off, Sergeant Major."

"Sergeant Savage, we need twenty more men to be positioned with another stout rope attached to the sleigh. Then, hopefully, we can get on with it," said Horrocks, somewhat exasperated and disappointed at the initial failure.

The extra men rushed in to attach the new rope. Finally, they were ready to go again.

"Right then, I want you to only listen to your team leader. We must pull together at the same time and on command. Shall we give it another go?"

Loud cheers of agreement went up from the ranks in response to the question, reverberating several times as an echo rolling over the hill and towards the camp.

"Capstan, ready?"

"Capstan ready, Sergeant Major."

"Sergeants and teams ready?"

"Sergeants and teams ready."

"On my orders, men. All together now, *heave!*"

"Heave!" shouted the NCOs.

With the men bracing themselves against the heavy load of the gun, it began to inch its way forward once more. The men at the sides and rear began levering furiously with crowbars to keep the sleigh travelling straight while the men on the ropes dug their heels hard into the ground. Any solid rut would do to support themselves and give them the leverage they needed to pull.

This time, the gun kept moving in a slow, deliberate trundle while the men on the capstan bent their backs to the wheel. A total of a hundred men were now being used on the ropes as the gun made its way from the landing site. However, the collective enthusiasm of the local crowd was still there and undiminished. They lined the hillside along the route the gun would take, encouraging and cheering the men on as they toiled away in the sunshine and heat of yet another glorious summer's day.

"Heave!" came the order, the men responding splendidly at each command.

In time, they began to slip into a routine of pull and rest, pull and rest, each of them intent on getting their pride and joy to the fort. Eventually, after an hour, Captain Marsh gave the order: "Lock-off capstan and make safe. Fit those wedges of wood under the rear rollers to prevent slipping back. Right then! Call the men to attention, Sergeant Savage."

"Yes, Captain. Attention!" he hollered.

Looking down over the heads of the soldiers gathered before him, Major Townsend called out from his vantage point, "Men! All of you will be pleased to know that we have moved the gun a total of twenty feet along the level in the last hour!"

Groans and moans came from the men after looking back and checking the distance for themselves.

"We cannot continue like this: it only moved four feet in the last fifteen minutes. What we do not want is any of you collapsing through exhaustion. However, we do have another plan. It will be in everyone's best interest to move the gun for forty minutes and rest for twenty each hour. In that time, you will be able to take refreshments from the water butts, use the latrines, or simply take a breather. It's crucial that anyone with injuries such as strains from pulling must immediately bring it to the attention of your section leaders, who will find a replacement." He gazed sternly down at them. "This is not a get-out for any malingerers amongst you, and you should know I will come down hard on anyone found doing so. The other thing you should know is that you will be required to be at your designated posts for the next pull. That, gentlemen, will start exactly on the hour, every hour, and woe betide anyone who is not in a position and ready to start on the whistle. It is most important that everyone knows the rules if we are to get this gun up there," he added, pointing towards the fort. "Is that clear?"

"Yes, sir," they chorused back at him.

"Good, then we all understand what must be done," he said. "We will have another hundred and twenty men on standby. One hundred of them will take over your duties tomorrow to allow you men to fully recover. We will then alternate the two groups of men every other day. The other twenty men will ensure we have adequate cover for any unfortunate injuries. That will enable us to pace ourselves sufficiently to keep the gun moving. All right, men, that's enough from me for now. We begin again on the hour."

Victoria had made a slow start at first with her duties in camp. After her baptism of fire reorganising the cookhouse schedule for the added workforce brought in, she began to relish her responsibilities. On discussing it with Sarah, she saw to it that regular supplies of cold drinking water were at hand in containers for the men on the day's slog. Physically pulling the gun all day in the heat would leave some spent and dehydrated, so plenty of water barrels – with cups attached – were essential. She knew herself that such a simple gesture would help breathe new life into tiring bodies.

When her premonition later proved true, Townsend began to warm to Victoria's foresight. It gave his men the strength and encouragement to carry on throughout the day.

The top of the hour soon drew near, and the NCOs blew their marshalling whistles to summon the men to their positions, ready for the next significant effort. They were given special permission to discard any clothing causing discomfort throughout the day, which resulted in large piles of tunics and helmets abandoned beside the roadway for recovery later.

After taking up position, and once the NCOs were satisfied, the sergeant major consulted his pocket watch and waited a few seconds. "Very well, men, on my orders. *Heave!*"

"*Heave!*" shouted the NCOs, and once again the gun moved off at a slow, laborious pace.

"*Heave!*" came the order again. The men responded with muscles and backs to the task, keeping it moving.

This work pattern continued for the next few days until, late one afternoon, they found themselves in the position to tackle the first gradient. The officers decided the day's toil should end at that point.

The capstan was locked off, with hammers again being used to drive large wooden wedges under the sleigh's rear rollers. With the cannon secured for another night, heavily armed soldiers were placed strategically around the gun. Simultaneously, those involved in pulling the weapon collected their uniforms and started dragging their tired bodies up the hill to camp.

As bedraggled groups of weary men moved towards the kitchens, some checked the new bruises and blisters they had collected from the day's toil. In contrast, some checked out their bruises and flaunted them like badges of honour. Others, who were more physically affected by the combined effort, took to emptying water over their heads and bodies to cool down their body heat and help them recover faster.

Each late afternoon, wives moved busily through the returning groups, asking if there were any repairs needed doing to clothing, or if there was anything that required washing. It was another way for the women to earn their keep, and it was not to be ignored or sniffed at; it was expected of them by the military in exchange for their food ration. Others tended to small cuts, bruises, and blisters – minor injuries not requiring a nurse or doctor. The ladies looking for work on passing also looked at some minor strains and aches. It never failed to amuse the officers how the women's hands had such a healing effect on the men.

Marsh had discovered that the question, "Is it sore, pet?" or even the words, "There, there," could often help instigate a quick recovery. The personal motherly concern they showed, rather than anything practical they did, assisted with the men's recovery – helping them to protect their masculinity.

Advancement up the hill towards the fort was painfully slow, and the men were beginning to lose the collective eagerness they had showed at the start of the climb. Townsend recognised that their enthusiasm was on the wane. So, to alleviate the physical boredom and lift the men's spirits, he ordered extra beer rations for anyone working with the gun each day, feeling they had earned it. It was a good move by Townsend, ensuring his men would all be keen to do their bit, if just for the ale. It also meant a comradely spirit grew between the officers and their men, which was necessary for everyone's welfare.

***

One such late afternoon, Victoria hurried through the returning throng to seek out her husband, who had informed her they were expecting dinner guests. She also caught the eye of Galea again, who smiled lecherously, then, on bowing deep, went on his way. Their chance meeting left her feeling cold, endorsing her first impression of him.

"How many are you inviting, so I can arrange it with the cook?" she asked, on finding his whereabouts.

"Oh, just Colonel Havers, Mr Copperfield, Sarah, and David. Maybe the doctor if he's not busy." He frowned. "Why? You look troubled."

"Not Galea, I hope?" she asked, pursing her lips. "Only, I caught him staring at you while you weren't looking when the gun first arrived, and I didn't like it. When he realised, I was watching him, he smirked and tried to flirt with me without reason. I found him charmless, false, and a little threatening – if I may say so, Robert."

"He bears a lot of responsibility, Victoria, and therefore, a measure of gruffness is understandable."

"Well, I would rather he did not attend, so that you know."

She left him to his reports, with which he busied himself until Marsh walked into the bell tent that served as the commander's office.

"Tell me, David, how did the men like the extra ration of drink?"

"A masterstroke, Robert. I'm glad I suggested it to you," he declared smugly – though he hadn't. "They will have earned every drop of the stuff by the time this little job's finished, I'll warrant."

Townsend chuckled. "I think we could do with a drop ourselves, don't you? Later, we will be playing host to Copperfield and Colonel Havers.

Victoria tells me the cook is baking something special for us. The colonel will be going to Fort Rinella tomorrow and then on to Fort Cambridge for a few days to sort out some new problems. Copperfield will go with him to make sure nothing impedes the other cannons' progress when the time comes. So, it's a farewell party of sorts."

"Isn't he supposed to oversee the gantry's dismantling, Robert?"

"No, Copperfield's biggest worry was the erection of it. He is the expert in all of this," Townsend reminded him. "He seems happy with our competence in moving it. I imagine that he and Havers will be busy for quite some time. All we must do in the meantime is concentrate on getting this armament up there to the fort. I'm glad to see them go, much as I like them; we can get on with it without being continually scrutinised."

David nodded his agreement. "Let's have that drink, Robert, before I get scrubbed up." He sniffed the air. "And I think you should too!"

Together, they walked off to seek out a barrel of the stuff in the officer's mess tent.

The soldiers were queuing in an orderly fashion to get into the cookhouse as the two officers passed; the rigours of another day had left them ravenous. As the men at the front moved on with their meals, others quickly replaced them, with tin plates and cups at the ready.

Two ladies of questionable virtue were staring at the body of men filing past them. Unofficially tolerated in the camp, these ladies gave necessary 'companionship' to the men, as very few had been allowed to bring their wives. Officially, sex was strictly prohibited and punished if found out, but it didn't put a stop to it.

"I never thought I'd see a whole lot of bloody men walk past me as though I wasn't there," moaned Maggie while edging her blouse down a little more.

"Aye, that's true! Not a wink or a grab at me wotsits," complained Flo. "They're like the walking dead, this bloody lot are." Flo looked Maggie up and down. "If yow lower yer blouse anymore, our kid, and one of them officer gentlemen sees yer, yow could be in big trouble, our Maggie. Yow could be thrown out of the camp, and me with yer. We gorra be careful yer know, luv," she implored in a thick English Black Country accent.

"Yeah. I suppose yume right, Flo. We'll come back to these buggers tomorra. Come on with me, then. Let's leave 'em and mingle on the other side of the camp, luv. See if we can cadge a couple of drinks from someone, eh?"

They moved off in the hope of finding others to appreciate their fragrant charms and flirtatious manner.

Then, Maggie nudged her friend. "Hey, Flo, I think we've gotta bloke interested; he's coming over now. I could do with earning a few coppers."

The man, who was shorter than both ladies, approached them. Then, looking the women up and down, he curtly demanded, "How much?"

"Two shillings," said Flo, giving a curt, brusque response.

"And you?" he asked, looking at Maggie.

"One and a tanner, handsome," she said, undercutting her friend and winking at him. "I've never failed to delight a customer."

The man, who had grizzled features and thick, heavy stubble on his chin – along with a smell on his breath to run from – looked her over and said, "You'll do, woman."

Maggie held her ground. Putting out her hand, she insisted, "Money first or nothing doing."

Taking her one and six, she gave it to Flo for safekeeping and took him off to sort him out, only to reappear later in a dishevelled state.

"Oh, Flo! He was an animal – on me as soon as I showed him our secret place," she told her, sorting out her hair. "He was frantic with me straight away. I said no to kissing, but he forced me to do it. The dirty git said it was part of the deal. It was awful. He stunk to high heaven, and he put his tongue in my mouth! Come with me to the washhouse, Flo, and hold my things. I've got to scrub his smell off me and out of my nose. I'll stick to soldiers in future – that little bastard has made me sore!"

"Well, if yer charged more, you'd get a better client," Flo said snootily as they walked towards the women's separate washrooms.

***

Gunners Pete Wilson and Jim Newberry had been two of the first to eat their fill, and now they were sitting down outside, talking about the day's events. By chance, Molly, the sutler, walked by, causing both men to ogle her as she passed.

"Where's she come from, Pete? Now that's what I call a woman if I know anything about women! Nice body on her."

"She's been around the camp a while, Jim. I'm surprised you've not seen her carrying out her duties."

"Where's she been hiding, then? I'm not one to forget a body like that, I can tell you. I wonder what her name is."

"Holly or Molly, or something like that," said Pete.

"Is she a cook or something?"

"Nah! She's nothing like that, or you would have seen her already, yer prick!" said his friend, cuffing his head. "She's one of the sutlers in camp. Stitches clothes too, so they tell me."

"Well, I'm sure I can find a shirt or something to rip and get the bitch to mend it."

"Try that on, and I'll see you in the guardhouse; she looks after Captain Hill's special needs, she does."

"Perhaps she'd like to earn a little extra on the side."

"Ha! Which side are you thinking of, then?"

"Well, I won't know unless I ask her."

"Don't even think of it if you value your freedom," Pete advised. "Besides, there's another who's just as pretty. Daisy looks after Major Carter in the same way, if you know what I mean," Pete said, tapping his nose with a grimy forefinger.

"So what?"

"So what, you say to me? *So*, they will have nothing to do with people like you. You won't see her touting for business, either, because the officers take good care of them. She's not like that Flo and Maggie; I saw you arguing with them some time ago. No, you've got no chance. A few nights back, I saw Captain Marsh talking to Molly or Holly or whatever her bloody name is."

"What were they talking about?"

"I couldn't hear, but I did see how friendly they were together."

Jim thought for a minute, then asked, "Has she gone to the cookhouse?"

"Aye, but not the way we go in. Officers and people like her – who look after them – go in and out on the other side. More select, you might say, so they don't have to rub shoulders with the likes of us."

"Have the officers eaten? Are they likely to go in yet?"

"Not yet, not for a while. Why do you ask?"

"Oh, nothing, Pete. Look, I'm going for a little walk. I'm feeling bloated, and I think I'll walk it off. See you later."

"Where are you going?"

But Jim strode off, ignoring the probing question.

Walking near the cookhouse tent, he casually looked around to ensure no one was watching him. Then, satisfied, he picked his way over and around the ground pegs and ropes that held up the cookhouse tent and the two supply tents tied up next to it. In passing, he heard the banter between a soldier and a woman coming from one of them. He then heard a loud slap followed by, "Ow!" as she metered out instant justice to his saucy demands. Not wanting to be discovered by them, he carefully avoided the rope awnings spread out like a spider's web in front, attempting to entangle him and trip him up.

He came out at the officers' entrance to the cookhouse to find no one there, but within seconds Molly emerged, only to find her way blocked in the narrow passage. He deliberately stood in her way, forcing her to speak.

"Can I come past, sir?" Molly asked politely.

"Well, what have we got here, then? Holly, isn't it?"

"The name is Molly. Can I come past?" she asked again. "You're in my way."

"Why yes, of course. But first, a little information. Are you a sutler?"

"Yes, I am. Why do you ask?"

"I've got a few jobs for you," he said, grinning lecherously.

She felt his eyes play on her body; he was blatant with it as he looked over her front and rear. She felt icy cold shivers running down her spine as he leered at her. "I can't help you there. You need to see one of the other ladies. Now, let me pass?"

"Now I see why they wanted to keep you to themselves; you're quite a pretty thing. Built for breeding, I'd say. But I want you to look after me like you look after Captain Marsh. I want a similar service, and I promise not to mention anything to Captain Hill."

She ignored what he said and attempted to squeeze past him, but he held her wrist, applying a small amount of pressure to force her to stay.

"Oh! You're hurting me. Please, let me go!"

As he held her there with one hand, he cupped her breast with the other, holding it softly as he felt its shape and fullness. "You know, my pretty, if you listen to me and do what I tell you, we could make plenty of money while we bivouac out here. With my 'know how to do' and your 'know what to do', we could make ourselves a tidy sum and flee this place together."

"But what of the cannon and the army?"

"Fuck the cannon! I don't care – it's not my worry – and the sooner I can shake this army shit off my boots, the better."

"I'm just trying to survive the best I can. I'm not the sort of girl you're looking for," said Molly firmly. "You have the wrong impression of me."

"Look, I'll give you a little time to think about it. Then, when I come looking for you, the answer had better be yes, or you might feel the sharpness of my knife drawn across that pretty throat of yours." He took half a step closer to her and added, "I'll be seeing you, and soon, Molly." With that he let go of her and returned the way he came, picking his way carefully over and around the web of ropes and back to Pete.

"Where have you been, Jim? What are you up to now?"

"I've had a word with Molly – who is some beauty. Best seen close-up, like, to take it all in. Well, I had a little chat with her, and I have to say she took a shine to me straight away, Pete. If I've gambled right, I wouldn't be surprised if I'm not bouncing off body beautiful real soon. For the right price, Pete, I would even let you have a go."

Pete shook his head. "I told you about messing with fire. Count me out; I don't want to know anything about your scheming."

It took a while for Molly to stop shaking while alone in her tent.

She massaged her wrist; the bruises the bastard had put on her were beginning to show on the arm he'd forcibly held back, and it was hurting her. She pondered his threat to tell Captain Hill about her dallying with David. She had no idea how he'd found out, but she would have to avoid him now as best she could.

***

During the evening meal in the cabin, Major Carter said, "I must congratulate you, Commander, on giving out the extra drink ration to the men. It gave them a brief spurt of energy for at least a day or two. It motivated them more, I felt."

"Yes," replied Townsend. Then, after further thought, he added, "To begin with, it did. But I'm sensing their combined spirit is beginning to flag again. It seems that we need something other than a drink to encourage them. Something else to inspire and fire the imagination."

"I thought our making of two teams out of them quite inspirational, sir," said Captain Hill. "I thought the rivalry between them would continue, but it seems not," he added.

Between chitter-chat with Sergeant Major Horrocks, Sarah and Victoria listened to the men's immediate worries. Concerned, Victoria asked, "What other types of rivalry could you use? Are there any? Surely there must be something to hold their interest for longer than a few days."

"That's the answer, sir," Marsh exclaimed. "Having listened to Victoria, the two teams we have should be made up of one team of sappers against one team of bombardiers. Make a race of it, and the competition will be fierce, I'm sure."

"Congratulations! That's exactly what we need, Captain Marsh, and well done – we have found the answer, thanks to my dear wife," said a much relieved Townsend. "The Royal Engineers' sappers will make up one team, with the Royal Artillery's bombardiers making up the second team. The healthy rivalry between them is to be encouraged to increase the distance the gun moves daily and to keep them all focused. By Jove,

Captain, that's the answer. We will inform the men of our plans first thing tomorrow."

The sergeant major was sitting between the two ladies, capturing both Victoria and Sarah's attention by entertaining them with his enthralling descriptions of the animals he'd seen on the vast plains of the African continent. Elephants with trunks and tusks and lions were of particular interest, firing their imaginations. His tale describing a tiger stalking a kill had both ladies wide-eyed and open-mouthed, enthralled at the life-and-death situation.

Having finished their meals, Colonel Havers and Copperfield stood close to the small, contained fire, warming their posteriors while being a complete heat block to the others. Sarah had now unwittingly become the centre of their attention.

"How are you coping with your duties?" asked Havers, resplendent in his impressive uniform. "Perhaps you can tell us what injuries you saw to, my dear?"

"Well, sir, you can be sure there were quite a few in the surgery," Sarah replied. "Why, the doctor went through them like a hot knife through a slab of salted butter," she said, exaggerating, "and if he thought there were any malingerers amongst them, they got short shrift, I can tell you. But overall, they mainly suffered from strains and pulled muscles – though nothing that won't heal, bless them."

"And you, my dear," said Copperfield quizzically while holding a candle to light his cigar, "what were you doing?"

"Oh, I was treating the men for cuts and bruises and that sort of thing," she told them. "The men seemed grateful I was treating them, sir. They were very patient and good and never complained, although I did notice my queue was always longer than the good doctor's."

"I'm sure the men appreciated your feminine touch more," said Copperfield, flirting with her.

Horrocks interrupted: "If I know the men, sir, I'd say it could just be an excuse for them to ogle the young nurse! Er… I mean, lady, sir. But as time goes by, the real shirkers will surface, sir. They always do!" he finished loudly, with the air of a man who has the sound experience to cover up his slip of the tongue.

Ushering Sarah away towards the door, Victoria told them, "If you will excuse us, Sarah and I will top up your glasses again, gentlemen."

"What, both of you?" questioned Townsend, puzzled.

Lowering her head and looking at him sternly, Victoria said forthrightly, "Yes, Robert, both of us. I do need some help." She held Sarah firmly by the arm and led her from the room.

205

"Women are wonderful creatures but completely unfathomable," remarked Townsend when they were gone.

"I know what you mean, Major. It even takes two to go to the lavatory," said Horrocks, to raucous laughter from the assembled men.

"Anyway, please continue, Sergeant Major. Would you have any idea who the future malingerers would be?" questioned Havers.

"Yes, sir. I have one or two in mind. Briggs, Smith, and – of course – Donkey."

"Donkey, Sergeant Major?" Havers asked naively. "But they are excellent at pulling things, aren't they?"

"Yes, sir, donkey – Prosser, the donkey. I'll have him up front where I can keep an eye on him and make the most of his ability to pull." He barked a laugh, and everyone but Havers joined in.

"Tell me, Sergeant Major. That's the reason he's called Donkey, is it? Because of his ability to pull?"

"Oh, no, sir." Looking at the others, he lowered his voice so that the ladies were unable to hear. "No. He's more than gifted in the wedding tackle department. He carries his very own one-hundred-ton gun, sir. I can vouch for it because I've seen it."

A round of loud cheers rang out as the colonel finally understood the joke and joined in. The drink had loosened their tongues – especially now that the ladies were gone – and they freely began to swap bawdy jokes.

This stopped when the women returned, giving the optical illusion of floating into the room, their hems brushing the floor with their feet hidden under full-length lace dresses.

"Well, I say," said Victoria, on hearing the laughter. Putting the drinks tray down on the table, she asked, "Are we getting tipsy and merry, then?"

"If we are drunk, we are drunk on the beauty of you two ladies," Havers declared while sipping his whisky. "You are an incredibly lucky man, Major."

"I've told him that," said Victoria with amusement. "Perhaps now he'll believe me," she added, smiling over at Sarah.

"Thank you, Colonel. I do appreciate how fortunate I am, and I am often told it," he replied, tongue in cheek.

Outside, the late evening saw the shadows lengthening across the camp. The previous hour had shown the men high-spirited, drinking their rewards for the day's toil. But now, they were gradually wandering off to their tents; the beds were acting like magnets, drawing them into a deep sleep for their tired bodies. As they succumbed to its request, the healing process started, each strained and tortured sinew desperately needing the rest.

The last refrains of the bugle died away into the night air as the formal dinner ended, with due regard for another early morning start. Suitably fed and watered, the men were given an armed guard to escort them back to their quarters in the camp. Since the episode with the prisoner, Townsend had decided to leave nothing to chance.

The crockery was spirited away by a lady from the camp kitchen, to be washed in the morning. "We are off then, madam. I hope everyone enjoyed the meal?"

"Yes, thank you, Sally, it was most delicious," said Victoria warmly. "Goodnight."

"Goodnight," Sally replied, departing with her helper and another armed escort.

Sarah saw them go. "I'm rather tired myself," she stated, a little disappointment etched into her voice. "I'm going to bed myself now, so goodnight," she finished, leaving them alone in the room.

"I noticed Sarah and David hardly spoke to each other this evening," Victoria observed quietly. "Things seemed somewhat quiet and strained between them."

"Oh, it's probably nothing. I promise I'll find out the cause in the morning," Townsend assured her.

"Did I make a good hostess with our guests, Robert?" Victoria asked, slightly unsure. "Were you proud of me?"

"Oh, more than ever, Vicky. Come here."

They lingered there a while, lightly embracing before he moved behind and rested his hands lightly on the bump growing inside her. Leaning her head onto his chest, she turned slightly and nestled her shoulder under his arm while reflecting on the day just gone.

"I didn't understand him at the time, but old Copperfield remarked on how you are in full bloom with our child. I can see it now, though." He kissed her tenderly on the head. "You're not just blooming; you're positively glowing, to boot."

"Robert, that same man frightened the life out of me earlier," Victoria remarked lightly. "I thought his beard would burst into flames each time he lit his cigar with the candle. I was worried he'd start a fire or something, dripping candle wax onto the stove." She was teasing him. Seeing a hint of a smile forming, she continued, "Why, I had towels and water at the ready to douse him down if he ignited."

Laughing, Townsend murmured, "Let's get to bed. I'm feeling rather tired myself."

Extinguishing the oil lamps, they left the darkened room behind them and walked toward the bedroom. The flickering candle Townsend held in his hand threw their distorted moving shadows along the length of the timbered wall.

"You took a while replenishing those drinks tonight."

"If you must know, Robert, we had to visit our private latrines. I had to take Sarah and show her where the new trench had been dug for our use. You forget it's changed since she last stayed here. To know of a potential mishap is to prevent one; that's what I like to think. Oh, and that seat you had made has proved most comfortable for both Sarah and myself!"

The remark caused a high-pitched nasal snort, and then a chuckle to escape his lips as he recalled what Horrocks had suggested.

Climbing into bed beside her, he blew out the candle. Then, pulling her in close, he whispered, "Come on, cuddle in here to me, and let's get that sleep we both desperately need."

Chapter 17

Maintaining a daily rhythm.
Shirkers and workers and the first casualty

THE BUGLE'S piercing refrain stirred the camp, but it wasn't the usual call; that morning, the bugler played 'Fall in, A. Fall in, B. Fall in, every company' loudly and urgently.

Well-versed in the bugle's calls, the men initially panicked as they tried to sort themselves out and line up outside their tents.

The military regulation of leaving rifles standing in pyramid fashion outside tents for quick retrieval caught sapper Guthrie out; he collided with those outside his tent, scattering the rifles across the ground.

Others had just attempted to do up shirt buttons and trouser flies, with various levels of success, when the next barked order was shouted out.

"Attention!" The sergeant major came striding over. "Get them rifles stood up!" he ordered.

The impressionable and eager-to-please Guthrie quickly obeyed before getting back in line.

"Now, men, before you lot go tear-arsing about, there's something I want you all to know. Immediately after today's roll call, the men on the gun pull will eat first. All others will take themselves to the cookhouse afterwards. It's to get the men out on the gun quickly and give us more time with it. We urgently need it up there in the fort. Do you understand, Briggs?"

"Yes, Sergeant Major."

"Yes, sir, Briggs!

"Yes, sir."

"Well, do you understand, Smith, or do I have to give you private instruction?"

Not expecting to be singled out, Smith stuttered back in alarm, "Y-yes, Sergeant, sir, Major!"

"No need to elaborate, Smith!" he spat. "'Yes, sir' will do, Smith. An officer on parade."

"Yes, sir," he replied.

"I've had reports from the physician that the shirkers amongst you are trying to pull the wool over his eyes as to your state of fitness. Real injuries picked up *might* get you excluded, but nothing else. Still, I tell you this: it will give me immense pleasure to administer instant justice to any hairy arse I find pulling a fast one!"

"*Yes, sir!*" they shouted back.

His voice softened at their instant response. "Good! Today, men on duty are to get themselves to the cookhouse smartly, without injuring either themselves or others. You will be needed on the cannon, and I'll be watching you all, be sure of it. Finally, report to your section officers for deployment down in the bay. Dismissed!"

The returning patrol was spotted approaching the camp as the designated team lined up at the cookhouse. The early morning and late afternoon patrols had been a regular feature since Townsend had decided to disrupt any illegal activity building up in the area. The times the patrols went out were also varied and not as rigid and regular as before, making them harder to avoid. It was agreed amongst the officers that the locals needed to have confidence in their ability to protect them, and this was the military's response.

"Patrol returning! Call the major!" the lookout shouted down.

Dismounting from his horse outside the command post, the patrol leader hurried towards the waiting Townsend. Saluting his commanding officer, Sergeant James was eager to give his report.

"Carry on, Sergeant. What have you found?"

"Criminal activity near Mellieha this time, sir. Another farmer has reported livestock stolen. We found out where the thieves had struck but lost the trail across the hard rock, sir."

"What was stolen?"

"I was told sheep, goats, and some chickens, sir. The farmer said he heard what was going on in the night but couldn't see them. He said he thought it was well organised because he thinks there were about five or six. Fearing for his family's safety, he stayed put."

"Thank you, Sergeant. Get yourselves a bite to eat."

"Yes, sir. Fall out, men!" he ordered, leading his troop away.

"Do you think something is going on, sir?" asked Marsh.

"It's hard to say, Captain, but I don't like it," said Townsend thoughtfully. "I had dismissed our previous encounters with armed insurgents as something that simply occurs occasionally out here, so far from Valletta – and given Malta's history. But I have to admit, that is the largest number of animals taken from one farm to date. These people are poor and can't replenish their livestock so easily." He shook his head in frustration. "We need a strategy to deal with it. We need proof or to catch them in the act. We have got to sort it out, and if we get our heads together, I am sure we can. I do not want the locals losing faith in us; besides, the governor wouldn't be best pleased."

"We could be getting ahead of ourselves, Major," Marsh reasoned. "Maybe it's just plain sheep rustling to sell on the market at Valletta for cash?"

"That is possible, Captain," Townsend agreed. "Have a semaphore sent to Valletta, asking them to watch for any suspicious sales of sheep or carcasses suddenly being sold there. That's a start, but somehow, I don't think that's the answer; in this heat, any carcasses would go off extremely quickly and wouldn't sell. They could herd the animals there, at the risk of being discovered, but then again... they could be willing to chance it." He sighed. "I have no idea, to be truthful. This whole thing feels like part of something else, something much bigger."

***

The men on pull duty began descending the hill to assemble at the gun. The sergeant major was striding down there, too, cutting a lonely figure as the men kept clear of his sharp tongue. Although possessing a fearsome temper, he was well respected by them as he'd seen action on the African continent.

Dismissing the guards at the gun, he gathered the men around him. "Are we all here?" he demanded of the NCOs as they began to check everyone in attendance.

"Davis is missing, Sergeant Major."

"Is he, now? Would that be the culprit over there?" he said, pointing his finger at a solitary figure scrambling down the hill towards them. He bellowed out, "Get down here quick, Davis, or I'll put you on a charge! Run, man, run! Can you not hear me? Get here now! You are holding the British Army up!"

The man slipped and fell before regaining his feet and finally arriving amongst the group, exhausted before his day had even begun.

"*Attention!* That is the last time you will be late, Davis, my little Welsh rarebit!" snapped the sergeant major. "That also goes for the rest of you. I want you all down here at eight o'clock sharp, refreshed and ready to go. For any of you with doubts, that is a bloody order! Now, the other team's bombardiers did all right yesterday, but I want you lads – you sappers – to do better! A wager has been placed on the two teams between the officers. So, it's a race between you both – a race I want my men to win, you understand. It's also permissible for you lot to have bets on the outcome of the race as well."

211

"Permission to speak, sir," said a young soldier, saluting.

"Sergeant Major to you, sonny. We're not on parade now! Yes, Smith, what is it?"

"How can we race when we only have one gun?"

The sergeant major repeated the question in a high-pitched, mocking voice: "How can we race when we only have one gun? You son of a strumpet, Smith! The race is the best distance a team can pull in a day, lad! When we get this gun inside our fort, the winning side – counting up the daily distances – can have a full day of sunbathing and swimming in Anchor Bay, washed down with an extra jug or two of ale. You have my word on it! Right, then, take up the positions given to you by your section NCOs and stick to them for the whole day. Remember, I have an empty guardroom that needs occupants and volunteers for latrine duty. Hey, you there, Peterson. Are you listening?"

"Er, yes, Sergeant Major," Peterson answered, startled.

"Good! I will not stand for any crap from people who claim they hadn't heard me!" he snapped. "You have five minutes to take up the positions you are given. Then we start." He picked his way through the clumsy, rushing men as the section leaders barked out their orders for assembling on the ropes.

"Aah! That man there. Hart, is it?" he asked, stopping the man from running past.

"Yes, Sergeant Major."

"Tell me, Hart. Have you got over that, er, spot of trouble you had? You know… that touch of sunstroke you suffered the other day?"

"Oh, yes! I'm much better, thanks, sir. But he won't get away with calling you names like Horrible Horrocks next time. I'll see to it," Hart said in a single-minded, fixated fashion.

"What's his name, Hart? Who is he?" Horrocks enquired in a whisper, leaning in close.

"Never you mind, and don't fret, sir. Leave it to me. I will get it sorted," he whispered back.

Horrocks had been bending forward with his hands behind his back, looking down at Hart, but he straightened upon hearing his disquieting response. Looking at Hart quizzically, he said, "Carry on, Hart. There's a good chap." He looked around him to see if anyone had heard and then – satisfied no one had – strode off, fully intending to look up Hart's army medical history.

"Right, then, you men should all be ready by now. *Capstan ready?*"

"*Capstan ready, Sergeant Major.*"

"*Section officers ready?*"

"*Section officers ready.*"

"On my order. *Heave!*"

"*Heave!*" shouted the section leaders as the men took up the strain. Soon, they got into a rhythm as the gun began inching forward once more.

Horrocks roared over their heads, "Remember, men! Forty minutes on and twenty minutes off. *Heave!*"

The gun moved off, slowly climbing the incline while Horrocks walked alongside the men, shouting encouragement to everyone – including the men he heard cursing through gritted teeth. They cussed at all and everything, even at the men beside them, as they kept the gun moving. They were all blind and deaf to everything around them, such as the views, the birds singing, or the profusion of spider orchids growing from the rocky slope beneath their feet. The compulsion to keep the gun moving had taken hold.

Much wiser now, the men's tunics had been left abandoned in their tents, along with unwanted helmets. Some had chosen to wear the pillbox forage caps as head protection from the hot sun, and most had their shirt sleeves rolled up in a determined fashion, ready to shift the gun.

"*Heave!*" became the background sound throughout another arduous day. Any injuries were dealt with immediately, the men replaced by others on standby to keep the gun constantly moving on towards their goal, until – towards the day's end – tiring muscles responded with ever-decreasing effort.

***

Victoria was enjoying her responsibilities more since becoming involved in the running of the camp. Getting around to see 'her ladies' was an ongoing priority that she particularly enjoyed. It was a tough job, but it also had its rewards: not least being called 'madam' (although she never really got used to it) and the profound respect for what she was doing. The women's welfare was vitally important to her, and Victoria would never knowingly refuse a plea for help.

That day, she was out and about, intent on chatting to all the women in turn because there were still some she hadn't met. As well as re-ordering diminishing supplies of material and cotton fabrics for repairing soldiers' clothing, she made a point to find out what orders the sutlers wanted to replenish their holding stock. Although it was all rather time-consuming, Victoria was determined to acquaint herself with all of 'her ladies' in time, if possible.

The sutlers had separate tents from the seamstresses. Occasionally, they would assist them in repairing or washing clothes whenever there was a lull in their jobs of providing for the men. They did it to keep busy, to pass the time and share friendly gossip.

"Good morrow, Molly! Have you come to give a hand, then?"

"A good morrow to you, Meg! Yes, I want to help you for a while. Daisy has taken the officers' orders. Nothing much they wanted, really, apart from tobacco and such. I'm bored and thought I would come down, help out, and have a chinwag with you and the girls." She looked around her, admiring the sewing skills of the women there.

"Well, there's a pair of trousers in front of you that have got a bad rip in them," said Meg cheerily. "You could start with them, girl, I suppose. I'm sure we can find you plenty to do – and pay you for your time, of course."

Molly bent down and picked up the frayed trousers, flinching and rubbing her arm in discomfort. She took a seat next to Meg, who began frowning in concern.

"Are you alright, Molly?" Meg asked. "You're not hurt, are you?"

"No! It's just a little strain I've picked up somehow or other, that's all. It should clear up soon, Meg – there's no need to fuss. Tell me, have you met the commander's wife yet? Is she pretty and kind, or a complete tartar of a woman?" she asked, trying and failing to thread the needle.

"That's not like you, Molly," Meg remarked, not put off by the change of subject. "You're usually very quick at doing that – you have better eyesight than I do. Are you sure you're all right, girl? You seem to be in pain. What have you been up to?"

"I said stop fussing, Meg," she whispered, disregarding her friend's concern. "I'll get it through in a minute. Have patience!" But she was unable to.

"Come here, child, and let me do it for you." When Meg took hold of the needle and thread from Molly's grasp, she felt her wince. "Molly, what's wrong? Is that a bruise I see on your arm?" Meg took hold of Molly's hand and pulled up the sleeve of her blouse. "God help us, child! What's happened here? Has someone done this to you?"

"Please don't fret so, Meg. I fell, that's all!"

"I don't think so, Molly," said Meg crossly. "You don't have the bruising that comes from a fall; I can see finger marks. You had better tell me, Molly dear, who's done this; otherwise, I'll find out for myself."

Faced with her friend's unyielding determination, Molly burst into tears.

"Come now, my girl, you can tell us," said Meg, putting a comforting arm around her shoulder. "We're all friends here," she added as the others gathered around to listen and give their support.

"Oh, Meg. There's a soldier, and he's been threatening me. I've been avoiding him like the plague. He wants me to lie on my back – charge for the pleasure and give him the money."

Meg tutted angrily. "Was it him that bruised you so?"

"Yes, Meg. He forced my arm behind my back to make me obey him. He said he would let me think about it, and the answer had better be yes. I've been too frightened to tell anyone."

"We'll see about that! What's his name, Molly?"

"I think his name is Jimbo. He's a gunner with the Royal Artillery, and that's all I know," she said tearfully. "I've seen him about the camp looking for me, and I'm frightened he'll find me."

"Does anyone here know him?" Meg asked, looking over her girls, but they all shook their heads. "He must have evil in his heart to frighten you the way he has, Molly. A few golden rules in life help a girl get through it, and most concern men. There are men, and then there are *men*: good men treat a woman like a lady. Some men who start roughly eventually treat their women like ladies, after a time – the time it takes will depend on the man. Then, there are shitholes like this Jimbo, who think they can go through life simply living off others' efforts. Keep well away from those types; that road will just lead to heartbreak, Molly. It's good you refused him." She patted Molly's back sympathetically.

"Thank you, Meg," said Molly, sniffling. "It feels a great weight has been lifted from me now that you know."

"That's good, dear. We'll get it sorted," Meg assured her. "Now, back to the repair on those trousers you have there. There's not enough grey thread to finish it, so you'd better get a new spool of grey from the small table in the opposite tent. You should also see more of this old material we use for patching up in a box there. Bring that too, if you can carry it, dear."

Glad of the opportunity to have a moment to pull herself together, Molly went to the other tent to collect the things she needed. While she was sorting through scraps of waste fabric, someone grabbed her from behind.

Molly let out a soft scream, quickly stifled by the cold blade pressed into her throat. She shook uncontrollably, knowing her tormentor had found her.

It was Jimbo. He had caught a glimpse of Molly entering the tent and, without drawing attention, had casually strode over and quietly entered himself. He had soon realised there was only her in there, and that she had her back to him.

"Molly, oh, Molly – where have you been? I've been looking for you," he whispered into her ear. He then kissed the side of her head, which made her shake even more, both in fear and disgust. "I hope you've missed me too, Molly." He tightened his grip across her chest.

"Aargh! Yes! Yes!" she cried, hoping that he might not hurt her if she told him what he wanted to hear.

He kissed her head again. "I've come to find out your answer to my question," he whispered. "Though I must confess, I know what it will be, Molly, my love." His hand slipped off her front and delved down inside her blouse as he said it. He felt for her breast and squeezed it roughly in his calloused hand, hurting her more.

Too afraid to move or fight, Molly was frozen to the spot, unable to prevent him from molesting her. She couldn't think. She could barely breathe and was shocked into silence.

"Wherever has that girl got to?" Meg said to the others. "She should have found it by now. I'll go and see what's going on." Meg walked briskly over into the other tent and was outraged at what she saw. "Leave that girl alone, you dirty bastard!" she screamed, seeing Jimbo assaulting Molly. "I said, leave her alone!"

At the sound of Meg's raised voice, the other ladies came hurrying over, blocking the tent entrance.

Jimbo quickly pulled his hand from Molly's blouse and slipped his knife back into its sheath on his belt, though not before Meg had seen it.

"What are you doing in here?" she wanted to know as Molly ran to the protection of the other women. "It's out of bounds to soldiers, and you know it is!"

"Steady," he said, with what he thought was a winning smile. "I'm courting this young lady, and it's none of your business."

"So, as well as being a shithole, you're a lying shithole into the bargain, are you?" Meg spat.

"Now I know who he is, Meg," said one of the women. "Jim Newberry. I saw him trying it on with that Maggie and her mate Flo not so long ago. Even they told him where to go! He's a real troublemaker if you ask me."

"Shut up! No one's asking you," said Jimbo hotly, spitting the words out.

"I wouldn't call the state Molly's in 'love', would you, girls?" Meg asked loudly.

"No, Meg, not at all," another answered.

The women began moving in on him. "What shall we do with him, girls?" asked Meg.

"Cut his dick off," someone threatened – a suggestion greeted with nods and increasing angry murmurs of agreement.

"Aye, and serve it up as pork sausage. The other buggers won't know the difference," said a man-hater. Another woman tugged menacingly at his trousers.

The soldier was visibly rattled, having underestimated the women's anger. His eyes darted desperately around, looking for a way out as they moved in towards him.

Another woman had positioned herself at the tent entrance, holding the flap back and keeping watch outside. Suddenly, she froze, then in a hard whisper said, "Meg! Stop! The commander's wife is coming and will be here soon. I've just seen her, so don't touch him for now!"

"Keep him here, girls," Meg ordered. "Don't let him get away while I have a word with her."

"No, Meg," he pleaded.

"Shut up. We've no sympathy for the likes of you," Meg said before stepping out of the tent to meet up with Victoria.

"Hello, Meg. I've come down to speak to you and the ladies and find out what needs ordering."

"Thank you, madam. Unfortunately, we have experienced a little trouble, and I would like to tell you about it and see if you can help."

After telling her story, Victoria looked past her toward the tent, clearly shocked. "I see, Meg. Thank you for that, but you mustn't harm him."

"Oh! That was only said to put the frighteners on him, madam." Meg grinned. "Apply pressure, if you will." It was a blatant lie, but she thought Mrs Townsend didn't need to know what may have happened.

"Right, then. Show me to him, please, Meg."

They entered the tent, with the ladies giving way to allow Victoria access to him.

"What's your name, soldier?"

"Jim Newberry. Gunner of the Royal Artillery," he said, standing to attention.

"Well, Gunner Newberry, get yourself away and expect a visit from an officer. There will be a charge laid before you as soon as I tell the commander. You can be sure of it."

Without saying a further word he walked out, cursing under his breath for getting caught with Molly.

***

Finally, seeing the flagging spirit of the men and the time of day, the sergeant major called a stop to yet another day's hard graft, having decided enough was enough.

After ordering the gun's sleigh to be made safe and the capstan locked off, he then ordered the men to stand down for the evening and get themselves off to the cookhouse when ready. Some men drank greedily and were grateful for the water butts. In contrast, others tipped the water over themselves to bring their body temperature down. Most lay down where they stood, far too tired to attempt the steep climb back, for a while at least.

Marsh had wandered down on his own. He was interested in the day's progress, eager to estimate how long it would take to get the gun to the hilltop. Therefore, at the end of each day, he jotted down the distance the cannon had travelled. Striding down against the flow of men returning, he found the sergeant major deploying the guards to protect the gun.

Horrocks saluted the approaching officer. "They have got into a routine now, sir, and are achieving better distances. It's still painfully slow, though, Captain."

"I see what you mean," he said, returning the salute. "It will take another good week at this rate to get anywhere near the first turn. However, with each day, we are getting better at it. How often are the guards replaced?"

"Every four hours, sir."

"From now on, they are to be relieved every two hours on the commander's orders. It's to keep the men on their toes and stop them from getting bored and careless."

"Yes, Captain. I'll see to it straight away."

Marsh headed back up the hill, ready to meet with Townsend to give his daily report, when he spotted Victoria. He reached Townsend slightly earlier than she did.

"Here comes your wife, Robert," he remarked. "She's not pleased about something, judging from the look on her face. Perhaps I should go."

"Robert, I must have a word with you at once," Victoria said, gasping with the effort it had taken her to find him. She nodded her head towards Marsh. "You might as well hear this, too, David."

Townsend put his arm around her shoulder. "Steady on. Take a deep breath and calm down. What's wrong?"

"While you've been gone today, I had a most unpleasant report from Meg, who runs the repair tent. A soldier from the Artillery has been threatening one of my ladies. It seems it's been going on for a little while. I met Meg on my rounds today and found out they had the man cornered in the supplies tent. Meg tells me she caught him mauling the girl in there. She was frightened of him but didn't know how to make him stop and leave her alone."

"Which of the ladies was it?"

"He was fondling young Molly."

Marsh gasped. "No!"

"Molly, you say, one of the sutlers?"

"Yes, Robert. A most discourteous and surly man was molesting her. He frightened me just to look at him. He wanted her to work the men for him, if you know what I mean, and to give him the money she charged them," she informed him, embarrassed.

"Do we know his name, Victoria?"

"Yes. It's Jim Newberry, and his nickname is Jimbo," Victoria replied as Marsh stewed.

"He missed his turn on the gun today. Sarah told me he claimed to have a badly strained arm. Now we know he hasn't."

"Well, he's in big trouble now. Avoiding duty is frowned on, too; it's a serious offence."

"Meg said it didn't look as if there was anything wrong with him," said Victoria angrily. "From what she saw, his arm was working perfectly when he held the knife to Molly's throat."

"The bastard!" Marsh cussed to himself in a sigh, passing unheard.

"Tell me, Victoria, how has Molly coped with his unwanted attention?" Townsend asked while glancing over at Marsh's reaction.

"Meg said Molly was frightened; she lost control of herself when he threatened her and wet herself through. She's been sick with the worry of it all because no one knew about it. She kept it to herself, poor lass."

"Newberry's one of our men," confirmed Townsend. "The question is how to deal with him? We could have him serve a sentence in the guardhouse, but I don't think that's good enough! Apart from molesting her, did he do anything else improper, Victoria?"

"No, Robert," she assured him. "He never got the chance."

"Well, I won't have him in camp a minute longer than necessary," said Townsend. "It's not good for morale. I'll send him back to face charges in Valletta, but in the meantime, David – throw him in the guardhouse."

"With pleasure," he growled.

Marsh took two armed soldiers along to look for Newberry in the camp and disarm him. Poking his head into the man's tent, he asked, "Where's Jimbo? I'm here to throw him in the guardhouse."

"He's not here, sir. I haven't seen him since he told me about Molly," Pete responded.

Marsh reacted swiftly. "Search the camp, men. He's here somewhere!"

The camp was thoroughly scoured before the men returned to Marsh, who was inspecting Jimbo's belongings.

"There's no sign of him, sir; we think he may have deserted. One of Galea's men said both his coat and shirt are missing."

"Would he be stupid enough to leave camp?" Marsh wondered out loud. "He's making things much harder for himself if he has deserted. No doubt we'll find his tunic dumped somewhere if he has … keep looking, men. We need to find him!" He returned to examining Newberry's kit bag and, shortly after, became aware of a commotion.

A soldier hurried over to him with a bundle under his arm. "Sir! Sir! We found his tunic hidden under some sacking."

"Sergeant Savage and Corporal Collins, take some men apiece and search outside the camp," Marsh ordered. "He could still be here somewhere if he's not panicked. He might just be hiding out."

"You search in that direction, Collins, and we'll search over there," Savage directed.

After a long hour of looking, they were about to give up when a search team member shouted, "He's here! I've found him."

They hurried over to him, and he moved aside a portion of the bushes under which Jim Newberry's lifeless form had been dragged and concealed. They saw that his body was covered in slash wounds.

"Bloody hell, look what someone's done to him!" Savage exclaimed. "Keep alert, men, and on your toes. Whoever did this could still be lurking about here somewhere. Let's get him back to camp where we can have a better look at him!"

"Search party returning!" shouted the guard. "Inform the major they're carrying a body back with them."

Townsend was told and hurried over to meet the returning men. They laid the corpse down for him to see it for himself. "Is it Jim Newberry? Can anyone identify him?" he asked.

As the men gathered about and stared down at the man's lifeless body, Gunner Pete Wilson stepped forward. "Aye, it's Jimbo, alright," he sighed. "He might have been rough and randy and spoke bullshit at times – and I know he's done wrong – but the man didn't deserve that!"

"Whoever did this wasn't interested in just killing him!" Marsh remarked. "The man's got lots of knife slashes over his body, yet we heard nothing. It seems he's been tortured."

Gunner Wilson corrected him. "No, sir, I've seen similar instances where a man has been stabbed and died. The slashes were done after, showing complete disrespect for the body."

While they talked, the gathering crowd inched forward, trying to get a better view of Jimbo.

"That's far enough, men!" said Townsend. "And keep the ladies away. They don't need to see any of this. Whoever did it must have surprised him and killed him before he could shout out a warning. It also suggests the camp is being watched."

Loud murmurs spread throughout the gathering as to who could have done it to Jimbo.

"All you men must be aware of that and act accordingly," Townsend continued. "In the meantime, I'm doubling the guard in camp and around the fort's perimeter. We'll get our men out and see if we can find a trail and track these murderers down. They won't go unpunished. I can assure you. Can we arrange a burial party for this man, Sergeant Savage? I need to fill out a full report of the incident and get it off to headquarters."

"Yes, sir! I'll get on with it now, so we can put the poor bugger to rest."

Galea and Khalif, being involved in the building work, could move unhindered about the camp and fort without causing suspicion. So, when they came across the crowd around Newberry's body, they moved seamlessly amongst the onlookers, where they could hear every word Townsend said.

Alarmed at the heightened security and increased patrols, Galea walked swiftly away, his faithful second on his heels. "Those sons of dogs have disobeyed me yet again! I want you to go and find the ones responsible and make an example of them to the others. Kill them, Khalif; we no longer have use for them. The success of our mission is paramount – they must not be discovered! They will not disobey me a second time, my friend. Too much planning and money have gone into this to allow those dogs to ruin everything!"

***

Following Newberry's murder, the days passed uneventfully until the cannon reached the first bend in its journey uphill. The effort put into it by the two teams was physically affecting their bodies: excess fat was burnt off, while definitive muscles formed in their arms and legs. The friendly banter and challenges between the two sides continued unabated as the distance the cannon was moved each day also visibly increased, much to the delight of Marsh. To assist them in the task of turning the gun, the Royal Engineers had seen to it that large boulders and heavy metal plates were buried in concrete on each of the corners of the roadway, allowing for the jacks to lean against them, pressing out and forcing the gun around.

"Right, men, we are about to turn it onto the next level at last!" Horrocks exclaimed as the men below him got themselves prepared. "Get those ropes fixed to the front and sides and fasten the remaining ropes to the rear sides. Brace the jacks against the plates and the cannon. As you men pull, the jacks will force the gun around the bend," he explained. "There will be two capstans in operation as we turn it. The second capstan will hold the full weight while we disconnect the first capstan and continue raising it. I hope that's all clear. On my command, then. *Both capstans ready?*"

"*Both capstans ready, Sergeant Major.*"

"*Section officers ready?*"

"*Section officers ready.*"

"*Heave!*"

As the cannon began to move, the jacks were slowly wound out, forcing out the back of the sleigh. The movement was accompanied by a loud, high-pitched screeching from the rollers digging into the road surface under the gun's weight, gouging out jagged bits of the road surface as they went.

The work was slow, moving a couple of inches at a time to steer it around the tight bend. While pulling on the ropes, the men could see the cannon slowly turning, giving them a second wind. The other capstan was now taking up the strain as the gun came around, continuing to scrape out and break up the road surface as it did so. The men on the inner ropes had to gather dangerously close together at the tight turn while the men on the outer ropes spread further apart. They all knew constant pressure had to be applied to keep the rollers turning and to keep them moving; otherwise, the benefit of their combined strength would be lost.

"*Heave!*" continued the order as the men laboured, faces scarlet with their efforts, backs and arms straining every sinew. "*Heave!*"

The rhythm continued, but the men on the inside were now in each other's way. Eventually, the inevitable happened.

"*Aaargh!*" a man screamed. "*My foot! My foot! Aaargh!* It's caught! It's caught! *Stop! Stop! Aaargh!*"

"Stop everything! Lock-off capstans!" shouted Section Officer Savage. His request was immediately obeyed. "*Man injured! Man injured!*" he bellowed.

"Get them wedges in quick at the back there!" ordered Horrocks as he ran to the man.

"*My foot! My foot!*" he kept screaming at them.

An immediate hush fell across the teams of men watching the drama unfold. Some had little stomach for the sight and turned away, while others worked tirelessly on ways to free him.

"We'll get you out," Horrocks promised. "We'll get you out, Barnes. Just hold on, lad!"

"I can't stand it! I can't stand it! Help me. *Help me, please!*" Barnes begged, holding both hands to his head as he writhed in agony on the ground, his foot held fast by the heavy load.

Seeing the man's distress and the detrimental effect it was having on the rest, Savage drew back his arm, clenched his fist, and hit Barnes squarely on the jaw. It knocked the man out, immediately rendering him unconscious.

"Well done, Savage. Well done, that man," said Marsh, who had heard the screams and had run over to see what was wrong. "You men, get crowbars ready. We can't get his foot out as it is, but we can release it if we use the crowbars and break the road surface away from under the foot. Get them at it, Sergeant Major, while he's still unconscious."

"Yes, sir. Come on, men, you heard!" he barked. "There's not a moment to lose."

The two men on the crowbars chipped away under the surface with a frenzy. Asphalt and stones broke apart and fell away until Barnes' foot was slowly and carefully freed from under the sleigh. With Barnes lifted clear, a soldier was physically sick at the sight of the mangled foot. Galvanised into action, two enterprising men took it upon themselves to create an emergency stretcher. Stripping off their shirts, they fed two crowbars through the shirt sleeves. On seeing this, others offered their shirts too, and soon, a well-padded, effective stretcher had been cobbled together.

"Well done, men," said Marsh, congratulating them on their ingenuity. "Let's get him on it and off to the doctor, fast. He may be able to save something of his foot if we hurry! You four, carry him up, and you there," he added, pointing to another, "get yourself off to the doctor fast and tell him a patient is on the way and give him the details. Get off, man, do it!"

After an explanation from the sergeant major about how the accident had occurred, Marsh looked over the stunned, listless men and called on them to finish for the day. He could clearly see their spirit was drained, and none had any inclination to carry on.

Later, when Marsh reported the incident to Townsend, they were both eager to visit the doctor's makeshift surgery and get his opinion, only to be informed that he had already amputated the leg between the foot and the knee.

"I could do nothing to save it," Doctor Charlton told them. "There was too much damage to the bones in the foot and ankle. It had to come off."

"Well, you did your best," said Townsend.

The doctor nodded briskly. "I have seen similar injuries before. It would have been a waste of time and effort."

"Where's Sarah?" enquired Marsh.

"She's in there with Barnes," said the doctor. "He doesn't know he's lost a foot yet. I should think he'll be unconscious for the best part of twenty-four hours. It's the shock, you see. After the amputation, I had to cauterise it by dousing it in brandy and setting it alight –he'll be bloody sore when he opens his eyes! But there won't be any infection; that's all I can be sure of."

"Good God!" exclaimed Marsh, his face visibly draining of colour.

"She's doing what she can to make him as comfortable as possible and has volunteered to stay here all night and keep an eye on him."

"All night?" asked Marsh, still feeling nauseous.

"Yes, but she'll call me if he wakes up. I'm in a nearby tent."

"As soon as he's able to travel, I'll arrange transport for him back to the military hospital in Valletta," said Townsend. "He'll stay there and be tended to while they arrange his shipment back home. We'll leave you now, sir, and thank you for everything you have managed to do for Barnes."

"That's what I'm here for, Commander," he replied graciously. "Good evening."

Outside, Townsend turned to Marsh. "At least we didn't have a death on our hands, which is good, but we will have to show caution approaching the gun's next turn." After pausing and giving a sideways glance at Marsh, he continued, "You and Sarah hardly spoke the other night. Why was that?"

"No reason, Robert," said Marsh evasively.

"Well, something was wrong between you two. Victoria noticed it. Could Sarah be wiser now, and won't give in to you as easily as the first time? Am I right?"

He realised pretending was a waste of time. "Well, she wouldn't!"

"So, you're in another state of petulance?" Townsend sighed. "How much longer will it last this time, I wonder?"

"I was too clever by half after that first meal you invited me to," he said sulkily. "I tried to humour my way back into her affections, but she was having none of it. The charm didn't work the second time, old boy. I've misjudged her, it's true, but I meant what I said. I do have deep feelings for her. I think I'm in love with her even more now she's refused me," he lamented.

"The answer is to woo her properly," said Townsend briskly. "That's what she secretly wants, anyway. I'll warrant she hasn't forgiven you for leaving Newcastle the way you did. I know we were following orders, but you made sure to sulk your way through and missed your opportunity to say goodbye. You should tell her the truth – forcefully, if necessary: that you did go back to look for her. Her family and friends can confirm it. It wasn't easy going with Victoria and me; you have to work hard at it."

Marsh sighed. "I know you're right, Robert, but every time I make a move to be friendly and tell her, she says she can see right through me and knows what I'm after."

"Well, aren't you? Sometimes, it refocuses the mind if you can't have what you want."

"Yes, you know I am, but not for the reasons she accuses me of," he complained, frustrated. "I want to hold her. I want to feel her body close to mine and passionately smother her in kisses. I want to smell her fragrance, *then* have sex with her as soon as possible and get on with it!"

Townsend's jaw dropped, mouth agape. "Bloody hell, you do have it bad for her, don't you? But at the same time, she knows she's right." He pondered their situation for a few moments, scratching at his chin as he did so, before offering a solution. "In a few days, Gunner Barnes will be moved to Valletta's military hospital. He'll go as soon as he's fit to travel. Sarah will travel with him to tend to him on the journey. If I arrange it for him to travel there in the empty supplies wagon, it will stay there overnight, then it can be loaded up with stores ready to travel back the next day. I want you to oversee the armed escort there and back, of course. It should give you a little time together, and you can concentrate on some serious wooing – if you see what I mean. You can stop overnight, of course, and be ready for the early start back. You have seen parts of Valletta for yourself. So, you could show her one or two of the sights there. What do you say, David?"

"Thanks, Robert. I appreciate it," he said gratefully. "She mustn't know we colluded, though, or I could be done for."

"Of course not. Capture the heart first – the body will follow. It always works. Ask Victoria if you doubt me," he said, winking at him. "And don't muck it up this time!"

"Thanks again, Robert, I mean it," Marsh said, beginning to cheer up.

"Come along. There's plenty to do before then," said Townsend, feeling happy with his scheming.

***

The next morning, Townsend received a report from one of the outlying sentries stating that he'd heard two shots fired in the early hours away in the distance. So, he ordered a patrol to investigate, but without results.

Unbeknownst to the men, the area they had searched fell short of where the incident had taken place. Hence, the bodies of the two murdered men lay there undiscovered. Justice had been served on Jim Newberry's killers, but not how Townsend had intended.

225

The two men who murdered Jimbo were dealt with in a cruel, brutal way, as did all who disobeyed Galea. After being gagged, Khalif's men had them staked out on the ground before cutting off a finger from each hand to slowly experience the excruciating pain. After falling unconscious from loss of blood, they were shot, and the bodies were left to rot. It was to act as a warning to anyone else who stepped out of line and ignored Galea's threats. The bodies were left uncovered as carrion for any birds of prey or passing wild dogs to feast on at their leisure. The shots reported by the sentry were never verified by anyone else. So, the incident was left to remain on file – eventually to be forgotten.

Chapter 18

Injuries mounting. Turning shirkers into workers. Unplanned trip to Valletta

GUNNER BARNES' unfortunate accident and amputation had weakened his body considerably. After regaining consciousness, the doctor had the unsavoury task of gently informing him about the loss of his foot. Barnes was inconsolable at the news, and beside himself with worry about how he would provide for his family. Mentally tormented, he could do little more than remain helpless on his sickbed.

Marsh visited him daily, attempting to reassure him that his family did have a future. Then, on one such visit he told him, "I've asked about your situation, and they tell me you will be employed in the workshops of Woolwich with the other veterans there," which partly restored his confidence.

After being given this fresh hope, Barnes began to come out from under his dark cloud of despair. Faltering at first, he managed to respond, "Thank you, most kindly, sir, from both myself and my family."

"Just see that your injury heals, and we will have you back with them in no time." After giving him the good news Marsh left him propped up in his bed, feeling much better now about his predicament.

Barnes wasn't the only one there now, in the makeshift field hospital; there were others needing treatment for pains and strains, or even rest from sheer exhaustion. As more came in, more room had to be found for the unintentional victims of the cannon, so another tent was erected to allow them to cope. Sarah was kept as busy as the doctor as she put her skills to the test on her patients.

On occasion, when the doctor thought the men were trying to shirk their duty, he passed their names to the sergeant major. His small guardroom – built to house four – currently held six, and he was thinking about having to take drastic action to deter others in camp from chancing it. Marsh nodded to Sarah on occasion as he left Barnes to recuperate, and she would nod back in acknowledgement. Sometimes they spoke to each other when they met, but not about anything of substance. It was merely strained and courteous talk to allow them to get through whatever awkward situation came about.

"If only I could convince her I care about her, and that she wasn't just a conquest!" he complained to Townsend before reaching the bell tent. "But how? I want to show her I'm really sincere."

"Change your approach, then, and set about courting her properly. It's all I can advise you to do," said a somewhat exasperated Townsend. "Most women like to be wooed and courted romantically. It's just how it is."

"I'll try harder then, if that's what it takes," he replied, disheartened.

***

The steady, torturous progress of getting the gun up the hill halted one late afternoon. "Lock off the capstan, men, and get them wedges driven in at the rear," ordered Horrocks.

The men's clothes looked worn, threadbare, and sullied with dirt and sweat as they complied with the daily ritual.

"We don't want to lose it now," was an afterthought he said at the end of each day, and some were getting rightly bored with it. "You men have done an excellent job getting it this far, and I'm rightly proud of both our teams for the effort being put in."

He often thought about the gun's slow pace and the constant presence of the men working themselves hard to achieve the summit. It made him all the angrier at those he thought were avoiding their duty, not just to the Crown but also to their friends and comrades.

"After it's made safe, get off to the cookhouse. I've got business to attend to in my guardroom." His voice was still in fine fettle, even after all the ordering, scolding, encouraging, and even swearing at everyone around him over the last few weeks. When the cannon was made fast, he yelled: "Guards! Get to this gun. Quickly now; I've got important business to attend to and must go."

With determined strides, he was soon up the hill and heading towards the guardroom, followed at a safe distance by a group of curious men wanting to see what was about to happen.

"Hollocks, it's Borrocks. I mean bollocks, it's Horrocks!" a worried guard declared after seeing him heading towards them. He started a coughing fit as he sought to smother and conceal his lit pipe. A sliver of skin, sticking to the end of its mouthpiece, was pulled painfully off his lip. He desperately tapped the contents onto the floor and then stood on them, hiding the clay pipe behind his hand – it was far too hot for his pocket. "Quick, smarten up! The old man's coming, and he doesn't look pleased!"

The second guard had just managed to button up his tunic when the sergeant major strode in through the door.

"Attention!" cried the corporal as the two-man guard froze.

"How many men...? No, I will rephrase that. How many malingerers are there here, Corporal?"

"Six, Sergeant Major."

"Six! Six, you say! So, we are doubling up now, are we? Get them out here now. Six, as many as that, eh! My guardroom is overflowing, lads, so I need to make space."

The corporal hurried to the cells. "All of you on your feet now! You have a visitor, so out!" he ordered.

"Fucking hell," whispered one to the other. "It's Horrible Horrocks, and the old man's ranting and cussing!"

They came running out of the cells at double-quick time and were halted in front of Horrocks by the corporal.

"What's up with you?"

"I have..."

"Salute and stand to attention when you speak to me. And you. What's up with you?"

"It's my leg. It hurts, Sergeant Major."

"You ran out here on it, all right!" he roared into the man's face. "You?"

"My arm hurts lifting it," stuttered the man.

"My arm, it hurts to lift it. What?"

"Sergeant Major."

"And you?"

"Same as him, Sergeant Major," the man replied, while pretending to struggle to salute.

"Well, does it, or doesn't it?"

"Yes, it does, Sergeant Major."

"Just as I thought. There's fuck all wrong with any of you. Officer of the guard!" he yelled.

"Yes, Sergeant Major," the man snapped back hurriedly.

"You will see that these poor excuses for soldiers will assemble outside in full military uniform in fifteen minutes flat, Corporal."

"Yes, Sergeant Major. Fifteen minutes flat!" he repeated. Then, turning to the men, he said, "You heard. Move your backsides and get your full kit on. Left-right, left-right, left-right!" he ordered as he marched them off.

After they disappeared, Horrocks sent a soldier to the kitchen to ask the cook for the loan of six large saucepans and a large spoon, which he had brought back to him.

"You've displeased him now, you idiots. Who knows what he will do with you," said the corporal. "Left-right, left-right, left-right!" Then, at their tents, he cried, "Halt! Fall out and get your full kit on now, and you'd better get a move on! We'll take it out on you later if he takes it out on us!"

Amidst the ensuing confusion, they managed to get their full kit on – despite taunts from the watching men.

Mills was first out; he nervously tried to connect his belt but ended up dropping his rifle instead. As he picked it up, his helmet fell off. Finally suitably kitted out, he spoke to the corporal out of the corner of his mouth, "Damn it, George. We're in for it now, aren't we?"

"Well, I can't see you lot getting your ration of ale for a while, Robbie lad."

As the six gathered, they were brought to attention by the corporal. "By the left, head back to the guardroom. Left-right, left-right, left-right," he called out before finally ordering, "Halt! Men fully kitted, Sergeant Major."

"Thank you, Corporal." His moustache twitched slightly under his nose as he considered the punishment he was about to give out. He circled the worried men lined up in single file, before stopping at the last two. His favoured way of making his point was to place his face between the heads of each two men, in turn, maintaining this method of attack along the line. "You men are supposed to be soldiers of the 'Realm'. You took the Queen's shilling!" he bellowed. Moving along, he stopped again. "To date, we are only getting a tanner's worth out of you." Moving on, he stopped between the last two. "In some cases, we're only getting thruppence' worth! We want a full bob's worth!" he raged at them. "Do we or do we not?"

"Yes, Sergeant Major," they answered in unison.

"Now, it's my job to realign your thinking. Why? Because I can. I have it in my power, you see, to ensure the Queen gets her money's worth! Usually, I find a follow-up is unnecessary, but it is there whenever I feel it's needed!" His words were greeted by silence from those feeling the lash of his tongue. They shuffled nervously, then jumped when he suddenly shouted, "Get them helmets off!"

As they obeyed, he walked along the line, placing large, heavy saucepans over each head in turn. He then left each man imprisoned with his thoughts for two minutes while the pans warmed in the heat of the afternoon sun. Finally, gripping the large metal spoon in his hand, he walked along the line and played his version of reveille on the tops and sides of each pan while making a loud tootling sound with his voice. His humiliating impression of the bugle brought roars of laughter from the men circling the scene, each wanting to see what he would do next. He then walked the line of men again, asking each in turn, "Can you hear me?" in a soft voice until one unfortunate miscreant mistakenly said, "Yes."

"Oh, the ringing in your fucking ears ain't loud enough?" he shouted. "Take that! And that! And that!" he yelled, pounding on the pan. "Can you still hear me?" he cooed. "Can you still hear me?" he repeated. There was no answer. "Good! That's what I want. Corporal, while these sons of strumpets are listening to the Great Bells of Bow ringing in their ears, have their knapsacks filled with sand."

"Yes, Sergeant Major."

When the knapsacks were duly filled, he turned to the watching men and said, "This is the best part. I like looking at their faces when I lift the pans."

When their pained faces were revealed, they all sported agonising, distorted expressions, their eyes rolling around like marbles.

"Right then!" Horrocks cried with glee. "You are to put on your knapsacks, which these lovely NCOs have lovingly prepared. They will take you running down to Anchor Bay to show you the lovely scenery down there. You will then turn back and have a lovely run back up here. The exercise will release the sudden build-up of wax you now have in your ears. You will do it ten times, and if any of you fail, you will be given another lap to do. These lovely NCOs don't want to kill you, you understand – because that pleasure would be all mine. Make this the last time I see your ugly faces today, as I've had an exhausting day, too! It's not easy shouting out orders all day, but I do it because it comes with this lovely uniform I wear. Oh, and before you go off with your lovely NCOs, I want to say something else. Because there are a few more days to go before this lovely gun reaches our lovely fort, I'm inviting you six to join the teams every day until we get it there! Right, then! Your NCOs will take you men away, and I'll see you all tomorrow, sharp! Carry on and get these malingerers out of my sight!"

"On the order, run to the bay. On order. Ready! Go!"

Four of the NCOs ran with them. They had agreed one would stay at the bottom, one at the halfway point to criticise anyone struggling, and the other two would run along to bully and chastise them every step of the way. They carried the task out with a perverse sense of enjoyment of the pain being inflicted on them.

Soon, the weight of the knapsacks and kit began to tell on the shirkers; their speed dropped dramatically to a forced march by the time they had completed several laps. When they were finished, each man collapsed on the

231

floor or fell to his knees, utterly exhausted. They had to be helped off with their knapsacks by others because the straps had rubbed away and cut into their chafed skin. The evening sunshine, still quite warm, had also taken its toll on them. Trickles of salty sweat ran down their bodies, searching out and settling painfully in areas that had been rubbed sore. Eventually, only one man had to do the extra lap, and a while later came struggling in, ending his own personal torment.

The bullying had long stopped, turning into encouragement as they cheered him on and watched as he collapsed afterwards. Although they had driven the men hard, the NCOs had begun to feel a tinge of compassion for what they had put them through. So, seeing the men's obvious discomfort and dehydration, they grabbed buckets of water and threw the liquid over them, saturating them with it. After the initial shock, the men were grateful and attempted to drink from the buckets.

"Right, we're done with yer," one of the NCOs declared. "Get yourselves off and have those injuries seen to. Have an early night, and make sure you are all on the gun tomorrow."

Ignoring the food on offer at the cookhouse afterwards, the men dragged their tired and bruised bodies off to their tents to sleep and escape the torture. All those watching them trudge away agreed that the malingerers had learned a good lesson that day, and further punishment shouldn't be necessary.

***

After Barnes' accident there had been no further severe injuries, so Sarah was able to get back from the field hospital to stay in the cabin again. The last few days had been particularly intense for her as she nursed the men during the day and stayed overnight to care for Barnes. She was now feeling in desperate need of a rest herself.

Because Barnes was now making a dignified recovery – both physically and mentally – it was decided by Doctor Charlton and Major Townsend that he was strong enough to make the journey to Valletta. The doctor informed Sarah that she would accompany him, setting off the next morning. She was delighted to be leaving the camp, although temporarily, and was looking forward to the change of scenery.

Her impulsive decision to answer the plea for a nursing volunteer and travel to Fort Anchor to serve her calling was a noble ideal. Still, the shock of her encountering Marsh had been unexpected. Along with the long hours on duty and the tetchiness that had grown between them, her initial enthusiasm to be there was rapidly wearing off.

"Good evening, Miss," said a polite sentry as she and her armed guard passed him.

"Oh, thank you – and to you," she replied.

Finally, she stopped outside the cabin and pulled the shawl on her head down onto her shoulders. She said goodnight to her armed guard and, pushing a few errant hairs back into place, entered.

"Hello Sarah," said Victoria, looking up from her store's ledger. "It's nice to know things are getting back to normal at the surgery. Come and sit here and tell me all about that poor mister Barnes. How on earth did you cope? You must tell me over a drink," she said, rising. "So, sit down there – though I must say you are looking a little tired and drawn yourself."

"Thank you, Victoria. Is it that obvious? I've been most desperate for your feminine company, too, I must say. Barnes has recovered well after that horrific injury he had. The deep depressing gloom concerning his family's future has also slowly lifted. Now he's looking forward to going home and seeing the work on offer at the Woolwich Arsenal."

"Oh, that's good to hear," said Victoria, showing her concern.

"After he began to stand and get around – clumsily at first – a soldier with carpentry skills made a crutch for him, fashioned out of a length of discarded wood. He's still learning to use it, of course, but I feel he is doing well, considering – but can I hear voices?"

"Yes, it's David. Following his discussion with the doctor, Robert has decided that David is to escort Barnes to Valletta tomorrow in the supply wagon, along with the armed guard."

"Oh!" exclaimed Sarah, disappointed. "I thought it would be someone else."

"Sarah, stop it! You both need to get talking again. David adores you – and you're fond of him, too, I know you are. From what Robert told me, David is besotted; he's beside himself with feelings for you. But he told Robert that each time he pays you a compliment, you throw it back in his face. He doesn't know what to say to you anymore."

Sarah threw up her arms in annoyance. "Because he's only after one thing! If I give in, I feel like he'll go off and leave me, just like he did before – and I won't ever let him do that to me again."

"Of course he's only after one thing, silly!" Victoria exclaimed. "He *is* a man, of course!

The trick is to get him involved emotionally. Then you'll have him right where you want him. As we're the stronger sex, it's only right to make him earn it. He's becoming a tinge jealous now: he's picked up on the odd whistle aimed your way, and he doesn't like it, so I'm told."

"Victoria, he took my virginity while I was under the influence of the drink that *he* gave me. He planned it to the end," she said hotly. "Then he left me high and dry in Newcastle, once he knew I was falling for him. That is hardly the act of a gentleman!"

"Sarah, you gave your heart too quickly. I know how it must have seemed at the time – a dalliance even – but I can let you in on a little secret," Victoria said, lowering her voice. "Do you know he went back looking for you after they were ordered back to Woolwich? I can tell by the look on your face that you didn't. David told Robert he went back to the Blue Boar and made enquiries about you with the proprietor. The landlord's wife gave him very short shrift on your behalf," she added, which drew a smile from Sarah.

"Good for Rose. I am so glad she did," she remarked with bitterness.

"You never told him you had to suspend a nursing career to look after your father, so he had no idea what happened to you," Victoria explained. "And the reason they left Newcastle as they did was because they were ordered to by Colonel Downing. It had nothing to do with David at all."

"I can understand that," said Sarah, "but he spent that last day sulking and refusing to speak to me, even when I was friendly towards him. He could so easily have left a message. I was at the Blue Boar for another three weeks before going back to nursing school."

"True," said Victoria, "and I do see what you mean, but from what I gather, it wasn't until he left you that he realised you meant more to him than he knew!" She shook her head dismissively, tiring of making the point. "At any rate, Robert has the whole camp to worry about and hasn't got time for two warring lovebirds with a spat on."

The words hit home – and they hurt. "I remember Robert did attempt to tell me, but I ignored what he had to say because I was so angry." Sarah sighed. "I just don't want to be hurt again. Nor do I want him to be hurting. You're right when you say I'm fond of him, but it's difficult to trust him after the way he behaved. I trust your judgement; if you really believe he is in earnest, I'll stop putting him down. I just hope he'll be as forgiving as I am." She gave a long yawn. "Oh, Victoria, I've been feeling so tired and down lately," she declared, refocussing her eyes on her.

"Perhaps a little flirting and forgiveness are just what is needed," Victoria replied with sympathy. "You could start right now. David is in the other room, after all."

"Is it too late for me to freshen up? I could wash and put something on to please him."

"If he even thinks of leaving, Sarah, why, I'll trip him up and sit on him, and with the weight of this baby bump, he'll not move until you get in there!" Victoria said, urging her to go. "I'll give it a few minutes, and then I'll go in and keep him talking so you can come in whenever you're ready."

"Oh, I've been such a fool," she said. "I'll be back soon – and thank you, Victoria." She then hitched up the front of her full nurse's dress and left through the doorway to her bedroom.

After listening to the men's conversation outside the door for a while, Victoria chose her moment carefully, walking in at an opportune moment.

"... we need to sort it out before too long, that's for sure."

Seeing her as he turned towards the door, Marsh livened up. "Ah, Victoria, I want to know how you can look so cool and gorgeous after the day's heat. It's been very humid today – a real killer," he moaned.

"You are an incessant flirt, David," she answered tolerantly. "I've suffered as much as anyone else. Ask Robert."

"Yes, but not everyone is pregnant, are they?" he asked, charming her with his answer.

They chatted amicably for a while before the door opened and in swept Sarah, looking stunning. Victoria smiled. Her friend looked happy and beautiful.

"Hello, David. Hello, Robert," she said as she glided into the room. "I thought I heard voices in here."

"Hello, Sarah," said Marsh, rather breathlessly, as he took in her beauty. "You're not with your patient, then?" he asked, taken aback by her friendliness.

"No need to now; he's mending well," she replied. "The doctor will listen out for him tonight. We're taking him to Valletta tomorrow, aren't we? Together, I mean!"

"You don't mind?" he asked, fearful of the answer.

"Of course I don't mind. Why might you think such a thing?"

He couldn't believe his ears. "You don't?"

"No, I don't," she tutted. "Why you would think that, I'm not sure."

Victoria mentally applauded her friend's cunning.

Now, David only had eyes for Sarah. She looked gorgeous, along with a freshness – gone was the dirt and sweat of the day. She had quickly washed, combed her hair, put on a low-cut emerald, green dress with lace-trimmed cuffs and hem, and was wearing matching emerald green earrings. The result was startling.

Victoria slipped her hand around Robert's waist as they watched the tension between the pair melt away into affection. Soon, they were talking to each other as if they were the only two in the room.

After a while, Marsh asked, "Would you sit with me outside for a while? The stars in the sky are crystal clear tonight and I would like to show them to you," he said, gaining in confidence.

"I would love to, David," Sarah replied, quickly glancing over at Victoria for a nod of encouragement. She returned the secretive gesture – meaning the plan had worked. Then, taking his offered arm, they made for the door.

Victoria felt rather pleased with herself as she watched them go.

"You spoke to Sarah, then?" her husband observed.

"Yes, Robert. I explained everything to her and why he had to leave Newcastle. She admitted she refused to believe he went back looking for her, but I must just say I think he hurt her badly."

"Well, let's hope they've made up for good, then," said Townsend. "Now, where are those important papers I've got to read? I've put them somewhere."

"Here they are, Robert," Victoria said, handing them over.

"What would I do without you?" he asked and pecked her cheek in appreciation.

***

Outside, the sentry saluted as Marsh and Sarah passed by. He walked her a little way before sitting down on a flat boulder, hoping she would join him.

"Look at this, Sarah – it's probably been here for millions of years and will probably be here for millions more," he said, feeling incredibly romantic under the star-laden sky.

"And had millions of bottoms sitting on it," said Sarah in an entertaining, dismissive sort of way. They both laughed, imagining the silliness of the thought.

She held onto a low branch of the Aleppo pine and looked out across the sea towards Gozo. It was another warm, cloudless night, with the light from the full moon shimmering and flickering on the still waters below. She could see the darkened outlines of Comino and the larger island of Gozo beyond it in the distance.

Because Sarah hadn't sat with him, Marsh walked over and stood behind her at the pine tree.

She sensed his closeness behind her. "You were right, David. The stars are wonderful tonight, aren't they?"

The scent she had dabbed at the nape of her neck had done the trick, hanging in the air around her and drawing him nearer. He realised just how desirable she was as he moved in close. "Yes, Sarah, but not as beautiful as the sparkle in your eyes when you smile."

She suddenly dropped all pretences. "That's a lovely thing to say, David, after the way I treated you. You said you went back, but I didn't believe you or Robert – I didn't *want* to. You hurt me very badly, you know. You should have insisted instead of staying silent."

His hand felt for her slim waist. When he found it, it rested there for a while and then slipped to her hips.

She forcefully pushed it away. "Why didn't you insist?" she asked him again while trying to stay focused. "I would never have believed you if Victoria hadn't repeated to me what Robert had told her. I could have been beastly to you forever and ever."

He didn't answer; he was busy nuzzling his nose into Sarah's hair, her femininity overcoming his senses as he did so. When he found the scented spot, he kissed it. Then, after a short pause, he said, "Because I didn't think it was so important, but I do now." He turned her to face him. "I do now," he repeated, and then he kissed her on the side of the cheek, slowly moving his lips and lightly brushing her face with them until they settled lovingly on hers.

"God! We've both been such fools," she whispered. Closing her eyes, she responded eagerly to his touch and kissed him back. "I'm sorry, David, for my part, I–"

He cut her words short as he kissed her passionately again. This time, a hand moved to her breast and held it there. Spellbound and light-headed with the romance of it all, she suddenly became aware of what he was doing. Pulling his hand away, she firmly smacked it. "No, you don't! You know we are taking Barnes to Valletta tomorrow, don't you?"

"Yes, so what?"

"I need my sleep," she retorted. "I'm exhausted, running after all the aches and sprains in the fort, and I'm to be up early in the morning to get Barnes ready for the journey."

"Yes, but so what?" he repeated.

"You are awful," she scolded him mildly.

"Look, when we get to Valletta tomorrow, we'll be staying overnight. You can share my room for the night if you want to?" he suggested. "It would save you a good penny or two."

She ignored the question. "Will you walk me back now, David? It has been such a long day, and I am tired." She was forced to use the back of her hand to stifle a yawn.

Doing as he was told, he walked her back to the cabin. Then, kissing her on the forehead, he bade her goodnight, safe in the knowledge he had plenty of time to work on her in Valletta.

Sarah stepped inside, watching through the small window as he made his way back into camp, then yawned again. A flicker of a smile crept across her face as she recalled their conversation.

It felt so right, being in his arms. His kisses still excite me, but I had to be quick to stamp on his advances. He's a mite too eager to forget everything else – and there will be plenty of time for that in Valletta.

We shall see, she thought. *We shall see!*

***

Early the next morning, Sarah arrived dutifully to help Barnes prepare for the journey and gather all his belongings. Large empty hessian sacks had thoughtfully been laid out in the back of the wagon for him to rest on and help absorb most of the bumps in the road. She had with her his medical record and papers, which Doctor Charlton had instructed her to hand over to the chief medical officer, along with Barnes, on their arrival.

"Good morning, Captain Marsh," said Sarah when Marsh arrived with his detail.

"Good morning, Miss Cummings," he replied. "I trust you slept well and are looking forward to the journey?"

"Oh, I'm looking forward to the journey," she confided. "It's staying overnight I'm worried about," she answered in a low voice only Marsh could just about hear.

He tried to gauge her meaning, but her expression gave nothing away. *Is there a double meaning there?* he wondered. *Is she consenting to stay with me or not? Or is she just teasing me?*

Before he could find out, Barnes came hopping out of the tent, holding a crutch under his arm. As he hobbled to the wagon, Marsh ordered two soldiers to help him clamber up. They soon had him inside, but he insisted on staying at the back when leaving camp to wish his comrades a last farewell.

Sarah sat next to Corporal Collins on the bench seat in front. He, in turn, was attempting to keep the eager horses in check: the team were keen to get going, neighing and pulling restlessly in their harnesses.

"Make sure those notes go everywhere with Barnes, will you, Sarah? And I'll see you when you get back tomorrow," said Charlton, looking over his patient for the last time.

"Of course, Doctor."

"Right, men, get mounted," ordered Marsh. Twisting in his saddle, he looked back to check they were ready. Then, calling, "Forward!" he led them off.

The small party began to move away, passing gathered friends who wished Barnes, "All the best and good luck," bringing a tear to his eyes. On riding out, Marsh returned the salute from the sentries at the camp entrance.

Townsend watched them depart, but he had other things on his mind. After many weeks of work, he was satisfied with how the fort had been completed. Most of the craftsmen had gone now, leaving it near finished and empty as his footsteps echoed on the bare flagstones he walked on. Lieutenant Berry and his crew had almost completed the roadway at the very top of the hill. He could start thinking now of having the rest of the armaments, including the Gatling gun, brought in. In preparation for the arrival of the only cannon, his fort would hold. The hundred-ton beast was still making its slow journey up-slope towards it.

"Good morning, Major."

"Ah, good morning, Mr Galea," said Townsend, raising a hand to greet the man. "Your men are nearly done here, aren't they? As soon as our gun arrives and you have the wall finished, there won't be anything left, I should imagine. What will you do next?"

"Something will turn up, Major. It usually does," said Galea, with an expansive shrug. "And you, Major, what will you do?"

"Oh, I'll be here! This fort will be fully fitted out by then. It will be armed to the teeth on a full war footing."

"Where will the main arsenal be situated, and how will the gun be armed and fired, Major?" Galea asked, interested.

"I can understand you're keen to know what will happen to the parts of the fort you helped to build, but you should know by now I can't divulge that sort of information, especially to a civilian," Townsend reminded him. "But suffice to say the large stores to be delivered here soon are all the components we'll need to keep the gun firing. The gantry assembly will start today, and the men charged with it assure me it will be finished well before the gun enters through the open parapet."

"That is good news," said Galea.

A call rang out from the sentry, cutting off their conversation. "Morning patrol returning! Inform the major!"

Townsend heard Sergeant Savage reply, "He's in the fort. They can make their report to him there." Townsend immediately turned away from Galea and walked out to meet with the patrol leader.

The corporal's boots could be heard hurrying over the Guthrie bridge and through the gate into the fort, and he saluted the major as soon as he came into sight. "Sir, we've had more reports of cattle and other livestock going missing from the local farmers. We found footmarks and tracks left on the soft ground. I have to report that it looked like a substantial number of men, sir."

"Where was it?" asked Townsend.

"At Cactus Forest, west of Mellieha Bay," said Corporal Reeves. "We followed the trail but lost it on the blasted hard ground again. There are also a few caves in the area, sir."

Townsend thought about this for a moment. "Tomorrow, I want you to take enough men and check those caves out," he ordered. "It was the same after Jim Newberry got killed. The tracks were lost across the hard ground. It's frustrating, but they will eventually give themselves away. If we could trace them back, we could bring this mystery to a successful conclusion, but we can't do that if we keep losing them!" He shook his head. "At least the local people are no longer being attacked or physically hurt, which is a relief, so thank you for your observations, Corporal. Take your men and get some well-earned refreshments."

He had now been joined by Captain Hill, attracted over by the commotion caused by the returning patrol. "Has it happened again, Major?"

"I'm afraid so. We must be wary in case something is going on, Captain. Ideally, we need to take prisoners and make them talk. Just one is all it would take. Looking back, it's a shame we didn't take greater care of the one prisoner we did have; we could have learned a lot from him. I feel he's connected to these other incidents somehow. Sergeant!" he called out.

Sergeant James stepped forward from the gathered group. "Yes, sir."

"I want you to have a signaller sent to me at the command tent. I need to inform the regiment of what's happened and ask what they wish me to do about it."

"At once, sir."

Galea, who had withdrawn silently to one side when the officers arrived, waited for them to leave before scoffing to Khalif, "Fools! They have nearly given the game away again, getting more food. You, Khalif, will go there. Tell those dogs I will personally rip their tongues out if they keep defying me. I will not be pleased, so remind them what happened to the other two who disobeyed my orders. Remind them to have patience while we get them more food and tell them to leave the caves because the British want to search them. There are other places to hide in without them being found. Tell them to take everything and leave nothing to show they were there. We must wait until the British gun is mounted, and then we can delay work on the wall to allow our men to get inside once they have practised firing the gun. It is vital to ensure all our men are ready at the same time. Then, after the gun is fired, we will take it over and bombard Valletta at our leisure. Our

people can then have their fun and revenge themselves against the British."
He relished the thought, imagining how his plan would unravel.

"I will see to it, Edoardo," the loyal Khalif promised.

Chapter 19

Quality time in Valletta.
Normal relations resumed

THEY MADE the usual slow progress, driving along the narrow dirt track to Valletta. That part of the journey made for a rough ride and put enormous strain on the wheels and axles – and the spines and backsides of those onboard the wagon.

"Hopefully this road will be improved now the fort has been built, sir," said Corporal Collins.

"It's just sections that need levelling out," Marsh replied, "but you will undoubtedly be delighted when I say future store deliveries will come by barge after today."

"That is good news, sir," Collins remarked earnestly. "I don't think my bones could have stood it much longer."

Apart from Barnes' odd moan or groan, the hessian sacks cushioned him well from most of the shocks and jerks as the wagon lumbered on. Sarah, however, had to hold on at times as the wheels jarred on the exposed rocks.

Before long they came across the working party of signallers, whose first thoughts were to pick up their rifles – only to put them down again, visibly relieved, on recognising the uniforms. They snapped to attention, saluting as the captain stopped his party beside the group.

"Durban, is it?" asked Marsh.

"No, sir. Durham."

"Have you or your men come across anything suspicious since we last met?"

"No, sir, but we have noticed how it's getting quieter as we get nearer the fort," he reported.

"How do you mean?"

"Well, we've been attracting local people and children along the route. They watched and asked questions about what we were doing. But we've had none of that for a few days."

"Mm," said Marsh thoughtfully. "Just keep yourselves alert and your eyes and ears open, and report anything you find odd. We are still having problems with insurgents around here."

"Yes, sir."

"Since we're here – and I think our passengers would be glad of a few minutes' rest –where is this thing you call a telephone? Can I see one? How does it work?" asked Marsh, showing a level of interest before dismounting.

"Here it is, sir," answered Durham, passing the telephone to him and pointing out the relevant parts. "You listen here and talk through there. You are familiar with Morse code and semaphore, sir?"

"Of course," Marsh replied, examining the curious device. "Get on with it."

"Well, sir, this makes those other two systems outdated. You can talk to someone at the other end and listen to the answer with this new contraption."

"What, like this?" he said, holding his arm out.

"No, sir, like this. You put it up to your ear first. Also, if I may say, you're holding it upside down! Then, you connect it to the line like this, before turning this handle, which is connected to a small generator. It will put an electric current down the line to ring the bell at the other end. On hearing the bell, someone will pick up their telephone and start talking back to you, like this."

To demonstrate, he rang the signals engineer at St. Elmo Fort, who picked his receiver up. "Hello, Billy. I'm testing the line again. I want you to speak to Captain Marsh, if you will."

His demonstration had gained everyone's full attention – including Sarah and the mounted soldiers.

"Greetings, sir."

Marsh immediately held the telephone at arm's length, staring at it before slowly placing it back to his ear. "Greetings to, er, you," he said falteringly. "Am I really talking to someone at Fort St. Elmo?"

The wonders of modern science, he thought. *Or is it the devil's work?*

"Yes, sir. It's me, Private Bill Watkins."

"Good Lord!" exclaimed Marsh, nearly dropping the device before handing it straight back to Durham. "Here, take it! I'm lost for words." Recovering his composure, he stammered, "Well, thank you, Durham. It's a shock at first, but I'm astonished by your instrument." He then gathered his troop together and remounted, directing his group on towards Valletta. The incident had caused a great stir amongst his small party, and they spoke of little else for the remainder of the journey.

The trail to Valletta twisted and turned, running to and from the cable line, the best footings for the wagon track having been used. The heavy-gauge telephone cable had been run out as straight as possible between the poles to reduce costs and inefficiency. It primarily ran parallel to the track, only to part company and disappear out of sight before rejoining it further on in the featureless expanse of scrubland.

Eventually, they reached the stream that marked the halfway point. Thankful for the respite, the men stretched their legs while Sarah checked on Barnes. Captain Marsh had decided to walk a short distance away to rid himself of the numbness he felt in his legs, only to stop beyond the first bend of the meandering stream – just out of view. Dipping his neckerchief into the cold water, he wiped the trail dust from his face. He stooped and soaked his neckerchief again. Then, taking his helmet off, he slowly squeezed it out above his head, thinking how good it felt. Suddenly he heard movement from behind and turned swiftly, half drawing his sword from its scabbard.

It was Sarah, who was gazing down at him. "I was told you came this way," she said, carefully holding up the hem of her dress from out of the water's edge. "Did you have to come out this far?" she chastised him before squealing as her foot dipped into the chilled water.

"You should never creep up on someone like that," he admonished. "You could get yourself hurt." He loosened his tight grip on the sword handle and pushed it back in its scabbard.

"Don't you snap at me, Captain David Marsh of the Royal Artillery," she said curtly. "I'm not in your flaming army." She cast him a flirtatious smile. "In any case, you being a world authority on birds, especially pigeons, I want to know what type of pigeon they are – those two, making all that noise above us." She pointed upwards.

"Ha!" He laughed, relaxing a little. "They're not pigeons, but turtle doves. They're feeling unsettled now, slowly gathering with others about here somewhere. That's why they're cooing. Later, when they feel safe and together, the flock will take off in small groups. Normally, they will fly around in a circle to get their bearings, then be off on migration to other lands." After a short silence, he added, "They are also a symbol of love, Sarah."

He moved towards her as he spoke, wanting to kiss her, but she side-stepped him and dodged his advances. "Where will they migrate to, David?" she asked, interested.

"Northern countries like England, mostly. Your town or backyard, who knows?" he shrugged, stepping closer once more. "It's a very romantic thought, don't you think? Eventually, they will return. One thing's for sure,

Sarah: they'll be home before us." He lightly bit his lip. "Have you thought any more about tonight?"

"Well, if it saves me good money from renting a room, I don't mind sharing with you – if you behave yourself. Promise?" she asked of him in a coquettishly flirtatious manner.

"Oh, I promise," he assured her, both hands raised and feeling pleased with her answer. "Come on, let's get back to the others."

As they trudged back to the wagon, he called out, "Gather the horses, men. It's time to leave!"

When Sarah was safely seated, it was just left to him to call the men to order. "Let's get going, then. *Forward!*"

The small party set off. Captain Marsh was more eager now than ever to get to Valletta.

***

Upon reaching the regimental hospital in the late afternoon, Sarah duly delivered Barnes and his case notes to the chief medical officer, who handed her a closed envelope to give to Doctor Charlton on her return. Finally released from duty, she went to wash and refresh herself with a change of clothes.

To Marsh's surprise, he had a passenger to take back. The brigadier called him into his office and told him that firing practice was to begin as soon as the gun was installed. "Any cookhouse staff and Royal Engineers surplus to requirements will leave and be redeployed elsewhere. As Fort Anchor becomes functional, it will have a cook, Corporal Harris, who will supervise the installation of all kitchen resources to his liking. He will travel back with you." He tapped a thick envelope on his desk. "This envelope contains Major Townsend's orders for the coming weeks and will be given to him on your return. Hopefully, we may be able to discuss further such orders over the telephone. Harris will meet with your men and stay with them; he will assist them in loading the supplies wagon tonight and meet up with you tomorrow morning, Captain."

"Yes, sir," he said, taking the envelope and saluting back.

Sarah was still at the hospital when Marsh – now off duty – went looking for somewhere for them to stay the night; when on their own time, officers often booked into local premises away from the military. Having found somewhere convenient, he paid for a double room and booked them in for the night. Then, after a welcome refreshing wash and shave, he was off out to find Sarah and show her the sights of Valletta. They had agreed to meet up in Palace Square near the Battery Street Inn where they would be staying.

At first, he couldn't see her through the crowds of people milling about in the square. Once, he caught a glimpse of someone he thought was her, but upon approaching, he found himself to be mistaken.

I'm too early for a change, he thought.

He was beginning to doubt she would join him when he saw her looking in the window of a milliner's shop, her overnight bag at her feet. Two soldiers stood at her side, trying to engage her in conversation. She was ignoring them while staring intently at the hats on display. He casually walked over and stood behind her, allowing his reflection to loom large over her shoulder in the window.

On recognising him, she smiled and turned around. "Oh, Captain Marsh, where have you been? Are you late, or am I early?" she asked nervously, patting at her hair.

"Hello, Sarah," he said. "It's probably me: it usually is." Hearing him speak and then seeing his rank sent the two soldiers slinking away, seeking other prey.

"My, you wash and brush up rather well, David!" she exclaimed. "And you've shaved too," she trilled admiringly.

"Thanks, Sarah," he replied, pleased. "The same goes for you! That blue dress is stunning. I'm honoured to be your escort," he said with true sincerity.

"I got cleaned up at the hospital," she admitted. "All the facilities were there and free, so I thought, why not?"

"Quite right too! What were you looking at in the window?"

"That lovely hat there," she told him, pointing it out. "The blue one. I can see myself in it, and I think it would go with this dress a real treat. It looks like a perfect match. I haven't the nerve to go in and try it on in case it does fit. Besides, there are too many people in there, and I was worried if I went in and it took time, I would have missed you."

"It matches your eyes, too, Sarah!" he remarked. "Perfectly, if I may say so."

"You often speak of my eyes, David," she romanticised with a coy shake of her shoulders and a tilt of her head. "Have you not noticed the rest of me?" she asked with an alluring modesty.

"Oh, very much so, and often," he said, taking her by the arm and lifting her overnight bag.

"Where are you taking me?"

"I know you and your family are churchgoers, so I thought I would show you St. John's Cathedral to see King John's Order of the Knights. Then, if you like, we'll visit the museum they're building to see the Michelangelo masterpiece of the death of St. John. What do you think?"

"Oh, I would love to," she said, thrilled with his plans.

***

A happy time was had amongst the buildings of the Christian heritage of Valletta.

After seeing some of the famous old buildings, Sarah turned to Marsh with a warmth he hadn't seen before. "Oh, David, I'm having such a wonderful time!" she exclaimed. "It's all so dramatic and beautiful. Words fail me. I want to stay here and paint these wonderful scenes – and I can't even paint!"

They laughed, profoundly engrossed and happy together.

"I want to take you back the way we came because I want to show you the superb natural views of the harbour before the night draws in," he offered, to which she readily agreed.

They linked their arms while walking through the square. Marsh hadn't noticed before but now he noted the number of admiring glances Sarah received from other men passing by. Robert was right – she was a head-turner – and he felt immensely proud to have her on his arm! He stopped her suddenly when passing the same hat shop he'd found her outside earlier.

"But before we go to see the gardens and harbour, we'll go in here and see that hat you liked so much," he announced, surprising her by pulling her inside. "If it fits, I want to buy it for you. As a memento of our visit here."

Sarah was amazed at the kind offer – and seemed in awe of everything in the shop – as she headed excitedly towards the hat stand, Marsh in tow. With only minor alterations made by the master milliner, it fitted her perfectly. He then gave her a striped hatbox to store it in.

They left the crowded premises with the empty hatbox safely tucked under Marsh's arm. Sarah was feeling extremely happy with the purchase – now sitting on her head – and the day so far in general. She was quiet as they walked on, for once finding herself lost for words with his generosity.

Is he softening my resistance? Bribery, I wonder? If he is, it's working a treat.

Next, Marsh insisted on showing her the gardens. Holding her hand protectively, he walked her past the Castille Palace and, among more admiring glances, to Grand Harbour. They spoke freely and happily together, enjoying the scenery but increasingly finding themselves in a world of their own.

The Grand Harbour spread out below them, full of ships at anchor and screeching gulls soaring high above the gradually darkening scene.

"Look, Sarah. They're carrying fresh supplies aboard that ship there, so it must be getting ready to sail. I can see bread, ship's biscuits, and barrels of grog being loaded," said Marsh, pointing it out.

"Grog! What's that, may I ask?"

"Oh, it's a mixture of rum, diluted with water and lime juice in the barrels."

"Oh yes, I think I heard about that in nursing school," she said. "It's to keep the sailors from sickening, I think."

"That's right."

Leaning against Marsh's chest, with her arms around him, Sarah declared, "How splendid the views are, David! They are to die for." Then, suddenly, she gave a great yawn as she nestled in closer to him. "Excuse me. I'm so sorry, but I'm getting tired. You packed such a lot into just a few hours… it's overwhelming me." She began to yawn again. Good manners demanded she cover her mouth with the palm of her hand, exactly as her mother had taught her to do.

Realising the long day was tiring her out, Marsh led her back to the Battery Street Inn.

"Stay here with your bag and hatbox while I sign us both in," he said, leaving her standing under a large painting of a biblical scene. "Can I have my room keys, please?" he asked at the desk.

"Yes, sir. Your names, please, and how long you are staying for?"

"Mr and Mrs Marsh," he replied. "Staying overnight."

Out of the corner of his eye, Marsh saw that Sarah had turned her face to the painting on the wall, pretending to study it. She was blushing profusely and using her hand to fan her hot cheeks, hoping her discomfort would go unnoticed by the clerk at the reception desk.

She climbed the stairs first while he carried her hatbox and baggage. He enjoyed the view of her rolling hips immensely – *deliciously different from how a man walks*, he thought.

"This is ours, in here," he said, stopping her and turning the key in the lock. He pushed the lightly creaking door open and showed Sarah in. It was a small room dominated in the middle by a double bed. There was a cupboard, a basin with a water jug, a chair, and a small table.

"It's not as good as the Blue Boar, Sarah, but it will do for tonight," he uttered.

"It should be alright," she replied, inspecting the furnishings, "the sheets are clean. I heard you say we were married downstairs. I know you weren't believed; I could tell from the clerk's expression."

"I know he didn't believe me, but he saw you and was green with envy for me," Marsh teased. "I felt he would have swapped with me anytime."

"It felt embarrassing at first, I must admit… but the words 'Mr and Mrs Marsh' did have a nice ring to it. I had no idea you–"

"Let me light this oil lamp before you go further," he interrupted her. His passion for her was beginning to take over.

She tried again. "I had no idea–"

Her words were cut short as he spun her around, kissing her passionately and longingly on the lips. "Shh," he whispered as he kissed her again, greedy for her response. "We'll talk about it tomorrow." He kissed her delightful lips again, but more tenderly this time.

She showed no resistance against his urgency to have her, though she did attempt to speak. Each time, however, he kissed her words away. He continued to stroke her body while fumbling to locate her dress buttons. *How can I get her out of the dress without ripping the material?* he wondered, the problem continuing to frustrate him.

After being taken unawares, she responded willingly to his pressing need for her. It was what they both wanted and knew would happen as she prepared to give in to his oh-so-obviously cunning and devious plan. Pushing him away, she calmly undid her dress and bodice herself, letting them fall to the floor, then stepped out of her frilly, long-legged drawers. Aware he was watching her, she bent over suggestively to pick her clothes up and lay them neatly on the table in a slow, measured way, giving him a show.

Now that his problem was solved Marsh undressed quickly, leaving his clothes where they fell in a heap before pulling Sarah to him and kissing her more.

"Let me go, David. Let me at least get into bed, for goodness' sake!" she said as he pressed more eagerly against her.

Reluctantly, he released her and watched as she slipped beneath the bedclothes. Fumbling and aroused, he put out the oil lamp and climbed in himself. He felt his way towards her in the dark before placing his head on her chest, where she held it.

"Thank you, David. I'll never forget today. It was breathtaking and most enjoyable."

Then she laughed, perhaps aware that he wasn't listening – he was pressing kisses to each of her breasts in turn. He'd started before her, and she had some catching up to do.

"David!" she gasped. "Please – please be gentle with me. Not like at the Blue Boar. My first time was in a drunken haze. Oh, you're such a tease! Oh, stop it, you bugger," she giggled, forcing his mouth off her nipple. "David, are you listening to me? I don't want it to be like the first time."

"I'm sorry, Sarah," he said, though he didn't sound it. "I was just teasing you. I realise now how lucky I am and how much you mean to me!" He moved closer, straddling her legs, and lowering himself to kiss her lips tenderly. "I've got every intention of being gentle with you, darling," he whispered passionately into her ear.

"I feel like I'm falling in love with you all over again," she said, then whimpered with pleasure as he slowly entered her. Gripping his shoulders, she murmured breathlessly, "Oh, yes, I do like that, David."

***

The morning came, and they were waiting at the predetermined spot to meet up with the supply wagon, which was tardy to say the least. His horse was tethered to the back, and Marsh went to pat its nose while undoing and holding onto its reins.

"Supply detail reporting, sir," said the corporal, jumping down and saluting.

"Thank you, Collins. What kept you?" Marsh asked, returning the salute.

"Harris, sir!"

"What went wrong?"

"Let him tell you himself, sir. Harris, get out here!" ordered Collins.

Harris climbed out of the wagon clumsily. "Sir," he said, standing upright and saluting.

"Well?" Marsh snapped.

"I needed my cooking utensils, sir. I couldn't leave them."

"You would have been given new ones," countered Marsh.

"No. It wouldn't do," the man insisted. "My pots and pans have got my name stamped on all of them, sir."

"He means burn marks, sir," said the corporal, who had been having this argument with others for some time.

"No. They've been broken in, sir. Like a good sword or gun, you get a certain feel for them."

"What he means, sir, is he's familiar with burning his spuds in these pots and roasting the guts out of his roasties, sir," said the corporal, laughing along with the others. "He's not known as Cannonball Harris for nothing. Or, so a little birdie told us, sir."

"They just don't appreciate good cooking, sir. They're mucky little commoners," said Harris in his defence.

"Get back in the wagon, then, Harris, and let's get going," said Marsh. "Even if you can't cook, you should provide good entertainment, for sure."

"I know plenty of funny tales, sir. Many you have probably never heard of," Harris said, completely misunderstanding the officer.

"Get in the wagon, Harris; we have no time for any of that." He helped Sarah up to sit next to Collins for the return trek. "Mount up, men." Then, after mounting himself, he turned in the saddle and called out, "Let's get back to the fort. *Forward!*"

The convoy moved off with an accompanying rattle of pots and pans. By the time they reached their scheduled stop at the stream, the rattling had become a cacophony of clanking. The noise had slowly increased as the wagon slipped, slithered, and bumped its way along.

Marsh dismounted with his men before handing the reins of his horse over to one of them. Looking into the back of the wagon, he found Harris buried beneath a pile of ovenware.

"You're certainly amusing, Harris. Now, see if you can batten that lot down and stop the bloody din in there. The area we're coming to is known for bandits, and we don't want them to ambush us, now, do we? Are those empty sacks still in there?"

"Yes, sir. But I'm sitting on them. It stops the jarring of the wagon over the bumps, sir," he whimpered as he shifted his position again.

"God help you if we have to make a run for it," Marsh growled. "Get them bloody pots and pans in the sacks now, and that's an order. If it's a toss-up between your comfort and the men and Miss Cummings being shot at, your backside will lose every time."

"Yes, sir. Right away, sir!" He scrambled to comply; the thought of gunfire had deeply unsettled him.

Marsh had barely spoken to Sarah during the journey back, but on catching her eye a time or two they'd shared a knowing, satisfied look, both inwardly smiling at the thoughts of their time together and the fun they'd had.

Once everyone had stretched their legs and refreshed themselves, they were soon off. Before long they came across the signallers again, digging in yet another pole to carry their treasured cable.

"Attention!" ordered Durham on seeing the wagon returning.

"Halt!" ordered Marsh, leaning forward and resting his arms on the saddle horn. "Stand at ease, men. Have you seen or heard anything unusual since yesterday, Corporal Durham?"

"No, sir, and still not seen any locals," he reported. "Rather odd, wouldn't you say, sir?"

"Yes, it is." He frowned. "It's as if the locals are afraid to be in the area. Do you think you will get this cable into the fort in readiness for the gun? I know the major is keen to get the fort kitted out and completed."

"I can't see why not, sir," Durham told him. "We seem to be on schedule, more or less."

"Good. We have our cook in the wagon for the fort. His name is Harris."

"What! Old Cannonball? We know him well, sir," said Durham.

"Fell off any ladders lately, Durham?" a voice from the wagon chimed in. "He's always doing it, sir, but still hasn't learned to fall properly." The men laughed as Harris continued, "Durham's nickname is 'Dropsy', sir."

"You two seem friendly," Marsh remarked, raising an eyebrow.

"We joined at the same time, sir," said Durham.

"Not another one from Burton-on-Trent, surely!"

"Where the good beer comes from!" the two men replied, singing it together.

"Bloody hell! It must be dangerous stuff; it's pickled both your brains," claimed the captain with a laugh. He waved his farewell before getting his team moving again.

***

"Inform the major the supplies wagon and escort are back," the sentry called down.

The wagon stopped briefly outside the cabin to let Sarah off with her baggage, then drove on to the command post for Marsh to make his report and hand over the new orders to Townsend.

Receiving them, he slapped them down onto his desk, saying, "I will look at those shortly, David. While you were gone, we had another instance of livestock being stolen. I had a semaphore sent to the regiment to inform them about what had happened and to ask what I should do about it. Their reply wasn't encouraging." He picked up the returned signal and tossed it to the end of his desk for Marsh to read for himself.

"It says here livestock stealing by organised gangs has gone on for many years, and usually stops once they realise we are out looking for them. There's no mention of the shooting at the signallers or the two soldiers killed. But they were informed by you, Robert, soon afterwards."

Robert sighed heavily. "The decision has been made for us, David. Let's just concentrate on that cannon."

***

"Victoria! Victoria! I'm back!" Sarah called out loudly as she neared the door.

Victoria saw her arrive and opened the door before she got to it.

"Oh, Victoria, I've had a superb time with David," gushed Sarah, striding in. "He showed me some of the sights of Valletta and bought me this gorgeous hat!" She took it out of the hatbox and placed it onto her head, spinning around on her heels as she did so, then posing in front of the solitary mirror.

Victoria clapped her hands in excitement. "Oh, it's lovely! But calm down; I can hardly keep up. Sit down here with me and tell me everything, but slowly. Don't miss anything out."

"Well," said Sarah, taking a deep breath, "he was such a gentleman and so romantic. Why, he signed us both in at a hostelry as 'Mr and Mrs Marsh'! I felt embarrassed at first, but then it felt so right, somehow. I'm almost sure he proposed to me, but my head was in the clouds, and now I can't be sure. He knew his way around Valletta, though I found some parts confusing. The sights he showed me there were stunning, and he was the perfect escort."

"Tell me more!" Victoria begged. "I can see he got what he was after, though."

"He may have, though I didn't say he did," Sarah said to her friend modestly.

"Well, whatever you two got up to certainly didn't do you any harm," said Victoria, amused. "You seem so different. More alive, somehow."

"Oh, is it that obvious?"

"I swear, Sarah – if you don't tell me, I'll go mad!" Victoria exclaimed dramatically.

Seeing she was captivated, Sarah began, "I was looking through the window of the milliner's shop in Palace Square. It was full of the most beautiful hats you could ever imagine. Two soldiers were standing there, trying hard to flirt with me. Well, I was having none of it..."

***

Khalif's spy network had doggedly followed the Signals working party, unseen, for several days. Though they recognised a cable was being run overhead towards the fort, neither they nor Galea understood what it was for. Not until two of Khalif's spies related the demonstration Corporal Durham had given to Captain Marsh – putting their whole invasion plans into instant jeopardy. Their knowledge of the fort's layout was good, gleaned from the idle chatter with the engineers building it. Next, they planned to find out how to fire the gun successfully using similar tactics. Therefore, it was essential to stop the British from contacting Valletta for reinforcements before they could fire the gun at the city. They had counted on easily disposing of the semaphore signals unit when necessary, but worryingly, the telephone cable was something else entirely.

That evening, while some of the merrier soldiers were in good voice, a huddle of men sat in a tent on the edge of the camp. Inside was Galea, Khalif, and Asif, quietly talking in hushed tones about this unexpected problem.

Galea was agitated. "We must not allow this to happen, Asif." In the gloom of the low adjusted flame of the oil lamp, his eyes turned to Khalif, his deep concern etched into his darkened facial features. "We must stop it no matter what the cost to ourselves. The British would be quickly upon us, and all would be lost. I repeat, we have to stop it."

"We know we can dispose of the signal party instantly," Asif said confidently.

Khalif agreed. "Yes, as planned. Our men have boasted to me that they have learned how to read and send semaphore signals themselves just by watching the British do it. We could send many messages together – once the attack starts – to confuse them."

"No, it wouldn't work, my friends. They would still be able to talk to each other. Maybe we could use explosives and blow part of it up? Though clumsy, it would work," Galea pondered.

Asif had another idea. "I have seen this cable close up and have handled it out of the sight of the soldiers. It has a soft metal on the outside. Two or three good strikes with a heavy sword will easily cut it through, Edoardo."

"That's it! That is the answer." He embraced each of the two men and kissed their foreheads in joy. "That is the answer," he repeated, delighted with the outcome.

They all agreed to cut through the cable immediately before the British could raise the alarm at St. Elmo. Galea was relieved to have found a relatively easy solution to a very tricky challenge. "We will get our hands on that gun," he said, clapping his cohorts on the back. "We will, my brothers – and soon!"

Chapter 20

Gun in sight of the fort. Trouble for the ladies. Burnt bums for Bombardiers

MAJOR TOWNSEND paced up and down the command tent. With him was Sergeant Major Horrocks, discussing the day's progress.

It had been a month since Barnes had been sent back to Valletta, and work had moved on a pace. After many gruelling weeks of sweat and toil, the gun was finally at the top of the last level in the road. The soldiers were exhausted, many of them nursing aches, bruises, and sprains – although Barnes' incident was by far the worst. Though tired, the men were in a jubilant mood, for this was the day the gun would begin its final approach to the fort.

It nearly hadn't happened, however. On the previous day, the gun had slipped back before they had time to drive in the wedges. It rolled back at an alarming pace, pulling the men with it four yards into the side of the hill, where it stopped abruptly – jamming itself into the hillside. Horrocks was thankful it had halted there, and no one was injured. He knew they had been fortunate. Had it rolled the other side towards the drop, then everyone would have to face pulling it up again from the bottom!

The big horses were being drafted in; now, they had the luxury of space to be used effectively. "We should soon get it to the fort, Sergeant Major. What do you think?" Townsend asked.

"We will see, sir," said Horrocks, who – for all his bluster – was a cautious man at heart. "Now we're on top of this hill, the going will be much easier. With the big Shire horses coming in, I can even see it being near the outer parapet wall sometime mid-day, if not sooner, sir."

"Give it your best, then," said Townsend. "Are your malingerers still at it? I noticed the guardroom has been relatively empty since your inspirational talk with them."

"Yes, sir. I have had them out there every day doing their bit on the pull," said Horrocks, grinning. "The penny has dropped with them, and now we have a better sense of achievement and understanding from them, if you don't mind me saying so. I don't think we'll have any more skiving, so I've eased off somewhat. But I should think they are more than happy to see the horses being drafted in," he added, tweaking his moustache.

"Very good. Carry on with it," said Townsend, pleased. "I think those scoundrels will be just as keen as everyone else to finally get it there. In the meantime, I'm wanted in the fort. Our steam experts will finish installing the boiler and the hydraulic accumulator today and plan to demonstrate it working. Also, the pulley system that went in yesterday is due for a test, and they want me to be familiar with it all. We will soon start taking delivery of the shells and charges from aboard the barges they will be sending here. Our Captain Marsh will be busy with that. So, it's all coming together at once, and it's beginning to get rather chaotic!"

Horrocks nodded, agreeing. "Always does! What type of shells will you be using in it, sir?"

"We will have four types in the shell store," he said, checking the ordnance list. "Let me see… there will be the common shell, the armour piercing, and the Palliser rounds. Then there is the shrapnel and case shot containing 2000 eight-ounce lead balls. That alone will take charges of 450lbs of the large black prismatic gunpowder to fire a one-ton shell at its maximum range. The amounts of charge will vary depending on the range, of course."

The sergeant major was impressed. "It's one hell of a gun, sir."

"That it is, Sergeant Major. That it is."

"Well, I can see you are a busy man, so I'm off to the gun with the men." Casually saluting his commanding officer, he left the tent, and within seconds he was barking out orders to his men to follow him to the gun.

He began by lecturing them on the benefit of the big muscular horses being brought in. "Right, get these big boys hitched up to the front of the sleigh," he said, pointing to the four Shire horses being led over to them by their handlers. "These magnificent beasts are indeed the workhorses of our Army, boys. Beasts of burden with a great temperament and willing to give excellent, noble service – unlike some horrible buggers we have here.

"They can easily pull wagons loaded with ammunition and men, or pull heavy cannons along difficult terrain," he waxed. "They can even pull the one thing they are renowned for, a dray wagon loaded with full beer barrels! The downside is: the teams of men upfront can stand down now to accommodate these big fellas." He was forced to stop his instructions amidst the backslapping and cheering of the men at hearing the good news. "The rest of you can take up positions with the ropes and crowbars and keep this thing heading straight towards the fort where we want it. You men at the back must be careful changing those pipe rollers from back to front; the last thing we want at this late stage is another Barnes-type incident!"

Although the work was hard, this far-flung, rough, beautiful area of Malta made for a magnificent setting, positioned as it was, overlooking Anchor Bay and on the extreme edge of the camp. In Horrocks' daydreaming mind, the cannon stood regally and with dignity – waiting patiently for the next stage of its transit. It was easy for him to imagine it holding its nose in the air while its minions scampered around to pander to its every need.

He snapped out of it when a horse snorted into his ear. "Right! Let's see how we go. *Are the section officers ready?*"

"*Section officers ready, Sergeant Major.*"

"*Horse handlers ready?*"

"*Horse handlers ready.*"

"On my command. *Heave!*"

Both the men and the horses took the strain, but the large load wouldn't budge. They stopped, and Horrocks inspected the gun, puzzled until he found the cause: it had been parked carelessly overnight near the edge of the road. Two rollers had broken off the edge of the roadstone and had made deep depressions into the softer, crumbling earth beside it.

With more encouragement from their handlers, the horses took the strain up again. "Come on. Come on there, walk on!" shouted the driver, shaking the reins at them.

His helper took hold of the leading horse's bridle, whistling shrilly to encourage Hercules to get the team moving. The cannon's muzzle glinted and dazzled in the sunshine as the horses hunched forward in pulling jerks, starting to find movement in the load. It began to shift as they took short, low strides, hauling the sleigh out from its deep rut. The combined strength in their haunches kept the load slowly moving, with the skilled men on crowbars guiding it along.

"Come on there. Giddy up, Dash! Pull, Jack, good lad! Pull, Bailey, that's my boy!"

With the driver continually shouting his encouragement, the four horses – working as a team, and pulling together – moved the gun on. The driver eased off from calling and shaking the reins as the gun trundled steadily on towards the fort.

***

Victoria's responsibilities were telling on her more now that her pregnancy was further along. On top of keeping all the ladies happy, Cook's orders for provisions had to be accounted for, too, so that none of the necessary food supplies were allowed to fall to a dangerous low level. She sensed a tension between Sally and Harris, the fort cook, which she always needed to navigate with sensitivity when speaking with either of them about their wanted stores. She worked hard to arrange for the men's clothes to be laundered, washed, and repaired by seamstresses as required. Also, she had to craftily make sure the sutlers only provided the men with authorised provisions with payment upfront, rather than selling them inappropriate things such as whisky and running up a bill for it. She could turn a blind eye to a certain amount of this to maintain good morale, but too much could cause problems. It was a punishable offence that could result in fines or eviction from the camp, which for some would mean destitution. There was always a delicate and intricate balance for her to maintain throughout her time in the camp.

Consequently, she was not too pleased to learn that some women in her charge had been fighting. Sally, a good source of information and – by this stage – a trusted confidante, was her first port of call.

"What's been happening, Sally?" Victoria enquired, meeting her. "What has been going on?"

"It's Fanny, madam," she replied wearily. "She caught that cow Maggie trying to give her Ossie a bit of the other. Fanny came across them haggling the price – he was going to take her up on it too! She sent him packing, though, with a flea in his ear, and swung Maggie around by her hair at the back of those tents just there," she continued, pointing out the spot. "She was left holding handfuls of it! Her mate Flo butted in with a mouthful of filth and got scratched across the face for her trouble. I've never seen Fanny like that before, madam, because she's usually got such a sweet nature. It's just not like her at all," she repeated. "The lass has been sorely provoked, and she has my every sympathy," she added.

"Yes, it sounds like it," said Victoria. "It seems tensions are getting higher the nearer the gun gets to the fort. Don't worry; I'll deal fairly with her. We're all under a lot of strain. Thank you for letting me know."

"You're welcome, madam. I know you'll do right by the girl."

Victoria found Fanny washing plates and cutlery in the next tent, smeared tear tracks still on her face. She had been crying, and recently too.

Gently, since Fanny was distressed, Victoria approached the woman. "What's been happening, Fanny?" she asked with sympathy. "You know we can't have this sort of thing going on. It's upsetting for everyone."

"I'm sorry, madam," she said, scrubbing at her face. "Things just got on top of me, that's all. Life's hard enough as it is without worrying if your old man has caught the clap," she added, then raged, "I'll kill Ossie if he took her up on it, so I will!"

"Calm down, Fanny," said Victoria reassuringly. "Sally tells me this is all out of character for you, and I believe her. I've had my suspicions about that pair – they're nothing but trouble. I intend to see to it that they're thrown out of camp. Leave it to me. I'll speak to my husband on the matter." She put a sisterly arm around the woman's waist. "Just see that this doesn't happen again, will you, Fanny dear?"

"Yes, madam, and thank you for being so understanding."

True to her word, both women were thrown out of camp and forced to return to Valletta on the barge that same day.

The ordnance was beginning to stack up inside the fort. The barge was making regular trips back and forth to Valletta, carrying everything the fort required. Wagon runs were now becoming a rarity. Thirty-three shells, each weighing a ton, were also delivered, plus the two automatic rammers used to push them and the gunpowder charges down the gun muzzle. The explosive charges and shells were kept separately down in the fort's magazines out of respect for potentially disastrous consequences. After some repair, the new road built to carry the gun up from Anchor Bay was put to productive use – getting everything up to the fort and over the Guthrie bridge, which was also completed. The courtyard to the rear of the final gun placement housed the water pumps, engine, accumulator, and the ever-growing amount of coal to stoke and fire the boilers with.

Towards early afternoon, the men became enthusiastic about finally getting the gun to the fort.

"Keep going, men!" the sergeant major shouted for the final time as they got close to the loading gantry. Even his voice was beginning to croak with the effort of many weeks of encouragement. "Almost there, almost there. We are there now! Stop the horses' driver!"

"Whoa! Whoa there, Hercules! Whoa, I say!" the driver shouted, pulling back hard on the reins.

All four horses stiffened at the haunches on command and slowed to a stop. With their highly defined muscles straining – and each snorting loudly with the combined effort it took to pull up – the horses slowly brought the load, juddering, to a standstill.

"Good lads, you all are. We are bloody well there!" Horrocks whooped in delight. "The team of horses have done sterling work, and that last pull left the gun extremely near to the lifting gantry. So, well done again to all of you. Cut those horses loose and feed and water them well; they have earned it. An absolute godsend!" he declared.

The horses were unshackled from the gun and led single file around the gantry in the courtyard, then back out through the gap in the parapet wall – along with congratulatory slaps from the appreciative men as they passed by. Beyond it, everyone who had been involved in getting the gun up the hill had massed together to see it reach its destination at last.

"We've done it! We've done it, Sergeant Major!" shouted Hart, shaking him intensely, his helmet nearly falling off.

"Yes, Hart, yes, yes. We've done it, so don't get carried away. Now get your hands off my uniform, or you'll be polishing the buttons for the rest of the day."

"Yes, Sergeant Major!" he shouted back as he released him. Then, after a long pause, he quietly added, "He did say you were horrible and ugly, sir."

Shooting a sharp glance at Hart, Horrocks stepped back a pace or two. "Fall in, Hart! That's a good chap." Mildly relieved that he did so without further comment, he then addressed the crowd. "Right, men, we're here now, and that's good news. The other good news is I've declared the race between the two teams a draw! You will *all* have the privilege of bathing in those crystal blue waters below where we stand. We'll forget protocol and formality all afternoon – so get yourselves down there, out of sight of the ladies, and give yourselves a good dipping in those warm Mediterranean waters they have here." He sniffed as they theatrically cheered. "God knows some of you need it! I have been given special permission by the Commander to give you all double rations of ale tonight." Another round of cheering followed. "Remember, I don't need permission to come down hard on anyone I find abusing the privilege, so take it steady, lads. Go on, get down there and enjoy it while you can. You have earned it."

He stood carefully out of the way as a mad race ensued to get to the water, the men joking and shouting as they ran. Some took off down the zig-zagged road, while others took the direct route straight down, tumbling and falling in a headlong dash to be the first to get into the crystal-clear waters below.

They hit the water with a tremendous communal splash, where they frolicked and splashed like children in the surf, hooting with laughter and wrestling each other on the sandy beach. Other, more adventurous souls saw fit to jump into the sea from overhanging rocks. The men's pent-up emotions – which had been bottled up while moving the gun – were released in minutes as they dived, swam, splashed, and relaxed, their group tension disappearing into the warm, blue Maltese waters. Some were stripped down to their long johns, but others were blatantly naked. It didn't stop the ladies in the camp from straining their necks to see what was going on. They had seen worse, after all.

"Some of them could put my Bert to shame, that's for sure," observed one lady wryly after a second and more lingering look.

"You are wicked, Hilda," said another. "Although, as you know, I'm not the bragging sort… but after seeing all the men, I can tell you my Frank is in a league of his own, for sure!"

The women cackled, using innuendo and humour to release the burden of tension they had also felt over the long, hot weeks while the gun had crept slowly towards its new home.

Only the officers and the armed guards remained above it all, the latter watching and grinning over their comrades. At the same time, the former recalled their own wilder days with amusement.

The commander joined Horrocks, overlooking the spectacle being played out before them.

"Thank you, sir," Horrocks said earnestly, "on behalf of the men. You should know how grateful they are. Getting the gun up here has been a difficult exercise for many of them, especially the older ones, sir."

"Thank you, Sergeant Major. It sometimes helps to let off steam, but none of this could have been achieved without your brand of encouragement and sterling input," he said, winking at him knowingly. "Anyhow, both Copperfield and Colonel Havers will be joining us again in the morning by barge, and I want these men to be in the right frame of mind to help get the gun mounted."

"They will be, sir," Horrocks assured him. "I'll see to it."

"Good. This place should start feeling more like a gun battery afterwards," Townsend stated with relief. "Colonel Havers wants to get on and align the cannon with the two loading portholes."

Together, they strolled over to the traversing platform, which sat directly under the gantry they had built. Large hooks were dangling down from the massive block and tackle, swinging slightly in the sea breeze. This behemoth of engineering was to be used soon to lift the gun onto its traversing platform.

"Those two muzzle rests must also be aligned to the cannon so that the gunpowder charges and shells can be rammed home cleanly, under steam power, by those two sixty-foot rammers lying down over there." Townsend pointed to the two implements on the floor. "You see, Sergeant Major, there is plenty for Colonel Havers to do."

"Yes, sir," said Horrocks. "I'm sure he'll find more work for my men in the process."

They were walking along inside the fort, discussing the minor problems they still faced there, when they heard excited voices echoing through the windows of the parapet. Ignoring them at first, Horrocks spoke affectionately of the gun. "Both cradle and platform are sitting there on the track, waiting for us to lift this lovely cannon onto it. The men want to see it fire, and frankly, so do I. Will it be soon, sir?"

But before Townsend could answer, the voices outside grew louder and more raucous, disturbing their conversation. Stepping back into the courtyard, they walked over to the unfinished parapet wall, where they saw an unusual sight. In their exuberant state, some of the men had thought it appropriate to sneak back once the officers had gone, clamber along the cannon's barrel, and sit on it. They were still laughing when the reappearance of the two officers instantly silenced them.

"What have we here then? Thought we'd gone, did you?" Horrocks shouted. Taking in the scene, he began to count them. Thirty-five men were astride the gun, with the last man clinging on doggedly. He was impressed with the total but couldn't allow the incident to undermine his authority.

"You on there! Yes, you! What's going on here, then? What have you to say for yourselves?"

Saluting the officers while still sitting astride the cannon, the soldier blustered out, "Sorry, Sergeant Major. We've never seen a gun this large before, and we wondered how many of us it would hold, so we climbed on top and took bets on it."

"I'm surprised you haven't burnt your bloody arses! It's been out in the full sun all morning."

"Well, it is getting uncomfortable, Sergeant Major!" said the man, about to climb down.

"You will get off when I say you can get off!" he roared, having already noticed the men's increasing discomfort. Intending to prevent such mischief in future, he deliberately asked them meaningless questions with an evil look in his eye, biding his time as their backsides warmed up. When steam began rising along the full length of the cannon, and he felt they had been suitably cooked, he allowed them off. "Right, boys, get down from there – carefully, if you can. It seems you're starting to dry out a little too fast if you ask me, so try not to leave any skin stuck to the gun. Think of who, out of you lot, will have the misfortune to clean and wipe it off."

A series of yelps, groans, and swearing poured forth as they delicately extricated themselves.

"You have a few hours to go, so get yourselves back down to the bay to enjoy the water – and stay there until your NCOs call you in," he advised.

He didn't need to repeat himself as they scampered off towards the beach, with many backsides red and sore – much to Horrocks' devilish delight.

"Don't be harsh on them, Sergeant Major," said Townsend, amused with how he'd handled it.

"Yes, sir – I mean, no, sir. Just maintaining discipline, sir," he replied as he wiped the smirk from his face. "I know they will have sore arses, though, when that saltwater gets to work." His grin had just returned when he spotted Victoria over the major's shoulder. She was looking for her husband as she tentatively picked her way through the debris strewn across the ground.

Clearing his throat, he said respectfully, "I think you are wanted, sir. Your good lady is on her way over," before turning and leaving them alone.

"Ah, Victoria," Townsend said, holding out a hand to steady her.

"I guess it won't be long now, will it, before the fort is ready?" she asked.

"Two to three weeks, we reckon – and then it will be a working fort," he told her. "And then, Victoria, we will be looking for somewhere for you to stay in Valletta, where you can have our baby peacefully."

She pressed her lips together momentarily like she did when she tried not to worry him, and Townsend braced himself.

"Robert, you know when you said you could feel the baby kicking you in your back again?" she asked.

"Yes, it was amazing!" he replied. "But I've felt the baby kicking for a while now."

She held his arm. "Yes, about that... I went to see Doctor Charlton with Sarah because she had become concerned for me. Well, he examined me and found I was a month further on in my pregnancy than I thought. Instead of coming up to seven months, he reckons it's more like eight! The doctor is also beginning to worry for me now. He said it would soon be too dangerous for me to travel. So, it looks like it's going to upset our plans. I'm sorry, Robert..." Her voice trailed off as she stood there with mixed feelings, plainly worried about his reaction.

He smiled wanly, with fatigue. "I'm not angry; it's just one of those things. Doctor Charlton tells me it's difficult to estimate when people conceived, and many get caught out." He chuckled. "I suppose he was trying to prepare me."

"Yes, he's not particularly subtle," Victoria reflected.

"It has forced our hand, that's all. Our baby is more important to both of us than anything. I was about to ask you to slow down because I felt you were doing too much. Come, I'll walk you back to the cabin, and we can talk some more. I don't want you coming to this part of the fort anymore.

The ground is unstable and littered with debris, and I don't want you to slip or fall and hurt the two of you."

Back at the cabin, he held her in his arms and kissed her gently. "I have to tell you something, my sweet, which I couldn't tell you before now. I received orders this morning for a general withdrawal of all the men and civilians surplus to the fort's requirements, beginning next week. I want you gone before then, especially after what you've told me. There's no sense in lingering now. I must see you gone before we start to regret it."

"But what of Sarah and the doctor?"

"They will go too, but later," he told her. "The Battery has no place for medical personnel at this time, so the only people left here will be David, myself, and enough men for Fort Anchor to function. So, the miscalculation with your pregnancy hasn't made a difference in the grand scheme of things."

"But I can't leave you so soon, darling," she implored him.

"You must, Victoria, though your time here has gone too fast for both of our liking. I have relished your presence, and you have done sterling work here with both the ladies and stores, but I want you on that barge to avoid any overcrowding later. Anyone in the field hospital will also go back with you to Valletta. Doctor Charlton will see to it."

"I must tell Sarah," she said rather weakly, plainly upset.

"You can tell her later. In the meantime, let's spend this hour together. Forget about outside and the others for now. Meanwhile, I need a strong drink," he sighed.

After a few moments of thought, she asked, "But all the Royal Engineers won't go, will they? The sergeant major, for all his bluster, is such fun! He's very likeable and amusing, and I did enjoy his company whenever he dined with us. He had such thrilling, entertaining tales to tell Sarah and me of what he had seen, and we heard so few. Surely, he won't go, Robert?"

"I'm afraid so," Townsend confirmed. "Horrocks will stay after the initial departure, along with a few engineers to carry out the mounting of the gun and to iron out any snags under Colonel Havers' direction. He goes when that's finished, and then we commence firing practice."

"Does David know?" asked Victoria. "He'll be concerned for Sarah."

"No. I will tell him later, along with Sarah and the sergeant major. With Havers and Copperfield returning, I want you to arrange our meals with Sally. I'll be asking them all to dine with us tomorrow night. Would you do that for me?"

"Yes, Robert, of course."

"Don't mention any of this to Cook until I've spoken with Havers and confirmed it."

"No, I won't, Robert," she assured him.

The dinner was held the following evening at the major's cabin. Colonel Havers, freshly returned from a stint at Fort Rinella, came into his own as he enthralled them all – especially the ladies – with his stories before describing how the gun would work and how they would set it up to work with the steam accumulator. This particularly interested Horrocks, who had no idea what an accumulator was or its function relating to the gun.

After the meal, the officers agreed on a plan to evacuate the civilians and surplus Army personnel. Then, when Victoria gently reminded them that this was supposed to be a social engagement, the men yielded to talk of lighter things, including Havers' anecdotes of the problems other gun batteries were having to get their cannons ashore.

"Oh, and there was that Captain Cuthbertson at Gibraltar having his men on the wrong lifting gantry, while the bigger of the two gantries was being used to lift some other great weight. Somehow or other, they failed to winch the gun out of the ship. It couldn't be raised quite high enough. The gun was hoisted to the gantry's maximum height, but it was still a few inches short, making it impossible to transfer it to the sleigh! The height needed to clear the ship's side hadn't occurred to him for some reason. Most amusing." He allowed a lengthy pause for them to finish laughing. "I doubt he will live that down anytime soon, poor chap! I did feel sorry for him. The gun was dangling there wrapped in its chains, so he ordered over one hundred tons of sand and rocks to be loaded on board." He laughed at the thought of it. "When that didn't work, because it wasn't enough, he added water containers and more men on board until it sank sufficiently for the cannon to clear the ship and get transferred onto its sleigh.

"We are optimistic for Fort Anchor, though," he added once his companions had stopped their laughing. "It will be the first to fire its gun, as Rinella and Cambridge won't be ready for a few months yet."

"I can't wait, sir, and look forward to it," said Marsh.

"Indeed, Captain. Once that gun is safely on its carriage on the traversing platform, the work will start to align the gun's muzzle with its two loading turrets. Then I'm off again to the other forts in turn. It's a bit of a merry-go-round at the moment! The accumulator and the rest will be in full working order by the time I get back, I'll wager."

"When will that be, sir?" asked Townsend.

"In about two weeks. So, I wish to take this opportunity to say what a pleasure it's been to meet you, Victoria," said Havers, raising his glass to her. "You have been the perfect hostess."

"Why, thank you, Colonel. Your stories have been most amusing and riveting. Both Sarah and I have enjoyed your company – including Mr Copperfield and the sergeant major, of course!"

The colonel kissed the back of her hand. "You must visit me in Valletta once you've had your baby, Victoria. I look forward to your company and to repay you in kind. Goodnight."

The men then stepped out into the dark to be escorted back to their tents by the guards.

Townsend deliberately held Marsh back to inform him of his latest orders regarding the early evacuation of the men and support staff within the week.

"Thank you, Robert," said Marsh. "At least we can make our plans for it." He caught the look of concern on Sarah's face. "We can work out the finer details and allay any fears the ladies may have." He kissed Sarah on the cheek and wished Victoria and Robert goodnight before stepping out into the night air himself.

Chapter 21

At last, the gun on its cradle. Security clampdown. Kitchen established

ARMED WITH crowbars, the men carried on from where they had left off the previous day. It took all of their combined strength to manoeuvre the gun, inch by torturous inch, and get it under the gantry.

"We are almost there, men. Just a little further!" Copperfield ordered.

As the gun crept forward, the heavily marked rollers – now showing considerable wear – were moved from the rear of the sleigh and placed under the front for the final time.

"Right, stop! We're well under the block and tackle now, men, so that will do it," advised Copperfield. "Get them hooks over the trunnions and brace them there. Sergeant Major, can we have the half-ton collar brought over and get it fitted?"

"Yes, sir! You men bring that collar here. It's got to be fitted first before we go any further."

"Can't we leave it off, Sergeant Major?" asked one naïve young man. "The gun would be a lot lighter and much easier to lift, surely? Just like we did up the hill."

"Can't we leave it off?" Horrocks repeated the words in a singsong, mocking fashion. "You know, Johnson, I fear for the Empire when I hear words like that. No, you can't, you idiot! It helps with the point of balance of the trunnions. If we lift that gun as it is, it will drop at the bottle end with the muzzle end straight up, vertical – just like your dick before you exercise it! You would never get it on the carriage that way. The collar is a counterbalance on the muzzle end and keeps it level! Got it? It evens out both ends. We can then mount it on the carriage and *bolt it up! Then take it off and leave it off.*" He emphasised the final words by tapping firmly on the man's helmet with the knuckles of his hand. "The collar comes off the gun afterwards, silly boy."

"I see, Sergeant Major. It makes sense to me now," he said meekly.

"Well, get it on, man, get it on!" Horrocks commanded. "Use that smaller block and tackle at the far end of the muzzle. Push the bogey with the collar over to the muzzle and get the tackle on it. You two men get around here and help him. Come on, get a move on!"

After attaching the chain's hook to the collar, it was rapidly hoisted up and bolted to the gun's muzzle. Now the point of even balance was at the trunnions. Enmeshed and bound with rope and chain, trussed up and tethered like the monster it was, the gun was ready for hoisting.

Only once Copperfield was absolutely satisfied with where to place the lifting tackle did he ask the sergeant major to give the order to lift.

At first the beast of a cannon began to slip and slide on its sleigh, being dragged to the vertical before the chains slipped, in gripping it tightly. The ropes and the whole wooden structure started to creak alarmingly loud with the strain until – suddenly – the gun was free. It dangled there in the air, a few feet off the ground, while the wooden gantry continued to moan and groan with the weight it held.

"Right, you men, get that bogey out of the way – quickly!" said Copperfield, directing the men standing around. "Those on the chains and pulleys start raising it higher. Good, stop there. That's high enough. The rest of you can begin pushing the gun over to that traversing platform there." High-pitched groans came from the men as they carried out the order. "More. More! Well done, men, now stop. We are over it. We have to let it down with the pulley and chains quickly now. I don't like the noises coming from the gantry."

The gun was successfully lowered onto the traversing platform amid jubilant huzzahs. It nestled perfectly on the platform while the men busied themselves, clearing away all the ropes and chains from underfoot in the messy and dangerous work area.

"I can't believe it's finally here and mounted. All the arguments and tears shed getting it here have suddenly become worth it," said one relieved man, wiping the sweat from his brow.

Horrocks nodded. "Well, let's just hope we'll be here to see the firing, because I've heard a rumour, we will all be off in a week or two to elsewhere on the island. However, if we don't see it, we will at least hear it fire – you can be sure of that."

***

"That's me about done here, then," said Copperfield to Havers. "They can dismantle the gantry and then, in a day or two, get it down to the barge and store it in Valletta until one of the other two forts are ready to use it."

Havers nodded in agreement, then thanked Copperfield for his help and assistance with the project. "It wasn't without its snags and hitches, but they've mostly been sorted out now, making installing the other guns much easier."

His mind was already concentrating on fitting the two large recoil cylinders to the rear of the gun. They were designed to absorb the strong kickback expected during firing. Now focused entirely on these dampers, and working with his specialist crew, Havers began fitting them to the rear of the weapon.

Soon after the gun had been fitted and securely bolted to its firing cradle, the throes of decampment began. A large body of surplus Royal Engineers had already prepared themselves for moving out.

Townsend had watched the gun being mounted with keen interest. With it now inside the fort, he urgently wanted the wall restored. "Get me the gangmaster, Sergeant. Tell him to meet me here at his earliest convenience."

"Yes, sir," said Savage, turning on his heels.

He found Galea talking to his foreman outside the gate of the fort. Neither looked particularly busy but they had their heads close together, urgently whispering.

Odd, thought Savage. *You'd think they would be more interested in the gun now it's in place.*

"Excuse me, Mr Galea," he said, and the two immediately separated. "The major would like to speak to you at the gun emplacement as soon as possible."

"Thank you. I'll come straight away."

Galea waited for the sergeant to walk out of earshot before turning to his foreman and saying, in a low voice, "With it now in the fort, Khalif, they will be sending back many more of their men. We need to slow down the wall's closing somehow to allow our men time to arrive in greater numbers; there are far fewer currently than we need to make our mission a success. Immediately after they have finished test-firing that gun, we must be ready to attack in force. We will surely fail if we allow the wall to be finished too quickly."

"But our men are arriving every night, Edoardo," Khalif told him. "Soon, it will become difficult to keep them all hidden."

"Listen to me, Khalif: there are other caves on Comino, and there is that tower our men could use. No one lives on the island, and it's deserted. It would be mocking the British indeed if the watchtower on Comino

269

that helped defeat our ancestors would now assist us in taking Malta back. We must be wary, though. Anyone travelling on foot from Gozo through Comino to Malta must be allowed safe passage. If they were to see any of our men, they must be quickly eliminated. Our men must stay hidden, away from the main path leading across the island. Remember, the full attack begins in just a short time. We must have patience," he implored him.

"Once we have control of that gun, we will be able to pound Valletta into submission and kill them all," he continued. "We will destroy the British at will, long before they can react to us. The other two forts won't be ready, so there will be nothing to stop us. We will devastate everything and take these islands that have caused so much heartache to our people. Remember, my friend, while we are destroying their fortifications, they will be in a state of panic."

"What of the ships and their crews anchored in the harbour, Edoardo?" Khalif asked thoughtfully. "Surely, they are a possible threat to our success!"

Galea scoffed. "Their crews will be ashore, drunk and helpless while cavorting with the whores. Our men will torch their ships at anchor. As soon as one ship is on fire, the flames will spread very quickly to the others, effectively blockading the harbour entrance and stopping the British warships from escaping the fury of the flames. It will be carnage – a sight to savour. The Barbary corsairs will be back with a vengeance."

"But what of the other fortifications?" Khalif asked. "The British will have us in their gunsights, I fear."

"Yes, they will try, but we are out of range of the guns capable of reaching us here." He laughed. "Not so for us, with this gun! We will have our men in place to pick out targets in Valletta and relay them back through our communication line. Their big guns face out to sea and will be useless against us. It would take them far too long to turn them and, therefore, they will be destroyed."

Slapping his foreman on the back, he then strode off to meet Townsend, confident that his plans would come to fruition without a hitch.

"Ah, Mr Galea," Townsend greeted him amiably. "I want you and your men to complete the wall as soon as the gantry is dismantled and out of the way. We have the gun sitting in its firing cradle now, and it's at its most vulnerable."

"Yes, of course. I'll have my men start as soon as the gantry is gone."

"How long will it take?"

Thinking fast, Galea responded matter-of-factly, "Why, Major, it should take no more than three weeks. Certainly, no more than that."

"I want that wall closed within two weeks at the very latest," Townsend informed him.

"I don't think we can do it in that time," he replied, stalling.

"That's an order, Mr Galea," said Townsend, with a touch of sternness. "To help you, I'll allocate more engineers."

"Oh, there's no need for that, Major," Galea assured him hurriedly. "My men will get it done on time. I have enough here to do it, despite letting many of them go."

"Very well, I will return more of our men to Valletta in the morning."

Galea inclined his head. "You can rely on me, Major."

"Good. Now, if you will excuse me, Mr Galea, I have to–"

"Oh, there is one other thing, Major," he interrupted. "My men tell me they are no longer allowed in parts of the fort, particularly near the loading chambers and turrets. Is there any reason for this, may I ask?"

"My orders went out as soon as the armaments were delivered – only Army personnel are allowed down there now. You should have been aware of this, Mr Galea. It was in the contract as a condition of your employment. Everything down there is out of bounds to civilians. There is absolutely no reason for you or any of your men to have further access below ground level. Do we understand each other, Mr Galea?"

"Of course, Major," he said, keeping a lid on his temper. "It's just that, after all this time spent here on the fort's construction, I felt it would have been an experience for my men and me to see the gun being loaded from below."

Townsend curtly slapped him down. "It's beyond your remit, sir. Good day."

Galea was inwardly seething as the two men parted. He had not expected to have been given such short shrift over his men's presence at the fort, and he realised he would have to change his strategy once again – and quickly. He would have liked to see the steam engine working, especially the hydraulics required to reload the gun from the shell magazines and loading bays; he needed to be able to fire the weapon efficiently and quickly when the time came. Otherwise, he would have to force the gunners to operate it for them under the threat of death – and he doubted many would take that deal, given their connections to Valletta.

He hurried back to the worksite, where he told Khalif about the further change of plans.

During the next few days, Galea instructed his men to work as closely as possible with the specialist engineers so they could eavesdrop, listening for information on firing the gun without raising suspicion. They could also use bribes such as tobacco to help loosen the engineers' tongues if necessary.

"The pigs want the wall finished in two weeks, with the roadway across the ditch demolished," Galea said, annoyed. "We must stall for more time – without raising suspicion – because that is now our only access into the fort."

"What if they bring in more soldiers, Edoardo?"

"The commander wanted to, but I persuaded him that our men would be able to finish in the two weeks he asked for," Galea assured him. "Once they are relying on us, we can delay the completion. Our army should be fully equipped and assembled by then and ready to attack. We only have a small number of men here on the island now and very few in Valletta. Under the guise of passengers on our merchantmen, some of our men will put ashore at Valletta. Once in under their guns, we can take the harbour and shatter its fortifications with ease. It has taken careful planning, Khalif; in our children's time, books will be written to tell of our great courage and revenge," he claimed pompously.

"When most of the British have withdrawn, that is when we strike, my brother," he continued passionately. "But tell our men: in no way must the major be harmed. It will be my particular pleasure to cut his throat."

Khalif pondered the question and suggested, "We could make part of the wall collapse, with fake injuries."

"Yes, Khalif," said Galea, "but we can do better than that. The injuries will be real: only afflicting those who have continually displeased me. A well-placed death or two will help motivate our men to stay focussed and keep the British unaware of what we have got planned for them."

"But what if they bring in more soldiers to assist, and we can't delay them? Then what?"

"They won't. Valletta is too far, and many of them are already travelling on to Rinella and Cambridge. The commander will be forced to rely on us entirely," Galea reminded him.

"Allah will help us," said Khalif, nodding his head.

Galea agreed. "With your god on our side, we can't fail. Eventually, they will all be gone from these lands, and the people of Malta will be forced to forget them and accept that their fate is now in our hands. So, come with me, Khalif. We will pay off all the locals we employ and secretly replace them with our men. Soon, they will all be in place, and the stupid British will have no idea of what has taken place under their noses. Now that more soldiers are leaving, and we know what their plans are, we will be able to get more of our men over here without fear or risk of discovery."

***

Within the fort, the kitchen and dining rooms were being furnished by Harris and a couple of men who'd been allocated to work with him. It had been set up between the gate and the engine and pump rooms for convenience, with the courtyard separating the two. The end of the courtyard was where large mounds of coal were stored to feed the fires under the boilers. That way, a good head of steam could be generated quite quickly in an emergency.

Even from outside, Harris could be heard bellowing orders on how he wanted his kitchen set up. It was his domain, and he revelled in it, ensuring everyone in earshot knew it. Under his watchful eye, two men placed the furniture exactly where he directed. Anything unable to be fitted to his liking was skilfully altered by the camp carpenter, with a little bribery from Harris. He was beginning to make himself at home with his precious blackened pots and pans and their historical dents and scratches – each of which meant so much to him. Next, he turned his attention to the oven.

It must be lit and tested, he thought. *Now is as good a time as any.*

So, gathering up the wood shavings thoughtlessly left behind on the floor by the carpenter, he used them to pack the fire grate under the boiler. Then he placed more kindling and wood on top of that, topping it off with copious amounts of coal and slack heaped up at the back with his shovel. Satisfied, he lit the fire and stood back, watching as it rapidly took hold of the wood shavings and started roaring in the grate. He was feeling well pleased with himself until, after a few minutes of lively burning, the fire started to darken and die back alarmingly, belching dark smoke that suffocated the flames.

Realising what was happening, he grabbed the bayonet from his rifle, which leaned against the wall, and used it to prod and lift the sticks to get more air into the fire.

After a few minutes of coaxing the fire to reignite, a spluttering soldier came in, fanning the smoke back into the courtyard behind him. "What are you doing with that bayonet?" he asked.

Unperturbed, Harris answered, "Napoleon once said, 'You can do anything with a bayonet except sit on it.' I'm lifting the bloody sticks with it, aren't I?"

"Blimey, Corporal! The smoke's choking the men out there! They were trying to dismantle the gantry, and the smoke forced them to abandon it and clear off. Some are retching up as we speak! Even Galea's men have fled the wall."

In a calm and unhurried voice, Harris replied, "That's Cook to you, sonny, and don't you forget it."

"Fine, Corporal Cook," the coughing soldier mocked. "The smoke from your fire is –"

"Yes! Yes, I understand. Let me go and see for myself."

Stepping into the courtyard, Harris could see the black smoke hanging heavy in the air. The gantry was barely visible, and the gun had all but disappeared. The men that had been standing there had now retreated to a safe distance while the thick, acrid smoke continued to billow out from the chimney.

"Bloody hell! I've overloaded the fire without giving it time to set alight and burn properly," he gasped. "Bloody hell," he swore again. "Bloody fucking hell!"

Sergeant Savage was standing up on the musketry parapet, the wind behind him, when the altercation started below. "Harris," he shouted down, "get that fire sorted quick, or you'll be put on a charge! What's the good of building this fort and hiding it from the enemy when you're busy letting them know where we are?"

"Yes, Sergeant. Right away, Sergeant," Harris replied, realising the enormity of his folly. He returned to the boiler in double-quick time to continue lifting the sticks and hot coals, but without success.

Desperate to relight the fire, he splattered paraffin from a nearby lamp into the smouldering grate, causing it to reignite with a bang. The loud noise made him step back in alarm as the flames licked hungrily along his arm, singeing the hair away. It left him smelling of seared pork – at least, that's what the others in the kitchen thought. Now well alight, the fire in the grate took hold greedily, spitting laughing sparks back at him as it ravenously consumed the fuel. Panicking, he quickly stepped back, brushing frantically at the large, red-hot missiles landing on him and painfully burning him through his clothes.

After brushing them off, he took a look outside and was relieved to see the smoke beginning to disperse from the enclosed courtyard. Upon hearing loud swearing, he glanced over towards the gantry; the men returning there were shaking their fists at him with murder in their eyes.

"We hope you cook better than you light bloody fires!" one shouted – amongst other, less pleasant things.

The insults rang in his ears and followed him back to the kitchen. Once he had got the fire safely under control, he felt strangely smug at their discomfort. Nonetheless, he decided to keep a low profile until the hatred towards him died down.

Galea's men were secretly delighted at Harris' misfortune. They retreated from the smoke with the others, pleased to find an excuse to waste even more time. Many pretended it had affected their breathing and began to fake coughing. In the ensuing confusion, they could stretch out a few more hours of inactivity, comfortable in the knowledge that Harris would be blamed.

Chapter 22

Reality comes calling. Killing of the innocents. Lights on the remote island

THE SUN was exceedingly hot, searing the ground beneath Victoria's feet as she stopped outside another of the menders' tents, where she was informed that a minor dispute needed a mediator. It was a petty-minded falling out, with no real beginning, and was quickly resolved.

She was about to sit with them for a heart-to-heart talk and to rest her tired feet – all the sorer now, with the late stages of her pregnancy – when she began to come over weak. Amid a wave of feebleness and faintness, she felt herself sway, and then she was on the floor, blinking up at a circle of worried faces.

"Oh, madam! Madam!" shouted Betty. "Quick, lay her on her side while I make a pillow for her head with this material."

The other woman did as she instructed, making her as comfortable as possible. Victoria wanted to resist – to insist that she was just fine, thank you very much – but she didn't have the energy.

Betty dipped a square offcut of cloth into a bowl of water and held it to her forehead while another woman held her hand to comfort and assure her. "It's the heat and her condition that's done it," said Betty. "It's finally taken its toll on her."

"Ooh! Whatever happened? Lying here will never do," Victoria groaned, embarrassed by the fuss. "I must get up," she added weakly, trying to bat away a well-intentioned hand on her arm. "There is such a lot to do. Help me up, ladies, please."

"No! No, stay there, madam," said Betty. "One of the girls has gone to fetch the doctor. He will want to make sure the baby is unhurt. He'll be here soon," she soothed, reassuring her while stroking her hand. She dipped the cloth into the cold water again and dabbed it across Victoria's face and brow. "Stay where you are a little longer. I'll just loosen the top buttons on your blouse to give you more air. There, madam, is that better?"

"Yes, thank you, Betty," she said as the spinning room began to stabilise. "I don't know what came over me."

"Can someone fetch the commander?" Betty asked. "I think he should know too."

"I'll go and get him," said Lizzie, quickly disappearing out the door.

Nancy and a worried-looking Doctor Charlton arrived first, red in the face themselves from running. Not long after the doctor had got down on his knees to examine Victoria, Lizzie appeared with the commander in tow.

"Are you alright, Victoria?" he asked, highly concerned.

"Yes, Robert. I am now. The ladies have tended to me very well."

He looked around at them. "I am most grateful to you, ladies," Townsend said to all those standing there.

Before saying anything else, the doctor intervened. "I need you to know, Major, your wife has suffered a mild heatstroke. As she is approaching the end of her pregnancy, I would suggest complete rest, followed by her making that journey to Valletta, preferably tomorrow. Neither mother nor baby was harmed, but it is in both their interests to go while she still can."

"My wife and baby are very precious to me, Doctor. I entirely agree with you."

Victoria had recovered sufficiently by now to be helped to her feet by the women, who all fussed over her, reassuring her with individual stories of each of their pregnancies and mishaps.

Taking the commander by the arm, Doctor Charlton led him a few feet away from the concerned ladies. "Look, Major, since the camp has started to wind down and we no longer have injuries on the scale we had before, I have found Sarah somewhat surplus to requirements. I want you to allow her to accompany Victoria back to Valletta to look after her. They have become particularly close friends, and Sarah has worked ridiculously hard for me. I think her dedication has taken a toll on her too, although she doesn't realise it. If you agree to my request, I would like to recommend her for a special leave concession to coincide with Victoria's pregnancy. She would be at hand for Victoria, and I think she also deserves a break."

"Can you get special leave for her?"

"Yes, there's no problem there," the doctor assured him. "Once I have recommended it, it will be cleared by the medical authorities in Valletta. It will be a mere formality, I'm sure."

"But what of yourself?" Townsend asked, showing concern. "You have to return soon. Can you cope until then?"

"Oh, I can manage – business is steady. When it's my turn, I will be ready to go."

"Well, it's just down to persuading Victoria, then," Townsend sighed.

"You have my sympathy. I'm sure it will be no easy matter," intoned the doctor.

"If you will excuse me, I'll take my wife back to the cabin to ensure she gets the rest you recommended. Thank you, sir."

"Just before you go, I want to send Sarah over today to look after her. Then we will both be certain she has rested up. I'll have her other effects sent over to you later."

"Of course. The barge is sailing back tomorrow with some of our equipment on board so that the ladies will have plenty of room. Thank you again and good day, sir," he finished, politely saluting him.

The doctor watched Townsend hold her at the waist with one reassuring hand while holding her arm firmly with the other before gently coaxing her to take a tentative, unsteady walk back to their quarters.

"Well, did you ever?" said Lizzie afterwards. "I never expected all that to happen."

"Get on with your sewing, girl, and stop your tittle-tattle. Get that shirt and trousers done; they will be wanting them soon enough!"

"Yes, Betty. I should think this will keep the gossips going a day or two." Lizzie looked about at the other women in the room, detecting raised brows and nods of agreement as she spoke.

**

Beyond the camp, Sergeant Savage was leading a small detail of men with a horse and wagon to gather timber and fell any diseased trees for firewood.

"Shush! Stop hacking! I think I can hear gunfire," said Bailey, his head snapping up from their task.

The men stopped cutting the wood and listened.

"Yeah, you're right. There it goes again – and not far away," Savage confirmed.

"What if they're insurgents, Sergeant? They might outnumber us. We need to get back to the camp and report it."

"Steady on, men," Savage advised. "The shots sound slow and random to me; I think if they were insurgents, the gunfire would be more rapid and urgent than that. There's no harm in finding out. You two men stay here with the horse and wagon while the rest of us take a closer look and see," said Savage calmly.

Cautiously making their way towards the gunfire, they reached a clearing in the thick shrubbery where they could observe, unseen, the rifle fire.

What they saw enraged Savage.

"Why, it's Wilson and two gunners from my old regiment!" he whispered. "This is the same Sergeant Wilson whose own men despised him as a bully," he growled. "A man that enjoyed taking the piss out of me whenever I was demoted to gunner – always after I lost my stripes, but never a word when I got them back!"

Wilson and his men were standing with some local Maltese friends of theirs. They were trading rifles and taking potshots at groups of small birds lured in by the cries of others they kept trapped in cages. The shot birds' broken bodies lay scattered on the ground, which angered Savage even more when he saw the indiscriminate carnage.

One of Savage's men nudged him in the arm, nodding up at a flock of swallows feeding on the wing. The little birds were twisting and turning skilfully in the sky, gulping down their fill of flying insects. Wilson and his friends aimed and fired, blasting them from the air. Some fell to the ground dead, while some lay there twitching before dying of shock. The men ruthlessly finished off any still alive by wringing their necks. Those that had fallen in obscured places were simply left to die where they fell.

Savage had seen enough. Seething with anger, he stood to his full height and strode out to confront them. "If we had been insurgents, you scum would be dead by now!" he roared.

The men turned quickly at the sound of his voice. Wilson's eyes narrowed and then widened as he realised who it was. He lowered his rifle. "There's no fear of that. You've only just arrived," he claimed.

"We've been here long enough to watch what you've been up to, Wilson, you insensitive bastard!"

Realising he had seen it all, Wilson took to besmirching his character. "I see you've got your stripes back again, for the umpteenth time. What gutter did they drag you out of this time, Savage?" he asked, laughing loudly and encouraging his friends to chuckle and sneer.

"The same one you'll end up in, Wilson."

The animosity between the two big men bristled in the air, creating tension so thick it electrified those watching the unfolding drama.

"Whenever I lost my stripes due to the drink, you'd be there, Wilson, deliberately goading me and getting under my skin. Never a word of encouragement or a helping hand. But that's typical of you: hiding behind your stripes, safe in the knowledge you outranked me. Once a man is down, you keep him down for your amusement. When I got my stripes back and carried equal authority, you never said a word. You and these other so-called 'hunters' have been killing these songbirds for your own gratification. Even the swallows, for no good reason!"

"So what? Who cares? The swallows are more difficult to hit, being more skilful and faster in the air."

"But why do it? They're too small to eat, so it's not for food. Do you and the others get some kind of perverse pleasure out of it?"

Forced to answer, Wilson spluttered and gesticulated wildly. "So? They all do it in Malta. It's a sport over here. Besides, they regard it as a sign of good marksmanship and manliness."

"A sign of ignorance, more like. These little swallows you're butchering are not native to Malta!" Savage cried, feeling very protective of the small, feathered things. "If you took the time to educate yourself, you would know they are born in Europe, far to the north of here. They migrate to South Africa, where some perish, crossing several deserts without food. They then fly thousands of miles on a round trip back to Europe, even Britain – to our own country – for our people to enjoy, you ignorant bastard! They feed here in Malta to help sustain them for the homeward flight. You're killing our very own wild birds from home, you idiot!"

As Savage spoke, Wilson's face turned red with rage at being embarrassed in front of the men. Placing his face close to Ned's, he looked him in the eyes and growled, "There's nothing illegal about what we're doing here, Savage, so kiss my arse!"

Unflinching, Savage glared back and said, "No, I'd rather kick it."

Wilson stepped back, surprised at his response. Then, sizing up his opponent, he decided. "Right, men. All of you are sworn to secrecy. What happens here stays here. I'm going to whip his arse good and proper and strangle an apology out of him. He's had this coming for some time, so get your bets on," he announced.

A quick flurry of betting followed as the two groups of men gathered around, settling the odds between them.

Wilson began by rolling his sleeves up. "Come on, Savage, out of that tunic. I'll not hit a man wearing the Queen's uniform. I've got my principles, you know."

Savage looked down and started to open the buttons. Just as he got to the last, a powerful roundhouse of a punch caught him on his cheek, spinning him around and dropping him to the floor, dazed. Wilson then straddled him and began slapping him across the face.

"Stand up, Savage!" he taunted. "There's more punishment to come. I'm not finished yet!"

As Ned attempted to stand, a knee caught him low down in the groin and then a rabbit punch hit him at the back of the neck. He dropped to his knees just as Wilson grabbed at his tunic and ripped it, disrespectfully and unceremoniously, off him. Standing above Savage, Wilson pressed the sole of his shoe into his face, pushing it down forcibly into the dirt. He then did it a second time, showing utter contempt and disregard for the man.

"Just as I thought, all talk and no trousers, with the backbone of a jellyfish," Wilson gloated. "You disappoint me, Savage. What's this myth about having red hair and a temper to match? Think you're a good fighter, eh?" He unleashed yet another fist which caught Savage on the side of the jaw, causing a trickle of blood to spill out from his mouth.

Ecstatic, Wilson's supporters cheered him on, while the men with Savage found it hard to watch.

Standing astride the helpless man, Wilson bent at the knees to get more power into his next punch, which again came with a defined sickening thud as it landed. Grabbing at his shirt, he hauled Savage back to his feet. His face was a bloody mess and, unable to stand unaided, his legs kept giving way as Wilson held him up. He could just make out Wilson's blurred face, grimacing menacingly at him with his saucer-shaped eyes and bared teeth.

Within the deep recesses of his consciousness, he could see and hear his deceased father. Rolling up his shirtsleeves and spitting into both hands, the spectre raised his fists and said, *"Ah, to be sure yer big lug, yer. Put yer dukes up and fight him like I taught yer. Now do it! Do it!"*

Wilson was enjoying the punishment he was meting out. "It's easy money, men!" he cried. "One more should be enough." Measuring his next blow to Savage's face, he brought his arm back and looked at the nose he was about to shatter before letting his fist go with every ounce of strength he had.

Somehow, Savage sensed it coming and managed to drop to his knees to avoid being hit. Wilson missed, going over Savage's shoulder and onto the ground behind him. As the basic urge to survive rushed through him, Savage looked down, vaguely making out Wilson's outline sprawled on the ground. He twisted his body and dropped down onto him, blindly groping for his face before forcing him into a headlock. Now it was the men backing Savage who cheered wildly – their man was fighting back!

Savage managed to link his arms tightly behind the man's neck and lock them in. Holding him there, it gave him the chance to take a breather and gather his senses as more blood trickled out from his mouth onto Wilson's head. He was expecting Wilson to struggle violently to free himself. Indeed, his left hand reached out backwards for Savage's face, to poke at his eyes with his fingers or to grab at something – anything.

But Savage was ready for him: he kept his head and face well back, out of reach. Leaning on his right arm to get leverage, Wilson bent further back still, desperately grasping and clawing for the face. It was what Savage was waiting for, and he pushed the man's left arm quickly down; hooking it with his leg to immobilise him further while continuing to apply neck pressure.

Savage had him! There was nothing Wilson could do as his struggles diminished, his breathing becoming more laboured as he slipped in and out of consciousness while, all the time, Savage's head was clearing. Having not seen that first punch coming, he had nearly paid the price.

Eventually he got up off his man and watched as Wilson slowly recovered his senses. Wilson shakily stood up and took a wild swing at him, but Savage pulled his head back slightly for it to miss. Good, his man was conscious enough now for Savage to see the fear in his eyes – and for him to sense something unpleasant was about to happen a split second before Ned's hammer of a right fist connected with his jaw, forcing him back. He followed it up with a left into his lower rib cage, then another. An audible crack was heard, and Wilson doubled up in pain. Finally, another right hook under the chin lifted him off his feet and left him out cold. But Savage hadn't finished – anger still raged within him. Grabbing Wilson by the collar, he tried to yank him back to his feet for yet more punishment, but the man was unconscious, so Ned backhanded him to the ground.

"Leave him, Ned. He's had it!" shouted Bailey, clearly worried. "Let him go! *Ned, let him go, or you'll kill him, I said!*"

Savage stared down hard at Wilson, wanting to hurt him more. He felt cheated – his revenge unsatisfied. While struggling with him, his men managed to pull him off the prostrate figure.

Seeing Wilson unconscious, the locals slunk away, leaving Savage's men to begin whooping about and expressing gratitude as they collected their winnings from Wilson's crew. Then, showing due respect, they gathered around and congratulated Savage. It was a tough fight, and at one point they had all thought he was finished.

"Well done, Ned. Well done!" said Bailey. "He had it coming. Let's get you back to camp and get you sorted out by that nice filly of a nurse they have in there. Those cuts need seeing to – you're in a fine mess from what he did to you."

"You could be right," he said, exhausted. "I don't feel too good. But first, open those cages and let the birds free."

They did as they were asked, then broke the cages up after the birds had taken flight.

Satisfied, he said, "Let's go. I think the others will have cut enough wood by the time we get back to them."

***

Captain Marsh had been deeply involved with Valletta's regimental quartermaster, rooting out any missing items on the quartermaster's checklist and inventory. Everything excess to requirements had to be returned – it had to be itemised, logged, and packed, ready for transit. All items were included, from the temporary gantry (now being dismantled) to the bell tents, the number of men returning, and the arms and ammunition each carried.

During this period of high activity, it came as a welcome relief when Marsh spotted Sarah taking a stroll near the camp's outskirts. She had only just finished tending to Savage's cuts and bruises moments earlier. After demanding to know how Savage got them, Sarah listened sympathetically to the whole of his story. Feeling he was fully justified in what he did, she agreed to keep the confrontation between the two men a secret. She was glad Wilson had been given a beating for what he had done and would have chastised him herself if she had known.

Taking his leave from the officious quartermaster and the men helping him, Marsh went over to talk with her, only to find her gazing trance-like towards the sea.

"Penny for your thoughts, Sarah?"

"Oh, I didn't hear you, David."

"I can see that. Anything troubling you?"

"I gather from your question you haven't spoken to Robert yet?"

"No. Why?"

She told him about Victoria's worrying collapse. "The doctor would like me to go back with Victoria for a rest myself and to look after her. He told me he could manage himself with the few people left in camp. He said I could stay with her until the baby was born. Then, afterwards, I will be working back at Valletta Hospital."

Marsh held her arm and moved her to the other side of the tree, out of sight of prying eyes. "You have to go, of course. We knew this would happen, didn't we?"

"Yes," she answered softly, "but I lost you once, and I don't want to lose you again. I fear I will." A tear trickled down her face at the very thought.

Gently, he wiped the tear away with his thumb. "Sarah, that will never happen again, I promise. Besides, this arrangement allows you and Victoria to stay together. Why, you can be Victoria's private nurse – and then we'll both know she and the baby are in safe hands. Of course, you will see Robert and me when we're on leave, and we can all go to the theatre together, or something of that nature. When is she due to travel there? In a few days?"

"Tomorrow," Sarah said in a whisper.

"What?" he exclaimed in horror. "Oh, damn it, as soon as that?" he stammered. "What will happen now?"

"I'm on my way over to meet with Victoria now. The bits and pieces I used in the surgery are being taken back to the cabin, and I'm just lingering here before going over. Doctor Charlton has been wonderful, though. He's arranged everything for me."

"So, you'll stay overnight with Victoria before travelling back on the barge tomorrow?"

She nodded. "Yes."

"Look," he said, trying to bury his pain, "smile at me. Would you like me to speak to Robert and ask him if I can stay with you tonight? Would you like that?"

"Oh, you know I would. It hurts to be going. Kiss me, David, and hold me, please!"

He duly obliged. "I'll come over later. We can leave Victoria and Robert alone – I feel sure they have plenty to say to each other, too. I want us to be on our own. We can sit down on the hill somewhere and talk – maybe look at those flickering lights over Gozo again. You never know, we might see a shooting star. From what I'm told, the locals often see them."

"That would be lovely, David. But I should go now."

Marsh pulled her in close. He could feel her whole body pressing against him as they kissed. It was hard to let her go. "I want you, Sarah," he muttered as they kissed again.

"What! Not here, I hope?"

"No," he chuckled. "It will have to wait for now."

She drew her fingernails lightly from his shoulder blades, moving them down his back, towards his waist. "I know you do, and I want you to. I'll see you later, David," she said as she planted another, softer kiss on his cheek. Then she left him there, reflecting on their future and the sudden abrupt changes tearing them apart once again.

Arriving at the cabin, Sarah found that Robert had already put Victoria to bed. "Do come in, Sarah! Victoria went to sleep as soon as she lay down. She's exhausted."

"I'm not surprised with all the stress. David knows, by the way. I told him what the doctor wanted of me."

"You don't mind, do you, Sarah?" he asked, his concern touching her. "I would be most grateful, knowing you were looking after them both. I'm afraid that being in the Army does no favours for family life whatsoever. Just lately, it seems there are never-ending problems to be sorted out in the camp, and it can overwhelm one at times. I'll be glad when it's over," he said despondently before turning to the drinks cabinet for comfort, replenishing his glass.

She patted his shoulder sympathetically. *He sounds disheartened. He must be feeling the strain too, poor Robert. Being the commander here must come with many pressures, and I can only guess what they are.* "Look, Robert, I would have felt most hurt if you and the good doctor had not asked me to do it," she told him firmly. "After your baby is born, I shall no longer be needed. Then I will return to my employment at Valletta Hospital and still be able to get over to see them daily. Life should settle down into some sort of routine, dull or otherwise. It will be a pleasure for me to see Victoria and your child every day. Of course, you will see them both on your home leave too, won't you?"

"Yes," he agreed, nodding. "As an officer of the Crown, I can get special dispensation to see them both once the baby is born." The thought suddenly lifted his gloom.

"Did you have any trouble with her agreeing to go?" Sarah asked, aware of her friend's strong spirit.

"At first... until I persuaded her that she could be putting our baby at risk."

"Honestly, what with supporting you in running this place and the baby too, it's a wonder she's lasted so long," said Sarah, voicing a long-held opinion.

Townsend nodded. "Once I told her you'd be looking after her, her mood changed and there was no argument. She hardly knows anyone in Valletta, so we both appreciate it." Feeling in a better frame of mind, he picked up his pith helmet and said, "Please excuse me, Sarah. I have a camp to run. I'll see you both later."

***

The evening saw Captain Marsh knocking on the cabin door. "I'll go," said Sarah excitedly, making sure to get to the door first. Knowing it was David out there, she had made a special effort to look her best for him. She delayed opening the door while checking her appearance for the umpteenth time in the mirror. *There! How could he not fail to be impressed?*

She quickly finished her outfit off with a bright yellow ribbon tied in her hair and then waited impatiently, willing him to knock on the door again. She was beginning to think he wouldn't. When he did, she opened the door slowly so that he could take in her appearance bit by bit. "Why, if it's not Captain Marsh," she said, standing in the open doorway. She swished her light lace-trimmed cotton dress at him flirtatiously and pretended to be surprised.

Clearing his throat, Marsh began to say, "Sarah, you are–"

"Come in, Captain," she said enticingly. "As this is our last night together, I thought I would leave an impression on you." He stood transfixed. "Now close that door and let's go in," she said, avoiding his clumsy attempts to kiss her. Her womanly wiles had worked perfectly, much to her delight.

"Good evening, Robert," he said, following her into the room.

"Hello, David. You're finally here, then? I worried Sarah would wear the mirror out waiting for you. It's the only full-length one we have here."

Sarah swatted at his arm in good humour.

Looking around, Marsh smiled. "Where's the patient, then?"

"Here I am," Victoria said, entering the room with one hand on her tummy.

"I heard what happened," he said with concern. "How are you?"

"Oh, so much better now I'm out of the sun, thank you. It's much cooler than it was earlier. Although, I must say, I am a little worried about the weather for tomorrow. I'm like you, David: I dread sailing now."

"There's no need to worry. They won't set sail if the sea is rough; a barge is rather shallow in the beam and would likely sink!"

"David, stop it! Victoria is in no mood for jokes of that nature," Sarah admonished, guiding Victoria to her seat. "I've told you what you must do tomorrow, Victoria. You must wear a similar lighter dress with fewer folds in the underskirt, and don't forget to leave a couple of buttons undone under the chin. Otherwise, there's a danger of heatstroke again."

"Yes, nurse," Victoria replied as the four friends chuckled at the formality of her response.

Taking care of her patient, Sarah left the room to get her more fresh water and a flannel.

"If you two don't mind, I'm taking Sarah to look out towards Gozo from the cliff," said Marsh. "A spot of courting is called for, and I don't want to disappoint her. I think you have plenty to talk about yourselves, so we'll leave you two alone."

"We would appreciate that, David," said Townsend, gazing lovingly at his wife.

"Sarah!" Marsh called. "I'm going to look over towards Gozo. Are you coming?"

She hurried back into the room. "Oh yes, David," she said, putting the rinsed flannel and bowl of water down close to Victoria. "See you both later," she called back, on leaving.

It wasn't a pathway Marsh took her along, so she had to hitch up the front of her dress to avoid it snagging as they negotiated several obstacles.

This gave him ample opportunity as he helped her to admire her shapely ankles. It was a secluded place where he knew they could enjoy each other's company without being disturbed by camp activity.

They sat together on the ground, talking about their future and the impending trip on the barge the ladies faced in the morning. Marsh decided to lay his head in her lap while Sarah softly ran her fingers through his wind tousled hair. They talked about everything and nothing, oblivious to the camp and fort behind them. Then, as the night drew in, they watched oil lanterns flicker into life on the small fishing boats out at sea, where the crews were settling down for the night's fishing vigil.

"David?" she said softly.

"Yes, Sarah?"

"Victoria and Robert will make such good parents and become a proper family when the baby is born, won't they?"

"Yes, I guess so," he said. "I think Victoria will have more, though, if Robert has his way. No doubt he will enjoy trying!"

"That's how it should be if you're happily married," said Sarah wistfully. "Do you love me? I mean, truly love me?" she asked, a slight trace of doubt in her voice.

"Of course I do, Sarah."

"Well, I want us to be like them," she said earnestly. "I want us to be happy, and I want to have children. Your children, David."

"I want children, too, but only three. One of each!"

Sarah stared at him blank-faced. "What do you mean, three? One of each?"

"A girl, a boy, and a military gent's barber will be fine by me."

"You are so silly," she replied with a laugh, swiping at him playfully. Then she bent down low and kissed him again. "You do amuse me, you bloody fool."

The romantic setting began to influence her as she sat there, watching the moon's reflection shimmering out of shape on the sea's calm surface.

It was influencing Marsh too. He took something from his inside pocket and held it teasingly in his closed hand.

She glanced at his hand several times, and then – after a long, uncomfortable silence – Sarah asked, "Well, what is it?"

Finally, with her patience running out, he opened the tiny box revealing a ring inside and asked, "Sarah, will you marry me?" He smiled boyishly while she inspected the ring, momentarily speechless.

"Yes, David! Oh, yes! Yes! I will. I will!" she shouted, beaming with happiness as he placed the ring onto her outstretched finger. Then, calming down and looking slightly puzzled, she asked, "But how did you know it would fit?"

"Victoria innocently told me your fingers were the same size. I just went and selected it at the goldsmith. You see, I am deeply sorry for how I behaved. I want you to know I lost you once, and I don't want to lose you again, ever. I have matured a lot since then. Now, at last, do you believe me?"

"I do," was her heartfelt, whispered response.

They cuddled more, warmly wrapped up in their embrace, safe from the stiffening breeze.

Suddenly, Marsh frowned. "Did you see those lights, Sarah?" he asked, pointing out to sea.

"What lights?"

"On that small island near Comino. There were a few of them," he said. "They were congregating together at its edge – bunching close together and making it difficult to count. They bobbed up and down on the swell before disappearing onto the island. It must be the local fishermen catching crabs, maybe."

"Sorry darling, I had my eyes closed. I was thinking about our life together. Will we always be this happy? I hope it lasts, David."

"Of course it will last," he promised. "Why would it not? Do you love me, or are you just marrying me for my pension?" he teased.

She let out a full-throated laugh. "Ha! You come with a pension, as well? I feel doubly blessed."

"Give me another kiss, and we'll forget about the lights."

For a while they just sat under the clear night sky, watching the stars twinkle above. In the diminished 'Camp City', behind them, someone played a mouth organ in accompaniment to others humming. Four small campfires were dotted about the camp, lending everything a romantic atmosphere.

"Oh, David, it's so beautiful," Sarah sighed. "I could stay here and live this moment forever." She put both her arms around his waist and nestled her head into his chest.

Marsh gently kissed the top of her head. "Me too. Me too," he replied thoughtfully. "You have become the most important person in the world to me, Sarah. Oh, I know I have been a bit of a rogue – before I met you, I might add – but my family were right, saying everything falls into place on meeting the right one. In my case, it's you, Sarah," he told her romantically.

It was getting late, the singing had stopped, and one of the campfires had been extinguished. Fearing it would be minutes before all the fires were doused, leaving them in total darkness, Marsh stirred himself. "Come on, Sarah, I think we should go."

As they walked back, he kept glancing over his shoulder towards the island, but he didn't see those lights again – just the romantic scene of the few fishing boats on the waters below them. Finally, he turned his head towards camp and walked off.

Unaware, the vessels positioned out there were not catching fish for Malta's market; they were helping to feed Galea's growing army.

Chapter 23

Sad refrain of 'Reveille.' A secret revealed and the long goodbye

THE BUGLER was hard to see but easily heard when he started playing from the fort's ramparts. The morning calls were, 'Charlie, Charlie, Get Out of Bed,' followed by, 'Come to the Cookhouse Door, Boys.'

He played, but it lacked the same urgency and tone it once had. The daily duty he had undertaken for months was finally ending. With the shrinking of the camp, the subdued refrain filled the campsite quickly, requiring less enthusiasm and gusto from him. Sadly, he too would soon be gone. His instrument's tone and resonance now sounded different, dampened by the collective knowledge of the impending departure. A part of him even missed his canine hecklers, who had been found homes together with a distant farmer.

Both Townsend and Marsh had risen like everyone else as soon as the bugle played. It was part and parcel of being officers and ensuring the soldiers obeyed the NCOs' orders, lest they be put on a charge.

The ladies were fussing around each other, anxious for the upcoming journey. "Let me help you, Victoria. I've done my packing already. Most of it yesterday, to tell you the truth, and I can see you're struggling."

"Bless you, Sarah," said Victoria with gratitude. "The dresses and things need folding into those packing cases, and the hats into those boxes there."

Amicably, they set to work. Finally, Victoria straightened up and rested her hands on her hips and aching back. "Sarah," she said, putting a significant emphasis on her friend's name.

"Yes, Victoria?"

"You haven't said anything about what you two got up to last night. Were you courted properly? Did you give in to his wanton desire for you?" Victoria teased. "Come, tell all!"

Sarah laughed at her interest. "Steady, now, Victoria! Otherwise, you will be having your baby here if you are not careful."

The girls giggled at the suggestion.

"I was going to tell you, but not until we were on the barge – I promise," Sarah claimed.

"Good lord, I can't wait that long!" Victoria remarked. "Spit it out, girl. How else will I tell Robert if not before we depart?"

There was more giggling, followed by a pause, before Sarah said, "He's asked me to marry him."

Victoria squealed in excitement. "What! I hope you said yes. He's quite a catch, you know!" More squealed laughter followed the revelation. "Look, I've got to sit down again," Victoria said, giggling between gasps. "You know, Sarah, it's what Robert and I have always wanted for you two, and now it's finally happened." She gave out a sigh of satisfaction at the thought of them together.

"You haven't noticed yet, Victoria, but I've got his ring on." Holding out her hand, Sarah proudly showed it off.

"So, that's what lay behind his questioning me on my ring. He asked if we were the same ring finger size – rather craftily, I might say – and I told him we were and what it was. I never realised that was his motive! It is beautiful, Sarah. Were you like jelly in his hands after that and let him do as he pleased? Tell me."

"Yes, I might have if he'd wanted, but we simply cuddled a lot and talked about our future." Then a naughtiness crept into her voice. "In any case, we did it later, after going to bed."

"What, in that old rickety thing?" Victoria asked, not believing her. "Well, I heard nothing before I went to sleep – not a thing," she admitted, before adding cheekily, "I did listen awhile."

The naughtiness remained in Sarah's voice. "We didn't want to wake you both, or disturb the guard nearby, so we put the flock mattress on the floor, and we did it there!"

Still chuckling at her escapade, Victoria had to stand up. "Oh, Sarah, I'm aching all over. Please don't make me laugh anymore! You will have to finish my packing for me," she said, leaning down hard on the back of a chair.

Realising there was an outside chance of her waters breaking prematurely, a worried Sarah lay her down on the bed to help calm and relax her.

***

The Signals Unit had finally brought the heavy-gauge telephone cable into the fort, and Townsend was out trying to find the engineer allotted to his command. It would be his responsibility to operate this 'new-fangled' gadget on all calls, take messages, and undertake any maintenance required to keep the telephone functioning. He would only fight and bear arms if the fort's safety was compromised; his telephone needed to be always close at hand. A room had been made available for the phone and its equipment at the rear of the fort, and that was where Townsend was headed.

On seeing his commanding officer approaching, the man stood to attention and saluted as he walked in.

"At ease, soldier. Your name is?"

"Miller, sir."

"Where is it, Miller? I've been outside and looked around and failed to see your cable or poles anywhere. What have you done with it?" he asked, somewhat baffled.

"You won't find it, sir," said Miller, with a grin. "The last 300 yards were dug into the ground by the working party to protect it from any enemy. Behind me is where it comes into the fort." He pointed to the lead-covered, thick-gauge cable sticking out from the wall. "I've still got to fit the field phone, the heavy batteries, and the hand-cranked generator. Once I've made a few test calls, it will be ready to use."

"What happens if Anchor gets a call?" Townsend asked.

"It will ring a bell on this equipment, and I'll answer it. It's all good, well-engineered stuff, sir. It will amaze you."

"You are still to convince me, Miller. Until then, I'm happy to stick to semaphore and mirror flash. They have been exceptionally reliable over the years."

"Everyone has to change with the times, sir, even you." Miller smiled as he said it.

Townsend chuckled, shaking his head. "Will I be able to speak to the governor?"

"Yes, sir. Fort Anchor, Fort Rinella, Fort Cambridge, and Fort St. Elmo will be linked for security reasons. If you want to speak to the governor, I will tell the operator, and you will be connected to him."

"Marvellous. It can be difficult to keep up with the modern world at times, Miller. Sometimes, though, I feel things are changing a little too fast!"

"I'll let you know when it's working, sir. I know you will want to try it."

"I will indeed, Miller, and I look forward to it."

Leaving Miller alone with his baffling contraption, Townsend stepped out into the sunlight. He saw that Marsh was deeply involved with the quartermaster, as the inventory continued to take shape. *That should keep him busy for the next day or two. He's the only one that knows where everything is.*

292

He strode purposely back through the camp, casually returning any salutes that came his way. Victoria's imminent departure was firmly on his mind, and he wanted to bid her farewell before she and Sarah left for Valletta. He stopped momentarily on the brow of the hill to look down into the bay at where the barge was moored. He saw it was being loaded, and he guessed they had about an hour before the ladies and their baggage were to embark.

Striding back the way he came, he found Marsh and got his attention. "Sarah will want to see you, Captain. There's only about an hour to go – if that."

"Yes, sir. I'll be up to see her as soon as I've finished this count."

Townsend nodded and hurried to the cabin. Then, after taking the guard's salute, he entered to find the women waiting for him. He saw that Victoria had acted on Sarah's advice and was wearing something light; he nodded his approval to her.

"Look, I know you two would like a little privacy with how little time we have left," said Sarah. "I'll go and find David."

"No, stay. He's with the quartermaster, signing things off," Townsend informed her. "I have told him, and he said he would follow me here!"

"Robert, the camp is disintegrating and falling apart before our eyes," observed Victoria, looking out the small window towards the tents.

"Yes, it seems that way," he said. "This cabin will be gone the day after tomorrow."

"It's a wonder it hasn't collapsed before now," Sarah said jokingly. "Tell me, where will you and David be staying?"

"Well, there won't be much left in here when Victoria's gone. I'm afraid it will be back in the bell tent for about a week. Then I shall live and sleep in Fort Anchor, as will David and the rest of my command."

"Poor things," said Sarah, sympathising.

There was a sudden and urgent rap on the door, and Marsh strode in. "The men are here for the baggage, sir."

"What, so soon!" Townsend gasped, aghast. "Alright, show them in. It's behind the door in the next room."

The baggage was carried out, and one of the crewmen said, "The skipper sends his regards and wants you to make your way down to the bay, sir. He wants to take advantage of the good weather and get back to Valletta. He thinks it's likely to roughen later."

"Of course." He turned back, saying, "It's time to go, Victoria," and reluctantly led the small party out of the cabin. He held her arm as he slowly and carefully walked her down the roadway towards the bay, accompanied by Sarah and Marsh.

"God bless you, madam," said Sally, who was waiting to see them off. "We might see you both again in Valletta sometime soon." The rest of the camp ladies had also come to give them their best wishes, forming a guard of honour of sorts down the hill towards the barge. They had both proved most popular with the women they were leaving behind.

"Oh, thank you, Sally. Thank you, everyone. Goodbye, ladies!" On reaching the barge, Victoria looked back and thought, *That cabin, although a draughty, temporary home, felt rather romantic, sitting up there on that hill.* She squeezed Robert's hand affectionately, the other resting protectively on her belly.

"That telephone thing being installed in the fort can be connected to the governor's residence, so I'll be here if you want to send a message and tell me about our baby," said Townsend, unable to dislodge the growing lump in his throat brought on at her leaving.

He glanced over at Sarah and David, who had said their bit and appeared to be eating each other. He held Victoria in his arms and gave her one last lingering kiss before whispering, "Life around here will be very dull and strange, Victoria. The nights are going to be especially lonely without you. I'm so used to having you around; you have spoiled me, can't you see?"

The barge's skipper signalled that they were about to leave by letting off the steam whistle twice, interrupting their conversation. Reluctantly, Marsh and Townsend stepped off the barge and watched as the crew slipped the grimy mooring ropes before jumping back onboard themselves. Slowly, the barge inched its way out of the bay and into the open sea.

"Don't forget, you two – you'll be met at Grand Harbour by Minton and taken to the governor's wife!" Townsend called after them. Then he began yelling louder over the rumble of the boat's engine. "She's arranged everything for your stay there!"

The barge moved beyond vocal range, and the four were reduced to waving at each other until it disappeared.

Townsend took a sideways glance at Marsh, who was more emotionally affected than he thought he would be. Sarah had undoubtedly left her mark; it left him heavy-hearted at Sarah's tearful parting.

It's been a long time since I first met David, he thought. *How circumstances have changed! Somehow, I never thought he would feel that way about a woman, but Sarah was always someone special to him. I can see that now. I must get him to snap out of his melancholy, though.*

"That's it, David, they have gone. Attention, Captain!" he barked, offering a salute.

"Yes, sir," Marsh said, arching his back and returning a subdued, slow salute.

"We are here to do a job, Captain, and we have to get on with it. Are you still involved with the quartermaster?"

"Yes, sir! Until tomorrow!"

"Good! Carry on with that, then. I need to talk to Galea. I want to see if he's started constructing the fort wall now the gantry has been cleared away. But, first, I need to attend to something else in the camp that needs my attention. Then, I think I'll be ready for a swig of beer or maybe a supping of brandy. Will you join me, Captain? You can return to the inventory afterwards."

"Yes, sir. I would be most happy to oblige."

"Good. I'll be at the command post in about an hour. Carry on, Captain."

Chapter 24

A dressing down for Galea. Cook reaches boiling point. More delaying tactics

AFTER CLIMBING back up the hill, Townsend tended to a minor problem concerning one of his men's welfare in the fast-shrinking camp. Then he went on and visited the gantry at the fort. Its extra-large wooden scaffolding framework had been completely dismantled. It was now laid out along the fort walls, ready for collection. The men involved with its recovery stood to attention, saluting their commanding officer as he approached.

"At ease, men. Tell me, Corporal: have both gantries been completely dismantled?"

"Yes, sir. Both are down and waiting to be loaded onto the barge as soon as space becomes available. We are just clearing away the debris now, and then it's all done."

"What time did you finish taking down the gantry?"

"About two hours ago, sir."

"Thank you," said Townsend, looking around. "Can you tell me where Mr Galea is? Or his workforce? No one seems to be about."

"We've not seen him, sir, nor any of his men," the corporal replied.

"Send Galea to me as soon as he shows up, will you?"

"Yes, sir."

Townsend met up with Marsh at the command post as planned. Due to the heat, they discarded their tunics to relax and then sat down, supping the beer drawn from the barrel. It had been hectic all morning, and both took a well-deserved rest. As officers of the Crown, they were always expected to wear the tunics in the men's presence, but the rigid rules were more relaxed in other officers' company.

"I wonder what the women are doing now," Marsh said, bringing them into the conversation. "Still on the barge, I should–"

A voice outside interrupted the discussion. "Major, are you in there?"

"Come in, Mr Galea. I've been expecting you."

Lifting the tent flap, he walked in. "I was told you wanted to speak to me, Major."

"Yes, I do," said Townsend. "I was at the gun earlier, and there was no sign of you or your men, and I made it clear you were to start closing the wall immediately after the gantry was down. Where were you, may I ask?"

"I was there earlier, and I thought it would probably be later in the afternoon when your engineers finished the dismantling. We would then be working in the hottest hours of the day, and it would be too hot to set the concrete properly. It would most likely dry out too quickly and crack. Therefore, I decided to leave it until tomorrow morning and make a fresh start when it was much cooler. We can make up the lost time then."

"That's not good enough, sir," Townsend said smartly. "You could have made some sort of start, even if only to dig out more rock for the concrete. I need the gun enclosed, and I should advise you not to compromise the men's and the fort's safety under my command. When I arrived at the wall, Mr Galea, I found the engineers had taken the rest of the framework down and carried the heavy wooden beams out of the courtyard, along with the relevant tools. They had everything stacked up outside in good order – including the hooks and chains – ready for easy recovery. However, all your men were gone! Where were they, may I ask?"

Galea licked his lips, visibly surprised at being interrogated. "The rocks for filling in the parapet wall," he said quickly. "We were… er… short, and we had to excavate more. Er… I needed all my men for the task, Major."

"Well, that sounds reasonable, but why didn't you realise this before?" the officer asked. "You must stay focused on your task. Remember, you have two weeks to reinstate the wall and parapet, Mr Galea, and I suggest you get on with it. Thank you for your time, sir," he snapped – bringing the session to a halt.

After Galea left, under a cloud of his own making, Townsend declared, "There's something about that man, David. I don't know what, but I dislike him. Victoria said she wouldn't arrange any meals if he were invited. She said she didn't like him either. I bow now to her good judgment."

"Me neither. Galea is a bit strange, although his work here has been extremely good," Marsh reflected, thinking over the last few months.

Townsend nursed the beer in his tin cup as he thought more of Galea and his list of excuses. Then, he spoke. "That prisoner you took. He recognised someone outside the guardroom window while I was interrogating him. The guard outside told me Galea was hanging around, along with a few others. Could it have been him the prisoner recognised? Do you think he could be the traitor? Or perhaps he knows who the traitor is?" Townsend shook his head. "He *has* asked the occasional brazen question about things that shouldn't concern him. He can be evasive and seems to have an excuse for everything."

"I know what you mean, Robert, but don't worry," Marsh reassured him. "He and his men will be gone, as soon as the wall is finished, and then we can forget them."

***

Galea returned to his tent, still inwardly fuming at what the major had said. When he entered, he let fly at the nearest person to him, slapping him hard across the face with the back of his hand. The man was sent sprawling to the floor, where he cowered down, knowing his life was in danger and that he must remain silent and very still if he wanted to live. His men had witnessed their leader's violent tantrums before – and the dire consequences.

"Edoardo! Edoardo, what is wrong?" asked Khalif tactfully, calming him down.

"Bah! The British pigs were at the wall today. They wanted to know why we had not started. I made excuses for it. I could not say we were out meeting up with our forces."

During the agitated and troubled discussion, the man on the floor was quietly ushered out by a comrade, unseen by Galea, as Khalif distracted him with further questions. "What if the British suspect something, my brother?"

"They do not suspect anything," he growled. "They have complete trust in us."

"What if they come to check the wall?"

"Simple. Our men will pretend to be working," Galea told him, beginning to calm down. "Once they have gone, we slow down again. Make sure all our men know what to do. Any delay is to our advantage." He spat on the ground. "The British will only discover our betrayal once it's too late, and our swords have run them through. We can enjoy the startled look on their faces as their blood is spilt and soaked into the ground we walk on. I cannot wait to savour the moment."

***

The next few days saw the continued rundown of the camp. The sergeant major and the main body of his men – along with the doctor – departed. The camp ladies and wives of the men were transported back, along with the cooks and sutlers. The camp cookhouse was taken down. Along with its pots and pans and other equipment, it was shipped back to Valletta. The cabin and gantries were also sent back to be transported to the other forts.

Finally, the last operation was to take back all tents, ammunition, and other stores not required. After that, a strange calm settled over the hillside. The only voices now came from those inside the fort.

The two officers and the rest of their highly trained gun crew had settled into their new home. These men were part of a functional unit headed by Commander Townsend, who had quickly brought in a strict code of security for safety reasons.

Water header tanks installed on the roof were filled daily by a man pumping up water from the deep well. The tanks' gravity then fed all the water needed for the fort to function successfully: water for drinking, for ablutions in the latrines, and to top up the boilers to operate the steam engine. Then the steam hydraulics could move the cannon as they practised manoeuvring and aiming it.

Townsend had a troop of thirty-five highly trained men drawn from the Royal Artillery and established inside the fort to run his one-gun battery efficiently. Those men whose jobs involved working below ground amongst the shells and charges, or providing the light below to see and work in – safely ensconced behind glass partitions – were issued unique anti-static duck uniforms with pillbox hats. These were to eliminate any chance of static sparks setting off the gunpowder prematurely, with all its unimaginable consequences.

Harris, the cook, and his chosen daily helpers had to feed them all, but not simultaneously. Different sitting times were arranged for small groups of men to eat. As each group of men gathered for their meals, many still felt animosity towards Harris' attempt to choke them at the gantry.

On this day, one joker shouted for all to hear, "Are we having smoked fish again today, Harris?"

"Everything's smoked. Take your pick," said a second, to the delight of the others waiting.

"Very funny," said Harris. "If you two aren't careful, I'll have you both in here peeling a hundredweight of spuds. I always need help in the kitchen," he threatened.

"Steady on, Cook! No offence meant."

"Head Cook to you, sonny."

"Head Cook, you say. You're the only bloody cook!" another soldier said to more howls of derision.

"Ideas of grandeur," said the first.

"Ideas of grandeur! I'll be blown away, as my mate said, trying to clear the smoke!"

"What have we got with the spuds today, Cook?"

Upset from their tiresome jokes, he wanted to get his own back. "Steak."

"Steak?" said the man, suitably impressed. "What sort of steak?"

"Horse steak."

"Horse steak! Yuk. I don't fancy that!" He spat the words out with a snarl.

"Don't worry, lad," Harris continued mercilessly, "it'll be freshly killed and hanging up in the larder soon for you all to enjoy. I'm looking for a volunteer, maybe two, to help me capture it out in the stables. I think it's run its last patrol. That reminds me, which one is yours?"

The jokes and laughter made for a healthy atmosphere in the fort as the men learned to live and work with each other at close quarters for what could be a lengthy and remote posting.

It sorely tested Harris to be teased and tormented time after time, but there was no helping it, and it was challenging to get the timings right for each sitting.

"Hey, Cook! What's wrong with these roasts of yours?" one man cried. "There's no bloody spud inside them. They're as hard as boiled eggs."

"Shut up and eat it. Eggs are good for you, didn't you know?"

More hilarity and laughter followed.

"More like bloody cannonballs," piped up another.

"Well, fire them from that new-fangled gun of yours."

"Hey, that's a clever idea, Cook. Fill them with ball bearings and nails, and we could! What do you think of that, then?"

The good-hearted banter continued amongst the men whenever meals were served.

***

The telephone was now in daily use, with the major kept informed of forts Rinella and Cambridge. Occasionally, he got the latest news from the governor on how Victoria was coping with the birth looming ever closer.

Out in the courtyard, the intense practising of loading the gun continued. After its full installation, Colonel Havers was finally happy with its operation and performance. Each action had to run smoothly as a well-oiled machine, and his men were beginning to hone the process to perfection.

Working down below the gun, two men were in the loading chamber. They loaded the dummy shells and charges using a chain and pulley system. They lifted the shells and charges from the loading trolley onto the hydraulically steam-operated ammunition lift, which raised the ordnance in the lift shaft up to the small loading port. Using the steam engine's movement and accumulator again to operate the hydraulics, they rammed the shell and its charge into the muzzle. Soon, they got it down to ten minutes.

Dummy shells and charges were being used, allowing it to be done repeatedly without wasting any live shells on the exercise. All were aware that if live rounds were loaded by mistake, they could not be extracted and would have to stay in place until fired.

***

Before he left for Fort Cambridge, Colonel Havers insisted, "Practise, practise, practise – and the time will surely come down."

So, day after day, they practised. Captain Marsh kept them hard at it until the time did come drastically down, eventually getting to a staggering six minutes. Aside from the timing, their uppermost fear was having problems with the steam engine or the accumulator breaking down. Therefore, the men had to load and fire the gun manually to ensure they could still operate it under less than optimum conditions. That was also practised stringently, using the four manual pumps connected to the hydraulic system, until they got that down to twenty minutes.

Townsend was pleased with their work rate, remarking to Marsh one time, "If enemy ships are spotted on the horizon, I think twenty minutes will be sufficient to fire it if need be."

Meanwhile, there was a growing concern among the officers and NCOs that the locals they encountered in their forays outside the fort seemed less and less inclined to meet with the soldiers. For this reason, Captain Johns, a no-nonsense career soldier, was given forty men from the regiment and sent to assist with contacting the farmers – since they felt this might be due to bandit activity in the area. He and his riflemen would be based at Anchor, answering directly to the commander.

In the meantime, Galea and his men (having been banned from inside the fort) could still watch them practising as they set about restoring the wall. Any hopes Galea had of delaying the wall from being built were diminishing. They were now under constant scrutiny by everyone around them.

"Good morning, Galea," said Townsend. "I see you're not much further on since we last spoke. Why not?" he asked brusquely.

"Ah, good morning, my friend. It has been somewhat difficult."

"Look, I am not your friend. Her Majesty's Government employs you to reinstate the wall, which you do not appear to be doing fast enough. Make your report, man, as I'm rapidly losing patience with your lame excuses."

"The inferior quality of the concrete was unfortunate," said Galea, gritting his teeth. "It was not sufficiently strong for laying on the bedrock,

301

Major. Because of the delay, it lost its strength and affected the masonry bedding. Then there was the extra stone brought up from the quarry to sit on the bedding. Up to now, it's taken ten tons of earth and debris to fill in the parapet and it hardly shows."

"Even so, the wall is barely one-quarter up!" Townsend complained. "Furthermore, why is the roadway still spanning the ditch? That alone is enough to compromise the fort's safety and also its men. I offered you extra men, and you declined it. Now, thanks to your stupidity, we're in this irritating mess."

Galea bristled, unaccustomed to being spoken to in such a disrespectful manner. "Yes, Major, but that part of the road is needed for my men to work off a wooden frame and help build the wall up safely outside the fort. I give you my word, I will have it dug up as soon as I can."

"I want the wall up and the roadway down as soon as possible," Townsend declared, slamming the flat of his hand down onto the stonework to emphasise the point. "If my orders are not complied with, you will find yourself on a serious charge, which will mean you will no longer be considered for government work. You understand the implication of your actions, sir?"

"Perfectly," Galea replied as he briskly turned and left, his hand squeezing the handle of the dagger at his hip with such force his knuckles whitened on the handle grip.

He returned to his men at the wall, where he was joined by Khalif. Wisely, his second in command took one look at his expression and waited quietly and patiently until Galea saw fit to speak. "I want you to promise me not one hair of the major's head will be touched; It will be a pleasure killing him slowly until he begs me to end his life. He must be made to apologise a thousand times for his insults. Then I will have the satisfaction of killing him all to myself."

"I promise you will have that satisfaction," said Khalif, inclining his head and agreeing. "I will ride out to the men and let them know it is time to bring more of them ashore in the next two nights. They are gathering in the caves on the small island and are keeping out of sight, but the food is becoming a big problem."

"Then we must provide more food, Khalif," said Galea, sighing. "I understand from what you have told me that it's getting difficult, and there is only one solution to our problem as we wait for our invasion plans to begin: we need to take over a complete farm! Local people have reported cows, horses, and goats going missing, causing anxiety. They have asked the British to stop it, and they are beginning to take notice.

But if we were to take over a farm completely, no one would be left alive to report us."

"I know of such a place," Khalif said, agreeing. "It is near to where our men come ashore from the island. But the problem is there are two farms there, close together, and then no other farms for as far as the eye can see."

"Do the soldiers ride there?" asked Galea, concerned they could be found out.

"No, they are too isolated, and the patrols ignore them because of the rough terrain and the difficulties in getting there."

"Then that is the answer! We will take over both farms and bring our men over in readiness for the invasion. We can hide all our men there for a few days more. There will be plenty of food, so they won't risk being discovered. Go, Khalif, and make it happen."

"But what is to be done with the people at the farms? There are men, women, and children there, but we do not know how many."

"I am not concerned about what you do with them, Khalif, as long as they do not raise the alarm," said Galea callously with a shrug. "My only concern is to make a success of this venture. First and foremost, we must succeed in outsmarting the British. If we were to fail now, just as our plans are working and coming together, we would never get another chance. Let us hope, Khalif, that our plans are not a misjudgement on our part."

"They will work, Edoardo. They have to," he replied, giving confidence to Galea's plan. Then, mounting his horse, he rode out from the fort.

A familiar face on Galea's work crew raised no suspicions from any of the guards whenever he came or went from the fort, and this occasion was no exception. He casually rode his horse until he was well clear of any soldiers that happened to be outside the confines of the fort. Then, once he was satisfied there was no one about, he rode faster, all the way to an isolated part of the coast. There he was met and taken by a small boat to the island near Comino to arrive at the secret hiding place his men shared. He found them sitting near small campfires in the dark and dank caves, well-hidden but despondent and low-spirited. He told them of Galea's plans, and every man there brightened up immediately. After many days cooped up in the caves, they were keen to get off the small island and change their meals from a mainly forced fish diet.

"Whatever happens, no one must be allowed to escape these farms and live to tell of our plans," Khalif ordered. "Once we have succeeded in taking the farms over, we can concentrate on getting more of our men there. It will be much safer, with little chance of being discovered, and we'll have plenty to eat."

"We have not had female company for a long time now, Khalif, and our men are in desperate need of women," one man stated. Several of his companions grunted their agreement. "What shall we do with the women we know are there?"

"It does not bother Galea what you do with them, Abdul. Have your way with them and see the men are satisfied – but make sure none escape. Tie them up each night, or even better, manacle them if necessary for further use. As far as the others are concerned… dispose of them."

"Thank you, Khalif. We will see to it at once," Abdul said with a lecherous, callous grin, knowing full well he would have the first choice of any women they found there.

Chapter 25

Extra men for patrols. Firing the monster cannon. Heartened by good cheer

A DETAIL of forty men in crimson uniform, led by an officer, came riding up to the bent entry approach to be met by two sentries.

"Captain Johns to speak to the commanding officer. I believe he's expecting me."

Seeing the officer dismount and walk towards them, the sentries saluted him.

"Yes, sir," one of them replied. "If you follow me, I'll take you to him."

The sentry led Johns past the bent entry and over the bridge to the gate, where he called out, "Guard, open the gate! Captain Johns to see the commander immediately!"

The squeal of ungreased steel bolts being drawn back on the other side of the reinforced gate made the sentry wince before the guard opened the smaller entrance door, which had been built into it to allow for restricted entry.

Inside, he was led to the command office where the major had been expecting him.

"Welcome, Captain. I trust your journey here was not too arduous; we are a long way out of Valletta. I heard you being challenged by our sentry out there. Good chap, that man, and keen for a stripe. But I didn't expect you here so soon, I admit. I forgot it's a quicker journey without a stores wagon to drive."

"Why, thank you, sir. Unfortunately, we have brought a change in the weather," said Johns. "Those black clouds out there need monitoring. Malta is well known for the severity of its storms, and they can begin at any time. The first time I experienced one, I was taken aback by its ferocity. Much different from the weather back home, sir. But the journey here, if nothing else, was certainly scenic. The view over to Gozo is stunning, and I look forward to serving under you, Major."

"I'm sure the dark clouds will blow over, Captain," he said casually, without having experienced any of Malta's ferocious storms before. "Our signals engineer took the message on the new telephone thingy to tell me you would be arriving sometime today. It seems you are to meet up with the locals at their homes and have a more in-depth talk with them, something our earlier patrols were not allowed to do."

"Yes, sir. We can find out more about what's happening in the area that way. We cannot rely upon the locals meeting up with our patrols while crossing their properties – or reporting information or any other problems, because that's stopped happening, especially here. There's some we never see or hear from, so now we're going to make sure we get around to see and talk to everyone."

"Then be aware, Captain – we've had cases of banditry out here, and it still surfaces from time to time."

"Oh, I am, Major! It's one of the reasons I have more troops with me to add to those already here. The aim is to flush them out if we come across any and, hopefully, dispose of them."

"Are your men new conscripts or experienced and capable?" Townsend asked.

"They're both experienced and competent, and I have to say I have great confidence in them – and Sergeant Clarke – to do a fine job," said Johns smartly.

"Good! I share your confidence, Captain. Now, turning to other matters: you and your men will bivouac outside the fort. The stables are there for your horses to eat and rest up, and you will eat in our small canteen. If there's any trouble, you are to get yourselves into the fort and assist in defending it until help arrives. I must tell you that you are incredibly lucky since you will witness for yourselves our gun firing for the very first time tomorrow. I can assure you it will be quite a sight, and you and your men are invited to watch if you so wish."

"We look forward to it, sir, and thank you," said Johns.

"Very well, consider it done. Also, I want to let you know that some government contractors are working here, and I expect them to leave as soon as the gap in the wall has been closed."

"Of course, sir. May I suggest our first patrol go out in the morning?"

"Excellent, Captain. I share in your enthusiasm. I'll get Sergeant Savage to accompany you and show you our fort. He can also help you with your map reading. I'll speak to you later, no doubt."

"Yes, sir, thank you," Johns saluted.

He returned to his men and ordered them to set up their new camp, take refreshments under Corporal Harris inside the fort, and then rest up from their difficult journey to the fort. Meanwhile, he and Sergeant Clarke walked through the old camp area and down along Anchor Bay before heading back up the fort's new road. They wanted to see what had been involved in getting the gun up to its lofty position and find out what all the fuss was about with this hundred-ton supergun – very much wanting to see it for themselves.

Sergeant Savage met them when they returned to the camp and proved a highly informative guide for their tour of the site, as well as helping them look at and read the area's maps. After admiring the gun with him, they saw for themselves the extraordinary effort it must have taken to get it up there and were impressed with the men's energy and dedication. Afterwards, they spent the rest of the day looking at maps of the area, getting their bearings, and setting up camp before the serious business of reaching the remote farms the very next day.

Although it was now within the fort, it was still customary for sentries to be posted on three-hour shifts throughout the night to protect the gun. They were the only people to witness the early morning patrol leave before the garrison stirred. Long gone were the bugle calls, trumpeting out their orders first thing in the morning. Although there was a bugler in the fort's contingency, he also acted as the semaphore signaller. So, it fell to the non-commissioned officers, such as Savage, to raise the men from their slumbers in another way. They settled for a large handheld bell, kept in the built-in guardroom behind the barrack rooms and next to the gate. Anyone finding it hard to extract themselves from their beds would have it rung mere inches from their ears until they got up. They reasoned it would be easier to comply with orders than to go deaf ignoring them.

"Take your bloody fingers out of your ears. They'll come down your bloody nose if you push them too far. Do you hear me?" Savage yelled over the bell.

He had learned from Horrocks that a little humour with the men would encourage them to comply with their orders more readily.

"Yes."

"Yes, Sergeant!" he reminded them. "Get it right, or I'll have you in my guardroom if I can find it. Have you got it, Willis?"

"No, Sergeant, I haven't got your guardroom, but it's around here somewhere," the man replied, eliciting mocking laughter.

"Clever arse, Willis! You're the joker who might be sent to look into it in a minute," he retorted, which caused more laughter. He let it pass – he

307

knew Willis wasn't insubordinate. "Now, when you men have eaten and seen to your ablutions, the commander wants us all to assemble in the courtyard. So, this morning, we don't want any fannying about wasting time, do we? You will all be expected in the yard in one hour. Let the Lord have mercy on anyone who fails to make it on time. I am aware my guardroom is empty and where it is. I feel that all it needs is a few volunteers to spend some time in there and break it in. Understood?"

"Yes, Sergeant," they chorused.

"Right, then, get moving. You're wasting precious time. Make your beds before you go and hurry up about it!"

Sergeant Savage had endorsed his authority, leaving nothing to chance. The constant drill procedure had turned each man into a part of a very efficient fighting machine. And now, after being suitably fed and watered by Harris (with only minor complaints at the standard of his cooking), the whole garrison lined up in the courtyard – including the lighting man and the two shell and charge loaders fully kitted out in their newly provided anti-spark duck uniforms and pillbox hats.

When he was satisfied, Townsend nodded, showing he was ready to begin.

"Attention!" ordered the NCO.

"Thank you, Sergeant Savage," said Townsend, his voice carrying clearly across the courtyard. "At ease, men. Today is the day all our hard work and dedication is to be tested." He paused; he was aware they were hanging on his every word. "Today is the day we fire our gun for the first time!" He was immediately forced to stop. Each utterance was drowned out by the boisterous cheers that greeted his announcement.

"Hurrah! Huzzah!" they cried excitedly.

Townsend raised his hands to calm them. "Steady, men. Regimental Headquarters have authorised us to fire up to four shells at a target ship out at sea. The target is a rusting hulk that has been tied up and left to disintegrate for several years at Grand Harbour. We will be doing the harbour master a big favour by disposing of it!"

The men chuckled and agreed.

"It will be towed into position at an appropriate distance by a naval frigate – it shouldn't be too much of a problem for us, whatever the distance. It's now time for us to justify the huge expense invested in ourselves and, more importantly, in this gun. Suitable charges will be chosen to fire shells up to the five-mile mark. Now, our range finders must be at their best because the towing ship will have official observers onboard watching how we make out." He paused and then raised his voice to emphasise the point: "*I do not want their bloody ship hit! Also, I do not want our shells to drop anywhere near it!* The turbulence the impact of these shells will generate in hitting the water could affect the frigate's stability carrying these observers. The last thing we want is for dignitaries to be thrown overboard!" As he spoke, the spectacle of what had happened to the Italians was firmly in his mind. "We are not tossing pebbles into puddles here. We must be spot on and sink the target ship if we want to impress them.

"From the information given to me over our telephone thing," he continued, "the target ship will be left at anchor for our gunners at about two o'clock this afternoon. This means they will get here at about one o'clock, which should give us more than enough time to work out the coordinates of the target. We will be ready to hit that ship – or get very bloody close to it – at two o'clock precisely because I want us to impress those observers and our betters. Therefore, I want our lads to go over the loading and firing routine several more times to be completely sure. You range finders have got to be accurate with your readings because firing the gun successfully depends on it." He clapped his hands. "Right then, men, let's get at it! I want the boilers lit and the accumulator working the hydraulics and the machinery in time, with a good head of steam up within two hours. And because Captain Marsh is your master gunner, you will take all your orders from him for the duration of the exercise. Dismissed, men, and wait for your orders."

There was great excitement amongst the men. At last, they would fire 'their gun,' as it was now known.

"Morning patrol returning, sir!" the sentry on the musket parapet shouted down.

The men came into camp on foot, guiding their horses towards the stables. Captain Johns made for the major to give his findings.

"Well, Captain, what is your report?"

Johns saluted. "Sir, the patrol split up this morning as we headed north-west. We were able to get to more farms that way. I have to report that neither group met any of the locals, although we went to two remote farms each."

"Were there any animals about, such as cattle, horses, or dogs?"

"There was livestock about but no dogs or people; that's what felt strange," said the captain. "Speaking to the men, they reckoned the owners would come out where the track passed the corner of their land – just for a talk because they see so few people from day to day out there – but even the young lads they said had been cheeky to them before didn't show up. There was no sign of them, sir, yet all the livestock was there. Maybe they've been helping out neighbours somewhere and got back after we left?"

309

"They were out and about around here a few months back. Why, they even helped cheer the men on when they started the big pull from Anchor Bay," Townsend remarked. "There should also be dogs running around. One of those families took the two stray dogs we had in camp." He thought for a moment, then added, "It's concerning me. I will let you have the names of the families living out there. Tomorrow, I want you and your men to conduct a more thorough search of their properties – break in, if necessary! There must be someone about to tend to the livestock. But for today, as promised, you and your men are invited to watch as we fire the gun for the first time. We will be firing at a decoy ship the Navy is towing over to us."

"We look forward to being there with you, sir." Johns saluted and left to convey the exciting news to his men.

***

That afternoon, under dark, rain-threatening skies, two ships hove into view from around the mainland.

"Ships on the horizon, sir!" the spotter shouted excitedly from his post.

Marsh put the telescope to his eye and looked to where he was pointing. "It's them, all right!" He focussed it first on the frigate and the dignitaries it carried and then scanned the length of the decrepit, neglected ship being towed behind it.

"They are coming about as we speak, Major."

"Good. The amount of charge we select will depend on the final distance, so we must delay loading it until our range finders can confirm the exact distance to the hulk of the target ship. As soon as we are given the information, the shells and the chosen charges we decide to use will be made ready to be loaded into the gun's muzzle by the rammer."

The anxious gun crew watched the ships draw nearer. They were wishfully talking between themselves for the frigate to hurry up so they could fire the monster cannon, but they had to calm themselves and wait for the official signal to open fire. The shell loaders below the huge gun also waited impatiently for the signal to send up the chosen shell and charge to load into the gun for firing.

Time was passing slowly for everyone in the fort when suddenly the shout went out: "Naval semaphore message coming in, sir!" said the lookout, peering through binoculars. "Message reads, 'When in position, towing shackles will be taken off and will drop the anchor of your target. Wait until the crew are clear, then fire at will.'"

"Reply, 'Message received and understood.'"

"Yes, sir." The man stood high on the fort wall and waved his flags in a very efficient military style, sending the semaphore message back to the ship. Only the sound of his flags rippling and slapping in the wind could be heard across the highly expectant scene.

Captain Johns, his men, and others not involved in the firing took up all available vantage points, eagerly wanting to witness the tense spectacle about to unfold before them.

"Master Gunner, I'll leave everything in your capable hands," said Townsend, sending a smile at his old friend before adding, "Good luck."

Galea had positioned himself carefully, as close to the range finders and Marsh as possible without raising suspicions from the major. He had a full view of the controls he would need to fire the gun when the time came.

"Thank you, sir," said Marsh, with a tense grin. "It shouldn't be long now."

They watched as the rowing boat with the skeleton crew on board left the ship at anchor and headed back to the relative safety of the British frigate. Another anxious wait followed when the frigate's captain decided to pull a little further away from the target ship for added safety. *Perhaps the Italian mishap was on his mind, too,* thought Marsh.

"Safely apart now, Captain!" came the call from the spotter.

"Right, men, give me the range of the ship so I can convert it." As Marsh waited for the exact readings, he eased himself down into the seat in the traversing recess under the thick, protective concrete cover.

"Range at four and a half miles, sir."

He loaded the distance, grid coordinates, and firing settings into the hydraulics controls while sighting the ship through the viewfinder, and then waited.

The men watched in awe as the cannon sprung into life with a series of metallic clunks. The machinery turned it mechanically on its traversing platform and stopped at the loading turret. The 60-foot rammer pushed the selected charge – and the one-ton shell that had been sent up – down the muzzle to load the gun before retracting itself. Then the huge gun turned mechanically on its traversing platform again, back towards the target ship, and stopped. Menacingly, it raised itself to the required angle for the chosen trajectory it had been given for firing the shell. Release valves hissed and blew steam while the steam accumulator constantly changed the differing pressures to allow for the intricate manoeuvres.

Although they had practised feeding coordinates into the controls of the gun and watched as it magically came to life many times, it always held them spellbound – and this time, it held an added frisson of excitement;

it was to be the first live firing of a one-ton shell, and the garrison of Fort Anchor felt under enormous pressure to get it done successfully.

Seated at the controls, Marsh was feeling the pressure, too. *It never felt like this while practising,* he reflected. *But the onus is on me now to demonstrate the power of the thing.* Keeping his nerve, he waited in the stifling, confined space for permission to shoot. *Damn it; my hands are shaking,* he thought, balling them into fists to help stop the shake.

Finally, the signaller cried, "The frigate has repeated the semaphore, Captain. Fire when ready."

Globules of sweat formed on his brow and trickled down his face as Marsh checked and rechecked his readings. Then, wiping away the sweat with the back of his hand, he watched the target ship through the viewfinder and checked the readings one final time with his range finders until wholly satisfied. "Prepare to fire!" he ordered his gunnery crew and then, after a few more seconds of delay, shouted, *"Fire!"*

The lanyard was pulled, causing sparks from the friction tube to light the primer gunpowder which, in turn, ignited the main charge.

The sound of the colossus firing was indescribable as it discharged its one-ton projectile towards the ship. Layers of dust were shaken from the fort's ramparts by the shockwaves caused by the explosion. The watching men had instinctively covered their ears, with some rocking back on their heels with the explosive force the gun generated. The noise of the shot reverberated throughout the fabric of the fort, causing glass to break. At the same time, a cloud of acrid smoke enveloped everyone watching from the battlements. Lit embers from the spent explosive charge dropped out from the muzzle's end to the ground, adding to the smoke-filled scene.

A secondary boom followed immediately after firing, somewhere high in the sky above, causing them to momentarily avert their eyes. Through the clearing smoke from the firing, the ship could be seen lengthways on and still riding the waves, untouched and in one piece, when an enormous waterspout erupted, towering high above and beyond the vessel, behind its bow.

A loud gasp went up from the men as they realised how close the shell had been, while the noise of the firing could be heard echoing in the hills around them. The targeted ship rocked violently from the shock waves, rolling vigorously from port to starboard and then back to port side again. The ship was seen to drag its anchor for a short distance until it caught fast on the seabed once more.

Marsh half-watched as he busily worked at the controls, fully aware everyone was relying on his accuracy with the gun. *It's firing a little high,* he thought. Below him, governing valves hissed with escaping steam as the accumulator moved the powerful gun once more.

The hydraulics operated the machinery, lowering the barrel and then swinging it, mechanically and effortlessly, to load turret number two. A sizeable wet swab was forced down the weapon's muzzle by the rammer. It doused the gunpowder residue and burnt embers from the previous charge with running water, washing it clean and cooling it down. Meanwhile, the men below began loading the hydraulic lift shaft with the next one-ton shell and its mighty charge. It raised the round to the loading turret, where again the rammer shoved both propellant and shell into the cannon's muzzle. It swung majestically back into firing position with the gun loaded and then raised its muzzle, threatening to fire again.

"Down elevation two degrees!" shouted the range finder while wiping insistent spots of rain from his instruments.

"Down elevation two degrees!" repeated Marsh loudly as he adjusted the shell's trajectory when leaving the gun. The muzzle visibly dropped as he altered it. His shirt was sticking to him with uncomfortable sweat as he hoped and prayed the next round would fly true to the target.

"Prepare to fire!"

All of the men there collectively held their breath.

"*Fire!*"

The lanyard was pulled against the primer firing charge, and the great gun belched out its projectile. Again, the watching men became enveloped in the billowing smoke. As the smoke lifted all eyes were trained on the ship, riding high on the waves, when the one-ton shell slammed into it just above the waterline. It tore through the vessel's lower decks, which rocked violently from side to side on impact. Then, like a wild horse attempting to throw its rider, the ship's stern rose rapidly with the massive force of the explosion inside it before dropping down, its back broken and sinking.

They watched as the ship disintegrated, with debris thrown high and wide into the air before raining down on the boiling, turbulent sea. The only evidence it had existed was the floating wreckage and debris bobbing up and down on the churned-up surface of the water. Meanwhile, the highly trained gunners had loaded the third shell and its explosive charge into the gun's muzzle.

Soldiers cheered, hugged, and slapped each other. They whooped loudly with helmets held aloft, ecstatic to have witnessed their cannon's awesome power and feeling immensely proud and privileged to have done so. As Captain Marsh appeared from the traversing recess, more cheering greeted him, ringing out loud above the scene.

"Well done, sir!" came the cries of his delighted men.

A huge grin spread across the master gunner's face as he came to terms with what he had just achieved. In his mind, he could now picture the utter devastation of any large ship that saw fit to attack these islands.

Major Townsend grabbed his hand and shook it vigorously. "Yes, very well done, and congratulations, Captain. That was an awesome example of lethal shooting. You should feel rightly proud of yourself and your gun crew for using just two shells out of the four."

"Thank you, sir. I was highly relieved when the second shot hit home, I must admit!"

He was aware Robert knew how much it meant to him to fire the beast. At last, his wish had been granted, and he felt highly satisfied. The urge to succeed had overridden all his thoughts leading up to the firing. Now he could relax, with the pressure off.

"I have to report that the gun has been reloaded, sir," said a loader in a duck suit, who had come up from below after hearing the cheering.

"Well, it will have to stay loaded for now," said Townsend. "There may be a use for it soon, though it wasn't needed today, thanks to Captain Marsh's excellent shooting! Your firing crew are to be commended for their efficiency, Captain."

"Message received by semaphore, sir," the signalman interrupted. "It reads: 'On the nose, Fort Anchor. Congratulations.' "There's also another message: 'Battery unseen from sea position.'" Shall I reply, sir?"

After careful consideration, Townsend said, "Yes, just reply: 'Very happy battery.'"

Other eyes had also watched the events unfold. "The great gun spoke today, Khalif. We will soon take it away from the British and start the destruction of their fortifications at Valletta. Once we open fire, it will signal our gathering men to start the full-scale invasion of Malta. It will belong to our people soon, and I can hardly wait to get started."

"Edoardo, I thought we would take over the fort once the first shots are fired!" Khalif exclaimed. "We could take over now if we wanted to."

"Be patient, my friend. We haven't enough men yet. We must wait for our forces to gather. When we do have enough men, my orders will go out for them to listen when the first shot strikes Valletta. That will be the true signal to start the invasion and no other. It is a short time to wait, considering our families have waited hundreds of years already. Our objective is to ensure the wall does not get too high, or there will be no way into the fort. I think we can stall them with the poor state of the concrete once again. That wall must not be allowed to thwart our efforts in overrunning the fort."

***

There was much merriment at the gun's success, and it carried on relentlessly, with everyone in a joyous mood.

At the nod from the major, Sergeant Savage bellowed, "Attention!" which instantly cut out the exuberant chatter.

"Men, I would like to say a deep, heartfelt thanks to you all for the hard work in getting this gun up here," said Townsend. "It's because of your hard work that today has been such a success. That's not to forget all the others who are not here to share the occasion with us. That said, I propose to unlock the storeroom where our barrels of beer are kept. Captain Marsh and I will be extremely happy to serve everyone a couple of cold beers to express our gratitude – but no more than that! So, follow me, men. I happen to have the keys here in my hand."

More cheering ensued. That day, each man was feeling a deep sense of achievement, as they had found a common purpose: to protect and work the gun as a highly effective fighting unit.

When they reached the stores, Townsend and Marsh ensured everyone had a tankard full of beer before speaking again.

"The firing and shattering of the decoy ship today was a truly awesome sight to see, and I want you all to drink a toast to the largest muzzle-loading cannon in the world – thanks to Mr Armstrong," Townsend said. "No other country has come close to building anything like it, men, so hearty cheers to everyone for getting it here!" Finally, he raised his tankard to his lips, along with the others, and drank it dry.

The others drank too, thankful for their two beers each, but some wanted to continue the celebration with the illegal stuff they had got hidden away in the fort.

Later, Marsh came across a drunk gunner, Bone, who refused to say where the stuff was kept. He had Savage throw him into the guardroom before informing Townsend.

The day's excitement ended abruptly under the threat of heavy rain from the quickly darkening skies; the first few drops that had fallen earlier when they fired the gun had only been the start. More rain fell, gently at first and then more urgently, from the angry clouds swirling above them.

Dutifully and quickly, Galea's men set about covering the large, exposed mounds of cement – currently being used to reinforce the brick and stonework in the wall – before the full storm could break. Malta was renowned for the ferocity of its rainstorms, so due care was taken to draw and secure large tarpaulin sheets over the exposed work area.

Suddenly, a tremendously loud thunderclap was heard above, followed by a great deluge of heavy rainfall that painfully splattered at the men's bodies. Lightning lit up the darkened sky in multiple, searing flashes, sending everyone scurrying for cover. Open stable doors were hastily slammed shut to help keep out the unnerving flashing and to divert the torrents of water rushing through the camp. At the same time inside, the grooms stroked and calmed the frightened animals, protecting them from the crashing noises outside. The torrential downpour drummed loudly on the substantial canvas tents, making it difficult for those sheltering inside to hear and talk to each other.

Then Khalif came up with an idea. "Edoardo, if we loosen the ropes on the tarpaulin sheets, the storm will destroy the cement and delay the finishing of the wall for good!" He shouted it as loud as he could over the noise of the deluge outside.

Galea shouted back, congratulating him, "Bravo, Khalif, it is an excellent idea! Send two of our men out there and have them loosen the ropes. Everyone has taken shelter and won't see them!" he bawled.

The two unlucky men chosen for the task slunk off into the downpour to do his bidding, looking deeply unhappy at having to go into the harsh electric storm howling and exploding above and around them. With daring bravado, they forced their way over to the cement pile and loosened the ropes to the tarpaulin sheets that covered them.

Afterwards, wet and bedraggled, they re-entered the tent and, while dripping water across the floor, stood before their masters. "It is done, Khalif," the man gasped. "The cement will be destroyed long before morning," he added with a proud hint of achievement.

Chapter 26

Discovering the missing families.
Back by the skin of their teeth

THE MORNING light revealed the extensive damage and destruction wrought throughout the camp. Unlike the more substantial bell tents, some ridge tents had been ripped from their awnings by the strong, gusting winds. Their occupants had been forced to seek new shelter elsewhere during the height of the ferocious storm. Thick layers of wet mud covered the ground while mounds of cement near the wall had hardened or washed away, leaving white streaks across the camp floor.

Galea immediately reported the cement loss to the commander, who was not pleased after listening to his men's storm damage reports.

"What? Is it too much to expect you and your men to have made sure the ropes were fast and firmly secured? You continue to disappoint me!" Townsend barked. "Now, we must get more supplies in because of your incompetence. It's put the completion of the wall back even further!"

"I will order more right away, Commander," Galea promised apologetically. "It was unfortunate the storm loosened the ropes on the sheets. Between the frequency of the thunderclaps and the ferocity of the lightning strikes, my men sought the safety of shelter like everyone else and were afraid of being struck. It may be the ropes were not tied tightly enough; we shall never know," he lied convincingly. "It came down very quickly, and I apologise again on behalf of all my men."

After the initial delay in cleaning up the storm damage – which had violently laid waste to the area – and recalling their own stories of what happened to them during the disordered commotion, the morning patrol set off and headed out towards the same farms they'd visited the day before. At a convenient point, they split the patrol up again. Captain John's party would travel on to the two remotest farms. The sergeant and his party were to visit the other two isolated farms, which they had found unusually quiet the previous day. If there was still no answer to their calls, they had been authorised by the commander to make forced entry into the premises and outside buildings.

"Who would want to eke out a living in these harsh conditions?" said Johns as the first rundown farm came into view.

The corporal agreed with him, shaking his head in disbelief. "I have no idea, sir. Not me, for sure. Perhaps it's been passed down in the family?"

The farmhouse had been built in a natural dip in the landscape, sheltering it from the fierce winds that often ravaged this remote, exposed area. As they rode slowly and carefully into the steep hollow, they were forced to lean back and sit tight in their saddles, which rolled alarmingly with every step the horses took.

Dismounting at the house, they tied the horses to the rail at the water trough to let them drink. Some men cupped their hands and scooped the water up to their mouths to drink as their eyes continually scoured the scene for the occupants.

"Anyone here?" called out the captain. There was no answer. "Hello there! Anyone home?" he called out again, more loudly.

There was still no answer. Sharing a look with the corporal and gesturing for the rest of the men to search the outbuildings, he opened the creaking door and stepped inside. The outside of the structure looked as if some maintenance was required, but inside the house, it was neat and tidy and felt quite homely. There was plenty of evidence of a good woman's influence. A little girl's rag doll sat on one of the seats and, on the floor, a boy's small wooden horse lay, carved from a sawn-off block of driftwood. Also, in a heap, were several women's dresses and undergarments waiting their turn to be washed in the water tub.

As the captain searched the house, his corporal joined him at the door. "We have scoured the farm; there's no one to be seen anywhere."

"They could have gone somewhere together, corporal, but it's odd and highly unlikely, I must say." He looked again at the children's toys. "I can't imagine the little tykes leaving their treasures behind. The place is deserted."

"The livestock that were here yesterday have all gone, sir," the corporal reported. "Our men have been over to the far fields, and they are empty too. There are no animals anywhere."

"Well, I can remember the pigs and cows there," recalled Captain Johns while removing his helmet and scratching his head. "It's all rather strange," he surmised, rubbing his chin as he looked about him.

"Don't forget that ram and three sheep. One was in lamb, sir," said the corporal. "They wouldn't normally have moved her, being in that condition."

"Look, men, there's something odd at work here," said the captain, emerging from the farmhouse. "Let's get ourselves over to the other farm and see what we can find there. Get the men mounted, Corporal. We move on to the next farm immediately."

The trail between the two farms flattened out and became easier to ride on, so they pushed their horses on at a steady pace.

As they went, the captain noticed that the ground had seen some heavy usage recently. *These tracks weren't there yesterday,* he thought. "Certainly, plenty of hoofmarks along here, Corporal. Was it the missing animals, I wonder?"

"Maybe the owners are moving their livestock over here, sir."

They shared a look that suggested neither man believed it. "Be on your guard, men," said the captain, suspicious.

An eerie silence hung over the scene as they approached the second farm. No birds were singing, unlike the day before when they had been present in abundance. The backs of the men's necks prickled, though they could see no cause for it.

The captain raised his arm, halting the riders outside the farmhouse. Then, standing up in the stirrups, he shaded his eyes against the sun with his hand as he peered into the distance.

"There's plenty of livestock in that field over yonder, sir," the corporal pointed out. "Strange… they all seem to be gathered in just the one field, and – if I'm not mistaken – the ram and the three sheep are in there from the other farm, including the pregnant ewe."

"Well, let's dismount, Corporal. We'll have a good look around and see what we can find. *Is there anyone here?*" Johns shouted, cupping his hand to his mouth. *"Anyone at home?"* There was still no answer, just a heavy, overbearing silence.

Taking his pistol from its holster, he let off two quick shots into the air and waited, hoping for a response.

"Nothing," said the corporal, shaking his head after a pause. "I don't like it, Captain. It's not normal."

They entered the house to see the table and chairs had been upset and there was broken crockery littering the floor. Clear signs there had been a violent struggle in there.

Outside, the rest of the patrol continued the search while two of them walked off towards the barn: a dilapidated building, long worn out, but somewhere to keep the animal feed and farm tools. They opened wide its rickety doors to allow the sunlight to stream in. As the hinges screeched from a lack of duck grease, the daylight lit up the dark interior, instantly throwing both their shadows onto the far wall of the barn.

"There's plenty of feed here for the animals, Bert, but where are the men, women, and little ones?" Les wondered aloud as they went further inside the dilapidated building.

"Wait," said Bert, concerned. He held his hand over his mouth. "There's a stench around here somewhere! Can you smell it, Les?"

"Aye, I can now," he replied with a screwed-up face. "There's no mistaking a smell like that: something has died. It's coming from the back there. Yes, something's dead all right," he confirmed while swatting away at the swarm of flies that had flown out. "Stay here while I go in and see."

Les did as he was told.

After a few seconds Bert exclaimed, "Oh my God!" He then stumbled a few feet back towards Les at the barn entrance before violently emptying the contents of his stomach on the ground. "They're all in there! Both families have been slaughtered, even the little girl and boy. There's also the bloated bodies of the two dogs from the camp."

Les hurried over and looked at where he'd pointed. "Bloody hell, it's horrible!" he gasped, feeling nauseous. "Get yourself out into the fresh air while I fetch the captain."

The captain and the rest of the men came running over in response to his frantic shouts.

"Let me go in and look," said Captain Johns. "Keep a sharp lookout, men. Those shots I fired, and our shouts, may have been heard – or we may have been seen."

He came out after a few minutes, grey and furious. "Bastards! They killed the men and two lads by cutting their throats. The women and their daughters have been violated most horribly, and those little ones never stood a chance. It looks like the dogs were killed trying to protect them. Let's get back to the fort and inform the major of what we found!"

"Wait, Captain. We can't leave the poor devils like that, surely?" Bill asked. "I think we should bury them first. With your permission, sir?"

"I'm inclined to agree, soldier. It's the least we can do," said Johns. "I saw several spades we can use in the barn. But listen, men, we must be quick about it and not stand on ceremony. We must return to the fort with our report. We can come back and do a better job of this later."

After the bodies had been brought out and buried, Captain Johns called his men together. "Right, that will have to do," he said. "Let's get back to the fort before we push our luck. Who knows – they could be watching us right now. Mount up!" he ordered as they climbed into their saddles.

"Forward!" he cried, and the patrol hastily rode off. "And keep your eyes focused! It's occurred to me, Corporal, that we may have stumbled across a big insurgency group, given the many tracks we've seen about here. Along with the murders and the missing livestock, it paints a rather dark picture. It's hard to believe, but it could also mean an invasion is being planned."

"I think you're right, sir," the corporal replied, still constantly on the lookout.

They rode on for some minutes before a sudden shout of alarm came from a man at the rear. "Bloody hell! There's a whole army after us, sir!"

Twisting in his saddle, Captain Johns saw a vast dust cloud on their heels, each billow telling of several pounding hooves. "At the gallop, men!" he shouted. "Give the horses their heads! It's us they want. Ride like the wind, and if anything happens, don't stop, no matter what! It's crucial someone gets back and warns Fort Anchor!"

They stretched out the horses' legs as they dashed for safety – trying to keep a safe distance between them and their pursuers. But the pursuers' horses were fresher, and they began to gain ground on the patrol. Soon shots rang out, and a soldier was brought down from his horse.

"Push on, men, and keep low; they're getting our range!" Johns shouted above the loud drumming of the horses' hooves.

Racing along at breakneck speed, they swiftly reached the point where the trail dropped to single file between the two farms. Out of nowhere, another group of attackers rose in ambush – but they were too eager. They showed themselves early, firing upon the approaching riders and giving away their position.

A man was shot dead close to the corporal as he drew his sabre for the fight; he fell from his horse with a dull thud and his companions' mounts trampled his corpse. The ambushers appeared to realise the patrol wasn't stopping and scrambled to get away, but not before two were shot in the back. The captain slew another with his sabre, opening the man's chest with a slashing motion. Two more were bowled over and sent sprawling onto the hard ground before being trampled under horses' hooves, cracking ribs and skulls. The patrol raced along without stopping, onward towards the single-line track, manipulating their horses into a single file as they rode into it.

As they all but disappeared, the last horse took bullets in its flanks, and the horse's rear legs collapsed; the soldier was tipped out from the saddle. Scared and alone, he got to his feet and emptied the chambers of his rifle and handgun at the chasing horde. Then, using his bayonet, he ran the first man through before a group of them were onto him, pinning him to the ground. The fleeing patrol could hear his screams behind them in the

321

distance as they repeatedly stabbed at him, but they couldn't go back. It was futile; they would all perish.

The fallen horse had blocked the narrow rocky trail for a few precious minutes before its carcass was unceremoniously dragged out of the way, giving the patrol valuable time to reach the first farm. Then began the tricky climb up and out of the hollow. They knew they had to get to the top to stand any chance of escape, but it was slow going. Most of the patrol had managed it, save the last two riders, when the killers caught up with them. Then more shots rang out.

"Aaargh!" screamed one. His back stiffened as he let go of the reins and bowled over and backwards from his horse's saddle, his lifeless body rolling down to the foot of the hollow.

"Dismount!" Johns ordered at the top. "You men take the reins of the horses! The rest of you, get your guns ready. We'll let them have it as they near the top. If we shoot enough, they will be more cautious about following us, hopefully giving us more time to escape. But if we fail to hold them back, it's imperative someone gets back to the fort to warn them about what we discovered here!"

They were well hidden on top of the ridge, lying in wait with their ambush ready and waiting for the chasing pack to arrive. The pursuers were fooled – thinking the soldiers had carried on, making good their escape – so they attempted to ride up the slope themselves.

"Make every shot count," Johns whispered. "Steady, men, steady. On my orders... *Now! Fire!*"

The remaining soldiers fired a salvo of shots that took out the leading horsemen, their bodies rolling back under their companions' horses' hooves. In turn these horses shied up in fright, unsaddling their riders.

"Another salvo, men, and individual fire," Johns ordered. "Don't forget the families they butchered. Remember those young kiddies' faces! Let's do it for them! Pick your targets and fire!"

The salvo was a deadly accurate, withering hail of fire that brought down many front riders. Bullets pinged all around the troops as they concentrated on taking out their targets.

"Good, we've got them pinned down. They don't know what to do now, sir. We have totally confused them," said the corporal.

As the pursuers' riderless horses panicked and raced every which way, the battle settled down to the two sides sniping at each other. Soon enough, the captain began to worry about the few men below them. He had seen with his own eyes there had been many more of them than that.

"Where are they all, Corporal? We know there's more. I don't like it!"

"They're planning something for sure, sir."

Suddenly a desperate cry rang out. "Sir! Sir! They're trying to get around us. What shall we do, sir?"

"We get the hell out of here, of course!" Captain Johns shouted. "Mount up, men! Let's go."

Yelling at their horses, they set off at a fast pace. Half of the pursuers below were stumbling about in confusion at the bottom of the hollow, while the main body of men were attempting to come round and outflank them. They found they could ride faster now as the trail widened out and the stony ground softened under the horses' hooves.

Leaving the farms behind, with only token shots following them, they made good their escape. Their horses had had the chance to rest while they'd been exchanging gunfire with the insurgents in the hollow, but the pursuers' horses were tiring. Having attempted to outflank the troops, they were still out of range for their guns to have any effect, and the distance between them began to grow.

Captain Johns and his men finally met up with the rest of the patrol, who had heard the shots and were now on full alert. The captain shouted urgently to the sergeant as the two groups met, "Did you meet up with any of the farmers?"

"Yes, sir. They were in the fields and were unaware of our previous visit."

"Well, we found out the reason for the theft from the farms, Sergeant. It's a large group of insurgents. They murdered the families at the other two farms, and now they're after us. We must get back to the fort and fast!" he shouted breathlessly.

Pointing behind them, Sergeant Clarke asked, "Is that dust cloud the insurgents, sir? Can we do anything to stop them?"

"Yes, Sergeant Clarke, it's them alright," he said, panicking. "You would be most wise to follow me now. We have already lost some good men; I don't want to lose more."

"No! We're with you, sir," Clarke said, concern etched into his features. The patrol set off to the fort without further talk, riding their horses as fast as possible.

"Patrol returning. Inform the major – something seems wrong!" shouted the sentry.

They were still at full gallop when they pulled the horses up sharp outside the fort, rear flanks sliding first, then digging, into the dirt, stopping them. A few of the patrol had lost their helmets, and their scarlet tunics looked dirty and unkempt. Some of the riderless horses had also returned with them, following their stablemates back to camp.

In total panic, the order was shouted for everyone to hear: "Put the horses in the stables and get into the fort now – and fast!"

Johns met Townsend at the gate as he dashed inside. "A large force of insurgents we discovered at the farms are pursuing us, sir!" he reported breathlessly. "We need to break out the rifles and get everyone inside. They're not far behind and are after our blood!"

Hearing the commotion, Galea arrived just in time to hear Captain Johns give his report, which confirmed his worst fears. Discovery was always his prime concern when trying to conceal his growing army. Now the soldiers knew about them – before they were ready – and he needed to act fast.

Grabbing his second in command by his coat, he ordered: "Khalif, send our men out now and have the cable cut," he wailed. "This is the worst possible time! The main body of our men have not yet arrived in Malta. Order the men in the hills to kill that semaphore unit immediately. No messages are to be allowed to reach Valletta at any cost; otherwise, all will be lost. They can slip out of the fort through the wall without anyone seeing them."

"Yes, Edoardo. At once."

"Then go now and arrange it before it is too late. Hurry! Hurry!"

Unseen amongst the commotion of getting the garrison armed, two men slipped out through the gap in the wall and crept away from the ensuing chaos to do Galea's bidding.

Chapter 27

Attempting a repair. Missing Signals Unit found. Charge of the fools brigade

THE MEN from the patrol quickly closed the gates on the horses' stables and hurried across the Guthrie bridge into the fort. As the last man passed over the threshold, the chasing horde's vanguard appeared and resumed firing. Bullets broke fragments off the newly built stonework and pinged dangerously off the metal gate.

"Quick, men! Pull the bridge in and close the gate!"

The bridge was then pulled in and the gate slammed shut and bolted in double quick time.

"Captain Marsh!" Townsend shouted.

"Yes, sir. I'm here, sir," he answered, hurrying over to him.

"Bring out the Gatling gun from the armoury and set it up in the middle of the courtyard covering the open wall."

He came running back moments later. "Sir, someone has sabotaged it. It can't be fired!"

"Damn it!" he exclaimed, thinking fast. "Break out the rifles. See that all the men are armed with plenty of ammunition. Captain Johns, get some of your men on the musketry parapet and reinforce the counterscarp gallery and the caponiers. Hurry it up. Get a move on – we have got a fight on our hands!"

"Yes, sir. Right away."

In the highly charged atmosphere, men ran through the passageways to take up their defensive positions while filling their pouches with cartridges from the opened ammunition boxes on the way.

"Sergeant Savage, get that blasted Galea and his men away from the wall. It's too late for that now. I want six men down at that open wall to shoot anyone trying to get inside. It's the weakest part of the fort and must be defended at all costs," ordered Townsend.

"Yes, sir. You three and you two, come with me!"

They ran over to the wall break, taking up defensive positions close to the cannon while ordering Galea and his men to move away.

"That man there!" Townsend barked. "Get over to Miller and tell him to speak to St. Elmo. They are to get reinforcements here as fast as they can. Tell them we are under attack from many rebels – two hundred or more at a guess – and keep your head down, or you might lose it!"

"Yes, sir," he said, scarpering off, only to reach the bottom of the stairs to find Miller running up past him back to the major.

"I can't connect with St. Elmo, sir," he reported, panting. "There must be some fault with the line, or likely cut!" he gasped.

With the telephone's introduction, Townsend had been distrustful of the new technology and had insisted that a Signals unit – using the trusted semaphore system, or mirror flash – be used as a backup at the fort. Two men of the Signals unit were posted high up in the hills and within powerful telescope range. It enabled them to read the messages from a great distance and then pass them on to the next Signals unit, repeated at various lengths back along the way to Valletta.

No signals had been sent that way since the telephone was installed, and the two men in the nearest unit to the fort had allowed a general lethargy to creep into their duties. One man was eating at the small campfire while he listened to the other talking, stretched out on a blanket on the ground, near the jutting stone crag.

"Look, I'm just saying, Corporal, that when I've seen my service out, I would like to stay here in Malta." He got to his feet. "No, there's nothing for me back home." Casually, he picked up his powerful telescope and looked over towards the fort, way off in the distance. "Crikey, Corporal, the fort is sending a signal to us: *'Under attack. Reinforcements urgent!'*"

"What! Quick, man, send confirmation and pass the message on. Hurry, for God's sake!"

Raising his flags, he had just begun to reply when they were both startled by loud, deliberate noises coming from behind them. Both turned to see men standing there, holding guns and swords.

One stepped forward with a wicked, evil sneer on his face and plunged his sword into the soldier, whose face bore a shocked expression as he stared at the man who had struck the deadly blow. Then, dropping both flags, he fell off the crag and down onto the rocks below.

The corporal instinctively reached down for his rifle to defend himself when a sword blade flashed downwards, cutting deep into his back and shoulder. He sank to the ground, his body convulsing and twitching before becoming still. His life's blood seeped from the gaping wound, forming an ever-widening pool in the dirt beside his body.

Lifting him unceremoniously by his arms and legs, the two men swung his body backwards and forwards before callously tossing it over the edge of the crag. The corpse hit the ground and rolled at first before sliding down further on the loose shale, finally coming to rest near the body of his colleague.

***

The semaphore had been sent as soon as they realised the telephone cable had been cut – but they hadn't been quick enough. The worried Signal engineer had been watching through his telescope as the message was repeatedly sent until, finally, the men answered them – but then they suddenly disappeared before finishing the acknowledgement.

"They were there, sir. I saw them," Miller gestured to the major. "But we haven't heard from them since. I fear they could be done for, sir!"

"Then we are effectively cut off from any help," said Townsend gravely. "Unless you can fix the cable fault, Miller. Well, can you?"

"I could easily mend it, sir, if I knew where it's cut," he said helplessly, "but it could be anywhere between here and St. Elmo."

"My instinct tells me it can't be far away," said Townsend. "It went down too quickly once they arrived here. Take two men with you, Miller, and see if you can find and fix it."

"Yes, sir."

A few minutes later, Miller scrambled out of the gap in the wall with a short length of cable over his shoulder, a pocket full of connectors, and the two sappers. They crawled through the breach in the wall and across the narrow roadway spanning the ditch, each keeping low so as not to be seen. They got around to the outside wall of the telephone room, and then, led by Miller, they headed off to find the damaged cable. From experience, he could see where the ground had been disturbed when digging the cable in and he followed it off towards the poles. Finally, they reached the last of the poles to find the cut cable dangling from it, swinging aimlessly in the wind.

"Can you mend it, Miller?" asked one, holding his rifle at the ready.

"Yes," he replied, looking at the cable. "But it's too short, with no slack in the cable to reterminate the wires with, so I will have to connect this cable length for the repair."

"Get on with it, then! I want to get back to the fort in one piece," the man whispered at him hurriedly while keeping watch.

Working quickly, Miller stripped back the lead cover on the heavy-gauge cable using the tools he'd brought with him. He then splayed the wires and paper insulation, doing the same to the pole's loosely hanging cable. Bringing the two ends of each wire together, he used his hand tools to join them with the bulky screw-in connectors.

"How much longer, Miller?" asked the sapper, wild-eyed and agitated, losing patience.

"Soon. I just need to join the other two ends, and then it will be ready to use. Then we can get ourselves back." He stripped the insulation back on both ends to expose the heavy-gauge copper wires again. While rummaging for the connectors, two bullets slammed into the pole, nearly taking his head off. Alarmed, he dived for cover. "Phew! Where are they?" Miller asked, anxious.

"We can't see them yet," one replied just as more shots were fired, forcing them to scurry for extra cover as bullets ricocheted off the rocks where they had stood.

"Look out!" shouted Miller, seeing two breaking cover with swords raised. They came running towards them, only to be stopped in their tracks when the sapper brandished his rifle and bayonet. His companion quickly aimed and fired, sending one man reeling. The two circled each other, and then the soldier lunged with his bayonet towards the man, missing him as he dodged it. He quickly did it a second time and pierced the man's body, which dropped, lifeless, at his feet.

"Hurry up, Miller," he hissed. "Get it fucking done! There will be more soon."

Miller's hands started shaking as he tried to work under the threat of a lethal bullet. He had never seen death before, but now he'd seen two in less than a minute, and it had unnerved him. He tried to steady himself by bracing his body to the pole, but it didn't work; his hands appeared to have a life of their own, shaking uncontrollably.

Now, other hostiles were turning up, and more shots were fired. His hands were still shaking when the decision was made to get back to the fort without finishing the repair – though he hoped to return later in the dark to finish. Dodging the bullets and the pursuing men, they managed to get back to their comrades at the wall, who quickly thrust out their arms and helped them in.

Clambering over the rough, unfinished stonework, the man behind Miller suddenly slumped down, shot in the back. Two defenders immediately stepped forward, grabbed his shoulder and belt, and unceremoniously hauled him in. Everywhere, bullets peppered the wall and ground around them, sending more dangerous pieces of sharp granite flying off in random directions.

After they made good their escape, some of the attackers gathered at the pole to find out what the soldiers had been doing with the cable. Seeing the attempted repair, the group leader lifted his rifle and, taking aim, shot through it. He pulled the damaged cable down before dragging it away and hiding it behind some rugged rocks.

On returning and coming face to face with the major, a dejected Miller confessed, "I couldn't repair it, sir. They were on top of us before I had time to complete it."

"You did your best, Miller. The downside is we've lost a good man and are a contingency of infantrymen down, so we must defend the fort the best we can. We have plenty of food and ammunition to withstand a siege; it just depends on us keeping them out at the wall."

"Someone will realise soon and come looking for us if we fail to make contact," assumed Marsh.

"I beg your pardon, sir; I would also like to report that the cable was deliberately cut. I can confirm it was sabotage," said Miller, still shaking from his life or death experience. "These men have only just started attacking the fort after chasing Captain Johns' patrol back here," he pointed out. "They have not had the time to get to know the area, so I reckon the cable has been cut by someone who knew where it was and its purpose. It had been deliberately hacked through at the pole. No one outside the fort would have known it was there."

"Thank you, Miller, but it's too late to flush him out now," said the major, realising the assassin was still amongst them somewhere. *That's the last thing I need… the saboteur. He's still about and active,* thought Townsend.

Suddenly, a heavy barrage of shots was fired at the men in the musket gallery, who quickly refocused their attention outside.

"Steady, men," ordered Marsh. "Individual fire, when ready!" he shouted for all to hear.

Immediately, two of the attackers were shot and brought down.

"Captain, is the cannon loaded and prepared to fire?"

"Yes, sir. It's been left loaded since we blew that target ship to bits. We also have a good head of steam up," Marsh reported.

"Good. We've stumbled across something big going on, and they could have a ship moored somewhere. Get someone to watch out for it beyond the bay. If it shows itself, we take it out."

"What makes you think that, Major?" Marsh asked.

"There's a small army of them out there, and they got here somehow. Let's hope we get our reinforcements – and soon," Townsend said ruefully. "They must be after the gun."

"If they are, they can't move it," surmised Marsh. "So… they must be after the gun to use it. Good grief!" he cried. "They want to fire it at Valletta! It's within range!"

Just as they realised the enormity of the situation, insurgents outside the fort began firing in earnest from all sides. Returning fire, the defenders picked off some of the attackers in the cleared killing area of the glacis. Their full-scale attack had been halted at the dry ditch, where they became easy targets to take out. Some who were shot fell into it, while others climbed down to find other ways of penetrating the fort's defences, including scaling the inner walls on the other side of the ditch. These quickly fell victim to the deadly fire of the soldiers in the caponiers. There was no escape for anyone caught down there!

A soldier fell, mortally wounded, on the musket gallery, while another died in the counterscarp, clutching at his face. A bullet found its way through the loophole and hit the wall recess before ricocheting into him.

Seeing they were making no headway the attackers changed tactics and concentrated all their might back on the unfinished gap in the wall. Attacking in force, they attempted to climb in. Still, the defenders kept them at bay, helping with their 'lungers' – a twenty-two-inch bayonet on the end of a rifle, giving it a greater reach than the sword. But it couldn't last.

The attackers began to push the defenders back through the sheer weight of numbers as the body count steadily mounted. The prolonged bitter fighting was starting to affect the tiring defenders; one after another fell victim to the bullet and the sword.

"Major, we can't hold them! They're breaking through!" Savage yelled in panic. He grabbed one attacker in the melee, reaching over the parapet to get him. He then pulled him in over the bodies and held him to be bayonetted by another.

Townsend had held twelve men back as a reserve in the courtyard, sheltered behind the wall between the pump rooms and dining room. They were there to reinforce any weakness in the defences and were much needed as backup.

Now, he shouted his orders at them: "You six men, bring your rifles and set yourselves up on the barracks' roof. Get up there as fast as you can and stay down! Cover the breach in the wall where Sergeant Savage and his men are. When I give the command, let some in, then open fire once our men are in the clear."

After a few nervous minutes the men settled into position, signalling they were ready as Townsend ordered Sergeant Savage and his men to move away. They jumped back from the fight and ran over to the far end of the courtyard to rest up and recover their strength.

Thinking they had succeeded in overwhelming the defenders, the shouts and bloodcurdling screams of the attackers grew in volume and pitch as they breached the defensive wall, looking for the defenders. The situation for the soldiers was becoming desperate as the major prepared his small force.

"Steady, men, steady. Volley then rapid fire. Steady now."

The insurgents could not pull the corpses away, blocking them from entering the fort, and so began climbing over them.

Holding his nerve to the last second, Townsend ordered, *"Fire!"*

The distinctive sound of the Martini-Henrys rang out, spitting out a deadly hail of bullets that ripped into the enemy. Shot from close range by these powerful rifles, some were thrown off their feet with the force of the impact but still more clambered in with a vengeance. Their comrades' deaths hadn't deterred them but had, in fact, spurred them on. Their simple sole objective was to capture the fort and kill everyone in it.

Sergeant Savage and his two men had settled next to where the rest of the six reserve soldiers were waiting, aware that one was the cook. "What are you shaking for, Harris? When this is over, there will be less cooking for you. You should be a happy man," he said, taunting him.

"It's not because of that. I signed up to cook and cater for you lot, not fight."

"Well, you have to fight now if you value your life. From the way you're bloody shaking, Harris, I don't suppose you can shoot straight anyway. Mind you, if it comes to it, you can take them out by throwing your bloody roast spuds at them. That should do it."

Even Harris managed a tight smile, the banter briefly helping to lift the air of desperation hanging over the huddled group.

***

Back at Fort St. Elmo, it had been noted that no communication of any sort had been received or acknowledged by Fort Anchor for a few hours, and they urgently needed to find out why. A semaphore signal was sent to Fort Anchor but failed to get through. There were no visible signs of the missing Signals unit by others waiting along the old line of semaphore communication. They had failed to acknowledge the daily routine message, so they reported it, which immediately became a big worry for the regiment.

331

The order was given for a platoon led by Lieutenant Terry to ride over there and find out what was afoot. He was to take a platoon sergeant, two corporals, and a body of thirty men. If the absence of contact was found to be negligence, this would be viewed as a dereliction of duty, and there would be a heavy price to pay.

After a gruelling, intense ride, they arrived at the last known location of the Signals unit. They rode up to the hilly position where the two men were supposedly bivouacked but found no one, nor their horses or equipment.

Noticing a small fire had recently been doused, they began a close search of the immediate area until one man found a trail of blood leading towards the overhanging crag. Casually, he stood at the edge and glanced down; what he saw filled him with horror. There, below him, were the two butchered men. Their bloodied bodies lay in unnatural, contorted positions – with bones broken from the fall.

He tried to call the others but, at first, he couldn't speak. "Here they are, sir," he finally croaked, pointing his finger below him. "Both are down there, sir."

Leaving the platoon's main body with the horses, some men scrambled down the sixty-foot drop. It soon became clear that the rest of the men's equipment had been tossed down also. The only things missing were the two horses, which they assumed had been taken.

"Bring the spades down with you, men!" the sergeant called up. "It seems we must bury them down here. It's impossible to get them back up."

Speaking in a soft, respectful voice as he gazed at the pitiful sight, the lieutenant asked, "Does anyone here know their names or anything about them? Do they have families?"

"I think they were both single, sir, but I'm not sure," said one.

"Regimental Headquarters will know who they are. We will inform them when we return," said the lieutenant.

A short prayer was spoken over the men before carrying out the burial.

"Murderers!" muttered one man, unable to hide his anger.

"Bastards, you mean, to do something like that!" cussed another, letting his emotions get the better of him in the highly charged atmosphere.

As they climbed tentatively back up, the enraged men were in a silent, sombre, vengeful mood.

Standing back on the crag, Lieutenant Terry – the young platoon commander – trained his binoculars towards the fort, way off in the distance. As he focused his sights on the fort, he didn't like what he saw. Although the gunfire couldn't be heard, he could see they were under some sort of attack. He could see men firing their rifles from positions on the fort's ramparts.

"They're definitely under attack, Sergeant. But by who and how many? It's hard to tell. We need to get closer to find out," he said, straining his eyes into the binoculars.

Just then, a soldier ran up. "Sir! We have located the next semaphore party, and they are waiting for your orders."

"Tell them Fort Anchor is under attack and to get heavy reinforcements over there fast. In the meantime, we'll get down there and see if we can help." After a second look through the binoculars, he ordered, "Mount up, men. Forward at a gallop!"

They rode off at a fast pace until they were approaching the siege. Here the platoon watched the fighting, unseen, from the shelter of convenient tall bushes and shrubs, while the horses – made uneasy by the gunfire – were calmed with reassuring strokes and soft words. The lieutenant and sergeant tried to assess the enemy's strength by the shots they were firing.

After listening for a few more moments, the young lieutenant concluded, "I believe we can take these on, Sergeant; what do you think?"

"They don't know we're here, sir, and I must admit, I can't hear as many guns firing at the fort as before. If there are more than we think, then the surprise element will increase the odds in our favour. But I'm not sure, sir, to be truthful."

"My instinct says we should, Sergeant."

"Yes, sir."

The lieutenant turned to his men and ordered them to draw sabres; he was keen to see some long-awaited action. It would be his first fight in battle, and he was determined to savour it.

The horses became more nervous in the expectant, charged atmosphere. Some pawed at the ground for the off, while others snorted hard, turning this way and that.

"On my orders, men, *Charge!*"

They came thundering out of the cover, shouting and lifting their swords as they followed their officer's example of racing headlong into the fray. The clamour halted the attackers in their tracks when they saw the mounted troops bearing down on them, and they began to scatter and run away in utter mad confusion.

***

"Sir! Sir! Come here, quick. They're here! The reinforcements are here!"

"What? Are you sure?" Marsh asked as he ran over to the man, followed by Townsend.

Spontaneous cheering began from the men along the front parapet as they watched.

"Yes, they're here, sir! The reinforcements to help us. Look, over there. The bugler's playing the charge, sir!"

Sneaking their heads above the parapet, they witnessed a full military charge taking place. At the forefront was the young lieutenant that Marsh vaguely remembered from Valletta, his sabre pointed forward, bravely leading the charge in classic textbook fashion. The horses careered into the nearest group, bowling men over then trampling them underfoot, while the riders slashed and stabbed down at those closest to them.

"The bloody fool!" shouted Townsend, looking on in horror. "He has no idea how many there are."

The cheering coming from his men immediately stopped as they realised the truth of the situation.

"He only has twenty to thirty men with him. Get back! Get back, for God's sake!" He uttered profanities as he stood up and revealed himself, desperately attempting to wave them back, but they rode on. "Keep firing, men! Give them supporting fire!" he shouted above the din around him.

It was then that Townsend saw himself in an attacker's rifle sights and line of fire. For a terrifying moment he was fixed to the spot, fully expecting his demise.

But then the man moved his rifle and shot dead the soldier standing next to him before scurrying away himself.

The incident had happened in a split second, and Townsend thought no more of it; his attention quickly returned to the scene being played out beyond the fort's walls as he safely ducked down behind the ramparts.

Still, the horsemen rode on – quickly cutting down the running men in front of them – when, suddenly, they pulled their mounts to a stop as rifle fire opened up on their flank.

Some soldiers were hit, including the lieutenant, who fell from his mount with a bullet in the throat. He died lying on the ground, writhing and clutching at his neck.

"Bugler, play 'The Retreat'. Quickly now, before they're massacred! For God's sake, man, blow it!" Townsend cried impatiently.

"Yes, sir."

The bugler blew as hard as he could. The men in the platoon heard the order to retreat, but it was too late; they were fully committed to the fray.

After the initial surprise, the attackers realised that this was just a small force. They began to stand their ground, turning on the soldiers with a vengeance. Some men were brought to the ground by slashing and cutting with swords at the rear flanks of the horses they rode, while others were dragged from the saddle.

Suddenly, the glory of the charge was marred by its inevitable aftermath of cost and gore. Horses bucked up high to throw their riders, while others with their hindquarters spouting blood struggled to stand on three legs. The scene was horrific. The fallen men on the ground around them were killed with swords, their arms slashed at and cut in a desperate attempt to ward off the killer blow. They died screaming – bleeding from terrible open wounds. Some men lay on the ground, gasping and writhing with their bowels protruding. In contrast, others cried before collapsing to the floor and expiring. Some, who were still in their saddles, were pulled off their mounts to be set upon with sadistic pleasure.

The romance of the charge was lost on these poor souls, suffering for their lieutenant's arrogance and self-satisfaction, thought Townsend sadly.

The bugler at the fort continued playing 'The Retreat', but it was too late; they couldn't extract themselves.

Once down, vicious hand-to-hand fighting took place. Even though they were heavily outnumbered, the soldiers began fighting with a fury that defied description. When others joined the fray, they succumbed to the insurgents' superior forces.

The men at the fort could only help their colleagues by putting down covering fire, but it proved of little use; they were forced to stop, fearing they might mistakenly hit their comrades. Simultaneously, they had to defend themselves as the attackers turned their full attention back to the fort.

"The only way to save themselves is to try and get here," said Townsend to those around him, reflecting on the unnecessary carnage being played out in front. He ordered the bugler, "Keep playing 'The Retreat', do not stop!"

With fully blown cheeks the bugler barely paused for breath, only nodding and repeating his plaintive call.

Marsh found it hard to watch as the slaughter continued. "Give me six good men, and I'll bring them back," he pleaded, full of anger and bravado.

Stretching to his full height, and protected behind the musketry parapet, Townsend put his face just inches from Marsh's. "How would that help? This battery would just lose another seven men!" he hissed. "I doubt you would reach halfway! How would I explain it to Sarah and Victoria? Neither would forgive me. Your request is refused, Captain," he said, glaring fiercely at him.

Marsh lowered his eyes and backed down.

The cleared glacis around the fort had effectively become a shooting gallery for those soldiers on the musketry parapet as they continued to take the attackers out with ease.

The bugler was still playing, when – through the mayhem and clouds of dust thrown up from the fighting – a small group of soldiers made a break for it, running across the open ground towards them. The three men ran to save themselves with the screaming killers in hot pursuit, intent on stopping them from reaching the fort and safety. They were catching up with the fleeing soldiers as the defenders waved them on and shouted encouragement. It was all they could do.

"Come on! Come on! You can do it!" they shouted, encouraging them on. "Yes! This way! Come on!"

The attackers nearer the fort also tried to stop them but were slow and taken out by marksmen upon the parapet. The mob caught up with the last man and murdered him, while another was dragged to the ground. He punched and kicked out, fighting wildly for his life, but to no avail; they fell on him, brandishing their knives and swords until his wretched screams stopped.

Miraculously, a lone rider broke away from the murderous henchmen surrounding him in the melee and galloped for all he was worth towards the fort. He couldn't do anything to save the two men, but as he approached the chasing pack, he lowered himself in the saddle and stabbed and slashed at them with his sabre as he passed by. Others were shot dead as the marksmen at the fort did their deadly work to ease his passage to safety.

The rider caught up with the solitary man, reaching down and shouting: "Give me your arm, quick!"

They clutched at each other's arms, the rider swinging him up onto his horse's back by using the momentum of the speeding horse as his frightened, wide-eyed charger galloped on, carrying them away from the carnage. While they escaped, shots were continually fired toward them, trying to fetch them both from the horse's back.

They had almost reached the safety of the fort when the horse was shot from under them, sending both crashing hard onto the ground. Getting up, both saw that the horse was obviously in great pain, whinnying pitifully while trying to stand. Though still being pursued, its rider acted quickly and shot the horse with his last bullet while pulling his hurt comrade forcefully towards the fort's sanctuary.

Then, witnessing this incredible moment of hope, Marsh decided to disobey orders, seeing Townsend elsewhere with his back turned. "Open the gate, men, and roll the bridge out. *You three, come with me now! Fix bayonets!*" he yelled as he took his from his rifle and, with a firm click, locked it into place on the end of the rifle barrel. Tentatively, he looked out through the gate but couldn't see the enemy.

"All clear, sir," came a helpful voice above him on the parapet.

"Follow me, men."

They furtively slunk outside, keeping close to the entrance wall without raising attention, watching as the two men fell again in their desperation to get to the safety of the fort.

Both men were now completely exhausted, devoid of energy, and unable to move. They lay on the ground, face down and breathless, expecting the deathly thrust of a sword into their backs or across their exposed necks at any moment. They heard their pursuers run up from behind and screwed their eyes shut, bracing themselves for the final blow they knew was coming – when shots from the rescue party stopped the killers from delivering them.

Marsh had them lifted to their feet, and helped towards the fort, and finally led across the bridge to the gate. Typically, he was the last to cross the bridge after giving covering fire, only to realise a man was racing up behind him.

Turning to face him and seeing him raise his sword to strike, Marsh instinctively raised his rifle to block the downward slicing blow that came angled across him. They looked at each other fleetingly, Marsh taking in the man's harsh features in a split-second glance. His were the eyes of an uncaring killer. He wore a cruel grimace, twisting into a snarl. Marsh blocked the next downward arc of the blade and, skilfully turning his rifle in, swiftly plunged the bayonet into the man. Twisting the gun to rid it of the airlock, it freed up the blade, allowing him to retract it. He watched as the man tottered and fell into the dry ditch from the bridge.

"Get in quick, sir. There's more coming!" The urgent shout from the loophole above jolted him into action.

Without waiting, he bounded across the bridge just as it was being rolled in. Shots peppered the closing gate as it was slammed shut and securely bolted behind him.

The two exhausted men were propped up against the nearest wall. In between coughing and gasping for air, the survivors of the fateful charge gathered their senses to confirm to the defenders that heavy reinforcements had been sent for and were on their way.

"We will have to hold out then until they get here," said a relieved Townsend.

"If only that bloody Galea had completed the wall on time. Then there would have been no question about it!" Marsh angrily retorted.

Chapter 28

Treachery out in the open. Bloody face off

AS THE attack on the fort continued, Galea and his men secretly armed themselves with weapons previously smuggled into Fort Anchor, hidden amongst the tools they had stored in the annexe of the storeroom. As civilian contractors, they had been given the protection of the fort only to abuse that trust with the undeclared weapons they'd smuggled in. They sat behind the wall across the courtyard next to the kitchen, directly opposite the six soldiers held in reserve. Sergeant Savage and the two men with him had returned to the parapet and were busy defending the fort.

Little notice was paid to Galea and his men as they secretly passed knives and guns behind their backs from the storeroom. A sly signal with the hand or a nod of the head was enough to understand each other. When fully armed, they waited on Galea to decide when to attack the soldiers held in reserve.

Realising they had to strike first before being discovered, Galea observed the chaos around the fort and felt the time was ripe. With the soldiers busy defending the fort from another headlong rush from the outside attackers, he swiftly led his men across the courtyard and attacked the six men in reserve. They were taken entirely unawares by men they were familiar – even friendly – with, and were ruthlessly murdered instantly and silently. Even Harris, who hated violence, had no time to shout a warning.

Galea had enjoyed the moment. "Excellent," he whispered when they were done and satisfied that they hadn't been seen. "By the time those imbeciles realised what was happening, it was too late. Now, keep low so no one from above can see us. We need to stop those on the roof from firing at our men at the wall. We can't get up there or behind them; they will see our guns. However, I think we can distract them. Khalif, I will walk out and speak to them. I will ask questions, and when their guard is down, we will surprise them with our guns and kill them also. Stay hidden while I walk out and talk with them."

"It's a good plan and should work," Khalif said, encouraging him.

As the firing continued from the parapets, the men attempting to get through the gap were forced to halt their attack. The heavy casualties they were taking had made them stop and reconsider their tactics yet again. The soldiers on the kitchen roof were thankful for the respite; visibly tired from the onslaught, they welcomed the sudden lull in the fighting so they could take a momentary rest from the battle's savagery.

Seizing the moment, Galea stepped out from behind the wall and shouted to the men above him on the low roof, "Ah, my British friends. Can we help you to defend the fort?"

The nearest soldier, Gunner Smith, heard him above the din of the fighting. "Piss off, Galea. You're civilians! If we need your help, no doubt we will ask for it!" he said as he loaded another round into the rifle breech. "Everyone here knows if you had done your job and finished the wall, we wouldn't be in this shit!"

Four others had placed their rifles down to let the hot barrels cool from the continuous firing, while Miller took his helmet off to wipe away the sweat dripping from his head and face.

"But my men are already armed, look!" Galea said, waving them out. He shot Smith before he could react, while the rest were executed within seconds. A macabre dance of death ensued as the bullets slammed into them. "We have done well, Khalif – no one has seen us. Now we can shoot these other swine in their backs at our leisure, but slowly, so they do not realise what is happening."

His eyes scanned the musket gallery as he spoke, looking for the major. He badly wanted the pleasure of snuffing out the man's life – it had become an obsession – and now was his opportunity. His men began to take up favoured positions in the courtyard, which would enable them to shoot the soldiers in the back before they were aware of what was happening.

Outside, the attackers were still taking casualties as they struggled to breach the fort's defences, while inside, unknown to Townsend, he was losing more men than he realised. Marsh, meanwhile, raced back and forth, checking on the men on the parapet and encouraging any wounded to keep fighting – if they were able.

Seeing him, the major urgently shouted, "Captain Marsh!"

"Yes, sir," he replied, bending low as he came to his side.

"Give me your report, Captain."

"Thirty men dead and five wounded, sir! One critical. Six of the twelve reserves are still on the roof, with six held back. The men on the gallery walls are holding their own, too, if the ammunition keeps coming. Caponiers and counterscarp gallery are having it relatively easy, though."

"Well, see to it they get all the ammunition they need, Captain," he ordered. "We can hold out at this rate, so let us hope the reinforcements get here soon. Otherwise, we are in deep trouble."

Just as his words died away, a terrified soldier hurried along the parapet, seeking him out. "Major! Major! They're getting through the gap in the wall!" he shouted in alarm. "There's no one to stop them. All the men on the roof are dead, sir!"

"What did you say?"

"I was taking the ammunition round and found the men dead! Galea and his lot have killed them – he's begun shooting our men in the back from the courtyard, sir," he said breathlessly.

"What!" Townsend exclaimed again, hardly believing his ears. Moving quickly over to the inner wall, he looked down into the courtyard where he saw the bodies of the reserve he had held back, lying there dead. He also saw Galea and his men sniping up at the soldiers on the fort's parapet from the courtyard below them.

"Captain Marsh, get every second man from the galleries and caponiers," Townsend snapped. "Put half at the dining room end of the courtyard and the other half through the back, and out at the storeroom. That will cut off Galea's escape. I'll get men from the musket gallery to join me behind the chimney wall on the roof of the kitchen. I want Galea alive – but show no mercy to the rest of them. Quickly, get on and do it before we lose more men!"

"Yes, sir!" barked Marsh. He kept low to avoid the ricochets of bullets as he hurried off inside the fort, shouting out his orders while on the move to the men on the lower gallery. Moving swiftly, he came across the lifeless body of Captain Johns, slumped against the wall as if in sleep.

"Caught one, I'm afraid, sir," said the sergeant.

"I'm sorry, Sergeant Clarke. Take every man you can spare up past the latrines to the dining room. Go through the kitchen and barrack rooms and then the storeroom to get yourselves there. I'll get men from the caponiers into the dining room. That traitor Galea and his men are in the courtyard shooting our lads in the back, and he must be stopped – but don't kill him. He's to answer to the major personally," he said breathlessly. "They're also beginning to get through the wall, so direct your fire immediately into the courtyard first and then the wall. Otherwise, there's a real chance we could be overrun and end up like Captain Johns."

"Yes, sir!" Clarke snapped back, already halfway out of the room.

Townsend grabbed four men from the musket gallery and ordered them to follow him as he led them onto the roof above the barracks and behind a small, low wall above the dining room. They got into position just as two more soldiers were shot in the back. His men now had the upper hand as they fired at will into the men in the courtyard. With nowhere to hide, the bullets tore into them. Trapped by their own cunning, they were cut down. Only Khalif survived by pressing his body hard into a small three-step gap in the wall beside the gun. It saved his life, but his left arm hung down from where a bullet had shattered the bone. His big hope now was to be rescued by his men clambering in through the unprotected wall.

With all the ammunition for his gun used up, Galea threw it to the ground and shouted out in a high-pitched wail, *"Don't shoot! Don't shoot! Please, please don't shoot!"* as he walked out, body half stooped, his arms fully extended.

Ignoring Galea, Marsh ordered his men to direct their fire back towards the unfinished wall. Taking quick aim with his rifle, he shot one running from the cover of the gun.

Leaving his men there, Townsend vaulted the low wall beside the kitchen chimney. He then crouched down and headed towards Galea, who was whimpering outside the pump rooms. Reaching the safety of the stairway – where he could shelter from enemy fire – he stood up, keeping his gun trained on the man below. He stared at Galea with hate in his heart. Galea stared defiantly back, sweating profusely, his chest heaving from the false screams he believed had saved his life.

"So, it was you all along?" Townsend snarled. "It was you that killed the prisoner, wasn't it, and not one of your men?"

"Yes, it was me, Major," Galea replied with contempt. "He died with the love of his God on his lips."

"The cable – you had that cut too, and you disarmed the Gatling gun, didn't you? Again, we thought it must be one of your men, but never you. Your actions show you to be lower than a snake's belly."

Galea's face twisted into a grinning scowl. He dropped all pretence as he spat back at the major, "Your Captain Johns had unwittingly discovered my men, who chased him and his soldiers back here. I knew we were found out, so I had the cable cut and the Gatling gun made useless."

"And the Signals unit up in the hills? You had them killed too, didn't you?"

"The fools were watched for days, unaware!" he spoke contemptuously of the two. "Because you were slow to get a message out, it was just a case of flashing an order to my men using a mirror signal to dispose of them.

341

They could not be allowed to send for help. So, for now, you are cut off from your precious Valletta."

"You had no intention of finishing the wall," Townsend continued angrily. "I understand why, now."

"No! Of course not. You stupid British fell for it. We had to delay attacking your fort until we were ready. But your Captain Johns forced our hand and brought the day for action forward. That's all, Major. It hasn't affected our plans for your cannon at all!" Galea laughed cruelly. "Surrender, and I will see that what's left of your garrison is spared," he said cold-heartedly, clearly bluffing.

"You forget you are in no position to make bargains. I'm holding the gun, and I have every right to shoot you like the treacherous, murdering rat you are."

He had his gun trained on Galea's chest; with his finger on the trigger, he caressed the Webley handle with the side of his thumb. It occurred to him that it would be far easier to shoot him there and then. He was just on the cusp of deciding to shoot him when he asked, "And Valletta? We now know you want to use it against Valletta but, by your admission, you said your men were discovered early. So, the number of men needed for this crazy invasion to work is many more than you have now. You will fail, Galea."

The man looked uncomfortable with the major's assumption. He countered, "Malta will undoubtedly belong to us, as we always dreamed it would. We have men on standby, waiting for this gun to fire at Valletta. Others will converge on Malta once they hear it and then attack in greater numbers."

"You won't live to see it, whatever your dreams are," Townsend told him, his finger tightening on the trigger.

"Come, come, Major! You won't pull that trigger," Galea taunted. "You British have too much of a sense of fair play instilled in you. It is a national trait and a weakness to be exploited whenever and wherever possible," he said, spitting on the floor in disdain.

Townsend's hand gripped the gun's handle more firmly as he pointed it at Galea. *Just one bullet is all it would take. It would be so easy to discharge it into the man, but I have never killed anyone in cold blood... although I could make Galea the exception.*

"You know, Galea, you have a point. But whether you're right or wrong, you won't leave this courtyard alive to benefit in any way from your betrayal. Pick up that soldier's sword."

Behind Galea, Townsend saw Marsh firing at the wall, still directing fire at the attackers while glancing over at them both. He felt sure he would shoot Galea dead if he came off worse from their swordplay.

"What do you get from all this bloodshed?" Townsend asked, stalling. "Money, I suppose."

"Correct, Major! I'm to be paid most handsomely for ridding these islands of you British," he said, grinning. "Gold beyond my wildest dreams will be mine for the asking – and more, if I choose. We have all your fortifications in Valletta plotted on our maps with position references. We will point this beautiful gun back at Valletta and destroy your soldiers and their forts at will with their own wonder gun. Ironic, don't you think? You see, we do have our spotters in place. Though it's imperative I get on with our plan, I'm sure it can wait for a few more minutes while I dispose of you. If you are brave enough, put your gun down and fight me, Major. I'm desperate to kill you and spill your blood here, where we stand, in this very courtyard."

Townsend put the Webley back into its leather holster and unbuckled his belt, allowing it to drop to the stairs before kicking it off towards the kitchen. He took his sword from his belt and, withdrawing it, threw the scabbard hard behind him, out of the way. "The treachery you have shown doesn't merit a second chance, but I dearly want to kill you, Galea, and kill you, I will."

The battle at Fort Anchor raged around them, but the two men only had thoughts for each other as Townsend slowly descended the last few steps.

"Aha! From no chance to every chance. A sporting chance, I think you call it, Major. That is probably your first mistake." His smirk changed to a snarl of determination as he bent down to pick up the dead soldier's sword. Expertly feeling the balance of the weapon in his hand, he made two practice slashes through the air. "The British sword is not my first choice, Major, but it will do the job for me," he said as they began to circle each other.

Suddenly, Galea lunged at him with his sword, but the major quickly stepped back and deflected its lethal thrust. His response was to bring his sword over in a swinging arc – trying to hit the man before he stepped back – but Galea expertly blocked it with his own.

"You won't get away with it! The survivors of the patrol your men wiped out informed me that a message was sent back for reinforcements. As soon as they get here, you and your men will be done for."

With that, Townsend chopped at Galea's defensive stance. The clashing of swords echoed in the courtyard as the noise from the blades resounded off the bare stone walls.

"I do not believe you, Major. As we speak, I have men coming over from the caves," he said, slashing back wildly at Townsend as he spoke. "As soon as we have dealt with your garrison, we will turn your gun on Valletta. It will signal our invasion of Malta, Major, and you British will be gone and forgotten. Your reinforcements won't change a thing. In six more days, we will be up to full invasion strength, and then you will yield to our demands."

"It won't happen, no matter how often you say it. You forget the Maltese people won't stand for it, you evil devil!"

Galea was forcing Townsend back, repeatedly lunging forward with the tip of his blade. Defending himself, Townsend was forced to give ground, parrying each deadly thrust of Galea's sword away until he abruptly stopped and winced, feeling the wooden bayonet practice frame hard against his aching sword arm. He evaded the next sweep of Galea's sabre as it cut through the rope, bringing down the hanging straw sack. The duel continued with the distinctive clink and clatter of the swords crossing, echoing loudly as Townsend desperately held a competent and powerful Galea off.

"You won't be able to stop them. It's futile!" Galea cried. "As for the Maltese people, they will do as we say, Major. They should make good slaves, don't you think?" With that, he chopped down wildly at Townsend again and again in a demented fashion, forcing the major nearly to his knees. Still, he recovered sufficiently to bring his sabre arcing back towards Galea, keeping him at bay.

The battle raging around them seemed dim and distant, all their thoughts still focused on each other. Both determined to win their own private war, they circled each other once more.

Yet again, Galea slashed wildly at Townsend. The blows missed him, but the toughened steel made sparks fly as it scraped the flinted stonework. Townsend immediately flinched away, feeling them graze his cheek. Both men's swordplay was sorely tested as they sweated and grunted, each determined to kill the other.

Townsend thrust his blade forward yet again, only for Galea to parry it away with ease before catching Townsend's leading shoulder with a tap from the sharp, deadly tip of the sabre. Blood trickled down his arm towards his elbow as he hurriedly stepped back in alarm.

"Ah! The first strike to me, Major, I think. I am enjoying this, and I will enjoy it even more after killing you," he boasted. He quickly lunged at Townsend again, intending to catch him off guard and making him step back fast to avoid the blade's follow-up slash. Unfortunately, while stepping back, Townsend fell over the body of the soldier whose sabre Galea was wielding with such extreme confidence.

"I apologise for you having such a torrid time, Major, what with losing your command here at Fort Anchor – along with the gun. You won't even see your beautiful wife again. I promise most sincerely to look after her for you when we have captured Valletta, no?" Galea taunted, trying to rile him. "She will join my harem, and I will introduce her to the more beautiful things in life. I might even make her my number one woman, with that red hair of hers! I have never known or owned or lain with such a creature before – a rarity in our part of the world, you will agree. I am sure she will show her appreciation to me – if she values her life," he scowled. "I look forward to finding out." He was confidently playing with Townsend's mind, intent on procuring every advantage over his adversary no matter how slight.

Still on the floor, holding the sword level, Townsend blocked the next downward arc of Galea's sabre. Galea quickly raised it and brought it down again, putting all his considerable strength behind the action. Townsend, however, managed to roll away, with the blade harmlessly striking the flagstones beside him, causing more sparks to fly. Getting quickly to his feet, he took up his defensive stance again. The sleeve of his tunic had now become uncomfortably wet with the blood seeping from his wound. It stuck to his arm, and he was beginning to feel decidedly weak.

Driving him back with a fresh onslaught, Galea continued, "Even the corpse of your soldier has conspired to help me by tripping you up, Major. Another sign your life is about to end, my friend."

As Townsend avoided the next intended killer blow, he realised he had seriously underestimated Galea's ability with a sword. Ducking below the slashing arc of the sabre, he stepped back. It missed him but cut through a second straw sack, spilling the straw contents onto the floor. Before Galea had a chance to bring his arm up and down again, Townsend smartly moved in and trapped it, holding his sword with both hands and pressing hard against Galea's weapon, effectively pinning his man against the wall.

The two men glared defiantly into each other's eyes, neither wishing to yield. With a hand on the handle grip and the other along the flat back of the blade, Townsend began to apply steady pressure, slowly pushing the deadly, honed cutting edge towards Galea's throat.

Globules of sweat dropped from Galea's face as he watched the deadly blade getting closer to his neck, inch by torturous inch. Unable to allow it to get any nearer, he suddenly kneed Townsend hard in the groin, doubling him up. Powerless to use his sword because of their proximity, Galea instead used the handle as a club, beating down on the back of Townsend's head with it.

As he raised his sword hand for another hit, Townsend groggily turned in his sabre and sank it firmly into the man. The blade passed unhindered through him, only to be stopped abruptly by the wall at his back.

"Argh!" Galea let out a stifled gasp and dropped his sword as the two men stood in a deadly embrace. With eyes bulging, he gave Townsend a wry, defiant smile. "You were lucky, Major, and you know it," he whispered, his mouth filling with blood. "Unlike you British, I am not afraid to die. Khalif's god has decreed that virgins await us for obeying his commands," he said in a weakened, faltering voice while his free hand felt for the knife at his side. He slid it out from its sheath. His only thought was to put all of his remaining strength into one last effort to kill his hated opponent.

But Townsend was wise to the move; before Galea could do it, the major grasped his knife hand tightly and stopped him. Then, twisting the sabre a little, he snuffed out Galea's life. The traitor slumped down to the floor, dead.

His vengeance fulfilled after killing the braggart, Townsend yanked his bloodied sword from the man's corpse, saying sarcastically, "Enjoy your virgins, Galea."

Chapter 29

Fighting a rear-guard action
and the consequences

AS THE violent struggle ended, urgent shouts from Marsh interrupted Townsend's thoughts. "They're in now, sir, and behind the gun! We couldn't hold them off any longer. That man Khalif is with them. He seems to be the leader; he's giving orders to everyone around him, sir!"

"Get those men off the musket parapet, Sergeant Savage. They're easy targets up there now!" Townsend bellowed, with this fresh emergency focusing his mind. "Get them into the dining room and storeroom to reinforce the men there!"

"Yes, sir."

As Savage turned to carry out the order, a barrage of rifle fire tore into his men at the storeroom entrance. Bits of clothing flew off as the bullets found their mark, killing some instantly and leaving others lying fatally wounded. The rest of the men from the parapet charged blindly across the courtyard, desperate to reach the safety of the storeroom.

Not all reached the beckoning refuge alive. Some were shot in the attempt, but enough got there to turn and engage in hand-to-hand fighting with the pursuing invaders. The insurgents fought viciously, forcing the soldiers further into the storeroom.

The major realised they needed to hold on to what they had if they were to have any chance of rescue. "Get the men out of the caponiers and the counterscarp gallery, Captain, and get them here as fast as possible, or else they'll be massacred down there. The enemy will work their way through the passages and kill them all, so get them out now!"

Marsh managed to empty two of the caponiers and the counterscarp gallery of men before they were shot at and quickly forced to retreat.

Having gained entry to the storeroom, the invaders split their forces. The first group made their way into both the loading chambers, where they quickly captured the lamp man and the two shell loaders. With no escape

347

route and the possibility of the whole armoury exploding if shots were fired down there, the soldiers offered no resistance when the enemy arrogantly strode in.

Grabbing them, the attackers viciously forced the men to their knees, being in no mood to take prisoners. They were about to execute them when Khalif stepped in.

"No! Stop! Do not harm them. Without Galea, I need these men to operate the gun."

"You'll get no help from me!" the lamp man snapped.

"Silence, dog!" he snarled, swiping the man's face with the back of his hand. It sent the soldier sprawling to the floor. As he walked past him, he kicked the unfortunate man in the ribs, then – bending over him – threatened, "If you value your life, you will do as I say, effendi. I will be back to you very soon for your answer."

***

The second group followed the narrow passageway slowly and cautiously towards the caponiers, where another five soldiers were firing from, unaware that the enemy had gained entry to the fort. They were still firing through the loopholes when the enemy reached them. The nearest three were immediately executed before the other two even realised what was happening.

The remaining soldiers shot the attackers as they stood over their comrades' bodies and then quickly found shelter behind one of the solid stone pillars between the loopholes.

"Bloody hell! How did they get in? Where's the rest of the lads?" one startled soldier shouted, kneeling and firing back from behind the pillar as his companion fired back, standing.

But it was a lost cause; the enemy, bolstered by others behind them, forced their way towards the two soldiers in increasing numbers.

Fumbling for more bullets in his pouch, the kneeling soldier cried in despair, "I've run out of ammo, Harry! I've run out of pissing ammunition!"

"Back, you bastards, back!" Harry screamed, checking the mob's stride with the lunger on the end of his six-foot rifle.

Superior to the sword in the confined space of the caponier, its length gave them a mild advantage. The enemy quickly learned to respect it as they backed away, just beyond the reach of the soldier who threatened them with it.

Still daring anyone to step forward – the long length of the rifle and bayonet backing him up – Harry fired his last bullets into the mob, killing the sneering men in front who were baying the loudest for their blood. He then quickly took his place next to his colleague, and they both threatened anyone who moved towards them with prods and a threatening slash of the bayonet.

All the time, the killers were inching forward as the impatient men at the back relentlessly pushed at those at the front, knowing there was less to fear now that the rifles were empty. The enemy's smirking faces stared back at the two men as they teased and parried at the threatening bayonets with their swords. They could have shot the soldiers there and then, but they wanted their sport.

Slowly, the soldiers were forced to inch back until, finally, they could back up no more, their heels scraping the end wall of the caponier.

Sensing they were about to be rushed, Harry hurriedly said, "Do you remember what our old sergeant said all those years back, Billy boy?" His shouted words had a finality to them.

"Aye, Harry lad. Stick, twist, and withdraw," Bill answered bravely, knowing the end was near. "But with a lot of shoulder behind it!" He laughed manically. "I wish he were here, but I don't think even he would be much help now, bonny lad."

The mob lurched towards them, only for the first two to be run through quickly.

Harry bawled: "*Stick, twist, and fucking withdraw!*"

Bill joined in as they both chanted the mantra. "*Stick, twist, and fucking withdraw! Stick, twist, and fucking withdraw!*" they shouted above the clamour as more of the mob moved in, trampling on the corpses of the fallen and overrunning the two men.

They grappled them to the floor, pinning the soldiers down while the knives of the mob did their grisly work.

Finally, standing up, the bloodied enemy screamed insults at what remained of the two soldiers, highly delighted with their handiwork. Vulgarities over, they took to hitting the corpses with shoes snatched from the dead soldiers' feet as a final insult to their bravery.

***

The diminishing band of soldiers fought a rear-guard action as they gathered at the fort's kitchen and dining rooms.

"Well, men, this is where we make our stand until help gets here," Townsend told them. "Don't get disheartened; we're not finished yet. You men cover the top of the stairs. Anyone below the latrines, shoot them. You there, take up a position covering the barrack room. Those trying that route, take them out. The door at the back of the kitchen leading to the storeroom is well boarded up and secure. I want a man positioned there, and if there's any suspicion of them trying to get in that way, fire through the damn door! You men get those two hefty tables turned over and put at the door and window to the courtyard. They are quite substantial and should give us good cover."

As Townsend was supervising their defences, one of the men firing through the loophole in the entrance gate cried out as a bullet found its mark. Clutching at his face, he fell back inside the fort, only to immediately be replaced by another.

"You there! Get this ammunition given out," Townsend ordered, his firmness keeping his men calm. "Be quick and make sure everyone has water at hand, too. At least we have plenty of both, which is more than can be said for our guests."

Desperate to take a well-earned rest for himself, Townsend slumped down on the floor next to Marsh and the remnants of his garrison. He then began dusting off his tunic, more nervous than he would allow his men to see. "Well done, Captain, for doing an excellent job with the men. I think you helped save a few lives there," he said, through gasps of exhaustion.

"Why, thank you, sir," Marsh replied with fierce pride in his voice.

Apart from the occasional ping of a bullet bouncing off the masonry, the remainder of the fort had gone comparatively quiet as the insurgents planned the best way to get at the besieged men.

Looking around at the remnants of his battery, Townsend couldn't help but feel depressed at what he saw. As they crouched in their positions, it was clear that the fighting had taken a heavy toll on their morale and well-being. Their burnt faces and bodies perspired heavily from hours of exposure to the searing sun while they waited, tired and anxious, for the enemy's next move.

While he waited, Townsend began reflecting on his own charmed life, utterly unaware of Galea's orders to spare him for his depraved revenge. He recalled how one attacker had him in his gunsight only to turn away in a split second and shoot the man standing next to him. He could only guess what would happen to him if he were to survive this embarrassment. *Loss of my commission and being drummed out of the regiment, no doubt, and unable to provide for my family. God, what a mess*, he thought solemnly.

"Sir, could I speak to you?" The words brought him abruptly out of his malaise. It was one of the men from the gate.

"What is it?"

"It's Bone, sir. He's still in the guardroom, and we think we should get him out."

"He's still in there, is he? The drunkard."

"Yes, sir. With the fighting and everything else, we completely forgot about him."

"Right, unlock the cell and give him a rifle," Townsend decided, "then point him in the general direction of the enemy. He's an extra man, though not the reinforcements I had in mind. But he should come in handy – we can but hope," he added, looking to the heavens for salvation.

"Yes, sir. I'll let him out, then." Returning, the soldier reached for the keys hanging on the outer guardroom wall, unlocked the cell door, and walked in. The stench of urine hit him immediately. "Bone, you dirty bastard, you smell of piss," he said, holding his nose. "Come on, come on. Get up off your backside."

"What! Why? What's up?" Bone asked, still in an alcohol-induced stupor.

"Can't you hear the bloody gunfire, you prick? The fort's been under attack for hours, and you can't hear a bloody thing!"

"Oh, is that what it is?" Bone said, rubbing his eyes and scratching his head in a daze.

"You had to go over the top, eh? That still the men had set up for brewing will be found now because of you. Now get that fucking rifle and help defend this place, or else you could be eating your testicles – especially if they smell alcohol on you."

The thought motivated Bone into action – after checking he still had everything God had given him. Tentatively, he poked the barrel of his rifle through the bars of the guardroom window before ducking down again immediately when bullets peppered the window frame and bounced off the stonework, both inside and out. This near miss sobered him up quickly, once again galvanising him into action and resulting in his returning fire.

The soldiers' slender grip on the fort – and, consequently, the gun ownership – was confined to the small area between the gate, kitchen, and dining room. Firing down the stairs past the latrines kept the enemy back, while only the most stupid attempted the courtyard route. Outside, one attacker survived the rifle fire and managed to press his body hard against the outside of the entrance gate. He waited until enough of a rifle barrel poked out from the loophole before grabbing it and then stabbing the man on the other side.

As he dropped, the cry went up: "There's one on the gate! Can you get him, Bone?"

A shot rang out, followed by much whooping from Bone. "Got him! Problem solved," he shouted from the guardroom, clearly enjoying himself.

***

Having been informed of Galea's death, Khalif was growing impatient. All methods to dislodge the defenders had failed, and time was all-important for the mission's success. He decided to turn his attention to firing the gun and getting the invasion underway; the heavily outnumbered soldiers weren't going anywhere and could be dealt with later.

Though Galea had had a good idea of how the gun should be fired, Khalif lacked his leader's confidence. So, he had the three captured men taken to the magazine to show him how the gun was loaded. In their dirtied duck suits, the two shell men dragged the block and tackle chain along the track until it rested above one of the large, one-ton shells in the magazine store.

Feeling they were not acting quickly enough and were stalling for time, Khalif screamed at them, "Faster, dogs! Faster!"

Fixing the chain to the shell, they raised it with the pulley and then slid it along on its track to the lift, which served the loading turret. Along with its charge, it was hydraulically raised to the gun, using the control valves they had down there.

"Is that all there is to it?" Khalif asked. "You sons of swine will die if you deceive me!"

The men didn't reply.

The gun was now in its loading position. The long automatic rammer pushed the selected charge and its shell deep down into the muzzle.

"It's double-shotted," whispered one of the shell men. "It's been loaded twice," he added as he realised the danger they were in.

By now, Khalif was getting short-tempered. He was missing the clear thinking and self-assured authority of Galea. When he heard whispering between the men, he rounded on them viciously. "What did you say, dog? I will not have you defying me and showing disrespect! Take these two away and dispose of them."

"No! I said the gun had to be loaded from each loading turret in turn," the soldier lied.

"Take them away! We have no further use for them."

"No! Please, Khalif, no!"

But he had closed his ears to their pleas for mercy. He turned to the lamp man and slapped him hard across the face. "The same fate awaits you if you disobey my orders."

The lamp man knew he had little time left. There was no means of getting out, and he knew he wouldn't be spared. Besides, he felt too weak from the beatings to attempt escape. Belittled and tortured, he realised he would be killed and discarded in much the same way as his companions. Their screams and pleading for clemency had affected him deeply, and he knew he would be unable to face that. He wanted a quick end. He felt resigned to it; he accepted his fate with a strong inner strength of character. His overriding thought was to take as many of these criminals with him on his journey as he possibly could.

The men defending the dining room could hear the cries for mercy from the two miserable wretches being dragged away from inside the loading bay. Some covered their ears to shut out their pitiful pleas and screams.

"That's our fate if they ever get hold of us," claimed a worried Marsh. A ripple of anxiety ran through the men at the very thought.

"The reinforcements are taking their bloody time, sir," said Savage.

"Look, men, our best chance of surviving is to stay just where we are and defend ourselves until they get here," declared Townsend. "We can outlast them. Just hold steady."

One of the men gave a hoarse cry. "Sir! Here, quick. There's movement near the gun. It looks like they have the lamp man with them. What's his name? Booker, that's it. They've hit him about the face and body a few times – he's bleeding badly, sir."

From the kitchen window, they could see Booker being dragged over to the gun. His pristine, anti-spark uniform looked dirtied, ripped, and bloodstained. Khalif stood near the firing seat while Booker was violently slapped and forced to give him instructions on how to manoeuvre and fire it. Khalif was growing angrier as he was made to wait; for the most part, it was information he couldn't grasp. Frustrated, he demanded the muzzle be set to the trajectory and distance he had on his paper, which he thrust into Booker's hands.

They watched tensely as the traversing platform brought the gun around to bear menacingly towards Fort St. Elmo. The hydraulics raised the gun's muzzle towards the heavens, to near the gun's maximum elevation.

Gleefully, Khalif got into the firing seat and demanded Booker get ready to say when he could fire the gun. Booker stood behind him, explaining the drill on how to fire the gun. He noticed his guards were no longer paying close attention, so when he turned his head towards the soldiers defending the dining room, none of them saw him wearily drawing his thumb across his throat in an exaggerated style towards his comrades.

"Why is he doing that, sir?"

"I don't know... unless it's some sort of signal. But for what, I have no idea," admitted Townsend.

"Bloody hell!" exclaimed Marsh. "They have made the lads in the loading bay double load the cannon! Booker's going to let them fire the gun and blow up everyone standing there with it!"

"Are you sure?" exclaimed Townsend in disbelief.

"Look at how he's left the loading turrets open, sir," Marsh insisted. "To allow the explosion flash to travel down and ignite both magazines below it!"

Townsend was on his feet at once. "Everybody out! Out!" he shouted. "Come on, men, everybody out through the gate! Let's take our chances outside; he's going to blow the whole fort up and everyone in it! Get out! We should just make it. He wants us out, and he's given us the chance to go. So go, get out!"

With no one bothering with rank, it became a scramble to get out of the fort. The men at the entrance gate flung it wide open before extending the bridge out on its rollers as fast as possible.

"Are we doing the right thing, sir? We were relatively safe where we were," Savage said breathlessly.

"You can defend a fort from an attack from outside, but you can't defend it from an attack from inside. It's nigh on impossible," Townsend wisely informed him. "The man is going to blow the gun up, Sergeant. The exploding flash will travel through the loading turrets to the charges and shells below. It doesn't bear thinking about, but the fort's destruction will be complete, I'm sure of that."

They were spotted trying to escape, which soon drew rifle fire towards them. "Quick, men, we don't have much time!" shouted Townsend.

They had no choice: they charged out of the gate and into the killing field, which was filled with the bodies of the fallen. One defender was shot, and a deadly sword swipe killed another. Both attackers were then shot dead for their misplaced bravery.

"We need cover, sir!" shouted Marsh, anxiously looking about him.

"This will have to do!" Townsend shouted back, pushing and shoving his men into the dip behind the substantial bent entry wall outside the gate as more bullets took pieces out of the stonework. The lethal ricochets and chipped masonry was flying off in all directions as they desperately tried to hug the ground as low as possible.

The attackers began streaming through the barrack rooms and passageways inside the fort. Climbing the steps, they passed the latrines and into the kitchen in a frantic search for the soldiers. Down beneath the great gun, in the holding magazines, some were examining the shells and charges kept separate in the storerooms down there.

Meanwhile, the soldiers outside were frantically trying to work out a strategy to shield themselves beside the wall and fight back. Townsend was shoving Savage, the last man, down when the cannon fired.

Seconds later the whole ground erupted.

Everything shuddered and shook as the great gun exploded with tremendous force, throwing Townsend off his feet and slamming him hard against the wall. A second massive explosion was heard and felt somewhere deep inside the fort. Then a third, even bigger explosion shook the fort on its foundations, erupting out from the bowels of the earth after both magazines detonated together.

The noise was extraordinary. The force of the explosion sent large chunks of granite from the walls of the upper gallery spinning into the air before crashing down into the dry ditch outside, sending up great sprays of rock and soil. The large boulders buried above the arsenal for protection against bombardment were hurled into the air, only to fall back down on those below, killing or maiming many.

Daytime instantly turned into night as thick black clouds of dust and debris billowed and swirled high into the sky before falling back to earth, covering everything in acrid, choking dust.

***

Sergeant Major Horrocks, who was leading a large contingent of mounted soldiers towards Fort Anchor, pulled them up hard on hearing the huge explosion. "Whoa!" he shouted.

The looming black plume of smoke on the horizon unsettled the men and spooked the horses; the animals became uneasy, snorting and whinnying out of formation, with some rearing up and throwing their riders hard to the ground. The shock waves caused by the massive explosion spread menacingly out along the ground in a blanketed thunder roll, the tremors of the explosions rumbling on all around them, shaking leaves from trees and felling branches.

"Sir, it looks like the fort!" shouted the newly promoted Sergeant Collins, attempting to calm his horse. "I think we may be too late to help."

"I think you may be right, Sergeant, I'm sorry to say." Horrocks grimaced. "We're about fifteen minutes' ride away, so calm the horses down. We must get over there smartly and find out what has happened."

The sudden loud noises had deeply unsettled the horses; more reared up, trying to throw their riders. It took a few minutes to bring the wild-eyed animals back under control until, finally, after snorting their unease and defiance, they were forced to carry on.

On reaching the fort, the reinforcements came across many dead and broken bodies as they rode along the fort's glacis. All of them were coated in inches of thick, grey dust, which was settling across the whole scene. They heard low mumblings, moaning, and choking from the dying, as the blood from the many corpses was absorbed into the thickly layered carpet of dust.

"What the bloody hell!" Horrocks could hardly believe his eyes; they narrowed as he took in the worrying scene. *Unbelievable*, he thought. *It has been a mere matter of days since the men moved* out. The fort had been buzzing with activity then – and now, this! It seems to me there has been a severe lack of Army Intelligence going on here, and someone will pay for it.

"You lads get yourself down and look for survivors amongst our men," he ordered. "Quickly now. There may be more of the enemy about – probably making a run for it. Sergeants Timms, Collins, and Peters, take some of the men and find them. Bring a prisoner or two back if you can: our Intelligence people will be desperate to get their hands on one after this."

"Yes, sir. Right away," one replied, and rode off.

As the men went around, calling out for survivors and checking the bodies, Horrocks was drawn to the fort's wreckage and, especially, the gun. *What's happened to it? Surely the gun has escaped the carnage*, he thought.

Reflecting on what had gone on at the fort in the preceding months, he crossed the Guthrie bridge, which was remarkably still in one piece. As he passed over it, he could see how the explosion had blown much of the parapet and most of the musket gallery apart and into the ditch below. Walking carefully through what was left of the gate, his eyes took in the biggest crater he had ever seen. Gone was the kitchen and dining room, and the whole of the courtyard and everything it contained. The extreme heat generated from the explosions had left molten rock at its core. Large spirals of smoke billowed up and out from its centre, making his breathing extremely difficult and laboured. He had to stop there; he could go no further, making sure to stand well back from the heat generated by the smouldering inferno.

The force of the explosion had lifted the heavy gun as if it were nothing and thrown it high and wide into the air, coming down to rest next to the battered remains of the parapet in the corner of the fort. Looking at it from a distance, Horrocks could see that an internal explosion had split the muzzle asunder from the inside. It made for a sorry sight, lying there, torn apart with its secretive array of tubes curled and twisting out like distorted metal innards. *Yes, an instrument of death, but a beautifully manufactured work of art too, as most weapons are,* he thought sadly.

His eyes began to moisten with the futility of the last few months. He reflected on the huge effort everyone had put into the project –

all for nothing. Then he heard a voice calling his rank, which made him turn.

"We've found some alive, Sergeant Major!"

Surprised, he started back outside immediately. "Where are they?"

"At the bent entry. The captain has just about managed to sit up, although he's very dizzy and dazed. He's got both hands over his ears and is in a very distressed state. There's eight of them altogether, some with burn marks."

"Is the commander one of them?"

"Yes, but he's unconscious and in bad shape. A heavy stone was dislodged in the explosion and rolled over onto his head and shoulders. He's got a small trickle of blood running from his ear, which could prove fatal, Sergeant Major."

Quickly striding back over the bridge to the bent entry, Horrocks could see the bedraggled band of men gathering their wits about them. They shuffled about, dazed, coughing, and spitting out the dust and dirt they had been forced to swallow.

All the survivors were tended to by Horrocks' men – apart from the major, who lay there, unmoving. Heavy, laboured breathing came from his blackened mouth as they bathed his face with water from a canteen. They washed away the layers of dirt and dust from his face, finally dripping some into his mouth to help aid his recovery.

Horrocks sprang into action. "Harness the horses to the wagons, men. We can't use the barge; it's damaged, and the bay is filled with rubble. We have got to get these men back to Valletta Hospital as soon as possible, or we could lose the commander of this garrison and one or two of the others."

"Yes, Sergeant Major," said Corporal Andrews smartly, gesturing for several men to carry the order out.

"Are there any others?"

"No, all dead," he said, with the grimness of a man who once had friends somewhere among them. "It seems those that survived the explosion and falling debris suffocated from inhaling the dust and choking smoke."

Walking around the scene of the cavalry charge beyond the fort, Horrocks came to one of his men holding a battered, broken, old type helmet in his hands. "This is all that's left of the patrol sent out earlier," the man reported. "We found the Lieutenant's body lying back over there. It looks like it was one hell of a fight, Sergeant Major. I've just pulled this old issue spiked helmet from the hand of one of our men. It has the name 'Hart' written inside it."

"Let me see it," Horrocks said, feeling an unexpected pang as he took the helmet from the man. Indeed, the name 'Hart' was scrawled on the dirtied webbing inside.

"Where is he?"

"Here he is, sir, surrounded by the enemy."

The sergeant major walked over to the dust pile the man was pointing at and immediately recognised the body of sapper Hart, surrounded by the dead who had attempted to take him on.

"After he emptied his gun, it seems he used his rifle and bayonet to good effect, until the last thing he had to defend himself with was this old issue British helmet! It was lodged in that one there," he explained, pointing out the unfortunate terrorist.

For a few minutes, Horrocks could hardly speak as Hart's memory – and also the memory of all the others in the fort – threatened to overwhelm him. Eventually, he said, "Yes, he had his odd ways. You know, soldier, I took this man and others for bayonet practice a time or two out here. He was an excellent soldier – a damn fine soldier. He was a veteran of the African Zulu Wars, much like myself. He behaved strangely at times, like keeping his old, spiked helmet and wearing it about the camp on occasion instead of the new issue. Of course I knew about it, but it wasn't regular, so I thought he wasn't harming anyone. But those who knew him best put it down to the sights he'd seen and the things he'd witnessed – and had been forced to participate in with others in the great African campaigns. It left a mark on the poor fellow. Apparently, he had no family – the army was his family – and he had no wish to leave it. I had a sneaky suspicion; he played me up at times, making deliberate fools of us all, but no one could ever prove it. He must have come out here with the platoon they sent and changed to his 'lucky helmet' before the fight," Horrocks continued wistfully. "He was nothing special at marching or other drills – a piss-taker if anything – but when he was cornered, he fought magnificently, as we can see. A little strange at times, maybe, but we can all be proud of him and how he and the others fought here."

His companion detected a deep personal sadness in the officer's voice. "Of course we are, Sergeant Major. It goes without saying," he said, gazing around at the bloodied scene.

Chapter 30

The fog of reason. Welcome addition.
Unexpected verdict

TOWNSEND WAS aware of very little save a swirling grey mist that had spread throughout his senses, along with a great numbness in his body. He tried to look around him but he couldn't move.

Where has everyone gone? Why have they left me? he wondered. *I'm alone and completely and utterly lost. Where am I?* He tried to call the names of his men, but no sound came from his mouth. Then he heard a voice speak softly, wafting over him and sounding vaguely familiar before penetrating through the foggy haze of his consciousness.

"Robert. Robert! I'm here, Robert," she spoke, her voice fraught with worry.

Victoria! he thought. *My wife's looking for me, but she shouldn't be in the fort. Her life's in danger.* He tried to call out and tell her to go back, but the words wouldn't come. Someone whose voice he failed to recognise said, "Good. He's beginning to respond. Say something else."

"Robert, it's me, darling. I'm here in the room with you now. Speak to me, Robert. Please!"

He heard her but still couldn't see her through the swirling grey mist that held him in its embrace.

The fog was all-consuming. "Where are you, Vicky?" he mumbled, but it didn't sound right.

With that first movement of his lips, the pain hit him; every part of his body hurt with hot searing agony. Panicking, he kicked out, trying to escape the heat burning into him.

"Steady, Robert! Steady there, steady now," said the stranger's voice as someone held him down. "Wipe his brow with the flannel, then hold it to his lips, please, Victoria. He's burning up," said the strange voice. "Can you hear me, Robert? You have been concussed. Can you hear me?"

A sort of realisation began to play across his senses and penetrate the thick fog his reasoning was trapped in, tugging at his consciousness. A man's face began to take on a more defined shape and, after a few moments, Townsend mumbled something to him.

The doctor leant over, putting his ear to the major's mouth for a few seconds. Then, smiling broadly, he stood up. "He's asking for you, Victoria. He wants his wife," he enthused. "But see that he drinks first: just a few drops. We must get water into him because he's severely dehydrated."

Victoria settled herself beside her husband, warm and reassuring. Gently, she cradled his head as he sipped from the glass she held.

The water was so cold it made him cough, but it soothed the heat he felt within his whole being.

"Look at you. You gave us all a terrible fright," Victoria said, and he could hear tears in her voice. "What were you thinking? Scaring us like that? We'll have to get that stubble off your face too. I want to see the handsome man I married." Her worried heartfelt words flowed freely from her thoughts, soothing him considerably.

Events slowly began to dawn on him and, finding a semblance of a voice, he managed to speak in a hoarse, croaking whisper. "David... men... where?"

"Hush now. There's no need to worry," she said, placing a finger to his lips. "David and the men you left the fort with survived." She kissed his heavily bruised and blistered brow softly and then, looking down at him, realised he had fallen into a deep slumber.

"He's sleeping, Victoria. It's to be expected; it has taken a lot out of him. Speaking of rest, I think you could do with some yourself. These last few days have been a strain on you, too. We can look after him for you now he's out of the coma. If you'd like to come back later, he should be more aware and easier to talk to."

Victoria reluctantly agreed, then dutifully returned some hours later to find that the nurses had managed to prop him up in bed with a few pillows. His head was freshly bandaged, and his injured arm supported by a sling. The relief she felt to have him back – and recovering – almost overwhelmed her as she walked towards him across the ward.

The nurses were amazed at her transformation as she passed them by, making her way to her husband's bed. "Oh, she has changed! Bit different to the last few days," said the nurse, stripping back the sheet from a vacant bed. "And all the better for it, I'd say."

"Oh, Winnie, what I'd give to have hair like that. It's so beautiful and on fire."

"What I'd give for a man like *that*," Winnie replied with a sigh. "Now, he's got a way about him, has that one. I've been watching him closely, and if I know men, she's a very lucky lass." Both giggled quietly to themselves at her naughty thoughts.

Townsend – who had been gazing around, heavy-lidded – brightened up considerably as Victoria approached his sickbed. Just seeing her was enough to lift his spirits.

"Hello. How's my brave soldier?" she asked him, her tone light and teasing with the relief of finding him awake and propped up in his bed.

He grimaced and moaned in pain, clearly intending to smile but simply unable to.

She leant down low and kissed him carefully on his blistered face.

"Vicky, I love you." He gasped and wheezed breathlessly with the effort.

"You are most definitely getting better, Robert. You only call me Vicky when you're feeling amorous." A short silence followed before she repeated his name. "Robert. Robert!"

He had fallen asleep again.

The nurse appeared, advising her to let him sleep and to come back tomorrow. Victoria left the hospital feeling disappointed; she had so much to tell him.

She shrugged it off. *Oh, it can wait! The main thing is for Robert to get better.*

As he gradually recovered over the next few days, he was allowed no visitors – except for Victoria. Hence, after each visit, she went straight to see David and Sarah, who were anxious for the latest news about him.

***

The days dragged by slowly for Townsend as the healing process continued. He passed long hours of tiresome quiet by sharing the odd joke and story with the patient in the next bed: an older chap whose passage back to England was already booked.

Lucky beggar, he thought.

"Hello, darling," said Victoria as she breezed in.

"They could have moved me from here," he told her. "Then you would be calling a stranger, darling."

"That's where you're wrong; I checked before I opened my mouth, so, there!" Victoria playfully stuck her tongue out and then smiled broadly.

She leaned forward to kiss Robert, and his free hand snaked around her waist and gripped her, holding her there. He was so pleased to see her again, while she, in turn, was thrilled to have her man back.

"Hello, you," he replied softly, his slightly runny eyes all that betrayed his happiness at seeing his wife there. It had been a while since they'd spent any time together. She smelt clean and fresh and was instantly desirable, but he pushed any thoughts of that to the back of his mind. "When can I get out of here?" he asked, releasing her. "The whole dull routine is boring me."

"Well, I've got good news for you. I've just spoken to your doctor, and he sees no reason why you shouldn't leave here in about two days, three at the most. Also, Robert, you've got visitors." She waved her hand to call them over.

Marsh came over first, limping slightly and still carrying the bruises and scars from the explosions. "Hello, Robert. It's good to see you," he said, with an overabundance of earnestness. "So, this is where they put you when you have a little accident, eh? With free bed and board. I must try it myself sometime! It beats having to pay for a tavern in Valletta each time."

They both saw the funny side of the remark, along with its hidden meaning, although it hurt Townsend to chuckle. "Where's Sarah? Is she with you?"

"She's coming over now," said Victoria, visibly excited.

Sarah walked over, carrying a small bundle in her arms. "I have something to show you, Robert," she said.

Recognising it as a small baby, he said, "I didn't know you were having a baby, Sarah! You kept that a well-guarded secret – unless I've been unconscious for longer than I thought." Townsend rubbed at his head; it still hurt and throbbed.

She giggled. "Oh, he's not mine," said Sarah as she calmly handed the bundle to Victoria.

Unable to keep quiet any longer, Victoria proudly blurted out, "Robert, he's ours! He's our very own baby."

Townsend shook his head sideways with the little movement he could manage. "I can't believe it!"

"I couldn't tell you before... not until you were strong enough to take it in." She placed the baby carefully in his arms so he could see him more clearly.

"You know, I was sure it would be a boy with all the movement I felt in my back," he said triumphantly.

Victoria laughed at the suggestion. "Well, I knew it was a boy because girls are much livelier than boys in the womb. Despite what you say, boys are generally lazier. All women know there's a difference; my mother Tilly told me." Sarah nodded in agreement.

Townsend's initial delight and wonderment suddenly turned to concern as he held their perfect baby in his arms. "Is he all right, Victoria? You know, all… right?" he asked, emphasising his meaning while staring at the baby in amazement.

"Of course, Robert. He's got two of everything, you silly thing."

"And twenty-one digits, Robert. I've counted them," said Marsh.

After the laughter died down, Townsend asked why he wasn't told.

"Well, it happened just after the communication cable to Fort Anchor was cut," Victoria explained. "The engineer couldn't get through to give you the news."

While having the details explained to him, the nurse brought a dispatch courier over to where they were talking – pointing out the major to him.

They all looked up as the courier approached his bed, then made way for him.

"Sir, are you the commander of the garrison at Fort Anchor? Major Townsend?"

"Yes, I am."

The courier saluted. "Sir, I have a dispatch from the War Office for you." He attempted to hand the papers to the major and then waited for him to pass his infant son back to Victoria. "Er, thank you, sir," he blustered before saluting and leaving the papers with him.

Silence fell on the small group gathered around the bed as he read the dispatch. Afterwards, he tossed it on the bed and declared, "It's from the War Office. I've been worried about it, and now it's here. They have held an emergency inquiry into the destruction of Fort Anchor. How it happened, why our intelligence people were never aware of it, any dereliction of duty on my part – the usual thing. There's a good chance of loss of rank if I'm found to be at fault. Cable messages have been flying back and forth between Whitehall and Regimental Headquarters in Valletta for days now, it seems."

"When do you have to go before them?" asked Marsh.

"Two weeks," said Townsend, rubbing his chin, "to hear the final summing up of the panel and to find out if any criminal proceedings and charges are to follow."

"Why haven't they asked David to appear, Robert?" Victoria asked. "Not that I want you to go through it, too," she added quickly.

Marsh assured her that he hadn't thought anything of the sort.

"Because, as the commanding officer, it was my responsibility. No one else's."

"We will be there to give you moral support, Robert," Sarah told him. "Both David and I want to help you in some way. That's the least we can do."

"Thanks, Sarah. I think I need all the help I can get; things are looking grim. But tell me, David, how did you and the others manage to survive the explosion?"

"Compared to you, Robert, we only had scratches and heavy bruising. You probably don't remember it now, but you were too busy getting everyone behind the entry wall," he reminded him. "Just as you followed the last man, Savage, it blew up – before you could get fully behind it. I saw a lump of masonry hit you, hence your concussion and such. Don't you remember any of it?"

"No! But I will thankfully take your word for it. If it was heroic and deserving of a medal instead of a court-martial, it would lift this cloud of gloom I'm under."

"All right, all right," said Marsh, throwing up his hands in self-defence. "Joking aside, I must tell you, I have already been interviewed by the panel. I had to supply character references too. Being second in command, they wanted to know if you made the right decisions given the circumstances. I told them everything about what led up to this sorry mess, and that you did what you could at the time."

"Thanks, David. It means so much to my family and me." Townsend sighed. "So, what happened to the fort?"

"The fort has been destroyed. The many rumours suggest they won't rebuild it; it was far too expensive. Although Rinella and Cambridge are to continue."

"And the gun?"

"That's been destroyed too; I went back to see it. It's just lying there with no guards around it, I'm sorry to say. Now, it's just one hundred and nine tons of expensive scrap metal." Marsh ran his hands through his hair in frustration. "It's lying in bits, waiting to be collected and probably melted back down. The explosion ripped out the guts of the gun." He shook his head, sighing. "It feels strange when I think about its destruction. That gun has played a big part in our lives; in fact, our lives revolved around it for a long time, and now it's just... well... gone."

"I can't believe it either," Townsend admitted. "It's sad, even criminal. Talking of criminals, Galea and Khalif didn't survive, did they?"

"No, certainly not Galea; you saw to that!" Marsh reported. "I can promise you Khalif never felt a thing when it blew up. There wasn't anything left of him or his henchmen to bury!"

Interrupting them, Sarah gave two small coughs and pointed to the baby, nestled safely back in his father's arms. "It looks like you two have bonded, if you ask me," she said. "He's fast asleep. Come on, David, let's have that walk you promised. We must leave these three to get to know each other better."

"Yes, of course. We will be outside, Victoria, when you leave. Goodbye for now, Robert."

Townsend said goodbye to his friends, then focused his attention on his wife and their son.

***

After being summoned, Townsend arrived at the Regimental Headquarters in Valletta. He reported in and was told to wait in a side room until called. Here, Townsend watched the people – those who had already testified before the Inquiry panel – arrive to hear the final verdict. Each one passed the small window he waited behind.

"My window on the world," he mused aloud. "God! I feel like a criminal, being held in here." He emphasised his helplessness by bringing the palm of his hand down on the window's solid frame. *The first thing I'll do when I get out of here is to go down to the nearest tavern for a pint of their best,* he thought, frustrated with the slowness of it all and the lack of anyone offering him, the condemned, any sustenance.

He saw Marsh come and go within minutes: completely unaware he was sitting behind the window within touching distance. He also saw Sergeant Major Horrocks, Major Carter, and Captain Hill walk past – and various others he had worked with and known. They had all turned up, curious to hear the verdict on their colleague, while he had to sit it out and wait, not even being invited to give his version of events.

The Inquiry team would deliver their verdict later that morning, after days of considering the facts, and Major Townsend had been ordered to be present to receive the final summary. He was also informed that a court-martial would surely follow if the Inquiry found against him and proved any dereliction of duty on his part.

The door eventually opened, and in stepped the court usher. He coughed politely and said, "Commander?"

He startled Townsend, who was deep in thought, considering what he should do if he were thrown out of the Artillery.

"Thank you for being patient, Commander," said the usher politely. "If you would kindly follow me, the panel wants you present as they deliver their verdict on this sorry affair."

He followed the court usher into a large room, where he was told to sit down in a chair in front of three high-ranking officers. A single armed soldier guarded each of several doors leading into this grand, ornate Victorian room. A full general sat at the desk opposite, flanked by two colonels. The dour look on each of their faces immediately depressed him. He recognised Colonel Downing from the Woolwich Arsenal as one, who, on hearing about the catastrophe at Fort Anchor, had successfully applied to sit on the panel to deal with any misconduct charges thrown at Townsend and to act as a character witness on his behalf.

General Mathews, tasked with chairing the meeting, began to speak in a slow, deliberate fashion so that none of his words could be misconstrued. "Commander Townsend, you do not need me to tell you of the considerable investment the War Office has put into this gun and Fort Anchor. But something went drastically wrong, as we have seen. This Inquiry was convened to determine what went wrong and where to apportion the blame, if any. We have spoken to many people about your character, leadership fitness, and behaviour under fire. They have all vouched for your exemplary actions and ability to get a job done.

"The contractor hired to assist with the building of the fort disappeared before the project's commencement, along with his family," the general continued. "We have established that, at least, and you were not to know about any of it. It was about then when Galea first appeared on the scene, carrying on with the contract and beginning the deception. Somehow, he and his compatriots found out about our wonder guns – and the three forts to house them – and concocted a grand scheme to take Malta from the Crusaders, as they often liked to describe us."

The general shook his head. "It was a wholly slipshod and incompetent plan, and how he managed to fool us for such a lengthy period, we will never know. You, quite rightly, dispatched the rogue to the hereafter. Again, you were not to know any of this because your job was to oversee the building of the fort, manage and run the camp, and achieve a fully working, commissioned fort – not to identify spies among the civilian contractors. Meanwhile, he gathered his army in caves and the two remote farms they had taken over after butchering the occupants.

"The routine of the patrols passing the farms – and expecting locals to meet with them to air their grievances – was poorly organised and implemented long before you took up your post, so any failure there cannot be attributed to you. Unfortunately, this allowed Galea the time and space he needed to build his ragtag army out of sight. Fortunately for us, they were discovered. So, any criticism of you on that score is also unfounded. You could have acted sooner, with hindsight, but you weren't to know why the farmers had failed to meet up with our men. Your primary concern was preparing a fort and successfully commissioning it into a self-contained fighting force.

"Captain Marsh had the fortune to see several night-time lamps shining briefly from the small, remote island adjacent to the island of Comino," the general continued as Townsend began to realise, he was not going to be summarily dismissed. "Our men investigated, and they found plenty of evidence that many men had been living in the caves there for a while. It was logical for Captain Marsh to believe it was fishermen at the time, so he saw no reason to report it. We now know it wasn't. They also found similar evidence of occupation on the island of Comino itself and on Gozo.

"This incident, although disastrous, will not stop the War Office from having Forts Rinella and Cambridge completed to guarantee safe passage for all our ships, including merchantmen. The route to the Suez Canal is far too important to stop that and, if anything, this incredibly sad episode has served to further impress its importance upon us." He paused for a moment, then continued, "Looking at the evidence collected during this Inquiry and how the events unfolded, it's hard to know what else you could have done in the circumstances. We, therefore, wish to fully exonerate you, my boy, of all the unproven charges."

Townsend felt his whole body flood with relief as all the built-up tension he'd been carrying inside him since waking up in the hospital drained away.

"Major Townsend is an excellent example of the quality of the officers we are training today," the general assured the assembled military men, "and we will leave it at that. Have you anything to say before I officially close the Inquiry down?"

Innocent and now officially cleared, Townsend could not help beaming back at them as he said, "I am indebted to the panel for reaching the verdict they have, but I am concerned that the adverse publicity from this incident could prove embarrassing to the Royal Artillery and, by implication, to the Crown. Can it be avoided, sir?"

"Indeed. Because it would prove embarrassing to our standing in the world, and with the Mediterranean being in such a volatile state, we cannot let that happen," the general agreed. "It could encourage serious trouble elsewhere. Consequently, the Fort Anchor incident will be completely sanitised, meaning it never happened and will be denied at every official level. We only want to promote positive images of Malta and Britain, Major."

"Yes, sir. I understand."

"Look, Major. You and your wife have been here in Malta for a while now, and we feel you would benefit from extended leave," said the general. "We understand you have a new addition to your family – I'm sure you would like to get to know him better. Although your time here has not been particularly long, in service terms, we feel further leave would help you immensely; you could spend it exploring this wonderful island, if you so wish. We believe you have been exposed to many unfortunate circumstances in a short space of time, something that could have unhinged many others. Your doctors inform us you are improving daily, both mentally and physically. Still, none here believe you are ready for full-time service yet. Naturally, this does not reflect on your good character. We understand from Captain Marsh – who himself, along with the rest of the survivors, is on extended leave, recovering from the blast – that you will be attending his wedding to nurse Sarah Cummings. My advice is to enjoy it and forget about what has happened. That's all very much in the past, my boy."

"Why, thank you, General," said Townsend gratefully. "The past few weeks have proved both hectic and worrying for my family, and I feel I still need further rest."

"That's all, then, Major. Take it with our blessing. Case closed."

They immediately shook hands, and Townsend saluted him.

"There's no reason to blame yourself for any of this," said the general, as the room began to stir. "You're free to go without a stain on your good character."

"Thank you. And before I go, sir, I would like to know – if possible – was Galea his real name?" Townsend asked. "Could he have been successful with his plan to take over Malta?"

"I haven't the answer to that at this time," the general replied. "Intelligence is still working on it. They think it probably was the fiend's real name because he had such arrogance and charisma in his manner when dealing with people. We will find out soon enough. As for his invasion plan working, he underestimated the British Army. On the day he was to signal its start, many hundreds of fresh battle-hardened troops destined for Aden and British Somaliland on the 'Horn of Africa' arrived at Grand Harbour aboard troop carriers. There was no chance his cunning plan would have worked. Our troops would have annihilated him and his men with or without him using the gun. Anyway, well done, my boy. Well done."

Colonel Downing leant forward, gripped Townsend's hand, and shook it robustly. "My advice is to put this unfortunate incident behind you, Robert. Forget it and carry on with your career. I'm sure your next commission won't be too long coming. I have every faith in you, Robert, and I hope to see you again soon after your full recovery. Goodbye!"

A relieved and grateful Townsend was immediately surrounded by well-wishers and army colleagues he had worked with, congratulating him for what he was called on to do in defending both fort and gun.

***

Marsh was waiting outside the building. The longer the tribunal took, the more anxious he became, knowing the many spurious charges Townsend faced. Understanding that his friend could be in serious trouble, he'd been too nervous to sit in on the verdict.

At last, Townsend appeared and came down the steps outside the building. Marsh tried to read his features and body language from a distance as he walked toward him, but he wasn't sure; it was difficult to tell. As he drew nearer Townsend showed a stern expression, before slowly breaking out into a smile. He was no longer fooling Marsh by staying silent.

"They've cleared you, haven't they?" exclaimed Marsh in jubilation as he firmly shook his hand. "Come on, let us have a drink or two to celebrate before we get back to the girls at the gardens and give them your good news. You can tell me everything that was said in there and what you made of it. I'm sorry, but I just couldn't bear sitting in there myself and listening to it."

"Agreed! Right, David, where's the nearest tavern? I wasn't given anything to drink while in there, and I've got one heck of a thirst," he declared, licking his lips. "I want a couple of beers, at least for starters. I feel I could drink a brewery dry!"

"I'll certainly drink to that," was Marsh's amusing reply.

With that the two walked off, relieved that the unfortunate experience – including the Inquiry – was finally over and behind them.

***

An hour later, after they'd been suitably refreshed, it was time for them to set off and meet the ladies in the gardens, as planned.

Victoria looked at Townsend's face and instantly knew the Inquiry had found in his favour. She squealed for joy as he embraced her while holding their baby boy between them. They then stood in a noisy huddle with Marsh and his joyful fiancée. Now, at last, the two of them were free to focus all their attention and planning on their upcoming wedding.

Together, the four friends (and one tiny Townsend) set off, determined to make the most of their extended leave in and around historic Valletta.

***

What remained of the gun was duly gathered up and secretly transported back to the factory furnaces where it had been manufactured. After that, the authorities forever denied its existence.

The remaining guns in Malta and Gibraltar were never fired in anger; the lasting strength of the cannons was their ability to keep the peace and act as a deterrent to frighten off potential enemies, which was beyond doubt.

Their reputation alone, of ferociously engineered weapons of war, prevented any further attacks.

The enormous shells they were capable of firing ensured peaceful order in the region for the British and their allies over the next few years, as well as safeguarding the passage to the Suez Canal for the ships of the merchant fleet.

Afterwards, the new breech-loading guns – using the slower burning, more powerful cordite as a propellant – finally replaced them, at which point the Armstrong one-hundred-ton superguns were successfully decommissioned and retired.

Even so, these cannons had allowed Malta to enjoy a peaceful era well into the next century – before the horrors of world conflict surfaced, once again, into a troubled Europe.